K

224/96014867
1216197*

20 025 326 00

KT-486-174

301
092
/Par

The A–Z Guide to

Modern Social and

Political Theorists

LEARNING AND INFORMATION
SERVICES
UNIVERSITY OF CUMBRIA

The A–Z Guide to Modern Social and Political Theorists

Edited by
Noel Parker and Stuart Sim

PRENTICE HALL
HARVESTER WHEATSHEAF

London   New York   Toronto   Sydney   Tokyo   Singapore
Madrid   Mexico City   Munich   Paris

First published 1997 by
Prentice Hall/Harvester Wheatsheaf
Campus 400, Maylands Avenue
Hemel Hempstead

Hertfordshire, HP2 7EZ
A division of
Simon & Schuster International Group

© Prentice Hall/Harvester Wheatsheaf 1997

All rights reserved. No part of this publication may be reproduced,
stored in a retrieval system, or transmitted, in any form, or by any
means, electronic, mechanical, photocopying, recording or otherwise,
without prior permission, in writing, from the publisher.

Typeset in 9/11 pt Palatino
by Hands Fotoset, Ratby, Leicester.

Printed and bound in Great Britain by
Hartnolls Limited, Bodmin, Cornwall

Library of Congress Cataloging-in-Publication Data

Available from the publisher

British Library Cataloguing in Publication Data

A catalogue record for this book is available from
the British Library

ISBN 0–13–524885–X pbk

1 2 3 4 5   01 00 99 98 97

UNIVERSITY OF
NORTHUMBRIA AT NEWCASTLE
LIBRARY
ITEM No.   CLASS No.
2002532699   301.092

Contents

Contents

Acknowledgements

Grateful acknowledgement is made for permission to reproduce in this book material previously published elsewhere. Every effort has been made to contact copyright holders, but if any have been inadvertently overlooked, the publisher will be pleased to make the necessary arrangement at the first opportunity.

Introduction

The A–Z Guide to Modern Social and Political Theorists forms a companion volume to *The A–Z Guide to Modern Literary and Cultural Theorists* (Harvester Wheatsheaf, 1995). Like the latter, it consists of a series of concise and accessible essays on key theorists whose researches have been instrumental in shaping their respective fields of discourse, and in setting the agenda for current enquiry in them, both inside and outside the academy; figures whose names are constantly met with in political and social discussions. The present work is designed to cover an even wider intellectual territory than the first, ranging as it does over the diversity of discourses that we group under the general heading of the 'social sciences'. Readers will thus find within these pages representatives from the following disciplines and areas of discourse:

Anthropology
Architecture
Comparative politics
Economics
Feminism
Futurology
International relations
History
Marxism and post-Marxism
Philosophy of science
Political economy
Political philosophy
Psychology
Psychoanalysis
Public choice theory
Social philosophy
Sociology
State theory
Theology

Given such a wide range of fields to cover, there have had to be some hard choices made as to who's in and who's out of the volume. Where we have had to restrict ourselves to only a few names in a field, we have opted for those we think most representative in terms of recent debate and asked contributors to bring out the significant quality of those theorists. In such cases it is likely that other names important within the field are also mentioned in the essay, thus giving as much sense of the discursive context as possible. Another criterion used is that the theorists selected have all had a noticeable impact outside their chosen field, or outside the academy altogether, and can thus be considered of wider social and political significance.

Some of the figures included here can also be found in *The A–Z Guide to Modern Literary and Cultural Theorists*, but where this is so the emphasis has changed to take account of the different context. Marx, for example, is viewed in much more specifically political and economic terms this time around, rather than in terms of his impact on aesthetic theory. A similar point can be made about Lukács. It is also worth pointing out that many of the remaining theorists in the current volume were considered for inclusion in the earlier one (where hard choices also had to be made), so that readers of the first volume will find that the second further extends their theoretical understanding – and vice versa.

As in the earlier *A–Z* we have interpreted the word 'modern' in a fairly generous way, reaching back into the nineteenth century for figures like Marx where necessary, and also including several figures from the earlier twentieth century (Simmel, Freud, etc.). In every case the criterion has been that these older figures inform so many current theoretical debates that they can hardly be omitted in any serious survey hoping to map out the social sciences now. The accent is firmly on recent debates, however, and there are many up-and-coming figures in these pages whose influence will undoubtedly increase over the next few years. Taken as a whole, the essays in this volume bear tribute to the richness of the theoretical work going on in the social sciences today, and will enable students, academic staff and the general reader to build up a comprehensive picture of that collective endeavour.

How to use the guide

Each entry is designed to give the essential information about the theorist in question in around 1,500 words. The format is as follows:

1. Theorist's name and dates.
2. Overview of academic and cultural background.
3. Exposition of main ideas.
4. Consideration of impact and influence.
5. Main published works.
6. Further reading (up to six selected secondary texts).
7. Glossary of technical terms (where they cannot easily be explained in the main body of the entry).

A line marks the division between sections 2, 3 and 4 of the individual entries. When cross-references are made to other entries, theorists' names are picked out in bold type. The heart of each entry is section 3, which aims to provide a quick and easy-to-follow rundown of the theorist's ideas – not neglecting to draw attention to any weak or problematical aspects. Section 2 varies in length from theorist to theorist – some people lead more interesting lives than others, and some people's lives have more relevance to an understanding of their work than is the case with others – as does section 4. Section 5 lists all the main works by which the theorist is known, in their most accessible editions (that is, in translation where the original work is not in English); while section 6 suggests further reading on the theorist up to six titles maximum. Technical terms are in general defined in the course of each entry, but where this has been felt to hold up the progress of the argument they can be found in the glossary at the conclusion of the entry.

The collective goal of the volume's many contributors has been to provide lively, concise and – as far as possible – jargon-free introductions to all the chosen theorists, and to direct readers to more specialist work should they choose to delve more deeply into the literature in future.

Noel Parker
Stuart Sim

Contributors

Kay Adamson
University of Sunderland

David Amigoni
University of Keele

Pamela Anderson
University of Sunderland

Samantha Ashenden
Birkbeck College

Holger Briel
University of Surrey

Alan Cochrane
Open University

John Corcoran
University of Sunderland

Peter Dempsey
University of Sunderland

Julie Dickinson
Birkbeck College

Keith Dowding
London School of Economics

Peter Durrans
University of Sunderland

Antony Easthope
Manchester Metropolitan University

Mark Erickson
University of Birmingham

Trine Flockhart
University of Sunderland

Sarah Gamble
University of Sunderland

Dong-sook Gills
University of Sunderland

Peter Hayes
University of Sunderland

Keith Lawler
University of Sunderland

Barry Lewis
University of Sunderland

Anthony McGowan
Open University

Meg McGuire
Kings College London

Norrie McQueen
University of Dundee

Don MacRaild
University of Sunderland

David Martin
University of Sheffield

Alisdair Milne
University of Surrey

David Morland
University of Northumbria

John Mullarkey
University of Sunderland

Shane O'Neill
Queens University Belfast

Noel Parker
University of Surrey

Danielle Ramsay
University of Newcastle

Alan Roulstone
University of Sunderland

Peter Rushton
University of Sunderland

Sean Sayers
University of Kent

Tom Shakespeare
University of Leeds

Stuart Sim
University of Sunderland

Tamsin Spargo
Liverpool John Moores University

Lloyd Spencer
Trinity & All Saints College, Leeds

John Storey
University of Sunderland

John Strachan
University of Sunderland

Graham Thompson
Open University

Colin Tipton
University of Surrey

Nigel Watson
University of Sunderland

Robert Wilkinson
Open University

Russell Williams
University of Sunderland

Robert Woodfield
University of Sunderland

Rob Wooffitt
University of Surrey

Pamela Anderson, Peter Dempsey, Sarah Gamble, Barry Lewis, Stuart Sim, John Storey and John Strachan are all members of the Raman Selden Centre for the Study of Textual and Cultural Theory, in the School of Arts, Design and Communications at the University of Sunderland.

A

Adorno, Theodor (1903–1969)

One of the most influential German thinkers of this century, Theodor Wiesengrund Adorno was born into a wealthy German–Jewish family. He moved from Frankfurt to Vienna and Berlin before Nazism forced his exile, first to work in Oxford with Gilbert Ryle, then to New York and the Princeton Radio Research Programme, then finally to Los Angeles. He returned to Germany after the war and worked with Max Horkheimer at the Frankfurt Institute for Social Research eventually becoming its director. His *oeuvre* is wide-ranging: including aesthetics, philosophy of music, music reviews, sociology and psychology. Thanks to this breadth, he has been accused of dabbling. But for all its scope, his vision and interdisciplinarity bring together different fields and create new venues for thinking. Hence, it can be argued that few thinkers had more influence on German post-war society than Adorno. With Horkheimer, Fromm and **Habermas** (one of his pupils), he was founder and propagator of a specific school of western Marxism, *Kritische Theorie* (Critical Theory), also known as 'the Frankfurt School'.

Adorno's first major publication, *Dialectic of Enlightenment*, written in Los Angeles with Max Horkheimer, provided a motif for what came later. It argued that the project of the Enlightenment, the liberation of mankind, was in danger of ending up as a new myth that would sustain the very status quo that the Enlightenment had originally set out to challenge. This danger was largely due to humanity's ever-increasing belief in the liberating powers of technology and its world of objects. Defending their belief in spiritual progress, Adorno and Horkheimer proposed an antidote: not just thinking the relations of *things*, but also, as an immediate second step, thinking *through* that thinking, self-reflexively. Technology is dangerous precisely because it lacks that self-reflexivity. Adorno and Horkheimer found in art a model of how to evade this risk. For art is an open-ended system with no fixed rules, and thus resistant to being turned into an object of technology.

Yet, in typical Adornean fashion, Adorno and Horkheimer use the example of Odysseus and the sirens to suggest that certain strictures apply even in art's supposedly liberating operations. So that Odysseus will not perish as he listens to the sirens, he has his crew tie him to the mast of the ship. The impact of art, insight into the necessity of changing one's life, must, they imply, be thwarted. For Adorno and Horkheimer, art cannot change society. But it can, and should, mirror it, holding out hope for the individual, without being able to satisfy that hope. As Adorno would say in one of his darkest theorems: 'There exists no correct life within the false one.' Human beings cannot escape their destiny in death; and, hence, for Adorno, every death was a murder. Yet through art, the sufferings of human destiny can be relieved: for at least art conveys the *need* for change.

Adorno's *Negative Dialectics* (1966) pursues Hegelian dialectics, but with an all-important difference: much as his bourgeois self wishes synthesis, Adorno believes that the twentieth century no longer allows synthesis. His dialectic moves from thesis to antithesis, new thesis, new antithesis and so forth indefinitely – without coming to a rest in any reassuring final synthesis. Indeed, in this respect one can see a close proximity between Adorno's thought and the ambiguous, ever-turning styles of deconstruction and postmodernism. There is one important difference; they regard philosophy's rationalist postulate of a singular truth as dangerous, and prefer to abandon dialectics completely.

Yet it was this proximity to deconstruction that has led to the recent interest in Adorno's thought in the English-speaking world. In Great Britain, a further link has been the ascendancy of Cultural Studies, which has elaborated upon the Frankfurt School's criticism of twentieth-century cultural phenomena. But, though his philosophical texts and cultural analyses have aroused interest, most of his sociological writing is still awaiting an audience. This is to be regretted, since his sociological studies give examples of how to apply his intrinsically theoretical meanderings through art and philosophy to the study of individuals in society.

It has been argued that, both in style and content, much of Adorno's philosophy is based on music. Adorno himself admitted the link. And if, as he stated in his *Aesthetic Theory*, form is coagulated contents, then it should be of great importance to understand his own style and form of writing. He adopted a difficult, hermetic writing style and presentation of his subjects, which do not easily lend themselves to translation – a further reason for his slow reception in the English-speaking world. His *Notes on Literature* expound his views on music, on his own use of foreign words, on poetry in society, and on his usage of the essay – because it is a smaller, freer form for writing philosophy. The *Notes* also demarcate the boundaries he acknowledges in his own thinking: the essay is an open form, ample enough to describe artistic endeavours, but not itself enough to do philosophy. For that a more rigorous approach is needed. For Adorno, it was High Modernism that had achieved that apex of formal rigour. Thus, he embraced the cerebral approach of Schönberg's atonal music, but opposed the chaotic direction adopted by Stravinsky's.

In his posthumously published *Aesthetic Theory* (1970) Adorno attempts to make more coherent his idea that the philosophy of literature is a means for cultural and ultimately social change. He traces the move into silence of his most cherished examples of literature (Beckett and Celan) as an indication of how the establishment constantly silences its detractors. He feared that, just as art was only able to promise the good life as unfulfilled prophecy, so the idea of systemic change could only be thought of as utopian.

What mitigates Adorno's often harsh criticisms and authoritarian judgements on art and society is the fact that for him one question always had to be foregrounded: '*Cui bono?*', for whose good? In his social research, he stressed the necessity to look first and foremost at the individual, to try and coax the individual out of the mass and trace the way in which she was treated by society. He always remained the advocate of the disenfranchised single human being, thinking which did not endear him to the empirical, positivistic mass sociology emerging in the United States after the Second World War. This did not stop him, however, from choosing to make his point, in his own, solitary way, with examples of High Modernism in art, a movement which could be described as bourgeois in its very form. His reasoning for this was simple. High Modernism exemplified the most advanced form of art for its time, *his* time. Adorno's complete rejection of Stravinsky, jazz, or newer art forms (such as 'happenings') showed that his ideal of art was firmly rooted in the late nineteenth and early twentieth century. He was simply not able to see the changes in society which had brought about, or necessitated, such new manifestations of art.

Much of Adorno's pessimism towards history was inextricably linked to his experience of the rise and rule of fascism. Fear of a recurrence of such atrocities informed most of his thinking. Despite the fact that Germany had become a federal republic, to which he himself had chosen to return, Adorno remained wary of the way her citizens developed. Culture for him was the best way to combat and, at least in a utopian vein, overcome the inequalities plaguing the lives of the many. But he feared and abhorred the ever-increasing power of the 'culture industry', over which most citizens had no control. He had coined the phrase in reaction to the way he saw culture presented to the masses in the United States. For him, the culture industry, particularly through television and film, was merely cultural mediation. It only gave the *illusion* of choice, e.g. which game show to watch on which channel. It did nothing to extend high culture's use of 'aporias', the points where order and rationality reach their limits, and hence make the individual come to grips with the struggle for a worthwhile and fulfilling life.

While Adorno was viewed by the establishment as a Marxist revolutionary and leftist seducer of the young, many of his own students were not able to come to terms with his ultimately defeatist thinking. It is true, he did have a major influence on the development of the student movement in Germany in the 1960s, but he himself did not support the unrest in 1967–8. He believed that such 'actionism' only helps the powers that be to demonstrate their strength and take away even the minute freedom that may still arise in society. His students did not share his pessimism and took over his institute – whereupon Adorno called in the police. They never forgave him, charging that he was all words. And that he was. But what forceful words!

Adorno inspired a multitude of intellectuals in Germany, many of whom now occupy important positions in German public life. His most famous follower was Jürgen **Habermas**, who inherited Adorno's acknowledged leading role in the Frankfurt School. And while much of the leftist revolutionary fervour of the 1960s has been lost or superseded by newer developments, one has to admit that it is Adorno's insistence on *critique* when dealing with all social phenomena that has become his lasting legacy.

Main works

Dialectic of Enlightenment (1947, with Max Horkheimer), trans. John Cumming, London and New York: Verso, 1972.

The Authoritarian Society (with Else Frenkel-Brunswik *et al.*), New York: Norton, 1950.

Negative Dialectics (1966), trans. E. B. Ashton, London: Routledge, 1973.

Aesthetic Theory (1970), trans. C. Lenhardt, London: Athlone, 1984.

Notes on Literature (1974), trans. Shierry Weber Nicholson, New York: Columbia University Press, 1991–2.

The Stars down to Earth and Other Essays on the Irrational in Culture, ed. with an Introduction by Stephen Crook, London: Routledge, 1994.

Further reading

Buck-Morrs, Susan, *The Origin of Negative Dialectics*, New York: Free Press, 1977.

Hohendahl, Peter-Uwe, *Reappraisals: Shifting alignments in postwar critical theory*, Ithaca, NY: Cornell University Press, 1991.

Jameson, Fredric, *Late Marxism: Adomo, or, the persistence of the dialectic*, London: Verso, 1990.

Jay, Martin, *Adorno*, Cambridge, MA: Harvard University Press, 1984.

Rose, Gillian, *The Melancholy Science: An introduction to the thought of Theodor W. Adorno*, London: Macmillan, 1978.

Althusser, Louis (1918–1990)

Louis Althusser was one of the most important and controversial Marxist thinkers of the twentieth century. Born in Algeria, he was educated in Lyon and became an activist in the Catholic youth movement during the 1930s. He spent the war in a German prison camp and then studied at the prestigious Ecole Normale Supérieure in Paris where he later became Professor of Philosophy. In 1948 he joined the French Communist Party. During the 1960s and 1970s his writings on Marxist theory were extremely influential amongst left-wing groups in Europe. Following the unsolved manslaughter of his wife in 1980, he spent most of his last years hospitalised.

Althusser's primary ambition was to re-establish the importance of Marxist theory in the international Communist movement. This could only be achieved by reconstructing Marxism as 'the revolutionary science of society'. The rationale behind this strategy was described by Althusser in his autobiography, *The Future Lasts a Long Time*:

> No form of political intervention was possible within the [French Communist] Party other than a purely theoretical one; it was even necessary to take the existing accepted theory and direct it against the Party's own use of it. And since the accepted theory no longer had anything to do with Marx, being based on very dangerous absurdities derived from the Soviet or rather Stalinist, interpretation of dialectical materialism, the only possible course of action was to go back to Marx, to a body of political thought which was fundamentally unchallenged because it was sacred, and show that Stalinist dialectical materialism, with all its theoretical, philosophical, ideological, and political consequences, was a total aberration.

The wider historical context for his theoretical intervention included the process of de-Stalinisation (after the criticism of the 'cult of personality' at the Soviet Communist Party Congress in 1956) the rise of Marxist humanism and the Sino–Soviet split in 1963.

Althusser's response to the mid-century developments in Commun- ism was a detailed reassessment of **Marx**'s works so as to highlight his methodological assumptions and his key concepts for analysing social structures. From Gaston Bachelard, the French philosopher of science, he adopted the idea of an 'epistemological break'. Such a break, Althusser claimed, had occurred in Marx's work in 1845, dividing the humanist

Marx from the scientific one. Before then, Marx's works were inspired by the humanist philosophies of Feuerbach and Hegel, which emphasised concepts of human essence and its loss in alienation. Thereafter, especially in *Capital*, Marx introduced a number of new concepts: the social formation, modes of production, forces of production, infrastructure, superstructure, the ruling class, the ruling ideology and class struggle. As a result, Marxism was transformed from an ideological philosophy into the scientific revolutionary theory of historical materialism. Althusser believed 'that Marx's discovery is a scientific discovery without historical precedent in its nature and its effects. Indeed . . . we may claim that Marx established a new science: the science of the history of "social formations".' He compared this scientific discovery with those of Galileo and Darwin. Thus, from 1845, Marx broke with the tradition of merely 'interpreting the world' and adopted the position of 'changing the world'. This meant not merely exposing the mechanisms of capitalist domination and exploitation but active involvement in the class struggles of the working class to overturn them. For the first time, there was a 'union between the labour and Marxist theory'.

Althusser was a so-called 'structural' Marxist, who divided the capitalist 'social formation' into three distinct 'levels': the economic, the political and the ideological, each 'relatively' independent from one another but contributing to the nature and development of the overall structure. To escape from crude economic reductionism, Althusser employed the concept of 'overdeterminism'. Determination by the economic base occurred only 'in the last instance', in shaping the relations and the relative impact of what happened at the different levels in the structure. Thus social change was caused by a combination of different elements: ideologies, national traditions, customs and accidents of history. There needed to be an accumulation of extreme circumstances fusing in what Althusser termed a 'ruptural unity'. But sometimes 'the lonely hour of the "last instance" never comes'.

Also crucial to Althusser's project of reconstructing Marxism was the concept of 'Ideological State Apparatus'. Classical Marxism had viewed the capitalist state as essentially a repressive ruling apparatus, which enables the ruling class to ensure their domination over the working class in order to exploit them. An essay by Althusser on the Marxist theory of the state was published in 1970, entitled 'Ideology and ideological state apparatuses (Notes towards an Investigation)' in *Lenin and Philosophy*. Althusser argued that what was important was the reproduction of the conditions and relations of capitalist production. This was guaranteed by the existence of both repressive and ideological state apparatuses. The former (police, courts, prisons, military, etc.) functioned primarily through the use of force. The function of the specialised ideological state apparatuses (schools, churches, mass media, etc.) was to persuade the mass or the population to accept the ruling ideology with its divisions between rulers and ruled, exploiters and exploited. The difference between the two types of apparatus was in the degree of repression or ideology which they used – though the ideological state apparatuses could also resort to repressive practices such as censorship. The diverse ideological state apparatuses are 'relatively autonomous', but unity was provided by the ruling ideology and the common function which they performed for the ruling class in perpetuating class oppression and exploitation. Althusser believed that the dominant ideological state apparatus in advanced capitalist societies was education, which had replaced the church in reproducing the relations of production. Schools provided pupils with the relevant knowledge and training for their future positions in the capitalist division of labour. It was from schools that pupils received a 'massive inculcation of the ideology of the ruling class'. Because no dominant class could maintain state power for any length of time if it lost hegemony over the ideological apparatuses. These are potential sites for intense class struggles, where 'the weapon of ideology' could be turned against the ruling class.

In the 'Ideological State Apparatus', Althusser also introduced the concept of 'interpellation' to account for how individuals become 'social subjects', adopting the role laid down in the oppressive stuctures of society. He uses the image of a policeman hailing a suspect: 'Hey, you there!'. Ideology's function is to 'interpellate' individuals, hail them in the terms of their intended role and thus adapt them to it. Thus, according to Althusser, individuals are always ('already') subjects before they are born: 'appointed as a subject' in and by the specific ideological configuration in which it is 'expected' once they have been conceived.

Althusser saw his entire project as liberating Marxist theory 'from confusions, mystifications and manipulations', many of them resulting from Stalinist distortions like 'economism'. A revolutionary science of society could only be developed through 'a return to Marx' and the development of new concepts. In one of his last speeches in 1977, he highlighted once again 'a theoretical crisis within Marxism' and publicly disagreed with Lenin's description of Marxism as a 'block of steel'. In reality, it contained 'difficulties, contradictions and gaps'. Althusser recognised the vital importance of theory and the creation of a 'theoretical culture' for revolutionary practice: 'there can be no good policy without theory'.

Althusser's attempts to reconstruct Marxism as a rigorous science of revolution had a world-wide appeal for left-wing intellectuals during the 1960s and 1970s. His version of Marxism also influenced academic research programmes and debates in the social sciences, cultural studies, gender studies, history and literary criticism.

He was, however, not without his critics. Some accused him of reading Marx selectively and ignoring texts which disproved his interpretation. Althusser's account of ideological state apparatus was criticised for neglecting ideologies of resistance and struggle against the capitalist state.

The Marxist historian **E. P. Thompson** attacked Althusser's 'ahistorical theoreticism' and static concepts as a complete travesty of Marx's own method, which was firmly rooted in history. Althusser's 'theoretical anti-humanism' was unable to handle culture, values and experience in the 'real world', except in the most abstract manner. The end-result was 'the poverty of theory'. Althusser was also criticised for not testing his theories against any analysis of the social structure of contemporary capitalist society. Others criticised his writings for their obscurity and pretentiousness.

Although Althusser published *Essays in Self-Criticism* in the early 1970s, a decade later Western Europe was experiencing both 'a crisis of Marxism' and a downturn in the class struggle. New social movements (feminism, environmentalism, nuclear disarmament, etc.) began seriously to compete with revolutionary movements for popular appeal. With the rise of new intellectual currents such as post-structuralism and post-modernism, Althusserian Marxism declined in influence, especially in France, where it was gradually relegated to a topic in the history of ideas. Yet a balanced assessment of his continued relevance was made by Douglas Johnson in 1993:

> Althusser moved Marxism away from a mechanical evocation of economic principles. His description of the ideological state apparatus which manipulates people into positions of oppressor and oppressed, through education, the family, the media, has never been more relevant. There are those who learn to rule, and there are those who learn to be ruled. (Introduction to *The Future Lasts a Long Time*)

Main works

For Marx, trans. Ben Brewster, London: New Left, 1969.

Reading Capital (with Etienne Balibar), trans. Ben Brewster, London: New Left, 1970.

Lenin and Philosophy and Other Essays, trans. Ben Brewster, London: New Left, 1971.

Politics and History: Montesquieu, Rousseau, Hegel and Marx, trans. Ben Brewster, London: New Left, 1972.

Essays in Self-Criticism, trans. Grahame Lock, London: New Left, 1972.

Philosophy and the Spontaneous Philosophy of the Scientists, trans. Ben Brewster *et al.*, London: New Left, 1990.

The Future Lasts a Long Time and The Facts, ed. Olivier Corpet and Yann Moulier Boutang, trans. Richard Veasey, London: Chatto and Windus, 1993.

Further reading

Benton, Ted, *The Rise and Fall of Structural Marxism,* London and Basingstoke: Macmillan, 1984.

Elliott, Gregory, *Althusser: The detour of theory,* London: Verso, 1987.

Elliott, Gregory ed., *Althusser: A critical reader,* Oxford: Basil Blackwell, 1994.

Kaplan, E. Ann and Michael Sprinker (eds), *The Althusserian Legacy,* London: Verso, 1993.

Majumdar, Margaret, *Althusser and the End of Leninism?* London: Pluto, 1995.

Thompson, E. P., *The Poverty of Theory and Other Essays,* London: Merlin, 1978.

Arendt, Hannah (1906–1975)

Hannah Arendt was a German–American academic, philosopher and political theorist. She was educated at the universities of Marburg, Freiburg and Heidelberg. Arendt studied with and was deeply influenced by the two main figures within twentieth-century German existentialism: Martin **Heidegger** at Marburg and Karl Jaspers at Heidelberg. In 1933, with the advent of the National Socialist regime, she left Germany for France after a brief period of imprisonment, the consequence of her involvement in German Zionism. In Paris, she worked for Zionist agencies which sent Jewish orphans to Palestine, whilst at the same time calling, somewhat idealistically, for the establishment of an Arab–Jewish state in Palestine. In 1941, after being interned by the collaborationist Vichy government, Arendt fled France for the United States. For the next decade, she worked for various Jewish relief agencies. After 1952 she worked mainly in an academic context, holding professorial positions at Princeton (where she was the first tenured woman faculty professor), the University of Chicago and the New School for Social Research in New York. Her most significant book is *The Origins of Totalitarianism* (1951), a study which argues that the twin evils of mid-twentieth-century politics, Nazism and Stalinism, were instances of a new form of political dominion, totalitarianism. Her most famous book is *Eichmann in Jerusalem: A report on the banality of evil* (1963), a contentious analysis of Nazi war crimes which was based on her first-hand observation of the 1961 trial of Adolf Eichmann in Israel. Arendt was one of a number of German exiles (**Adorno** and **Marcuse** of the Frankfurt School, the iconoclast Leo Strauss, Hans **Morgenthau**) who, in different ways, had a major influence on the development of post-war political thought in the American academy.

In terms of political theory, Arendt's most significant book is her first, *The Origins of Totalitarianism*. Though she did not coin the term 'totalitarianism', Arendt's was the earliest sustained theoretical account of the phenomenon and provided the basis for its later discussion. She argues that the twentieth century has seen the emergence of a new political system which is qualitatively distinct from previous forms of oppression: 'totalitarian government is different from dictatorships and tyrannies'. The older forms of coercive government, despotism and dictatorship, only seek limited, generally political, control and either term is inadequate to describe a form of social organisation which attempts to dominate all aspects of a nation's life. This 'newest form of government' systematically uses terror in the service of its ideological project and to achieve its goal of national, and in the end, world 'domination'. Fascism itself need not necessarily be totalitarian; Mussolini's Italy, for example, was not 'a full-fledged totalitarian regime'. Neither is this form of government limited to fascist states; Stalin's Soviet Union is also totalitarian. Arendt's study not only describes totalitarianism; it also describes its antecedents. Totalitarianism has its origins in several things: the degeneration of the legacy of the idealism of the French Revolution and Romanticism into fanaticism and racism; the failure of nineteenth-century European liberalism evident in post-First World War Europe; anti-semitism; the tendency of nationalism to descend into racism; and European imperialism.

In terms of philosophy, Arendt's most significant book is *The Human Condition*. Basing her analysis on the Greek city-state, she divides the modes of human activity into a hierarchy of forms. The human condition divides into the life of thought (the *vita contemplativa*) and the life of action (the *vita activa*). Repudiating contemporary liberalism for what she sees as its privileging of the realm of private experience, Arendt's focus is on the *vita activa*, which is subdivided into labour, work and action. Labour is simply the toil necessary for the maintenance of life. Repudiating Marxist thought for its materialism, Arendt criticises **Marx** for his overriding emphasis upon labour. Thus Arendt is involved in a twin-pronged assault upon the two main strands of contemporary political philosophy, socialism and liberalism. An egotistical attention to private selfhood on the one hand or a concentration on labour on the other preclude the individual from being fully human. Higher than labour is work, an activity which produces durable objects, from the chair of the carpenter to the artist's painting. Superior to labour is action, which involves the individual leaving the 'private realm' to interact and debate with other people in the 'public realm'. Given her Heideggerian antecedents, it is hardly surprising that Arendt addresses ontological issues. However, she firmly links the question of being to politics. Politics is the highest form of action. Lamenting what she sees as the disappearance of a Greek ethic which tied political action to private thought, Arendt endorses what she sees as the classical position of obtaining a 'space' within which the individual can be truly free. Action 'corresponds to the human condition of plurality' and Arendt's notion of good government is pluralistic, a vision of power being exercised by agreement after debate. In the opposite of the totalitarian exercise of power, power amended is derived from the process of 'acting together'.

Arendt's next book was her most contentious. In *Eichmann in Jerusalem*, she worked up her reports of the Eichmann war crimes trial for *The New Yorker* into a criminological meditation; part reportage, part biography, part political philosophy. Arendt was attacked for downplaying Jewish resistance to Nazism, for her refusal to grant Eichmann the status of a uniquely depraved individual, for implicitly acceding to his defence that he was simply obeying the orders of his superiors and for her awareness that many people would have acted in a similar fashion in the same dark context of totalitarianism. However, these points should not be divorced from their context in her argument; Arendt does not condone Eichmann. Though Eichmann's evil was 'banal' (because of his mindless refusal to contemplate the significance and nature of his own actions), Arendt does not shy away from condemnation of his human 'wickedness'. Eichmann was, in Arendt's most famous phrase, 'terribly and terrifyingly normal'. He was not a superhumanly villainous individual, 'not Iago and not Macbeth', but part of a totalitarian bureaucracy devoted to providing a machinery of 'administrative massacre'. However, though Arendt's critics have seen this as a capitulation to Eichmann's own defence, that he was simply a 'tiny cog' in the machinery of the Final Solution, her position is slightly different. For her, though the Holocaust was implemented by the 'giant bureaucracy' of totalitarian government, this does not excuse the human actions implicit in acceding to the state. 'Far from being a dehumanised cog, all the cogs in the machinery, no matter how insignificant, are in court forthwith transformed into perpetrators, that is to say, into human beings.' Finally, though Arendt makes the painful acknowledgement that many people would have behaved in 'just the same' manner as Eichmann, his condemnation is not 'any the less correct for that reason'.

Arendt's later works develop the issues raised in *Totalitarianism* and *The Human Condition*. In *On Revolution*, she returns to the notion of French Revolutionary philosophy's degeneration (caused by its inability to maintain a public space for political action) from its honourable, well-intentioned beginnings into the barbarous sham of the terroristic imposition of a supposedly egalitarian ideology in the Soviet Union. Whilst condemning *dirigiste* Stalinism, she praises the near-anarchic manifestation of the workers' councils established during the short-lived 1956 Hungarian Revolution as something approaching her concept of ideal political action. *Crises of the Republic* returns to the concept of power as mutual action, whilst her last work, *The Life of the Mind*, is an unfinished attempt to engage with the philosophical life of the mind which she had bracketed out of her discussion in *The Human Condition*.

Arendt's work defies orthodox categorisations of left- and right-wing philosophy and the assessment of her influence and achievement is rendered still more problematical by her overt refusal to offer a systematising vision. Arendt's work was intended to prompt debate rather than to found a coherent school of thought. In this she has been successful. After her death, as during her life, her work remains contentious. Her admirers celebrate her originality and eclecticism; her critics, in Sir Isaiah **Berlin**'s famous phrase, disparage the 'metaphysical free-association' evident in her work. Much recent criticism has been antipathetic. Her account of Nazism and the resistance to it continues to prompt antipathy amongst Jewish writers, Marxists berate her anti-materialism, feminist philosophers have disparaged her almost total inattention to issues of gender and theorists of post-colonialism (notably Said) have faulted her for the allegedly ethnocentric bias apparent even in her attention to the nature of imperialism.

Main works

The Origins of Totalitarianism, New York: Harcourt, Brace, Jovanovich, 1951.

The Human Condition, Chicago: University of Chicago Press, 1958.

Eichmann in Jerusalem: A report on the banality of evil, New York: Viking, 1963.

On Revolution, New York: Viking Press, 1963.

Crises of the Republic, New York: Harcourt, Brace, Jovanovich, 1972.

The Life of the Mind, 2 vols, New York: Harcourt, Brace, Jovanovich, 1978.

Further reading

Bradshaw, L., *Acting and Thinking: The political thought of Hannah Arendt*, Toronto: University of Toronto Press, 1989.

Canovan, M., *Hannah Arendt: A reinterpretation of her political thought*, Cambridge: Cambridge University Press, 1992.

Kateb, George, *Hannah Arendt: Politics, conscience, evil*, Oxford: Martin Robertson, 1984.

Passerin D'Entrèves, Maurizio, *The Political Philosophy of Hannah Arendt*, London and New York: Routledge, 1994.

Young-Bruehl, Elisabeth, *Hannah Arendt: For love of the world*, New Haven, CT: Yale University Press, 1982.

Aron, Raymond (1905–1983)

Aron was educated at Ecole Normale Supérieure in the class of 1924 – the same year group as Sartre and Canguilhem. Aron's education prepared him for an academic career, but following the fall of France and Aron's escape to England in 1940, he was drawn into journalism, writing for the Free French review *La France Libre*. On returning to France in 1944, Aron briefly worked for the de Gaulle Government in the Ministry of Information before committing himself to journalism, writing firstly editorials for *Combat* and then moving to *Le Figaro*, a connection Aron maintained even after he moved permanently into academic life. Aron was made Professor of Sociology at the Sorbonne in 1955, subsequently becoming a Director of Studies at the Ecole Pratique des Hautes Etudes in 1960 and Professor of the Sociology of European Civilisation at the Collège de France from 1969 until his retirement in 1978. Aron was widely regarded as one of France's leading post-war intellectuals and was a prolific writer until his death.

Raymond Aron, throughout his life and work, represented the tradition of liberal humanistic rationalism, and personified the archetypal intellectual. Aron frequently acknowledges the influence of the work of **Weber**, and comparisons between Aron and Weber are not inappropriate: both had wide-ranging spheres of interests and a prolific output, and neither concentrated on purely academic audiences. Aron's range of interests makes it difficult to typify him: he was primarily a sociologist, but contributed to the study of international relations, political theory, and the philosophy of history. Aron published some forty books in his lifetime, many hundreds of articles and some four thousand newspaper and magazine articles: he was undoubtedly one of France's most famous intellectuals of the post-war years.

Aron's influence on the French intellectual community is marked by a number of decisive texts. His doctoral thesis *Introduction to the Philosophy of History* (1948) provides a Weberian account of the ways in which history can achieve objectivity, and focuses on the need to oppose scientific rationalism and positivism in historical analysis. Aron's Weberian approach identifies the fragmentary determinism of history that denies the possibility of any purely causal analysis, whilst maintaining the necessity of historical analysis to provide understanding of society. However, Aron's opposition to historical determinism pushes him towards a historical relativism, a position he attempts to avoid by advocating the need for the historian to use absoluteness of decision and resoluteness of choice. Aron's liberalism is further evident in his advocacy of the need for the empirical study of modern regimes to aid people to choose a political regime for themselves. Such an approach, relying as it does on the need for rational choice and commitment, marks the course that much of Aron's later work takes.

Aron's liberal approach to the political and economic spheres is again encapsulated in his next major work. Deeply opposed to the rising Stalinism he felt characterised French intellectual thought of the 1950s, *The Opium of the Intellectuals* (1955) is a trenchant attack on Marxism and existentialism, and marked the end of the collaboration between Sartre and Aron in the journal they founded together in 1944, *Les Temps modernes*. Aron's polemic is not directed against the ideology of Marxism so much as at the communist 'fellow-travellers' he identified, notably Sartre and Merleau-Ponty. Aron denounces as 'myths' the key tenets of the ideology and political strategy of the left, and characterises as 'fruitless' the accompanying search for universality, but does this from a sociological rather than political perspective. *The Opium of the Intellectuals*, with its sustained attack on Marxist political action, provides the starting point for a sociology of intellectuals, delineating and analysing as it does the meanings and actions of the intelligentsia. Aron's conclusion, suggesting that there may be an end to the ideological age and a possible rise of political tolerance and scepticism, need not be seen as naïve given that Aron bases his conjecture on an analysis of class conflict between the proletariat and the bourgeoisie: this was not analogous to the fundamental class conflict between the aristocracy and bourgeoisie of pre-industrial society, rather it is a difference of lifestyles and values. Aron seeks to abolish fanaticism in all its forms: 'the true Left is that which continues to invoke, not liberty or equality, but fraternity, in other words, love' (*The Opium of the Intellectuals*). On publication, *The Opium of the Intellectuals* was the subject of strong attacks from the French intelligentsia and received hostile notices in the press. This served to cut Aron off from much of the French intellectual community, which was still largely adhering to the Hegelian–Marxist orthodoxy at this time.

In the late 1950s, Aron turned his attention to international relations, producing his classic study and magnum opus *Peace and War* in 1962. Aron argues the need for a historical sociology of war, such that reductive analyses ascribing the origins of war to human psychological characteristics could be opposed by a science of international relations that identifies different orientations towards war and peace on the part of leaders. *Peace and War* attempts to provide the basis for such a science by systematically analysing the basic concepts of war, such as power, force and diplomacy, and proceeding to investigate diplomatic–strategic behaviour and strategic decisions.

Aron's writings on international relations are varied, but focus on a central theme; the limits of the realist–idealist dichotomy. Aron challenges both approaches, and rejects them for their attempt to overcome politics. It is only through the construction of a political science that recognises the reality of diverse human communities and human values that attempts can be made to offer advice to statesmen attempting to secure peaceful co-existence. Aron preaches a morality of prudence, and attempts to utilise rational analysis to identify the essentially political nature of the human condition. Given the turbulent international conditions Aron was writing under, his account of possible strategies for analysis of international relations, whilst not overly optimistic, retains a humane and prudent character.

Aron's influence on French intellectual life was closely tied to shifts in political climate. Following the publication of *The Opium of the Intellectuals* he was in the wilderness, isolated from the dominant left, but the events of May 1968, the publication of Solzhenitsyn's *Gulag Archipelago*, and the rise of a new generation of thinkers, critical of Marxist orthodoxy, drew Aron back towards the mainstream. By the early 1980s Aron was considered to be one of the most influential thinkers in France and his work was documented extensively by the French media. Aron's legacy is far reaching: his work challenges fundamental assumptions of modern thought through its sustained attempt to provide understanding rather than rhetoric, and his opposition to totalitarianism in politics and in theory provides strategies for action and resistance that promote human freedom and human reason. Indeed, it could be claimed that the collapse of communism in Europe vindicates Aron's sociological and philosophical perspectives on the indomitability of the human spirit.

Main works

Introduction to the Philosophy of History (1948), Boston, MA: Beacon, 1961.

The Opium of the Intellectuals (1955), London: Martin Secker and Warburg, 1957.

The Dawn of Universal History, London: Weidenfeld and Nicholson, 1961.

Peace and War: A theory of international relations (1962), New York: Doubleday, 1966.

'Social class, political class, ruling class', in R. Bendix and S. M. Lipset (eds), *Class, Status and Power*, New York: Free Press, 1966.

Progress and Disillusion, Harmondsworth: Penguin, 1972.

History, Truth, Liberty: Selected writings of Raymond Aron, ed. F. Draus. Chicago: Chicago University Press, 1985.

Further reading

Colquhoun, R., *Raymond Aron: The philosopher in history 1905–1955*, London: Sage, 1986.

Colquhoun, R., *Raymond Aron: The sociologist in society 1955–1983*, London: Sage, 1986.

Draus, F., 'Introduction', in F. Draus (ed.), *History, Truth, Liberty: Selected writings of Raymond Aron*, Chicago: Chicago University Press, 1985.

Hall, J., *Diagnoses of Our Time: Six views on our social condition*, London: Heinemann, 1981.

Mahoney, D. J., *The Liberal Political Science of Raymond Aron: A critical introduction*, Lanham, MD: Rowman and Littlefield, 1992.

Pierce, R., *Contemporary French Political Thought*, Oxford: Oxford University Press, 1966.

Arrow, Kenneth J. (1921–)

Born of Rumanian–Jewish extraction, Kenneth Arrow was educated in the New York school system. The great depression ended his father's banking career, but encouraged Arrow's interest in economic problems, scepticism about the nostrums of market economics and sense of social responsibility. He studied mathematics and economics at City College,

New York and at Columbia University. In 1951, he was awarded a Ph.D. by Columbia for his ground-breaking work on the axiomatic analysis of mechanisms of social choice (published as *Social Choice and Individual Values*). He became Professor of Economics, Statistics and Operations Research at Stanford University in 1953, and there (in collaboration with Gerald Debreu and others) pursued his seminal work on the mathematical theory of general market equilibrium, the economics of uncertainty and information, and the theory of fixed capital and inventory investment. In 1968 he moved to Harvard University. In 1972 he became the youngest ever recipient of the Nobel Prize for Economics. In 1974 he returned to Stanford where he is currently emeritus professor.

Kenneth Arrow's seminal intellectual contribution has been the application of axiomatic methods to problems in economic and social theory. He epitomises the shift towards mathematical methods in economics which gathered pace over the past half century and now dominates departments of economics in both the United States and Western Europe. Though often technical and inaccessible, this 'mathematical economics' has profound implications for social and political theory.

Post-war mathematical economics has often been labelled 'neo-classical', on the grounds that formal methods hide a bias towards a market allocation of resources. Its general assumption that individuals seek to maximise their own well-being (expressed in some utility function) fails, critics argue, to incorporate the social dimension of economic interactions. This charge certainly cannot be made against Arrow, whose analytical techniques co-exist with scepticism about market forces achieving desirable social outcomes.

Arrow's doctoral thesis was his celebrated 'impossibility theorem'. The basic assumption is that individuals have 'preference orderings' about outcomes – i.e. they can order all possible outcomes from the most to the least desirable. A well-known instance of failing to establish a social ordering (known to Condorcet in the eighteenth century) is pair-wise majority voting. Suppose a majority vote for outcome A over outcome B, and a majority also votes for outcome B in preference to outcome C: a majority may perfectly well vote as well for outcome C over outcome A. Arrow's theorem shows that difficulties like these can arise with *any* system of resolving social preferences out of only individual preferences. More complex mechanisms (such as the single transferable vote) do not resolve such paradoxes.

The question for Arrow was whether there is a reasonable mechanism for deriving a *collective* ordering for individual preferences for possible outcomes. The task requires some basic assumptions (axioms) about what are reasonable mechanisms for establishing collective preferences. Arrow imposed four. His 'theorem' shows that it is impossible to find a mechanism for establishing social preferences which satisfy all of his four axioms.

The first three axioms are uncontroversial: the mechanism should order all possible outcomes (have 'unrestricted domain'); it should not depend on the preferences of one individual (should be 'non-dictatorial'); and, if all individuals prefer outcome A over outcome B, there should also be a *social* preference of A over B (it should be '**Pareto**-optimal'). The fourth, apparently quite mild assumption was the so-called 'independence of irrelevant alternatives'. An alternative to any two possible outcomes is 'irrelevant' if *either* all individuals would prefer the 'irrelevant' one to *both* the outcomes under consideration *or* all individuals would prefer *both* those outcomes to the 'irrelevant' alternative. Arrow's fourth axiom is that the introduction of irrelevant alternatives does not affect the collective ordering of any two given outcomes: 'irrelevant' alternatives would not alter individuals' preferences *amongst* the alternatives already on offer.

Amongst economists, Arrow is best known for his theory of general market equilibrium. With Debreu, he provided the first description of equilibrium in a market economy. He again used the axiomatic method, establishing a mathematical statement of the conditions for equilibrium in an economy where household utility and profits are maximised; namely, a set of relative prices which ensure that supply always equals demand. This opened up a field of economics which went beyond the traditional *partial* equilibrium analysis, in which the price of each *single* good ensures that supply equals demand, to examine how prices may ensure equilibrium in the markets for *all* goods. Because a change in one price potentially effects supply and demand in all other markets, this is technically a difficult problem.

General equilibrium, the view ascribed by **Keynes** to the classical economists, is the opposite of Keynes's own analysis, which suggests that general equilibrium can *not* be achieved: prices (particularly for labour) do *not* adjust; factors of production remain idle and output below its potential. None of this would happen in a so-called 'Arrow–Debreu' economy. However, as another of Arrow's collaborators, Frank Hahn, has often emphasised, general equilibrium theory does not justify the market as the sole mechanism for the allocation of economic resources. On the contrary, the axiomatic method reveals just how strong are the assumptions needed for market allocations to generate an optimal outcome. Judged by the standards of general equilibrium theory, market allocation in the real world is usually very far from optimal. General equilibrium theory provides a precise guide to the circumstances where the market might be improved upon – though that does not establish that the alternatives would perform any better.

Symmetric information is one of the conditions for general equilibrium: all agents (households or firms) must share the same information. The crucial point is the symmetry. It is does not matter if some information is unknown (the weather next summer, for example), provided everyone is equally ignorant on the point. Arrow used the device of 'contingent commodity markets' to show that, provided information is symmetric, the standard results of general equilibrium theory apply even when there is uncertainty. He distinguished commodities and their values according to the outcome of uncertain events: an umbrella in a wet summer is treated as a different commodity from one in a dry summer. Provided there is a market price for every 'contingent commodity', and assymetries of information are excluded, this kind of uncertainty remains quite consistent with general equilibrium analysis.

Yet Arrow has also provided analyses of allocation mechanisms where information is asymmetric rather than symmetric. Particularly influential was his 1964 paper on uncertainty and the welfare economics of medical care. This highlighted the difficulties of market allocation in medical care because the producer (the physician) has greater information about the commodity being sold than does the purchaser (the patient). Alternative (institutionally mediated) methods of allocation, in particular a code of professional ethics, therefore have to play a central allocative role. The paper can also be seen as the forerunner to the explosion of literature on the economics of information.

The concern with assymetries of information is pursued more broadly in Arrow's accessible public lectures, *The Limits of Organization*, which analyse the role of organizations in economic allocation. In Arrow's view, a central reason for these alternatives to market mechanisms is that information held by some has to be transmitted to others, a process not usually achieved effectively by market relationships: examples include the internal allocation of resources within firms, non-profit-making trusts, social and ethical conventions, even the operations of government itself. In this way, Arrow has been a pioneer in the so-called 'new institutional economics', which seeks to understand non-market institutions as real-world departures from the strict assumptions of general equilibrium theory.

Arrow's most direct influence has been the subdiscipline of axiomatic social choice theory, which was created *de novo* by his doctoral thesis. Social choice theory presents many attempts to get around his impossibility theorem (mostly by relaxation of the axiom of irrelevant alternatives) and many additional impossibility results. While the technical details are mostly of interest to *aficionados*, the general perspective of social choice theory has had a wider influence, especially on contractarian political thinkers such as John **Rawls**.

Because of its technical nature, general equilibrium analysis has had little influence outside the economics profession. But two connected results from this literature, the first and second 'theorems of welfare economics', have had a direct impact on wider political and social thought. They state mathematically precise conditions for general market equilibrium to achieve a **Pareto**-efficient allocation of welfare resources. They imply that there is no conflict between equity and efficiency in the strict Arrow–Debreu economy; but (as with that economy) stringent conditions must be satisfied if market allocations are to be the socially optimal course.

The economics of information which Arrow pioneered has been applied to financial and insurance markets, investment in education, labour markets and the process of research and development. Meanwhile the new institutional economics exerts a growing influence on social and political thinking, replacing the simple ideological dichotomy between interventionist and market-orientated economics with an understanding of how government itself is subject to the problems of limited information, and how a range of other non-market institutions can serve to correct deficiencies in market allocations.

Arrow, unlike **Keynes** or **Friedman**, is not associated with any particular economic policy doctrines. Nonetheless, one can fairly view Arrow as the leading thinker of the modern economic middle ground: that which grasps both the benefits of market allocation and the role of non-market institutions in improving on pure market outcomes. As the Keynesian critique of market economics retreats in the face of seemingly intractable social and economic problems, this newer economics is becoming the principal alternative to simple pro-market thinking.

Main works

Social Choice and Individual Values (2nd edn), New York: Wiley, 1963.

General Competitive Analysis (with F. H. Hahn), San Francisco, CA: Holden Day, 1971.

Essays in the Theory of Risk-Bearing, Amsterdam: North-Holland, 1971.

The Limits of Organization, New York: Norton, 1974.

Collected Papers of Kenneth J. Arrow, Vol. i; *Social Choice and Justice* (1983), Vol. ii: *General Equilibrium* (1983), Vol. iii: *Individual Choice under Certainty and Uncertainty* (1984), Vol. iv: *The Economics of Information* (1984), Vol. v: *Production and Capital* (1985), Vol. vi: *Applied Economics*, Cambridge, MA: Harvard University Press.

Further reading

Feiwel, George R. (ed.), *Arrow and the Ascent of Modem Economic Theory*, London: Macmillan, 1987.

Feiwel, George R. (ed.), *Arrow and the Foundations of the Theory of Economic Policy*, London: Macmillan, 1987.

Sen, Amartya, *Collective Choice and Social Welfare*, San Francisco, CA: Holden Day, 1970.

B

Beauvoir, Simone de (1908–1986)

Simone de Beauvoir was born in Paris to bourgeois parents, to become the elder of two daughters. Beauvoir attended a Catholic girls' school and later was enrolled at the Sorbonne. While preparing for the highly competitive French national examination (*l'agrégation*) she attended some philosophy lectures at the prestigious *Ecole Normale Supérieure*, at that time, strictly an all-male institution for the education of the academic elite. In 1929 as the youngest ever candidate of either gender for the *agrégation* in philosophy, Beauvoir came second to Jean-Paul Sartre. However, despite competing and achieving recognition with men at the highest level of national standing in philosophy Beauvoir never stressed her distinctiveness as a woman or her achievements as a philosopher. Instead she saw herself, along with other women of her generation who attained impressive public standing, as having become – at most – equal to men. Such were Beauvoir's modern liberal views of equality, human freedom and the individual subject.

The most frequently quoted phrase from all of Beauvoir's writings, including her several novels and her autobiographical works, remains the assertion from *The Second Sex*, published in French in 1949: 'One is not born, but rather becomes, a woman' encapsulates the hugely significant idea for the mid-twentieth century that femininity is a social construction. This assertion became central to subsequent feminist politics and fundamental to much social and political inquiry into the sexual division of labour, women's health, familial relations and popular culture.

In the same work, Beauvoir also asserts that women assume the status of the Other. Such otherness is not biologically created; it is socially constructed yet can be transcended by the individual subject. To remain the Other is to be the negative of man, to be passive not active; and this is to accept the immanence which culturally women become, but do not have to be. Reflecting Sartre's existentialist conception of being condemned to freedom, Beauvoir insists that women are ultimately free to transcend their situation of otherness; the problem is that they have been complicit in accepting their subordinate status. To become fully themselves, instead of remaining man's Other, a woman needs to be courageous to face her freedom and to recognise herself as a subject.

The tension in these two assertions, between being socially constructed and individually free to change one's situation, raises certain questions. How much does Beauvoir's philosophy owe to Sartre's existentialism? And how much was she constrained by his philosophy? Michèle Le Doeuff has argued that Beauvoir created her own philosophy, even though she was unaware of doing so. For subsequent women philosophers the difficulty with Beauvoir is, in part, her failure to claim the title of philosopher, restricting it to Sartre. In other part, Beauvoir is constrained by Sartre's notion of transcendence as conceived in opposition to immanence, the body, and hence to what might still be called the feminine.

Generally in her writings Beauvoir holds to the existentialist tenet that we can constantly and deliberately take responsibility for our situations and actions, and even for our response to the imperatives of our own bodies. Her novels, such as her first, *She Came to Stay*, and her Prix Goncourt winner, *The Mandarins*, suggest that to be truly ethical subjects we must transcend both our social and physical conditions as much as possible. And to be truly free women, like men, must learn to take responsibility for their own lives, alone and courageously. In the past women have often attempted to imprison men in the feminine world of domestic and bodily relations. But in the future women can move out of traditional domestic relations and demand respect, freedom and equality. In Sartrean terms, a woman remains man's Other out of bad faith or self-deception, supporting his transcendence while being complicit as an immanent object. Yet in the end Beauvoir moves beyond Sartre in offering a new understanding of social relations between men and women. She introduces the philosophical distinction that femininity has been a state of being Other to oneself, whereas men have been other than the Other.

Her life and her works suggest that access to the world of men is possible for women. In fact this should be women's goal. Such access is achievable once women recognise themselves as equal. Now equality is the pivotal term which distinguishes Beauvoir as a so-called first wave feminist from subsequent or second wave feminists; the latter insist on the importance of women's distinctiveness or difference. For example, equal is the critical word linking Beauvoir in a dialectical manner to contemporary French feminism. If equality means to have equal rights in the world of individual subjects, this is no longer enough or even the primary issue for French feminists such as Luce Irigaray. Whereas Beauvoir insists that access to the world of (male) subjects is achievable once a woman sees herself as equal, Irigaray counters with the claim that women need to create difference. In contrast to Beauvoir's earlier liberal feminism, feminists have come to recognise that their task must be to unearth sexual difference in order to become self-defined women.

In a popular essay, 'Equal or different?', first published in 1986 at the time of Beauvoir's death, Irigaray praises Beauvoir's achievements on behalf of all women and for modern feminism. Yet she insists that it is necessary to develop a new feminism of sexual difference. Irigaray provocatively questions the idea of equality. When modern feminists insist upon equality, to whom do they want to be equal? And to what laws are they making themselves equal? In Irigaray's words:

> To demand equality as women is . . . a mistaken expression of a real objective. The demand to be equal presupposes a point of comparison. To whom or to what do women want to be equalised? To men? To a salary? To a public office? To what standard? Why not to themselves? (Irigaray 1993: 12)

Beauvoir's account of the Other describes woman's situation as the other of the same; but to accept equality to the same is to accept the laws of men; the laws of the self-same subject are male, since they exclude or repress sexual difference. Irigaray argues that women's specific differences are not represented by our present laws, language or culture; she aims to move beyond Beauvoir with a radical transformation of the world of men. It is not enough to claim equality with men; rather women must first discover and then express sexual difference.

In being recognised as an independent, intellectual woman Simone de Beauvoir gave many twentieth-century women a significant role model. But at the same time Beauvoir has been treated with suspicion by subsequent feminists, frequently because of her life-long relationship with Jean-Paul Sartre. According to Beauvoir herself, Sartre was 'the philosopher'; it was he who insisted that she write on the myths which had shaped her upbringing as a woman. The result was *The Second Sex*. Yet Le Doeuff contends that Beauvoir produced influential philosophy for the next generation of women.

In *The Second Sex*, Beauvoir presented a crucial and formative feminist argument concerning a woman's status. She developed from Sartre's existentialism an account of woman's otherness and of the need for every woman to transcend her situation as the Other in order to become a subject. Her conclusion proposes a political project of liberation requiring that men and women work together in solidarity. However, Beauvoir's distinctiveness seems to rest upon a certain degree of awareness of women's oppression and of the social construction of every self as a gendered being. Precisely in revealing the social constraints on women's free choice she departs from the strict tenets of Sartrean existentialism and liberal individualism. Today we can see in the light of her writings what Beauvoir failed to recognise fully for herself: that women have lived constrained by the contradictions of individual freedom and social oppression.

Major works

She Came to Stay (1943), trans. Yvonne Moyse and Roger Senhouse, London: Fontana, 1984.

The Ethics of Ambiguity (1947), trans. Bernard Frechtman, New York: Citadel Press, 1976.

The Second Sex (1949), trans. H. M. Parshley, Harmondsworth: Penguin, 1984.

The Mandarins (1954), trans. Leonard M. Friedman, London: Fontana, 1986.

Memoirs of a Dutiful Daughter (1958), trans. James Kirkup, Harmondsworth: Penguin, 1987.

Force of Circumstance (1960), trans. Richard Howard, Harmondsworth: Penguin, 1987.

Further reading

Al-Hibri, Azizah Y. and Margaret A. Simons (eds), *Hypatia Reborn: Essays in feminist philosophy*, Part III: 'Beauvoir and feminist philosophy', Bloomington: Indiana University Press, 1990.

Green, Karen, *The Woman of Reason: Feminism, humanism and political thought*, Cambridge: Polity, 1995.

Irigaray, Luce, 'Equal or different?' in *Je, Tu, Nous: Toward a culture of difference* (1986), trans. Alison Martin, London: Routledge, 1993.

Le Doeuff, Michèle, *Hipparchia's Choice: An essay concerning women, philosophy, etc.*, Oxford: Basil Blackwell, 1991.

Moi, Toril, *Simone de Beauvoir: The making of an intellectual woman*, Oxford: Basil Blackwell, 1994.

Simons, Margaret A., 'Two interviews with Simone de Beauvoir', *Hypatia*, Special Issue on French Feminist Philosophy, 3 (1989), pp. 11–27.

Bell, Daniel (1919–)

Daniel Bell is an eminent and celebrated American scholar who has spent a large part of his professional career at Harvard University. He recently joined the prestigious American Academy of Arts and Sciences. His prolific output over the last three decades embraces the diverse areas of social and political theory, futurism, cultural and economic analysis, and his academic writings appeal in much the same way that J. K. Galbraith's do, targeting a wide audience and imparting a refreshing 'American' style and scope to often inaccessible, arcane and arid intellectual debates.

Bell first achieved international recognition in 1960 with the publication of *The End of Ideology*, a major work which generated widespread debates among American social and political theorists in the 1960s. Moreover, the book engendered a 'school' of thought, the prominent leader of which was Francis Fukuyama. Fukuyama, and other disciples following Bell's intellectual lead, declared 'history' was at an 'end', in so far as all alternatives to Western political liberalism were exhausted. This contro-versial philosophical proposition, that 'history' and the development of political ideology were exhausted particularly in rich countries, generated a fierce counterblast from the American sociological theorist C. **Wright Mills**, in 1961. In *A Letter to the New Left*, surprisingly not published until 1969, Wright Mills argued that Bell's view concerning the 'end' of history and ideology was lacking in academic objectivity. Wright Mills reasoned that 'endism' was merely a political fashion statement that ignored obvious realities in poor countries; moreover, he maintained and demon-strated that 'end of' concepts and views are not fully fledged political doctrines but merely offer veiled defences for political apathy and the status quo. Wright Mills argued that Bell's proposition of 'endism' was itself an ideology, not an 'end of' ideology. To a large extent, Wright Mills's critique of Bell's views on endism are now accepted as the established rebuttal of the central message contained in *The End of Ideology*; none-theless the work produced a massive literature.

In 1973 Bell published what was to become perhaps his most influen-tial piece, namely, *The Coming of Post-Industrial Society: A venture in social forecasting*, a work which placed Bell at the forefront of the futurist movement in the United States. In this study, which attracted consider-able attention at the time and has continued to do so up to the present day, Bell presented new choices, dilemmas and debates for rich 'high mass consumption' societies. In rich industrial economies the shift from agricultural into factory, and hence service, employment for much of the workforce, became the universal phenomenon associated with economic growth and 'high living standards'. Bell outlined a further possible phase of capitalist economic, social and political development into post-industrial service-based 'high mass consumption' societies.

The Coming of Post-Industrial Society offers an ideological framework containing four key analytical tenets. These are that in post-industrial society (a) societal divisions of social stratification, polity and culture are inextricably linked with 'mass' high-level consumption; (b) a 'new intellectual property' class emerges, segmented into scientific, techno-logical, administrative and cultural estates; (c) a growing incompatibility evolves between post-industrial rationalisation, democratic participation and apathy; and (d) a tacit choice approaches between technocratic meritocracy and 'hedonism'.

Bell faced criticism on these points from several commentators. Peter Kivisto (1981), for example, argued with others that Bell's four key areas of analysis were unconvincing because the eschatological and determinist tendencies of these concepts were questionable, and that he had failed to consider the bourgeoisie's potential for durability. That Bell had ascribed a 'benign' label to the technocracy was seen as a serious limitation too. Moreover, Bell's assumption that mankind will in the future control the means of producing its own social order is highly debatable, as witness the current instabilities in Eastern Europe.

In 1978, Bell produced another influential paper 'Modernism and capitalism', which stressed the cultural contradictions of capitalism. Using the concepts of 'axial principals' and 'axial structures', ideal types are considered in terms of technological economies, politics and culture. Bell regards history as an attempt by culture to produce unity through art. As a type of protest against order, modernism demolished this unity with its fundamental emphasis on the new. Bell argued here that although modernism and capitalism possess a common origin in so far as they both reject past traditions and socio-economic authority, they nevertheless differ, because modernism stresses impulsiveness whereas capitalism emphasises constraints. Culture had, according to Bell, become a major source of change. Modernism, however, then emerged to mirror the work of the masses rather than individuals with strong convictions. So, rather than persisting with its innovating themes, modernism became otiose in its repetition of past trends.

In 'Resolving the contradictions of modernity and modernism' (1990), Bell argued that modernity represents a basic change of consciousness. For example, modernity acknowledges the variability of human nature defined by history and culture, replacing the classical idea of human universals. He contends, moreover, that society is not a natural order but a social contract in which the individual, and not the community, is the essential element whose rights determine the basis of political order. Such a line of argument reveals the classic 'American' tone to Bell's writings.

Bell's academic focus began to shift in the 1990s into the domain of political economy. Thus in 1991 he published two papers on the Soviet economic system. In 'Behind the Soviet economic crisis: A background paper' (1991), and 'Socialism and planning: beyond the Soviet economic crisis' (1991), Bell basically contends that the collapse of the Soviet econ-omy was due to the fact that its pre-1991 socially minded management styles produced excessive bureaucratisation and concomitant inefficien-cies. Bell proposes that the failure of the Soviet economic system indicates that it was a mobilised rather than a planned economy, and that the distortions in the economy were due to the fact that the direction of planning was dictated by the political value system. According to Bell's 'ideal' Soviet style planning should be conceived as a model of different value systems that in turn reveal viable alternative patterns of growth and costs. Bell's analysis of Soviet economic philosophy fails to centre on the fundamental issues of central planning, which as Hayek correctly highlighted years before, involve information networks, co-ordination failures and lack of market knowledge – hence no 'single mind' can know the data needed for successful planning.

In 1993 Bell published 'The downfall of business giants: as American capitalism changes', primarily a study of the recent decline in market shares experienced by IBM, GM and US Steel. This study is far less innovative than the earlier ones on post-industrial society and modernism, since the central theme of the tract stresses the conventional wisdom that market dominance declines if competition from new entrants with superior technologies occurs.

The switch of focus in Bell's writings in the 1990s possibly reflects his sensitivity to the criticism put forward by many left-wing sociologists that his earlier ideas on the 'end of ideology' and post-industrial society are obsolete. It is clear that in the 1980s Bell was angered by the criticism that he belonged to the intellectual Right. Bell's writings over the last thirty years have generated seminal debates and critiques from leading theorists. His work on post-industrial society, modernism and post-modernism has been extremely influential in shaping the intellectual agenda in social and cultural theory since the sixties. *The Coming of Post-Industrial Society* should be seen as a landmark study in the sociology of futurism.

Main works

The End of Ideology, Cambridge, MA: Harvard University Press, 1960.

The Coming of Post-Industrial Society: A venture in social forecasting, New York: Basic Books, 1973.

'Modernism and capitalism', *Partisan Review*, 45 (1978), pp. 206–22.

'The new class: a muddled concept', *Society*, 16 (1979), pp. 15–23.

'The revolt against modernity', *Public Interest*, 81 (1985), pp. 42–63.

'The world and the United States in 2013', *Daedalus*, 116 (1987), pp. 1–31.

'Resolving the contradictions of modernity and modernism', *Society*, 27 (1990), pp. 43–50.

'Behind the Soviet economic crisis: a background paper', *Dissent*, 38 (1991), pp. 46–9.

'Socialism and planning: beyond the Soviet economic crisis', *Dissent*, 38 (1991), pp. 50–4.

'The downfall of the business giants: as American capitalism changes', *Dissent*, 40 (1993), pp. 316–23.

Further reading

Gibon-Donald, E., 'Post-industrialism: prosperity of decline?', *Sociological Focus*, 26 (1994), pp. 147–63.

Kivisto, Peter, 'The theorist as seer: the case of Bell's post-industrial society', *Quarterly Journal of Ideology*, 5 (1981), pp. 39–43.

Longstaff, S.-A., 'Daniel Bell and political reconciliation', *Queen's Quarterly*, 94 (1987), pp. 660–5.

Marien, M., 'Daniel Bell and the end of normal science', *Futurists*, 7 (1973), pp. 262–8.

O'Neil, Joan, 'Religion and post-modernism: the Durkheimian bond in Bell and Jameson', *Theory, Culture and Society*, 5 (1988), pp. 493–508.

Phillips, Mark, 'The coming post-industrial society: a review symposium', *Summation*, 2 (1973), pp. 60–103.

Glossary

Post-industrialism The age succeeding the decline of heavy labour-intensive technologies, towards capital-intensive computerised or digitised technology where service industries dominate.

Berlin, Isaiah (1906–)

Isaiah Berlin was born in 1906 in Riga, now the capital of independent Lithuania, then under Russian control. His family moved to Petrograd in 1917, where he witnessed both the revolutions of that year. His parents brought him to England in 1921. He gained a scholarship to study at Oxford, where, with the exception of wartime Government posts in New York, Washington and Moscow, he has spent all his working life. In the 1930s Berlin taught philosophy at Oxford, forming an influential discussion group with, among others, A. J. Ayer, Stuart Hampshire and J. L. Austin. After the war he moved away from 'pure philosophy' into that unfashionable academic suburb, the history of ideas. Most of Berlin's published work consists of collections of essays, among which *Four Essays on Liberty* (1969) has proved the most influential. Isaiah Berlin was Professor of Social and Political Theory in Oxford from 1957–67 and president of the British Academy from 1974–8. He was knighted in 1957.

Isaiah Berlin has drawn a famous distinction between writers who, like the hedgehog, have one big idea, and those who, like the fox, have many. Hedgehogs interpret the world in the light of a single, all-embracing system; the foxes attempt to understand the world as endlessly complex, its plurality requiring a plurality of theoretical approaches. Despite the great range of his writing and his evident preference for the foxes, Berlin is himself something of a hedgehog (although his one big idea is an ultimate justification for the foxes): almost all of his work is dedicated to showing that there are a variety of human values, moral principles and ethical systems which cannot, ultimately, be reconciled.

Berlin's massive erudition, grand historical vision and penetrating intelligence, along with his big idea, are all on display in a short essay he wrote on 'The originality of Machiavelli' (published in *Against the Current*). Berlin surveys the bewildering variety of interpretations that Machiavelli's *The Prince* and *Discourses* have attracted since the seventeenth century. Was the author a black satirist or a realistic politician? A ruthless monarchist, a stern republican or a democrat? A revolutionary or a reactionary? An anguished humanist or an evil, satanic manipulator? Berlin picks apart the various Machiavellis showing how each interpreter reveals more about his own time and interests than about the original. For Berlin, this failure to agree on the meaning of *The Prince* does more than demonstrate the inadequacies of any particular interpretation. Berlin argues that we can find two quite different value systems in Machiavelli's work, two systems which, although both coherent, and morally defensible, are completely incompatible: the Christian and the pagan. The Christian virtues (charity, mercy, the love of God, forgiveness of enemies, etc.) are fine and noble things, but, for Machiavelli (or rather Berlin's Machiavelli) they are incompatible with the Renaissance world of bitter political struggle, warfare and intrigue. If a state is to survive, its citizens must embrace the martial values of courage, fortitude and ruthlessness – the virtues on which Rome's greatness was built.

It is the failure to understand that there can be such things as incompatible values that has brought about the uncertainty over the meaning of Machiavelli. We too often assume that there must be some overarching system which can accommodate all those things which we take to be worthwhile. For Berlin, the central fact of human existence is that there can be no such unifying system. We want different things, we value things differently; frequently there will be no reconciliation. Berlin's 'liberalism' is based on the acceptance that society must be plural, that we cannot argue or rationalise our way out of the confusion of human values, into a simpler world. To be human is to differ.

It is this insight that inspires Berlin's greatest contribution to political and social philosophy: his work on the idea of freedom. This is given its most potent statement in his essay 'Two concepts of liberty' (in *Four Essays on Liberty*). Berlin argues that there are two conceptions of liberty which, if not incompatible conceptually, have always, historically, come into conflict. 'Negative freedom' is the freedom from interference, the freedom to pursue whatever goals we choose without active hindrance from other people. Negative freedoms can be vital, such as the freedom to speak freely, or 'trivial', such as the freedom to carry weapons. A government might be justified in curtailing the latter where it can show that other rights would be endangered, but it is nevertheless a restriction on (negative) liberty.

'Positive freedom' is a rather more complex concept, present in some degree in the work of Rousseau, Kant, Hegel and **Marx**. Individual positive freedom is the idea of being one's own master, deciding by what rules and principles one should live. From the perspective of positive freedom, a society is free when it subjects itself to rational self-government under some such principle as the general will. Berlin argues that this benign-seeming concept is, by its nature, anti-pluralist: it does not involve the freedom to choose between competing goals, but instructs us to follow a particular path. Only by following that path, the advocates of positive freedom maintain, can we truly be free. The doctrine of positive freedom almost inevitably becomes oppressive because of the failure to realise that people have differing, and indeed incompatible goals. It assumes that a person might be mistaken about what he or she really wants, that our true interests may be quite different from what we believe them to be. Positive freedom has been too easily appropriated by authoritarians of both the left and the right as a justification for oppression and leads ultimately to the gas chamber or the gulag.

Negative freedom can also be abused: too much liberty for the wolves means less liberty for the sheep. Berlin fully supports the safety-net of the welfare state, and legislation protecting workers from exploitation by ruthless employers. Nevertheless, only the concept of negative liberty can form the basis of a humane society, and only under a capitalist system with a democratic government can the plurality of human aspirations be accommodated.

Berlin's pluralism follows from his rejection of the idea that there is a single human nature. People, for Berlin, are products of the enormously complex web of influences specific to particular cultures and times, and he has always championed those thinkers, such as Vico and Herder, who have recognised this specificity. Giambattista Vico (1668–1744) was among the first to realise the imaginative leap needed to enter the minds of those living in earlier historical periods. Johann Gottfried von Herder (1744–1803) carried Vico's insights further, emphasising the particularity of different contemporary cultures, moulded by their separate geographies, histories, languages and myths. Berlin, although temperamentally a man of the Enlightenment, feels that these figures of the 'counter-Enlightenment' were a necessary corrective to the rationalist belief in the unity of mankind and the inevitability of progress.

Although, for Berlin, we are the products of our times, he retains a place for a (limited) freedom of choice for the human subject. In his essay 'Historical inevitability' (*Four Essays on Liberty*) he argues that without this freedom our concept of morality, our legal system and our view of history would have no meaning. Introducing an element of free choice means abandoning historicist, deterministic accounts of human history – there are times when the actions of great leaders have changed history, and those actions were, at least partially, the result of free choices. History therefore can have no master-plan, no fixed pattern.

Along with Karl **Popper**, Isaiah Berlin has been the most influential theorist of liberalism since the Second World War. As with Popper, it is an influence felt more in the wider world of cultural discourse than among professional philosophers. His liberalism is both more humane and conceptually much richer than such neo-liberals as **Friedman**, **Hayek** and **Nozick**, but for that reason it came to seem a little dated in the 1970s and 1980s. Berlin has done much to bring respectability to the history of ideas, although it remains a Cinderella discipline in the English-speaking world.

Main works

Four Essays on Liberty, London: Oxford University Press, 1969.

Vico and Herder, London: Hogarth Press, 1976.

Concepts and Categories: Philosophical essays, ed. Henry Hardy, London: Hogarth Press, 1978.

Karl Marx: His life and environment, 4th edn, Oxford: Oxford University Press, 1978.

Russian Thinkers, ed. Henry Hardy and Aileen Kelly, London: Hogarth, 1978.

Against the Current: Essays in the history of ideas, ed. Henry Hardy, London: Hogarth, 1979.

Personal Impressions, ed. Henry Hardy, London: Hogarth, 1980.

The Crooked Timber of Humanity: Chapters in the history of ideas, London: John Murray, 1991.

The Magus of the North: J. G. Hamann and the origins of modern irrationalism, London: John Murray, 1993.

Further reading

Galipeau, Claude, *History, Pluralism and Liberty: A study of Isaiah Berlin's political thought*, Oxford: Oxford University Press, 1993.

Gay, John, *Isaiah Berlin*, London: HarperCollins, 1995.

Jahanbegloo, Ramin, *Conversations with Isaiah Berlin*, London: Peter Halban, 1992.

Margalit, Edna and Avishai (eds), *Isaiah Berlin: A celebration*, London: Hogarth, 1991.

Ryan, Alan (ed.), *The Idea of Freedom: Essays in honour of Isaiah Berlin*, Oxford: Oxford University Press, 1979.

Bonhoeffer, Dietrich (1906–1945)

Dietrich Bonhoeffer, the German theologian, academic and Lutheran pastor is notable as one of the century's most influential theologians and one of its most significant martyrs. Born into a prosperous and liberal family, Bonhoeffer studied theology at Tübingen, Rome and Berlin where he came under the influence of Karl Barth. Bonhoeffer became a lecturer at Berlin in 1930 and was ordained in the following year, but his conventional life of scholarship was changed in 1933 when the National Socialists came to power. From the start Bonhoeffer was involved in opposition to fascism. Abandoning his academic life, which now seemed without meaning, Bonhoeffer took an active part in the political struggle within his own church. Some elements of the church, the pro-Nazi 'German Christians', argued for collaboration with the government and a synthesis of National Socialist ideology with Christianity. Bonhoeffer, like Barth, repudiated the notion of the adulteration of Christianity with fascism and became involved in the founding of the 'Confessing Church' from the sections of the Lutheran church which opposed Hitler. After a period in London as the pastor of a German-speaking congregation, Bonhoeffer returned to Germany to lead the Finkenwalde preachers' seminary. After the Gestapo closed the seminary down, Bonhoeffer spent some time in the United States. However, in 1939 Bonhoeffer spurned the chance of a secure job in exile in the United States and returned to Germany for the war years. Abandoning his *quondam* pacifism, Bonhoeffer became an active member of the resistance movement and part of a conspiracy to murder Hitler. In April 1943 the Gestapo arrested him and he was imprisoned in Buchenwald concentration camp. He spent the last two years of his life in several prisons, from where he produced his important *Letters and Papers from Prison*. Bonhoeffer's most influential work, *The Cost of Discipleship* (1937), insists that Christian belief is 'costly' and involves huge personal sacrifice in the modern secular world. So it proved for Bonhoeffer, who was executed in April 1945.

Though his theology developed and changed over his short career, Bonhoeffer is consistent in his preoccupation with Jesus Christ and the role of the Christian within both secular and religious communities. His work demonstrates a profound concern with discipleship and martyrdom, traditional Christian themes which were given new potency in the context of Bonhoeffer's life. Bonhoeffer's life was spent in the midst of the darkest manifestation of human society and his work engages with the place of faith amidst oppression and suffering.

Bonhoeffer's early theology demonstrates a strong reaction against nineteenth-century liberal (that is post-Enlightenment, optimistic, scientific) theology which is dismissed in favour of a neo-orthodoxy (that is the post-existentialist restatement of Reformation principles) which was much influenced by Barth. In his unfinished lecture series, *Christology*, which dates from 1933, Bonhoeffer rejects the liberal theologians' non-incarnational conception of Christ as a religious pioneer and insists upon the notion of Christ as a divine saviour. Bonhoeffer examines what he sees as the central role of Christ in human experience and this theme is one which he returned to throughout his life. For him, only through Christ can human history and human nature be explained and interpreted. And human history and politics are vital parts of Bonhoeffer's thought. He is concerned with the things of this life as much as those of the next. Christians must serve their fellow men in a world of pain and suffering. The great example is Christ, 'there only for others', whose life is one of costly sacrifice. In his *Ethics*, upon which he was working at the time of his arrest, Bonhoeffer argues that though Christianity addresses the 'ultimate' (the transcendental and the eschato-logical 'last things'), the Christian lives in a 'penultimate' world (the 'things before the last') and must address the everyday ethical and social responsibilities of the quotidian world. The Christian has a duty to speak out against oppression in its various forms (racism, totalitarianism, war).

In the most important of his books to be published during his lifetime, *The Cost of Discipleship*, Bonhoeffer is preoccupied with the question of what the call to discipleship means for the Christian in a secular society, for 'the only way to follow Jesus was by living in the world'. What does discipleship mean for 'the worker, the business man, the squire and the soldier'? Bonhoeffer offers a sustained exposition of the Sermon on the Mount which is not to be dismissed as demanding an impossibly ideal standard of behaviour. For discipleship is 'costly'. Repudiating the 'cheap grace' of conventional bourgeois lip-service to religious doctrine, Bonhoeffer insists on 'costly grace', which may cost 'a man his life . . . and cost God the life of his Son'.

In Bonhoeffer's next significant work, the privately circulated *Life Together*, he drew on his experiences at the Finkenwalde seminary which had been closed by the Nazis. The religious community (the 'House of Brethren') which Bonhoeffer had established at Finkenwalde is used as the model for his advocacy of communal existence in monastic-style communities. In the midst of a society gone mad, Bonhoeffer meditates on the notion of a true Christian vision of brotherhood.

Bonhoeffer's theological achievement in his last writings, the material collected in his *Letters and Papers from Prison* is not easy to assess, given its dependence upon fragmentary papers which were written in the most wretched of circumstances and smuggled from under the gaze of the Gestapo. Bonhoeffer died before he could complete a systematic account of the innovative concepts such as 'worldly Christianity' of which he offers tantalising glimpses in his prison letters. However, it is fair to say that *Letters and Papers from Prison* shows Bonhoeffer's thought beginning to strike out in new theological directions. He criticises the most significant post-liberal thinkers, Barth, Tillich, Bultmann, and begins to look for a new way ahead which is suitable for 'a world come of age'. The most striking and influential conceptions found in Bonhoeffer's late theology are the notions of 'secular holiness' and 'religionless Christianity'. Bonhoeffer argues that man must be able 'to live in the world as if there is not God', must take responsibility for his own actions, and also not rely upon God to be rescued from the consequences of error. Religion which simply acts as a kind of psychological crutch is worthless. In a world which has come of age, 'God is teaching us that we must live as well as men who can get along very well without him.' Religion should not be based on fear or insecurity, but upon a sense of responsibility towards other human beings, 'holy worldliness', for, in a phrase which offers an emblematic summary of Bonhoeffer's entire thought, 'the Christian life is to be lived in the world'.

It is undeniable that Bonhoeffer's renown is, to a large degree, dependent upon his life and, in particular, his death, rather than his work. The image of the youthful martyr to fascism has inspired both liberation theologians and wider Christian opposition to oppressive political regimes. However, Bonhoeffer's thought, fragmentary though it is, has not been without influence. In particular, Bonhoeffer's prison letters have had a profound influence on the development of post-war theology in Europe, America and the Third World. Bonhoeffer has been claimed by a wide variety of spiritual movements: liberation theology, theologians of secularity, ecumenism, the 1960s counter-cultural 'death-of-God theology', as well as more conventional theological thought.

Main works

Christology (1933), trans. Edwin Robertson, London: Collins, 1978.

The Cost of Discipleship (1937), trans. Reginald Fuller, London: SCM, 1959.

Life Together, trans. John Doberstein, London: SCM, 1954.

Ethics, trans. Neville Horton Smith, London: Collins, 1964.

Letters and Papers from Prison, ed. Etherhard Bethge, trans. Frank Clark *et al.*, London: Collins, 1967.

Further reading

Bethge, Eberhard, *Dietrich Bonhoeffer: Theologian, Christian, contemporary*, trans. E. Mosbacher *et al.*, London: Collins, 1970.

Bethge, Eberhard, *Bonhoeffer: Exile and martyr*, trans. Eberhard Bethge and John W. de Gruchy, London: Collins, 1975.

Feil, Ernst, *The Theology of Dietrich Bonhoeffer*, Philadelphia: Forest, 1985.

Godsey, J. D., *The Theology of Dietrich Bonhoeffer*, London: SCM, 1960.

Phillips, John A., *The Form of Christ in the World: A study of Bonhoeffer's Christology*, London: Collins, 1967.

Bourdieu, Pierre (1930–)

Pierre Bourdieu was born and raised in a village community in the French Pyrenees mountains. He first studied philosophy, but soon switched to the social sciences. During the Algerian nationalists' struggle for independence from French colonial domination, Bourdieu worked amongst the Kabyle peasantry as a field sociologist and ethnographer. On returning to Paris in the early 19606, Bourdieu worked at the universities of the Sorbonne, Lille and, in 1964, was elected to the Ecole des Haute Etudes et

Sciences Sociales. Bourdieu was working in Paris during the events of May 1968, a critical moment for a generation of French intellectuals and theoreticians. He is currently Professor of Sociology at the Collège de France.

Bourdieu's intellectual trajectory has resulted in work which traverses the disciplines of ethnography and anthropology, sociology, philosophy and linguistics. From this multidisciplinary base his project has sought to overcome the classical antinomies of the social sciences: objectivism and subjectivism; structure and agency; symbolic and material. In addition, whilst it is clear that Bourdieu's work has been conditioned by the linguistic turn in the human sciences, it claims to move beyond the theoretical polarities represented by Saussure and Chomsky. Beginning always with strenuous acts of self-reflexive positioning, Bourdieu's work asks how relations of domination are reproduced in objective social spaces through agents whose subjectivities are themselves the product of complex, but objective, historical determinations. This is answered through a methodology which privileges two concepts: the field and the habitus.

Fields are objective domains of social activity which consist of shifting relations between positions grounded in forms of power. Power, for Bourdieu, is best characterised as 'capital', which should not be equated simply with concentrations of economic wealth, nor with the 'rational' logic of political economy: a Kabyle peasant family may buy an excess yoke of oxen, and then sell it during the ploughing season, when it would be most economically logical to retain it: yet they would still have accumulated social capital from the possession because of the prestige it bestowed upon the family during marriage negotiations, a central practice in establishing relations of domination. Such empirical data from Bourdieu's ethnographic field work, theoretically framed in perhaps his most important methodological statement, *Outline of a Theory of Practice* (1972), suggest that the 'economic' is merely one of many fields. More important to fields in general is the exercise of symbolic violence and the 'practical' logic which determines the means by which an appropriate form of capital is accumulated, exchanged and converted into positions of power. Indeed, capital – derived from the symbolic violence exercised through the possession of objects as divergent as oxen in peasant societies and educational qualifications in modern societies – is the stake which drives the pursuit of profit, and structures relations of domination, in any given field.

The habitus is the concept which Bourdieu uses to account objectively for the varieties of subjective disposition deployed in the pursuit of this activity: a habitus is a subjective but not individual system of internalised structures, schemes of perception, conceptions and actions common to all members of the same class or group (*Outline*, p. 86); it is the objective consequence of a forgotten history of class which has taken root in the body. Particular fields structure particular kinds of habitus, and reciprocally, a habitus comes to view a specific field as a knowable and meaningful world in which it is worthwhile to invest time and energy. It is in this context that Bourdieu's extensive work on the educational and academic field should be read. *Homo Academicus* (1984), Bourdieu's freeze-frame analysis of the French higher education system in 1968, revealed that a large proportion of in-post senior academics, especially in the arts and humanities, were the children of academic and professional families. In other words, success in the academic field could be traced back to a specific kind of habitus, and a consequent willingness to invest time and energy in the pursuit of professorial discourse, a form of symbolic power which, as Bourdieu argued as early as 1965 in his joint publication *Academic Discourse*, is premised on the reproduction of widespread incomprehension amongst the student body, and a limited success rate in mastery over the discourse.

Bourdieu's interpretation of the academic habitus also reveals the symbolic violence that goes misrecognised beneath the notions of 'culture' and 'taste'. In *Distinction* (1979), Bourdieu engages in a 'making strange' of the classical maps of aesthetics, including the ideas of universality and disinterestedness articulated in Kant's *Critique of Judgement*. Bourdieu argues that competence in the academic field, measured in terms of academic qualifications, legitimises the accumulation of cultural capital: educational capital, which denotes competence, can be exchanged for prestigious cultural capital – vested in the acquisition of knowledge of certain kinds of literature, music, and visual art – which is held to be aesthetically 'distinctive', and which is, homologically, a mark of social distinction.

A consequence of Bourdieu's sociological coupling of education and culture is a critique of the traditional political field. Apt to encourage its misrecognition as the expression of popular opinion and the sovereign will of the nation, the political field, for Bourdieu, is constituted by certain types of discourse whose practices are homologically linked to the discourses of the academic field. The political and cultural fields, though autonomous, are still linked through their common adherence to distinctions measured through the possession of educational competence and forms of discourse which are highly valued in an overlapping linguistic marketplace: for Bourdieu, people who express no opinion in response to a question posed by an opinion poll are not abrogating their democratic responsibility: instead, they are recognising their dependency on opinion-producing apparatuses.

In thus subjecting the constituted political field to critique, and acknowledging the power of language in constituting and delimiting the field, Bourdieu might seem to be in tune with a generation of French intellectuals who, especially in response to the events of May 1968, politicised language and translated politics into linguistic categories. Certainly Bourdieu's ethnographic work was influenced by **Lévi-Strauss's** structuralism. However, Bourdieu was never at one with the Saussurean objective linguistic model on which structuralism rested. Instead, and rejecting simultaneously the theory for which other opponents of Saussure reached – Chomsky's idealist grammar – Bourdieu came to view language as a performative practice, generated out of a habitus and exchangeable in the embattled linguistic marketplace of a field. Indeed, it is significant that in his analysis of the 1968 French university crisis in *Homo Academicus*, the texts of **Foucault**, Barthes and Derrida are viewed as acts towards a struggle for prestige within a deeply divided academic field. A methodological sense of social forces, structures and determinations is required to contextualise these acts and thus to understand the intersecting social trends which increased the value of post-structuralism and deconstruction in the post-1968 academic marketplace. And whereas these latter critical tendencies eschew scientism, Bourdieu remains committed to the scientific goals of social science.

In reinstating a genetic account of human agency in social theory, Bourdieu is arguing against the anti-humanist Marxist and psycho-analytic offshoots of structuralism (the subtext of *Outline*). However, the concept of the habitus may still be as deterministic as anything proposed by Althusser, and may, beneath theoretical sophistication, be harbouring a fairly traditional class analysis which is better at observing continuities than grasping the nature of contradiction and contestation. In an otherwise sympathetic appraisal of his work, John B. Thompson has argued that Bourdieu's model of social reproduction is overly consensual, and relies on inadequately theorized notions of misrecognition and recognition.

English translations of Bourdieu's texts have appeared somewhat erratically: for instance, published originally in 1965, *Academic Discourse* did not appear in English until 1994. As a result, English-speaking social and political theorists have perhaps found it difficult to assess the full impact of his work. But with translations now having appeared, allied to the publication of book length studies of Bourdieu, something like a proper appraisal is now possible: and this should be set alongside the more localised impact that Bourdieu's work has already had on cultural studies – including the study of cultural institutions such as museums – and educational theory.

Main works

Academic Discourse: Linguistic misunderstanding and professorial power (with Jean-Claude Passeron and Monique de Saint Martin, 1965), trans. Richard Teese, Cambridge: Polity, 1994.

Outline of a Theory of Practice (1972), trans. Richard Nice, Cambridge: Cambridge University Press, 1979.

Distinction: A social critique of the judgment of taste (1979), trans. Richard Nice, London: Routledge, 1989.

Language and Symbolic Power (1982), trans. Gino Raymond and Matthew Adamson, Cambridge: Polity, 1992.

Homo Academicus (1984), trans. Peter Collier, Cambridge: Polity, 1988.

Further reading

Brubaker, R., 'Rethinking classical social theory: the sociological vision of Pierre Bourdieu', *Theory and Society*, 14 (1985), pp. 745–75.

Garnham, N. and R. Williams, 'Pierre Bourdieu and the sociology of culture: an introduction', *Media, Culture and Society*, 2 (1980), pp. 209–23.

Jenkins, R., *Pierre Bourdieu*, London: Routledge, 1992.

Layder, D., *Understanding Social Theory*, London: Sage, 1994.

Thompson, J. B., *Studies in the Theory of Ideology*, Cambridge: Polity, 1984.

Wacquant, L. J. D. (with P. Bourdieu), *An Invitation to Reflexive Sociology*, Cambridge: Polity, 1992.

Braudel, Fernand (1902–1985)

Braudel's wide-ranging historical works represent one of the most impressive conceptualisations of European social and economic development to be written in the twentieth century. From the 1940s to the 1980s Braudel was the premier historian in France and heir to the *Annales* tradition of Marc Bloch and Lucien Febvre. He studied history at the Sorbonne and, while preparing his doctoral thesis on the Mediterranean and Philip ɪɪ, he held a number of teaching posts in Algeria and Paris (1923–35); between 1935 and 1938, he worked at the University of São Paulo. During the war Braudel was held in a German prisoner-of-war camp, where he wrote up his doctoral research in exercise books, mainly from memory, posting it in sections to Febvre. The thesis, defended in 1947, was published as *The Mediterranean and the Mediterranean World in the Age of Philip II* (1949) and is now regarded as one of the finest books of its age. Braudel was appointed professor at the Collège de France (1949) and president of the Sixth Section (Economic and Social Sciences) of the Ecole Pratique des Hautes Etudes (1956–72). From 1956 to 1968 he edited the journal, established by Bloch and Febvre, *Annales d'histoire économique et sociale*. In 1963 he founded the Maison des Sciences de L'Homme, dedicated to the promotion of interdisciplinary research.

Braudel was perhaps the greatest scholar of the Annales school. His monumental works, though principally concerned with the early modern period (1400–1800), made regular reference to earlier periods and were written with one eye to the modern Europe of the author's day. Although he was a committed European, his perspective on history was global. Yet most of his works are written around a European/non-European dichotomy and France remains central to all that he penned. Braudel was concerned to write what he called 'total history' (*histoire totale*) over the long term (*longue durée*) and he echoed **Marx**'s emphasis upon the material dimension. However, at best Braudel was ambivalent to Marx, and some have described him as anti-Marxist as it is clear he tried to formulate an alternative to historical materialism. Just as Marxism has been criticised on the grounds of economic determinism, Braudel's history was charged with being 'ecologically' determined, and central to his writings is the struggle between humans and nature.

The main influence on Braudel came from the early Annalistes, and particularly Lucien Febvre. Like Bloch and Febvre, Braudel was anxious to promote the interdisciplinary nature of history; to harness its study to the works of sociologists, economists and geographers. Braudel's geographical approach – which he himself termed 'geo-history' – was much influenced by Vidal de la Blache and Friedrich Ratzel. Other early influences include the Belgian medieval historian, Henri Pirenne, whose work stressed an understanding of European history by reference to a wider geopolitical arena. Braudel's later works owe something to a number of historians, geographers and economists such as Immanuel **Wallerstein**, Karl Polyani and, probably, Oswald Spengler.

Braudel's classic book, *The Mediterranean* perhaps came closer than any other to total history. The first of its three sections deals with the seemingly timeless relationship between humans and their environment. The second deals with the changing economic, social and political systems of civilisation. The third examines the fast-moving history of events. In each section, Braudel was, like other Annalistes, concerned to express the limitations of traditionalist, nineteenth-century modes of historical writing with their emphasis upon men and men's actions. *The*

Mediterranean was, more than any book of its time, an attempt to reverse the increasing fragmentation and thematic specialisation of history, which had been a feature of the 1920s and 1930s outside the Annales school. John Tosh writes that Braudel's aim was 'to recapture human life in its variety' (*The Pursuit of History*); and James Henretta describes his work as 'a comprehensive, multidimensional cubist portrait of society' ('Social History as Lived and Written', *American Historical Review*, 84 (1979)). Braudel contrasts the eastern and western Mediterranean worlds ruled by Turkey and Spain, but he concluded that these worlds were more unified than Europe itself because they were shaped by a common environment, by common produce and by a similar reliance on the sea itself for trade and food. Braudel's *The Mediterranean* has been likened to Gibbon's *Decline and Fall of the Roman Empire*, for both authors display a vast historical knowledge concluding that the Roman and Spanish empires were each crushed by their own weight.

Braudel's other great work – known in English as *Civilisation and Capitalism* – is similar in organisation to *The Mediterranean* which preceded it. Originally intended to complement volumes by Febvre (who died before they could be written), *Civilisation and Capitalism* bears a striking structural resemblance to a Marxist conception of society. Its three volumes are principally concerned with modes and impacts of consumption, distribution and production in the old regime (1400–1800). The project constitutes a genuine attempt to write world history, for in it Braudel attempts systematically to unite, by comparison, the major civilisations of the eastern and western worlds – India, China, Japan and Indonesia, the Americas and Europe. In so doing, it combines the 'history of everyday life' with greater social and economic developments. Its central quest is to discover the material culture of the period.

While lauded by many as one of the greatest historians of the twentieth century, Braudel also had his critics. It has been said that 'total history' is impossible beyond the local level: that something as big as the Mediterranean world cannot be treated inclusively. Moreover, as Tosh claims, 'Braudel and his followers have conspicuously failed to develop a satisfactory model for integrating political history with environmental and demographic studies' and he goes on to add: 'In this respect at least, it must be counted as inferior to Marxist history with its emphasis upon the reciprocal interaction between the productive forces, the relations of production and the superstructure' (*The Pursuit of History*). Marxists, like Eugene and Elizabeth Genovese, condemned Braudel because his work, with its 'structural interpretation, with its anthropological, ecological and archaeological predilections, implicitly negates the historical process itself'. Braudel has also been criticised because he failed adequately to account for the role of human agency and class formation in the process of historical change. For Braudel, historical 'man' was relegated as a 'prisoner' of his environment; and the early modern world Braudel recreated, said one reviewer, is 'unresponsive to human control'. *The Mediterranean* in particular evinced little concern with mentalities and ideas, eschewing such important phenomena as manners and customs. Within the historical world, Braudel's influence was considerable. The roll-call of historians who developed under his aegis is impressive indeed. Pierre Chaunu ascribes his own interest in the Mediterranean to hearing Braudel lecture, while Emmanuel le Roy Ladurie, the most important of the third generation of *Annales* historians, wrote his doctoral thesis on the peasants of Mediterranean France under Braudel's directorship. LeRoy Ladurie succeeded Braudel at the Collège de France, and his thesis, published as *The Peasants of the Languedoc* (1966) is, like Braudel's works, a 'total history. Just as Braudel's history was 'global', so his influence extended beyond France. In Italy and Poland, Braudel's work was well received at the time of publication and the American historian, N. J. K. Pounds, is a notable follower of Braudelian method. In Germany and Britain, however, the *Annales* tradition enjoyed less success until recently. While German historians of Braudel's generation were preoccupied with their own turbulent political history, empirically minded British historians tended to dislike the style of the *Annales*. Moreover, words such as *mentalités* are difficult to translate into English. British historians of the 1940s and 1950s, with the exception of pioneers like W. G. Hoskins, tended to view Braudel's work as generalised and unsubstantiated. Since the 1960s, however, notable English proponents of the *Annales* tradition include Peter Burke and Keith Thomas.

Main works

'Les espagnols et l'Afrique du Nord', *Revue africaine*, 69 (1928), pp. 184–233, 351–410.

The Mediterranean and the Mediterranean World in the Age of Philip II (1949), London: HarperCollins, 1972.

'Présence de Lucien Febvre', *Eventail de l'histoire vivante* (1953), pp. 1–16.

'Georges Gurvitch et la discontinuité du social', *Annales*, 12 (1953), pp. 347–61.

'Lucien Febvre et l'histoire', *Cahiers internationaux de sociologie*, 22 (1957), pp. 15–20.

'Marc Bloch', *International Encyclopaedia of the Social Sciences*, 5 (1968), pp. 348–50.

'Personal testimony', *Journal of Modern History*, 44 (1972), pp. 448–67.

Afterthoughts on Material Civilisation, London: Johns Hopkins University Press, 1979.

On History, London: Weidenfeld and Nicholson, 1980.

'The rejection of the Reformation in France', in H. Lloyd-Jones (ed.), *History and Imagination*, London: Duckworth, 1981.

Civilisation and Capitalism, Vol. I: *The Structures of Everyday Life*, Vol. II: *The Wheels of Commerce*, Vol. III: *The Perspective of the World*, London: Collins, 1984.

The Identity of France, Vol. I: *History and Environment*, Vol. II: *People and Production*, London: HarperCollins, 1988.

A History of Civilisations, London: Allen Lane, 1994.

Further reading

Bailyn, B., 'Braudel's geohistory – a reconsideration', *Journal of Economic History*, 11 (1951), pp. 277–82.

Burke, Peter, *The French Historical Revolution: The Annales school, 1929–1989*, Oxford: Polity, 1990.

Burke, P., 'Fernand Braudel', in John Cannon (ed.), *The Historian at Work*, London: Allen and Unwin, 1980, pp. 188–202.

Tosh, John, *The Pursuit of History*, 2nd edn, London: Longman, 1990.

Trevor-Roper, Hugh, 'Fernand Braudel, the Annales, and the Mediterranean', *Journal of Modern History*, 44 (1972), pp. 468–79.

Wesseling, H., 'Fernand Braudel, historian of the Longue Durée', *Itinerario*, 5 (1981), pp. 16–29.

Burnham, James (1905–1987)

James Burnham was an American academic and political theorist. Although he had an academic base, his writing was principally intended to influence wider political debates. In the course of his career, he moved from a position on the left of US politics (associated with the Trotskyist movement) to one on the libertarian right. Although his work largely drew on and synthesised the arguments of others, it was also influential in shaping contemporary debates.

In his book *The Managerial Revolution* (first published in 1941) Burnham developed the thesis that the world was passing through a fundamental structural change, in which capitalism was being superseded by a new social formation. Capitalism, however, was not – as Marxists might suggest – under challenge from socialism, or at risk of being overcome through working-class revolution. On the contrary, said Burnham, the new line of development might best be characterised as 'managerialism'. What was happening was a global trend for managers as a social group to seek political and economic power in their own right, as a form of ruling class. In this context, 'managers' were defined as those responsible for 'the technical direction and co-ordination of the process of pro-duction' (as distinct from the capitalists, who might continue to own industry).

Although Burnham's ideas initially developed in the context of debates within the American Trotskyist movement about the nature of the Soviet Union, the claims he made were much wider, since they identified a global trend, rather than one restricted to any particular country. For Trotskyists in the 1930s, the choice was between characterising the Soviet Union either as a workers' state or a capitalist state. **Trotsky**'s own position (expressed in 1937 in *The Revolution Betrayed*) was that the Soviet Union was a degenerated workers' state – horribly deformed, since Stalinism was a parasitic bureaucracy with no progressive historic role. Because it was no longer capitalist, however, the Soviet Union had to be defended by socialists when under attack. For Burnham (and a number of others, including Schachtman) this position was unsustainable: such was the extent of deformation that the Soviet Union could not be defended. Instead, it was increasingly seen to represent a third option, neither capitalist nor socialist, but what some called 'bureaucratic collectivist' and Burnham came to label 'managerial society'.

The importance of the Soviet case was that it seemed to provide the most developed instance of what Burnham argued was a universal tendency. In his letter of resignation from the Workers' Party (of which he was briefly a member after leaving the Trotskyist Socialist Workers' Party), Burnham writes that a 'new form of exploitive society (what I call "managerial society") is not only possible as an alternative to capitalism but is a more probable outcome of the present period than socialism'. He argued that the managers ruled in the Soviet Union, because they effectively owned the state. The system was capitalistic because it was still based on the extraction of a surplus from the working class; but it was also socialistic because it was based on state ownership. It was relatively easy to draw analogies between the Soviet model and that of Nazi Germany. Burnham did so, concluding that Germany was at an earlier stage of development along these lines than Russia (since it retained more capitalist elements) but nevertheless emphasising that the managers understood that the society which was developing was *their* society.

Extending the argument beyond these two cases may seem rather more difficult, but Burnham confidently moved towards analysing

US society in the same way. Managers, he wrote, included 'business executives, technicians, bureaucrats and soldiers at the top of US power elite, as well as Soviet party managers'. The moves towards proto-Keynesian policies in the era of Roosevelt's New Deal simply heralded the broader shifts Burnham had analysed elsewhere. Although he admitted that it did so in a more confused way, Burnham highlighted the extent to which 'New Dealism' laid stress on the state as against the individual, and on planning rather than private industry. The New Deal may have been committed to capitalism, but its protagonists' belief in technocratic solutions through state investment in major infra-structural schemes made it part of the general trend towards a managerial society. Technocracy and the New Deal were, said Burnham, 'less developed primitive native-American managerial ideologies'.

For Burnham, the managerial economy was necessarily an exploiting economy; but it was based on corporate exploitation rather than private exploitation. The worldwide basis for change was the gradual extension of state ownership. The logical end point of the process implied the elimination of capitalists from the control of economy. In a managerial society, politics and economics so fused that totalitarianism was presented as its fullest and most complete expression (although – drawing on the analogy of capitalism – Burnham did hold out the distant hope that a more democratic phase might emerge in the future). The new world was to be dominated by two or three massive continental superstates, covering Europe, Asia and America. When he wrote *The Managerial Revolution*, Burnham suggested that the global process of change was in mid-course and still incomplete; but he took an almost fatalistic view, stressing the inevitability of the 'revolution' he had identified. All of the evidence, he suggested, pointed to a breakdown of capitalist society in an irreversible trend towards managerial society.

Burnham's approach raises questions about theories which claim that powerful elites can ever be effectively overthrown, whether by democratic or revolutionary means. For him, all that is possible is the replacement of one elite by another. In *The Machiavellians* (which followed *The Managerial Revolution*), Burnham explicitly draws on the elite theories of **Michels**, Mosca and **Pareto** to argue that all politics is about the manipulation of the masses to achieve (or sustain) power for particular elites. The only political change which takes place, he suggests, is between elites.

In his later writing, however, (such as *The Struggle for the World* (1949), *The Coming Defeat of Communism* (1950) and *Suicide of the West* (1964)), Burnham turns to the individualist American way as an alternative which needs to be defended from the incursions of communism and collectivism. In this discussion of the managerial revolution, Burnham also suggested that the world would soon be divided between a limited number of superpowers. As Burnham saw it, conflict between superpowers ruling Europe, Asia and North America would be dominant (with the United Kingdom in an ambivalent position between Europe and North America). The importance of these conflicts was reinforced by Burnham's growing critique of communism, which he explicitly interpreted as a worldwide conspiracy for power in the context of capitalist decline. Although he appeared to retain the belief that global defeat for individualist capitalism may in the end be inevitable, Burnham also seems to have come to the conclusion that some resistance was possible. In the struggle for 'world empire' between the United States and the Soviet Union, he enthusiastically supported the United States, because – despite being affected by creeping collectivism – it continues to allow some space for individualism.

Burnham's writing in the 1940s had an impact which went beyond its intrinsic merit or originality. His books are sustained essays, which seem to have resonated powerfully with contemporary concerns, both during and after the Second World War, both because of their stress on global change and the emergence of continental *superpowers*, and because of their focus on new (totalitarian) managerial elites. The analysis of *The Managerial Revolution* undoubtedly finds a clear resonance, for example, in George Orwell's *1984*, although Orwell also distanced himself from some of Burnham's arguments. As contributions to social and political theory, however, Burnham's writings are less impressive. The transformation of managers into a social (or political) class, for example, is never fully explained. The differences between those he describes as managers are often as great as the similarities between them; while the tension between 'inevitability' and resistance remains problematic. His discussion of elites adds little to the classic theories on which he drew. As Orwell pointed out at the time, while Burnham's predictions are superficially convincing, in practice they do not seem to have been realised in the ways he expected.

Main works

The Managerial Revolution: What is happening in the world, New York: Greenwood, 1941.

The Machiavellians: Defenders of freedom, Freeport, NY: Books for Libraries, 1943.

The Struggle for the World, London: Jonathan Cape, 1949.

The Coming Defeat of Communism, New York: Greenwood, 1950.

The Suicide of the West: An essay on the meaning and destiny of liberalism, New Rochelle: Arlington House, 1964.

Further reading

Bottomore, T. B., *Elites and Society*, London: C. A. Watts, 1964.

Orwell, G., 'James Burnham and the managerial revolution', in *In Front of Your Nose, 1945–1950: The collected essays and letters of George Orwell*, Vol. IV, London: Secker and Warburg, 1968, pp. 160–81.

Orwell, G., 'Burnham's view of the contemporary world struggle', in *In Front of Your Nose, 1945–1950: The collected essays and letters of George Orwell*, Vol. IV, London: Secker and Warburg, 1968, pp. 313–26.

Wright Mills, C., 'A Marx for managers', in I. L. Horowitz (ed.), *Power, Politics and People: The collected essays of C. Wright Mills*, New York: Oxford University Press, 1963.

D

Dahl, Robert A. (1915–)

Robert Dahl is the best-known modern American pluralist. A long-time writer on democracy and democratic values from an essentially empirical viewpoint, he is known as the defender of polyarchy and pluralism, and is often seen as an apologist of American democracy as it exists today. In fact, his thought is much more radical than his critics allow. Dahl wrote his doctoral dissertation at Yale between September 1939 and May 1940. This was a time of the Nazi–Soviet pact and the invasions of Poland, Norway, the Netherlands and Belgium. The dissertation was entitled *Socialist Programs and Democratic Politics: An analysis*. It was a discussion of possibilities of democratic socialism, concluding with the belief that democratic socialism required market processes. During the war years he first worked for the government and then fought in the US Army, receiving the Bronze Star with Cluster. He joined the Faculty at Yale in 1946 where he has remained and is now Sterling Professor of Political Science Emeritus. He was President of the American Political Science Association 1966–7 and has won numerous awards for his work.

Dahl's concern with the possibilities of democratic socialism emerges in his dissertation and in an early joint work *Economics, Politics and Welfare* (1953) with Charles Lindblom. But one also finds the ideas of polyarchy and pluralism, concepts which it is easy to confuse, as indeed Dahl sometimes does himself. Polyarchy takes on diverse meanings through Dahl's work: a set of institutions necessary for democracy; a system of political rights; the historical outcome of the attempt of nation-states to liberalise and democratise; a Schumpeterian battle for the people's vote; and a distinctive political order or regime. In *Polyarchy* (1971), Dahl introduces a two-dimensional scale for the concept: on one axis is liberalisation in the form of public contestation, on the other inclusiveness or participation. With low orders on both scales we have a closed hegemony; as both liberalisation and inclusiveness go up, we move toward polyarchy. Dahl makes clear his preference for writing about polyarchy, rather than democracy, because he believes that no existing system is fully democratic. It is on this issue that many of his critics misunderstand Dahl. He is often seen as an apologist for American democracy who makes the United States and other democracies appear in a better light than they are. But Dahl champions polyarchy only because it is preferable to hegemony or dictatorial regimes, and believes that polyarchy too can be improved and made more democratic by increasing participation and public contestation. As his later work explicitly reveals, he thinks that a democracy requires democratic institutions throughout society: not only in elections for national (or federal), state and local government, but also for clubs and firms. Without democracy in the workplace, national politics becomes dominated by business and the needs of capital, rather than the needs of the citizens. This conclusion, in *Economics, Politics and Welfare* is surprising to those who have only read, or read about, the Dahl of *Who Governs?*

The second strand in Dahl's work is pluralism and *Who Governs?* stands as the classic pluralist text. Dahl's work has always remained tied to both theory and empirical research. In the late 1950s, criticising the methods and conclusions of earlier elite studies, he set up a project to examine the structures of power in an American city (New Haven, where his own university is). He examined three key decisions facing the government of New Haven: redevelopment, public (i.e. non-private) schools and a new city charter. The issues were chosen by examining the topics most discussed in the local news media. The key finding of *Who Governs?* is that there is no single elite running New Haven: different sets of people are powerful or influential in the different issue-areas. In keeping with modern elite theory, the mayor and the business community were the key actors in the redevelopment of the inner-city area. However, even the most powerful did not always get their way. New Haven is pluralist: power is dispersed amongst many different groups.

Critics have seized upon the power dispersion as an apology for American democracy. They argue that whilst there may not be a single elite, many groups are not, and some may never be, included in the political process, or, if included, they are virtually ignored. Dahl answers that opportunity costs must be included in any measure of power; so any organisation which brings costs to the decision-makers, even if its demands are not met, has some power. Secondly, we can only expect representation for legitimate groups and cannot expect it for, say, communists. These replies seem to equate pluralism, which is about the distribution of power, with polyarchy, which is about institutional rights. In *Dilemmas of a Pluralist Democracy*, Dahl says that democratic pluralism is the existence of a plurality of relatively autonomous organisations within the state: a country is a pluralist *democracy* if it is a polyarchy and important organisations are relatively autonomous.

In *Who Governs?* Dahl creates the idea of *homo civicus* and *homo politicus*. Unless they feel their interests are threatened, the former do not engage much in politics beyond, perhaps, voting. *Homo politicus*, however, is a political animal that constantly tries to lead and persuade *homo civicus*. In this way Dahl tries to explain how pluralism and polyarchy work together to provide representation for people. Most people are happy to let the politicians and planners get on with ruling. Only when they feel their interests threatened will they form organisations to promote those interests.

It is this cosy version of pluralism that Dahl's later critics seize upon. For the costs of forming organisations to defend interests vary enormously across different groups of people, so many may not bother to engage in politics at all. This is known as the 'collective action problem' (see the entry under Mancur **Olson**). It implies that the range of interest groups does not match the range of threatened interests. For example, race relations was not an issue in *Who Governs?*; for it was not in the media much and few organisations promoting the interests of blacks were influential. But someone today writing a history of New Haven in the 1950s could not ignore racial issues. This mistake is also seen in *A Preface to Democratic Theory*, where Dahl assumes that one can evaluate the intensity of individuals' political preferences by examining the leisure time they are prepared to give up in political disputes. That neither takes account of initial endowments of money and time, nor differences in individuals' assessment of the pleasure afforded by leisure. Poor behavioural theory led Dahl astray.

Dahl has constantly worried about who 'the people' are in polyarchy. How does one decide the proper boundaries of the state and the scope of citizenship? But a more general problem is involved in aggregating the views of 'the people' once we have decided who is to be included. His concentration upon polyarchial institutions has left him less interested in the problem, which so besets other democratic theorists (e.g. **Arrow**), of aggregating preferences. Despite a discussion of it in *A Preface to Democratic Theory*, his underlying assumption is that aggregation is not a major predicament. Rather, what concerns Dahl is stopping the tyranny of the minority and of the majority. This seems to entail that the constitutional requirements of a liberal order are prior to, and more important than the wishes of some plurality or majority. Yet Dahl writes less about rights than one would expect. In work on ethnically divided societies, for example, Dahl takes political rights of self-government to be as important as any constitutionally guaranteed rights. Rather than rights, Dahl concentrates upon equality. Ever the pragmatist, he suggests that advanced democratic orders should concentrate upon reducing gross political inequalities. For him (see *A Preface to Economic Democracy*), that means introducing workplace democracy: the interests of stock-holders should not be given weight in proportion to how much they own of a firm; rather each person with an investment, be they employee or investor, must be taken equally *qua* individual.

Dahl's later writings come back to his early dissertation and look to market socialism (with full employment) as an answer to the demands of democracy. This is a far cry from the picture of Dahl that his anti-pluralist critics paint and shows Dahl to be more radical in his thought than often acknowledged. Yet his *Preface to Democratic Theory* remains today the classic text with reference to all versions of pluralism. Dahl's combination of normative values with concepts amenable to comparative analysis has given his thought a continuing relevance for study of and debates about democratic institutions and values throughout the contemporary world.

Main works

Congress and Foreign Policy, New York: Harcourt Brace, 1950.

Democratic Control of Atomic Energy (with R. S. Browne), New York: Social Science Research Council, 1951.

Economics, Politics and Welfare (with Charles Lindblom, 1953), 2nd edn, Chicago: Chicago University Press, 1976.

A Preface to Democratic Theory, Chicago: Chicago University Press, 1956.

Who Governs?, New Haven, CT: Yale University Press, 1961.

After the Revolution: Authority in a good society?, New Haven, CT: Yale University Press, 1970.

Polyarchy, New Haven, CT: Yale University Press, 1971.

Dilemmas of a Pluralist Democracy, New Haven, CT: Yale University Press, 1982.

A Preface to Economic Democracy, Cambridge: Polity, 1985.

Democracy, Liberty and Equality, London: Norwegian University Press, 1986 (collection of essays, including three early ones).

Democracy and its Critics, New Haven, CT: Yale University Press, 1989, is seen by Dahl as the summation of his thoughts on democracy.

Further reading

Domhoff, G. W., *Who Really Rules: New Haven and community power re-examined*, Brunswick, NJ: Transaction, 1978.

Dowding, Keith, *Rational Choice and Political Power*, Aldershot: Edward Elgar, 1991.

Dunleavy, Patrick and Brendan O'Leary, *Theories of the State*, Houndmills: Macmillan, 1987.

Held, David, *Models of Democracy*, Cambridge: Polity, 1987.

Isaac, J., *Power and Marxist Theory: A Realist View*, Ithaca, NY: Cornell University Press, 1987.

Shapiro, Ian and Grant Reacher (eds), *Power, Inequality and Democratic Politics: Essays in honour of Robert S. Dahl*, Boulder, Co: Westview Press, 1988.

Deutsch, Karl Wolfgang (1912–)

Although mainly a political scientist, particularly within the field of international relations, Karl Deutsch can also be classified as a historian and scholar of nationalism. Deutsch was born in Prague where he studied at the Charles University. Having finished his studies in Prague, Deutsch emigrated to the United States receiving both his MA in 1941 and his Ph.D. in 1951 from Harvard University. He returned to Harvard as Professor of Government in 1967, after having taught at the Massachusetts Institute of Technology and having been Professor of Political Science at Yale. He also spent time as visiting professor at Princeton, the University of Chicago and Heidelberg University.

Karl Deutsch has written on a wide variety of subjects including comparative government and international relations theory, although his name is mainly associated with his work on nationalism and regional integration, particularly the concept of security community. His research has elegantly combined the different fields that he has worked with, starting with his work on nationalism which gradually progressed towards his later work on regional integration and the creation of political communities. However, in whatever field Deutsch has turned to, his work has been unconventional and radical in its approach, and heavily influenced by the behavioural sciences.

The radicalism and unconventional approach of Deutsch's was clearly evident in his first major work *Nationalism and Social Communications: An inquiry into the foundations of nationality* (1953). In *Nationalism and Social Communications* Deutsch breaks with the conventional study of nationalism, which stressed its qualitative aspects, and turned instead to his own unique approach combining many fields and research methods, including communications theory and cybernetics, leading to a structural quantitative analysis of nationalism. Deutsch suggested that the best test of nationalism was not the traditional political, cultural and economic factors, but was the ability of members of a group to communicate with each other. According to Deutsch, the essence of a people is communication, the ability to convey messages, to have them quickly and accurately understood, and to predict one another's behaviour from introspection. Hence the key to understanding nationalism would be to measure the degree of social communication.

From his work focused on nationalism in terms of the nation-state, Deutsch moved over the following decade towards linking up his work on nationalism with the concept of regional integration, particularly the relationship between the presence and strength of international communities and international peace (*Political Community at the International Level: Problems of definition and measurement*, 1954). Again much of his research was centred around levels of communications also known as the transaction approach. Here, drawing upon earlier findings from his research on nationalism, Deutsch suggested that international community could be ascertained and measured by examining the volume, content and scope of international transactions, where a high degree of transactions over multiple ranges of social, economic, cultural and political concerns would indicate the presence and strength of international community. Intensification of transaction patterns across borders would indicate international community formation.

The relevance of Deutsch's transaction analysis for the study of regional integration has been the subject of controversy, particularly the question of whether transaction analysis can carry research beyond the level of pure description. There can be little doubt that Deutsch's transaction analysis describes the process of regional integration quite well, but a serious question mark has to remain as to whether it actually offers any explanations of the phenomenon. It may well be that an intensification of transaction patterns is merely part of the regional integration process, but that intensified transaction patterns do not actually cause regional integration to take place. Whether this is a particular problem for Deutsch's transactions approach, or simply an inherent problem of inductive research methods is another cause of debate. Certainly the main critique of Deutsch's transactions approach was that it did not lead to a coherent explanatory theory of the formation of international communities, but simply generated a huge number of different variables.

Deutsch's integration concept is not like most other integration theories based on institution-building in the form of either national or supranational structures. Rather the process towards integration is characterised by increasing levels of transactions between people from separate social entities. This is a process that can be observed throughout history, both at the nation-state level and at the international level. At the nation-state level a process of nation-building has taken place, gradually creating viable degrees of unity, adaptation and a sense of national identity among the people of a territory leading to the establishment of a state or a sense of nationhood within an already existing state. At the international level a similar process takes place (the increased levels of transactions) except that the end result of the integration process will be the establishment of political communities that may or may not achieve the higher degree of integration to become *security communities*. In other words whether at the international or the national level, people learn to consider themselves members of a community as a result of human communications patterns.

Deutsch's main work (with seven other authors) on the formation and definition of political and security communities is *Political Community and the North Atlantic Area* (1957). A security community is characterised by Deutsch *et al.* as

> one in which there is real assurance that the members of the security community will not fight each other physically, but will settle their disputes in some other way. If the entire world were integrated as a security community, wars would automatically be eliminated. (p. 5)

Political communities on the other hand, whilst being the result of increased levels of transaction, are not necessarily able to prevent war within the area that they cover. Hence what is of real interest is the concept of security community as a measure towards ensuring world peace.

The Deutsch group distinguishes between security communities that are amalgamated and those that are pluralistic. An amalgamated security community is where two or more previously independent units merge into a single larger unit, with some type of common government after amalgamation. The common government may be either unitary or federal. The United States is an example of an amalgamated security community. More contentiously, it could be argued that the Federal Republic of Yugoslavia appeared to be an amalgamated security community, but the suddenness and speed with which it disintegrated would seem to suggest either that the concept is not that helpful, or that in fact Yugoslavia was not a security community.

The pluralistic security community, on the other hand, retains the legal independence of separate governments, but achieves, like the amalgamated security community, also a firm expectation that violent resolution of disputes no longer exists. The example mentioned by the authors is the relationship between Canada and the United States, but Scandinavia is also commonly mentioned as an example of a pluralistic security community. Since the formulation of the concept during the early years of West European integration, it has obviously remained the main question whether the European Community/Union, and particularly France and

Germany, can be said to have developed into a security community. This is a question that exists independently from the general ups and downs of the more formal aspects of European integration, as the Deutsch group do not postulate a necessary existence of supranational structures, nor do they imply a transfer of loyalties to some new larger political entity.

The concept of security community has had a significant impact within integration theory, and has recently experienced a revival, as the international relations community ponders whether a security community between the former Eastern and Western Europe can be established in place of the Cold War division. It must also be acknowledged that more work on the concept is needed. It is not clear how stable a security community is, nor is it clear under what circumstances it develops and collapses. Even so Deutsch's work on political community is considered by many, including Ernest Haas, as important pioneering work in the field of regional integration. Deutsch raised many of the main questions and introduced many of the concepts that still preoccupy and guide the research effort.

Main works

Nationalism and Social Communication: An inquiry into the foundation of nationality (1953), Cambridge, MA: MIT Press, 1966.

Political Community at the International Level: Problems of definition and measurement (1954), Garden City, NY: Archon, 1970.

Political Community and the North Atlantic Area: International organisation in the light of historical experience (with Sidney A. Burrell, Robert A. Kann et al., 1957), New York: Greenwood, 1969.

Nation-building (ed. with W. Foltz), New York: Atherton, 1963.

The Nerves of Government: Models of political communication and control, New York: Free Press of Glencoe, 1963.

The Analysis of International Relations (1968), Hemel Hempstead: Harvester Wheatsheaf, 1988.

Nationalism and its Alternatives, New York: Alfred A. Knopf, 1969.

Further reading

Cobb, Roger W. and Charles Elder, *International Community: A regional and global study*, New York: Holt, Rinehart and Winston, 1970.

Dougherty, James E. and Robert L. Pfaltzgraff, Jr, *Contending Theories of International Relations: A comprehensive survey*, rev. edn, New York: HarperCollins, 1990.

Merritt, Richard L. and Bruce M. Russett (eds), *From National Development to Global Community: Essays in honour of Karl W. Deutsch*, London: Allen and Unwin, 1981.

Puchala, Donald J., 'International transactions and regional integration', and Ernst B. Haas, 'The study of regional integration: reflections on the joy and anguish of pretheorizing', both in Leon N. Lindberg and S. A. Scheingold (eds), *Regional Integration: Theory and research*, Cambridge, MA: Harvard University Press, 1971.

Dilthey, Wilhelm (1831–1911)

An eminent Japanese philosopher of the twentieth century, Nishida Kitaro, summarised his life in the remark that for the first part of it he sat facing a blackboard, while in the second part he sat with his back to a blackboard, and much the same can be said of the life of Wilhelm Dilthey: outwardly uneventful, it was a life devoted to learning, passed in a small number of European university cities. The son of a clergyman, Dilthey was born in Biebrich am Rhein and after schooling in Weisbaden he was sent to the University of Heidelberg to study theology. After a year he moved to Berlin, becoming increasingly absorbed in the study of history and philosophy. Having obtained his doctorate at Berlin (1864), his first major appointment was as professor of philosophy at Basle (1867). Further appointments at Kiel (1868) and Breslau (1871) preceded his return to Berlin in 1882, where he succeeded Hermann Lotze in the professorship once held by Hegel. He remained in Berlin until his death.

Though in his lifetime his reputation rested to some extent on his published work as a historian of ideas, Dilthey's importance is now regarded as derived from his major philosophical enterprise, which was to provide a sound methodological basis for what he called the human studies or *Geisteswissenschaften*. By this term he means history, philology, jurisprudence, comparative religion, criticism of the arts, psychology, economics and sociology. Dilthey was convinced by his own work as a historian that the attempts prevailing at his time to give these studies a theoretical basis were deeply in error. The first of these was that of the positivist school, in both its English version, exemplified in the work of John Stuart Mill, and the French version, epitomised by the philosophy of

Auguste Comte. Common to both forms of positivism is the assumption that all knowledge worthy of the name is scientific, and arrived at by the methods of the natural sciences. Positivists had attempted to apply the methods of the natural sciences to the human studies, where they had been found not to work, and in addition could give no real account of certain distinctive and important human attributes, notably the creative imagination. The second major school of thought in this area, which one can call that of Romantic individualism, had a great deal of value to say about the imagination, but with its stress on individual intuition as the means to knowledge had done nothing to provide the human studies with a codifiable, impersonal and intellectually respectable method. Dilthey's major assertion is that there is such a method, and that it is distinct from that of the natural sciences.

The human sciences have a method distinct from that of the natural sciences because they have a distinct subject matter, which Dilthey called 'lived experience' (*das Erlebnis*). Human experience or mental life is known to us in a unique and privileged way. While external objects are known to us only as appearances, mental events are known by direct acquaintance, from within: they are, as Dilthey puts it, 'real realities' (*reale Realitäten*). We are only observers of the external world, but human experience, and human nature, we know from the inside. Further, human experience has a central and important property, which is that it tends to express or objectify itself: such expressions may be voluntary or involuntary, gestural or conceptual, or a blend of these. It is because of this tendency to expression that knowledge of minds, both our own and those of others, is possible. Introspection unaided would be unable to grasp the flux of experience: by contrast, expression keeps experience before the mind for a manageable length of time, thus clarifying it and allowing us to study it, both in ourselves and others.

Knowledge of the experience of other minds, Dilthey argues, is possible because of a natural psychological process in human beings, namely that, under normal conditions, every physical event which is the expression of someone's inner life can evoke a corresponding experience in the mind of an observer: the expression sets up a reproduction (*Nachbild*) of itself in my consciousness. This reproduction is not an inferential process, but an immediate evocation. I live over again (*nacherlebe*) the experience of the other in my own mind, yet with one crucial difference: the *Nachbild* is not present to my consciousness as would be one of my own experiences (e.g. it does not operate as a motive for action or cue for emotion as do our own experiences). Instead it is 'bracketed' (*eingeklammert*) from the stream of my own experiences. This bracketing is natural to us – we do not need to learn how to do it or bring it into play by an act of will. Again, Dilthey stresses that the process of reliving the experiences of others in this bracketed way, whilst it involves some logical reasoning of the kind summed up in textbooks of logic, is not primarily ratiocinative in that manner, but rather a process of imaginative amplification. It is more akin to direct vision than to arriving at a conclusion by means of deductive reasoning. The whole process of coming to know mental life, both in ourselves and others, is called by Dilthey understanding (*das Verstehen*), and so this term has a technical sense in his writings.

While expressions of experience take many forms, from gestures to the construction of visible objects or music, the pre-eminent mode of human expression (Dilthey argues) is linguistic, and the great majority of linguistic expressions are studied in the form of written texts. These texts are often opaque, and yield their full significance only when properly interpreted. The interpretation of texts has a respectable methodology, which Dilthey, following the theologian and scholar Friedrich Schleiermacher (1768–1834), calls hermeneutics. The most significant feature of this method is the not altogether aptly named 'hermeneutic circle' (inaptly because the method does not result in circularity but in progressive understanding). The 'circle' arises from the fact that the objects studied in the *Geisteswissenschaften* are wholes composed of parts. Now parts gain their meaning from their place in the whole, yet the whole can oniy be understood by means of an understanding of its parts. Dilthey argues that the process of understanding is one of oscillation between part and whole: we make provisional assumptions about the meaning of the whole and of the parts, and revise these assumptions as our scrutiny of each proceeds. This applies equally to understanding a sentence via its constituent words, a text via its sentences or the complete work of a writer from individual texts: the pre-eminent example of this Dilthey saw in Schleiermacher's interpretation of Plato's dialogues. This process of revision of understanding of part and whole each in the light of the other Dilthey held to be central to hermeneutics, and distinct from the method which he regarded as typical of the natural sciences, namely to explain the particular in terms of the general. (It must be made clear, however, that he did not regard this methodological division as absolute, though certainly as very typical.)

A further important property of the human studies, in Dilthey's view, is that they cannot be value-free (*Wertfrei*). They all rest on axiological presuppositions, i.e. they select their facts and formulate their questions from the standpoint of certain presuppositions concerning value. This follows from Dilthey's philosophy of action: human action is always purposive, and what furthers our purposes we call good, and what frustrates them, bad. Hence no understanding of human beings is possible unless we have grasped their standards of value. Our own standards of value play a key role in the human studies, since they determine our choice of subject – we study what in our value-system is important.

Again, it follows from Dilthey's analysis of the methodology of the human studies that the various discipline branches are not ordered in a hierarchy: having rejected the view that the only respectable method is that followed in the natural sciences, Dilthey dismisses the consequence which Comte had drawn from its acceptance, namely that disciplines of study are arranged pyramidally, with a scientific sociology at the apex of the structure. For Dilthey, the human studies exist in relations of mutual dependence, just as, in human relations, self-knowledge is enriched by knowledge of others and knowledge of others is possible only because we have self-knowledge. Thus biography and history complement each other, as do psychology and sociology. (This at least is the point of view which follows from Dilthey's major assertions: occasionally he writes as if he believed that one or other branch of the human studies could be regarded as more 'basic' than the rest, but his opinions as to which remain inconclusive).

A further major consequence of Dilthey's views is his perspectivism, a variety of what has since been labelled anti-foundationalism. All human thought is ineludibly of a particular place and a particular time, and this applies not only to transient fashions but also to what many have regarded as irrefragible 'first principles'. These too, Dilthey argues, have a history and a geographical distribution – in the *Introduction to the Human Studies*, he gives an example of what he means, tracing at some length the history of the metaphysical concept of substantial form, once regarded as a major advance on mythopoeic explanation, but now swept aside by the scientific outlook. The obvious objection to this view is that it appears to be self-refuting: if there are no absolutes, but only perspectives, then the thesis that there are only perspectives is itself only a perspective. Dilthey was perfectly aware of this, but was untroubled by it: we must simply recognise that we do not have absolute knowledge, and must limit our epistemological pretensions.

Rather than pursue an unattainable 'absolute' point of view, Dilthey argues, a more profitable way to proceed is to study the perspectives or belief sets which human beings have evolved in order to make sense of their experience. Human beings are indivisible wholes: we think, feel and desire. These aspects of the person are interwoven and constantly in play, and each has associated with it a set of beliefs and principles: a set of factual beliefs about the way the world is; a related system of preferences, expressed in value judgements, and, consequent on these first two elements, a system of ends, duties, practical rules and principles. Further, all human beings are at some time exercised by questions raised by the major features of the human predicament, e.g. the place of life in the cosmos; whether the cosmos is purposive; whether there is an afterlife, and so on. Awareness of these issues gives rise to what Dilthey calls the metaphysical consciousness (*das metaphysische Bewusstsein*), and our answers to these profoundest of questions are generally expressed in religion, art and philosophy. Taken together, all the above elements make up a world-view or *Weltanschauung*. One of the principle roles of philosophy, once it has abandoned its unrealisable pretension to arrive at an absolute and final systematic view of all there is, will be to study these world-views. Dilthey envisages a new branch of the subject, *Weltanschauungslehre*, devoted to a comparative analysis of such world-views.

Different aspects of Dilthey's thought have had a major influence on a number of currents of thought in continental Europe and, via that route, on those parts of the anglophone world sympathetic to continental thought. The notion of bracketing became a major element in the phenomenology of Husserl, and the existentialist **Heidegger** was avowedly indebted to Dilthey. Again, the greatest Spanish philosopher of the twentieth century, José **Ortega** y Gasset, adopted a version of historicist perspectivism almost identical to Dilthey's, which, granted Ortega's pre-eminence in the Hispanic language communities, has had and still has a considerable influence in Latin America as well as Spain. Also deeply indebted to Dilthey were Max **Weber**, Gadamer and many literary critics, theologians and theoreticians of the social sciences sympathetic to the hermeneutic method.

Main works

Collections: a number of editions of Dilthey's *Gesammelte Schriften* (Collected Writings) have been issued since 1914, usually in twelve volumes.

Thanks to work on his papers, the 1974 edition includes twenty-five volumes (Stuttgart: Teubner and Göttingen: Vandenbroeck and Ruprecht).

English translations

Selected Works (5 vols), Princeton, NJ: Princeton University Press, 1985, contains many important writings.

The following should also be mentioned:

Introduction to the Human Studies, trans. Ramon J. Betanzos, Detroit: Wayne State University Press, 1988.

The Essence of Philosophy, trans. Stephen A. Emery and William T. Emery, Chapel Hill: University of North Carolina Press, 1969.

Dilthey's Philosophy of Existence, trans. William Kluback and Martin Weinbaum, London: Vision 1960.

Selected Writings, ed. and trans. H. P. Rickman, Cambridge: Cambridge University Press, 1976.

Further reading

Bulhof, I.M., *Wilhelm Dilthey: A hermeneutic approach to the study of history and culture*, The Hague: Nijoff, 1980.

Ermath, M., *Wilhelm Dilthey: The critique of historical reason*, Chicago: Chicago University Press, 1981.

Hodges, H. A., *The Philosophy of Wilhelm Dilthey*, London: Routledge and Kegan Paul, 1952.

Hodges, H. A., *Wilhelm Dilthey: An introduction*, London: Routledge and Kegan Paul, 1944.

Plantinga, T., *Historical Understanding in the Thought of Wilhelm Dilthey*, Lewiston: Edwin Mellen, 1992.

Rickman, H. P., *Wilhelm Dilthey, Pioneer of the Human Studies*, Berkeley and London: University of California Press and Elek, 1979.

Glossary

Hermeneutics   A method for the interpretation of texts, derived from the study of scripture, held to result in progressively more exhaustive and interpersonally valid exegeses of their meaning.

Durkheim, Emile (1858–1917)

Born in Alsace of Jewish parentage, Durkheim was educated at the Ecole Normale Supérieure, and taught both sociology and education at the University of Bordeaux (1887–1902) and the Sorbonne (1902–17). Usually hailed as the inspiration of sociology's scientific pretensions and of much twentieth-century sociology, he battled with more psychologically oriented contemporaries such as Gabriel Tarde. As a secular Jew, he shared the unease over the religiously inspired prejudice of France during the Dreyfus affair, and concerned himself with civil rights and educational secularisation. Like other theoretical French sociologists, he evinced profound anxiety about modernity and sought to intervene decisively for the better in the development of the present.

Durkheim wanted to establish both the subject matter of sociology and the scientific status of its methodology. His first two major works, *The Division of Labour in Society* and *The Rules of Sociological Method*, envisaged society as consisting of powerful 'social facts' constraining its members: two kinds were defined, the structure of the division of labour, and the collective culture – the norms and representations of the *collective conscience*. This is a base/superstructure model in which the social structure, determined by division of labour, in turn creates the cultural and moral environment of society. The two work together in a state of necessary functional compatibility to shape the individual. As techno-logical and economic development become more sophisticated, society is dominated by increasing social *differentiation*. Corresponding to this differentiation, Durkheim proposed, an appropriate and functional form of normative order and law would unfold, as a pre-industrial society based on status (fixed hierarchies of groups) would be replaced by one founded on individual contracts. In effect, he accepted the image of modern society promulgated by the *laissez-faire* individualist social theorists inspired by Adam Smith, but tried to show that no increasingly individualistic society could be satisfactorily explained except in terms of its necessarily collective culture. The greater *interdependence* of an advanced economy produces the paradox of a more individualised, yet still integrated, society of 'moral individualism'. Models of rational indi-vidualism in capitalist society have therefore missed the key normative element of values such as personal commitment to contracts, mutual trust between contractees and the presumption of honesty in dealings, by which behaviour in such a society must be governed. While Durkheim later became anxious as to whether modern economic life was in fact subject to normative control, he initially thought that social order is both functional and normative: the division of labour requires successful economic interconnections and the members of the society must share the consensus of values and ideals.

Durkheim's methodological prescription for scientific sociology was based on these social or collective facts, which famously he held to be *sui generis*: sociological data did not consist of the facts about individuals except where they reflect society's characteristics. In effect he stressed the role of unconscious forces – the social in the individual – providing social theory with the most determinist model before **Althusser**. His was not the only, but among the first, attempts to abolish the 'subject' and individual action in twentieth-century French thought, but his target was the rational individual in free-market theory. His famous work on suicide was not accidentally chosen, for if he could explain these most private acts in terms of social forces rather than personal motivation, then sociology could be demonstrated to be truly 'scientific'.

Durkheim recognised, however, that deviance from norms was common in society. The questions of individuality and normative control pervaded much of his work, and his concentration on law as the best exemplar of the collective conscience was deliberate. While social order could mostly be guaranteed by the successful socialisation of individuals, the norms of society had to be constantly reaffirmed through the punishment of deviants. The state is a prime force here, as an organ of communication of 'social thought', though not its originator, for this is provided by the *conscience collective*. Durkheim's evolutionary schema proposed that while traditional societies are characterised by strong regulation, modern society needs, instead of comprehensive control, less moral integration, and consequently stands in danger of normative collapse – 'anomie' – both collectively and individually. As he expressed it, society has evolved from *mechanical* to *organic* solidarity: whereas the former requires all the cogs to fit perfectly in the machine, modern society permits a degree of individuality while also needing to maintain common values. Modern law is therefore less repressive, permitting the development of 'restitutive' techniques of punishment which reinforce social relations and restore deviant individuals to society once they have compensated for any damage. Instead of banishment or death, criminals are subject to resocialisation before being returned to society. Yet the use of punishment provides constant reminders of the society's distinctive common values defining deviance. This perspective presaged both later relativist perspectives on deviance and analyses of punishment stressing its effect on social order rather than its consequences for the criminal.

In explaining another crucial area of common culture, religious beliefs, Durkheim rejected evolutionary theories which dismissed magic and religion as a series of mistakes which would eventually be replaced by science. Religious beliefs and representations, he thought, reflect the underlying social structure: this is most obvious in totemic systems where each social unit has a totem (much as landed titled families have a coat of arms). The *sacred*, of which these totems and other representations form a part, is integral to the collective conscience, a social fact contrasted with the personal, variable or *profane*. Because of its social character, the sacred is the primary object of religious worship, while magic was thought to be so personal and profane as to be incapable of sustaining a social structure: magic has no 'church'. In worship, therefore, people gathering in their significant social groupings and worshipping their sacred object reaffirm the social structure and teach it to the next generation. Consequently, religious phenomena, Durkheim said, are naturally divided into beliefs and rites – in effect, theory and practice in mutual support. Religious practice expresses a social truth, for in worshipping the sacred people are worshipping society itself. While the sacred's form may change with secularisation, socially sacred objects remain untouched by the dominance of modern science, for they cannot be disproved by science's intellectual achievements. Social solidarity *requires* the maintenance of significant collective sacred objects, even if they are now constitutional traditions or institutions.

The decline of these strong collective ideals with the rise of individualism aroused Durkheim's anxiety, for modern economies could become, if not completely anomic, devoted to individual ends rather than social objectives. His discussion of socialism, morality and material excess was directed towards an ethical restatement of socialist social relations (that is, a new form of moral regulation, reached by agreement between the different occupational groups). He recognised the uniqueness of the present in that, for the first time, modern society requires the means to negotiate a moral consensus: one could no longer be inherited or left to arise naturally out of the relationships of a divided society.

Durkheim's impact on subsequent sociological theory has been paradoxical: in some ways he was the dominant influence on functionalist sociology, but his standing has waned with its demise and his work is due for serious re-evaluation. Yet in the anthropological interpretations of religion and ritual, and in the development of Lévi-Straussian structuralism, the legacy remains strong. Less acknowledged, though equally important, was his model of the state and of changes in social punishments: while much conservative sociology of deviance paid him homage, **Foucault's** radical theorising in *Discipline and Punish* also owes him much. Overall, he shared the denial of action in the French tradition of social and cultural theory, foreshadowing the agonising difficulty subsequent generations found in absorbing hermeneutic and phenomenological perspectives.

Main works

Elementary Forms of the Religious Life, trans. J. W. Swain, London: George Allen and Unwin, 1915.

Moral Education: A study in the theory and application of the theory of education, trans. E. K. Wilson and H. Schnurer, 1925, ed. E. K. Wilson; repr. New York: Free Press of Glencoe, 1961.

The Division of Labour in Society, trans. George Simpson, New York: Macmillan, 1933; repr. London and New York: Collier-Macmillan, 1964.

The Rules of Sociological Method, trans. S. A. Solway and J. H. Mueller, ed. G. E. G. Catlin, London and New York: Collier-Macmillan, 1938; repr. New York: The Free Press, 1964.

Suicide: A study in sociology, trans. J. A. Spaulding and G. Simpson, London: Routledge and Kegan Paul, 1952.

Socialism, trans. Charlotte Sattler, London and New York: Collier-Macmillan, 1962.

Primitive Classification (with Marcel Mauss), trans. Rodney Needham, London: Cohen and West, 1965.

Further reading

Giddens, A., *Durkheim*, Hemel Hempstead: Harvester Wheatsheaf, 1978.

Thompson, K., *Emile Durkheim*, Chichester: Ellis Horwood, and London: Tavistock, 1982.

Lukes, S., *Emile Durkheim: His life and work*, London: Allen Lane, 1973.

Taylor, S., *Durkheim and the Study of Suicide*, London: Macmillan, 1982.

Fenton, S., *Durkheim and Modern Sociology*, Cambridge: Cambridge University Press, 1984.

Gane, M. (ed.), *The Radical Sociology of Durkheim and Mauss*, London: Routledge, 1992.

Dworkin, Andrea (1946–)

An American feminist writer of both fiction and non-fiction, speaker and activist, Dworkin is particularly associated with the radical feminist fight against pornography. In the mid-1980s, together with the lawyer Catherine MacKinnon, she drafted the Mackinnon–Dworkin Anti-Pornography Ordinance, which attempted to control pornography by making it a civil rights violation against women. Although anti-pornography ordinances were passed in Minneapolis and Indianapolis, these were later overturned by the US Supreme Court in 1986 on the grounds that they violated the First Amendment right to free speech. However, Dworkin continues to campaign on the issue, both in person and in print.

It is the work of Andrea Dworkin that is primarily responsible for making pornography a continuing issue within feminism. Unlike some feminists, who draw, for example, a line between pornography (which degrades women) and erotica (which is a healthy celebration of sexuality), Dworkin's views are absolutely uncompromising, and make no such distinctions. 'The word pornography does not mean "writing about sex" or "depictions of the erotic" . . . or any other such euphemism. It means the graphic depiction of women as whores' (*Pornography*). Pornography has 'presented the contemporary women's movement with an emergency of staggering proportions [where] sexual sadism against women is mass entertainment . . . [and] the sexual violation of women in the pornography itself is protected by the courts as "speech"' (Russell, *Making Violence Sexy*).

Dworkin's concern is twofold. Firstly, she is concerned with the many thousands of women who are exploited by pornography, either directly or indirectly. The women who actually perform in front of the camera, according to Dworkin, always do so as a result of force, be it economic necessity or physical intimidation, and that performance inevitably leads to their torture, degradation, and sometimes even death for the sexual gratification of the male spectator. But Dworkin also makes a direct, and controversial, connection between pornography and violence against women in general; it is not only the woman in the pornographic picture who is pornography's victim, but also 'the women against whom the picture is used, to make them do what the woman in the picture is doing' (Itzan, *Pornography*).

Secondly, therefore, Dworkin is not merely concerned with pornography *per se*, but with the larger social and ideological system within which it operates, arguing that 'the ways and means of pornography are the ways and means of male power' (Dworkin, *Pornography*). In other words, pornography at once illustrates and perpetuates the brutal inequalities of a patriarchal system which valorises male authority through the enforced submission of women. Men do not merely have the social upper hand, but also possess the much more fundamental power of naming, 'a great and sublime power . . . [which] enables men to define experience, to articulate boundaries and values . . . to determine what can and cannot be expressed, to control perception itself' (*Pornography*). Sexual violence against women is thus sanctioned because they are constructed within this system of signification as sexually voracious creatures who both desire and deserve exploitation and abuse. This cruelly reductive view is not just confined to the men and women who work within the pornography industry itself, but affects all men's treatment of all women.

Pornography is thus a system which not only denies woman a voice, but ensures she remains voiceless, and it is this rationale which lay behind the Anti-Pornography Ordinance drawn up by Dworkin and MacKinnon. Their intention was not necessarily to ban pornography altogether – although that is indeed Dworkin's ultimate aim – but to enable women who felt themselves to be its victims to gain some redress in law.

> Any woman – or man, child, or transsexual used in the place of a woman – should be granted a legal cause of action if she is coerced into a pornographic performance, has pornography forced on her, or has been assaulted or attacked because of a particular piece of pornography. (Tong, *Feminist Thought*)

The fact that the Ordinance was eventually overturned on the grounds that it was an attack on the American right to freedom of speech is, in the context of Dworkin's argument, bitterly ironic.

Because of the uncompromising nature of her views, Dworkin has always been an easy target for criticism. Indeed, she has pursued several unsuccessful libel actions against the more personal of these attacks. While hostility originating from within the pornography industry is predictable, it is less easy, perhaps, to understand the opposition to her views from within feminism itself. The issue of pornography, however, has motivated a bitter debate between the 'radical' and 'liberal' sections of the movement. While radical feminists such as Dworkin assert that pornography is an essential factor in the perpetuation of male dominance, liberal feminists argue that this is a sweeping and simplistic analysis which leads to the damagingly negative portrayal of women as men's helpless prey, incapable of acting as the autonomous agents of their own sexuality. Naomi Wolf sums up this view when she brands Dworkin's ideology 'victim feminism [which] is when a woman seeks power through an identity of powerlessness' (*Fire with Fire*).

Moreover, liberal feminists express a concern with the whole notion of the abolition of pornography, not only on the grounds that a straightforward relationship between pornographic material and violence against women has not been proved, but also because they construe such an action as potentially dangerous censorship. While Dworkin and MacKinnon were attempting to make pornography a civil rights rather than a moral issue, it was argued by those who opposed them that their campaign was playing into the hands of the moral right-wing who could turn such legislation against women. It was this belief which motivated such groups as the Feminist Anti-Censorship Taskforce (FACT) to participate in the defeat of the Anti-Pornography Ordinance.

Dworkin's critics have also focused on what they interpret as her own unhealthy fascination with pornography. Her sexually explicit fiction has been widely attacked for adopting the very discourse against which she is supposed to be campaigning, and her analysis of pornography and violence, *Pornography: Men possessing women*, has also been criticised for its lengthy, detailed descriptions of particularly unpleasant pornographic material. This portrayal of Dworkin as salivating over the very material she is condemning is, however, rather unfair. She is insistent in her claim that most feminists speak up in pornography's defence from a position of ignorance – they simply have no idea of the horrors that are perpetrated in its name. In the afterword to *Pornography*, she writes at length of 'the nausea, the isolation, the despair' she experienced while researching the book; research which, however distasteful, she regards as absolutely necessary if her aim is to be achieved.

Dworkin has not yet succeeded in her campaign to have pornography controlled on the grounds that it is defamatory to women. However, her passionate polemic ensures that it remains a hotly contested issue both within feminism and outside it. Currently, the tide of feminist debate appears to have turned somewhat against Dworkin, with younger feminists such as Naomi Wolf dismissing her argument as outdated, for it 'derives from conditions that once applied more than they do now ... the rationale of this kind of feminism is becoming obsolete' (*Fire with Fire*). Whatever one might think of Wolf's sweeping dismissal of Dworkin, she speaks for a popularised liberal feminism which is much more palatable to the mainstream than Dworkin's angry, unsettling and uncompromising crusade.

Nevertheless, Dworkin remains probably the most widely known – and reviled – of the American radical feminists, and her name has become virtually synonymous with the movement she represents. Just as her anti-pornography campaign has been accused of being appropriable by right-wing moralisers, so the term 'Dworkinite' has become an unkind and crudely sweeping term used by those unsympathetic to feminism to indicate what they believe to be its man-hating, dungaree-wearing, lesbian extremes. This image of her, however, entirely obliterates both the range and conviction of her views.

Main works

Woman Hating: A radical look at sexuality, New York: Dutton, 1974.

Pornography: Men possessing women, London: Women's Press, 1981.

Our Blood: Prophecies and discourses on sexual politics, London: Women's Press, 1982.

Right Wing Women: The politics of domesticated females, London: Women's Press, 1982.

Intercourse, London: Secker and Warburg, 1987.

Letters from a War Zone: Writings 1976–1987, London: Secker and Warburg, 1988.

Mercy, London: Secker and Warburg, 1990.

Further reading

Assiter, Alison, *Pornography, Feminism and the Individual*, London: Pluto, 1989.

Berger, Ronald J., Patricia Searles and Charles E. Cottle, *Feminism and Pornography*, Westport: Praeger, 1991.

Itzan, Catherine (ed.), *Pornography: Women, violence and civil liberties*, Oxford: Oxford University Press, 1992.

Russell, Diana E. H. (ed.), *Making Violence Sexy: Feminist views on pornography*, Buckingham: Open University Press, 1993.

Tong, Rosemarie, *Feminist Thought: A comprehensive introduction*, London: Unwin Hyman, 1989.

Wolf, Naomi, *Fire with Fire*, London: Chatto and Windus, 1993.

Dworkin, Ronald (1931–)

Ronald Dworkin is one of the foremost advocates of contemporary liberalism. He first made an impression with a series of influential essays on jurisprudence and he is now regarded by some as the most important philosopher of law ever to emerge out of the United States. His right-based egalitarian moral theory has also had an impact in political philosophical debates. He has held posts on both sides of the Atlantic for a number of years, as Professor of Jurisprudence at Oxford University since 1969, and as Professor of Law at New York University since 1976. Having studied at Harvard University and at Oxford, he worked in legal practice for a number of years before teaching for much of the 1960s at Yale University Law School. He was politically active in the US Democratic Party in the 1970s and he remains an articulate defender of many liberal causes in the public domain. His regular contributions to the *New York Review of Books* are noteworthy as incisive explorations of practical problems through an accessible application of philosophical theory.

Legal reasoning is for Dworkin more concrete than traditional political philosophy yet more principled than political practice. It is, for him, the most appropriate mode of reflection on our public commitments, on the principles that underlie them and on what those commitments may require in new circumstances. In modem democratic societies we are subject to the rule of law. Law constitutes us, individually, as citizens and, collectively, as members of a particular political community. The thread that has guided Dworkin's writings on legal theory is the idea that the rule of law must flow from a coherent moral vision of what justice and fairness requires both of our legal practices as a whole and of our institutions in concrete cases. His rejection of a strict separation of law and morality represents a challenge to the theory of legal positivism which he identified, in his early work, as a ruling orthodoxy. Both legal positivism and utilitarian normative theory are grounded in the philosophy of law that was developed by Jeremy Bentham. Dworkin presents an alternative, right-based, liberal theory which opposes both the legal positivism and the utilitarian moral reasoning that inform Bentham's general theory of law.

One of the main problems with legal positivism, for Dworkin, is that it only recognises those rights that have been created historically by explicit political decisions or social practices. These rights are enshrined in the collection of rules that regulate the life of a political community. This conventional understanding of law insists on a conceptual separation of law and morality which reduces the law to a system of rules. Dworkin maintains, in contrast, that individuals do have legal rights that are not created by explicit decision or by particular social practices. These rights are the moral principles that inform our understanding of justice and fairness. Considerations of moral principle should, and do, figure in the reasoning of a judge who is seeking to determine what the law requires in particular cases.

Dworkin believes that any conception of law, including both legal positivism and his own alternative, must make some controversial assumptions about political morality. Legal positivists' denial of this fact leads to further problems in their understanding of how judges are to adjudicate in 'hard cases'. In such a case, no legal rule seems to yield a decision and so, according to the positivist, there is no right answer. Judges must therefore use their discretion by introducing new rules that add to the law. Dworkin rejects this view by arguing that there usually is a right answer even in such a difficult case. His argument stresses the role that moral principles play in deciding these cases. Considerations of principle are right-based in that they point to the impact a decision might have on particular people rather than its consequences for the general welfare. Judges typically present arguments of principle in their efforts to reach a decision in a difficult case. They may well, in this way, be drawn eventually into an assessment of general claims of political morality or of the best justification of the legal system's social role. While lawyers and judges may disagree, and mistakes are always possible, the practice of legal adjudication rests on the assumption that a right answer can be found in every case. The right answer is not demonstrated or proven but it rests, rather, on the weight of reasons that can be drawn on to defend a moral argument for making a certain decision.

In *Law's Empire* Dworkin gives his most complete account of law. He presents a conception of law as an interpretive ideal of integrity. Judges are constrained in their adjudication in that their decisions must fit within a coherent general interpretation of the community's legal and political culture. The moral convictions of a judge are therefore held in check by the political history of the community. In a hard case, two or more interpretations of the law can pass this threshold of fitness. Then the decision must be made by assessing which of the interpretations presents the community's institutions in their best light by the standards of political morality. It is at this stage that judges must draw on their own moral convictions in presenting arguments of principle. But these arguments must also consider the best justification of the community's legal practices as a whole. These criteria of 'fit' and 'best light' express a judge's commitment to integrity by revealing the way in which legal reasoning is an exercise in constructive interpretation of the community's public commitments.

Dworkin has developed the core ideas of his legal theory in ways which have had a significant impact in political theory. Most notable in this regard is his critique of utilitarianism and the defence of a conception of individual rights that 'trump' any consideration of the general welfare. Rights are moral principles which inform legal decisions as a means of protecting individuals in a culture where the dominant morality is some form of utilitarianism. While we normally argue about the merits of a particular policy with a view to its consequences for the well-being of the community as a whole, we must, if we are to take rights seriously, distinguish between such considerations and an argument of principle. Rights trump collective goals whenever a consideration of the general welfare offers insufficient grounds for justification of a policy that has a serious impact on an individual's well-being. Dworkin notes that the main appeal of utilitarianism is the concern that each individual is to be treated as an equal. If this concern is not to be undermined then we must ensure that, in seeking to justify particular policies, we consider only the personal preferences of each individual for certain goods and opportunities and not their external preferences as to how they want goods and opportunities to be distributed to others. Since it is not always possible in practice to count only personal preferences we need rights so as to protect individuals, as a matter of moral principle, from the external preferences of others. Dworkin has used this distinction between right-based arguments of principle and goal-based arguments of policy to intervene in numerous issues of topical concern. He defends, for example, practices of positive discrimination in procedures of admission to university by insisting that these programmes have typically not been guilty of a failure to respect the right of each citizen to be treated as an equal. They are, he insists, to be justified not in terms of a right-based argument of principle but rather on the grounds that, as a matter of policy, they help to produce a more egalitarian, and just, society. On the other hand, he makes a principled argument against the censorship of sexually explicit material, by appealing to the individual right to moral independence. His contributions on these and other controversies, including questions of civil disobedience and freedom of the press, are collected in *Taking Rights Seriously* and *A Matter of Principle*.

Dworkin's most notable intervention, however, in controversies of public concern is *Life's Dominion*. Here he presents a sophisticated liberal argument about abortion and euthanasia. Dworkin reinterprets the conflict between pro-life and pro-choice perspectives in the abortion debate, as a question not about rights, but rather about the intrinsic value, or sanctity, of life. He insists that the state should maintain an environment where decisions about life and death, including decisions about abortion and euthanasia, are made in a way that takes seriously the intrinsic value of human life. But he also insists that the state must not determine how the sanctity of life is to be weighed in individual cases. We must respect life's intrinsic value by treating such decisions as the moral responsibility of the particular individual directly involved.

The key value of liberalism is, for Dworkin, not liberty but equality. In a series of essays about equality, he explores the political theoretical consequences of the idea that each citizen has a right to equal concern and respect. He argues that the state must be morally neutral since it would fail to treat every individual as an equal if it sought to enforce, or to promote, the conception of the good held by a particular group, or even a large majority, of citizens. From this liberal egalitarian perspective the market is indispensable as a mechanism for distributing goods in a way that allows people's genuine choices to make a difference. But liberals must also be careful to ensure that market allocations do not favour some people simply because of their good fortune. It is a matter of luck if an individual inherits wealth and property, or if she is especially talented or intelligent. The state should introduce redistributive programmes that aim to bring people closer to the share of resources they would have had were it not for such differences in fortune.

Dworkin's legal theory represents the most coherent alternative to legal positivism. His insistence that rights are 'taken seriously' has had an extraordinary impact in contemporary philosophy of law. As a political theorist his liberal egalitarian perspective on distributive justice offers a strong challenge to rival positions put forward by libertarians, socialists and conservatives. His stress on the foundational value of equality has in many ways framed recent debates about liberal justice. Dworkin's reflections on the character of a liberal political community are notable as contributions to the encounter between liberals and communitarians. His influence has been most forceful however as an insightful advocate of liberal positions in the public domain. His writings on issues such as abortion, positive discrimination and civil disobedience combine intellectual rigour with a welcome sense of urgency.

Main works

Philosophy of Law (ed.), Oxford: Oxford University Press, 1977.

Taking Rights Seriously, 2nd edn with a Reply to Critics, London: Duckworth, 1978.

'What is equality? Part I: Equality of welfare; Part II: Equality of resources', *Philosophy and Public Affairs*, 10 (1981), pp. 185–246, 283–345.

'In defence of equality', *Social Philosophy and Policy*, 1 (1983), pp. 24–40.

A Matter of Principle, Cambridge, MA: Harvard University Press, 1985.

Law's Empire, London: Fontana, 1986.

'What is equality? Part III: The place of liberty', *Iowa Law Review*, 73 (1987), pp. 1–54.

'What is equality? Part IV: Political equality', *University of San Francisco Law Review*, 22 (1988), pp. 1–30.

'Foundations of liberal equality', in Grethe B. Peterson (ed.), *The Tanner Lectures on Human Values*, Vol. XI, Salt Lake City: University of Utah Press, 1990.

'Liberal community', in Shlomo Avineri and Avner de-Shalit (eds), *Communitarianism and Individualism*, Oxford: Oxford University Press, 1992.

Life's Dominion: An argument about abortion, euthanasia and individual freedom, London: HarperCollins, 1993.

Further reading

Burley, J. (ed.), *Reading Dworkin*, Oxford: Basil Blackwell, 1996.

Cohen, Marshall (ed.), *Ronald Dworkin and Contemporary Jurisprudence*, London: Duckworth, 1984.

Guest, Stephen, *Ronald Dworkin*, Edinburgh: Edinburgh University Press, 1992.

Hunt, Alan (ed.), *Reading Dworkin Critically*, New York: Berg, 1992.

Narveson, Jan, 'On Dworkinian equality', *Social Philosophy and Policy*, 1 (1983), pp. 1–23.

Wolfe, C., 'Liberalism and paternalism: a critique of Ronald Dworkin', *Review of Politics*, 56 (1994), pp. 614–40.

E

Elias, Norbert (1897 –1990)

Norbert Elias was born into a well-off Jewish household in Breslau (Wroclaw), where his father owned a clothing company. After studying medicine and philosophy, he became assistant to Karl **Mannheim**, then one of the most prominent sociologists in Germany, following him in 1929 from the University of Heidelberg to the Institute for Social Research in Frankfurt. Here he met **Adorno**, Horkheimer, Fromm and Löwenthal, who would have a strong impact on his work. He left for Paris after Hitler had taken power and then in 1935 moved to London. Here he started work on *The Civilising Process*, his most successful text. He took a lectureship at Leicester in 1954. From 1962–4 he was Visiting Professor of Sociology in Ghana, from 1969–71 in Amsterdam, where his public influence increased steadily. From 1979–84 he lived and worked at the University of Bielefeld. Elias died in 1990 in Amsterdam.

'But perhaps a certain irregularity is welcome': this quote might stand as a motto for Elias's work. He always aspired to an interdisciplinary approach to his search for knowledge. He had a Hegelian drive to discover the dialectics of the ages of world history, but it was coupled with the very un-Hegelian look at the microcosm of people's individualities in relation to their overall cultural habitus or milieu. It was the mundane, the ancilliary that caught his eye. The way people ate, drank and had sexual relations; the way they perceived time; the changes from one age to the next: all these interested Elias and he attempted to account for all of them with a theory of civilisation. Because his interests were so diverse and he wrote in various languages, for most of his life he fell between the cracks of academia. Only in his later years did he receive the academic accolades that were his due, among them the 1977 Adorno–Preis and the 1988 Premio Europeo Amalfi.

Elias's most influential text is *The Civilising Process* of 1939: most of the others are concerned to enlarge on the central theses presented here. Already its title is telling. Elias's work has been called 'figurational' sociology, mapping out historic contexts that are similar to what Benjamin called thought 'configurations'. Taking issue with his contemporary nomenclature, the title eschewed the term 'history', which Elias viewed as too static a concept, in favour of 'process', which describes the gradual changes in, and of, the world much better. Fear of process itself would haunt him through all his life. While in the 1960s and 1970s he would be charged with being too much of an empiricist, earlier it was the opposite: he was charged with being too philosophical for a sociologist. Yet his stress would always lie with the individual and how this individual fits into society at large. His intention was to give humans the tools to improve their 'means of orientation' in this world.

The Civilising Process looked at how social manners and the state (especially its monopoly on force) had changed from the Middle Ages to today. He saw civilisation as a process of internalising controls, a move from external constraints (*Fremdzwängen*) to internal restraints (*Selbstzwängen*). This line of thinking led him to theorise that humans in their own individual history undergo on a small scale the same changes that the human race itself has undergone in its development: (social) 'ontogenesis' mirroring 'sociogenesis'. Things that were being openly expressed in medieval times, were going on only 'behind the social scene' after the Renaissance. Sexual matters, dying, table manners; all these became matters of delicate social interventions and double talk. In the second part of *The Civilising Process*, Elias analyses the formation of states. Starting with the move from feudalism to bourgeois society, he detects in society a monopolising tendency, moving from private, internalised constraints to the public sphere, and ultimately leading to a power monopoly by the state. Elias viewed this power monopoly on the part of the state as one of the most problematic facts of modern society. Extrapolating from this model, he established a ranking of 'open' and 'closed' societies. The levels of social control over individuals, the state's ability to control natural forces and the state's control of human forces figure in the ranking.

In the 1970s, this line of thought would lead Elias to involve himself in the terrorism debates in Germany. Elias had long felt that as a sociologist it was his duty to intervene in present-day society, to become engaged. Needless to say, in the hysterical atmosphere prevalent in Germany at the time, this did not endear him to many. It appeared that his model, though quite useful in itself, would, if used without regard to the different histories of different states, prove problematic. This led to attacks on the whole body of his teachings.

One of Elias's most valuable texts is *Time: An essay*. It is typical of what makes Elias's work so interesting: his ability to defamiliarise things taken for granted, such as the structuring of time. It can be taken as paradigm of his methods, both in its success and in its problems. Published in 1984, it examines how the system of time-keeping can structure societies, placing personal time and state time at odds. Elias speaks of the dialectics of time:

how time changes us and long-term historical processes. For Elias, time is a concept about behaviour, a structure placed upon us to attain certain goals. He shows very clearly, with a non-European example (taken from Chinua Achebe's writing), how the structure of time has changed over the centuries and enslaved humans – especially the western world – in the process. As with all of his writings, his aim is to liberate his readers from unreflective simplification and propel human development forward.

The last text published before Elias's death (but not yet translated into English) was *Studien über die Deutschen* (On the Germans). In it, he expressed his principle thoughts on Germany and its historical processes. In line with his earlier writing, he states that much of Germany's destructive twentieth-century history was the result of the formation of the first German Reich in 1871. Elias contends that the feudal order gained a victory over bourgeois, civil forces at that time, throwing Germany's social development backwards. Other societies (such as the French or, more prominently, the Dutch) became much more open, comprising citizens who were amenable to the shared, common life of their society (*homines apertii*), rather than people who were closed in on themselves (*homo clausus*). While this model might hold in many respects, it is its universalistic claim to validity across the board, not allowing for societies in a transitional state, which makes it problematic.

Norbert Elias was a prolific writer over fifty years, and several languages and countries. His multifaceted interests led him to tackle such wide-ranging topics as terrorism, eating orders and disorders in medieval times, sports, the theory of nature, children–parent relationships and his own poetry. His surprising and insightful analyses, both on a micro-sociological and a macro-sociological level, provide a large body of disparate texts. A definitive list does not as yet exist, making his reception problematic. But one gets the feeling that he would have liked it that way.

Main works

The Civilising Process (1939), Vol. I: *The History of Manners*, Oxford: Basil Blackwell, 1978.

What is Sociology? (1970), London: Hutchinson, 1978.

Adorno-Rede: Respekt und Kritik in: Elias, Norbert and Wolfgang Lepenies. Zwei Reden anläßich der Verleihung des Adomo-Preises 1977, Frankfurt: Suhrkamp, 1977.

The Civilising Process, Vol II: *State Formation and Civilisation*, Oxford: Basil Blackwell, 1982.

Time: An essay (1984), Oxford: Basil Blackwell, 1992.

The Society of Individuals (1987), Oxford: Basil Blackwell, 1991.

Los der Menschen: Gedichte/Nachdichtungen. Frankfurt: Suhrkamp, 1987.

Studien über die Deutschen. Frankfurt: Suhrkamp, 1989.

Further reading

Kilminster, Richard, 'Structuration theory as a world view', in C. G. A. Bryant and David Jary (eds), *Giddens' Theory of Structuration*, London: Routledge, 1991.

van Krieken, Robert, 'The organisation of the soul: Elias and Foucault on discipline and the self', *Archives européennes de sociologie*, 31 (1990), pp. 353–71.

Mennell, Stephen, *Norbert Elias: An introduction*, Oxford: Basil Blackwell, 1992.

F

Fanon, Frantz (1925–1961)

Frantz Fanon was born on Martinique in the French Caribbean. During the Second World War, when the island was controlled by the Vichy regime, Fanon slipped away and volunteered to fight with the Free French forces in Algeria and France. After the war he became a student of medicine at Lyons, qualifying to become a Doctor of Psychiatry. In 1953 Fanon took up a hospital appointment in Blida in Algeria. The following year the National Liberation Front (FLN) began its guerrilla war to free Algeria from French colonial rule. Fanon became a vocal supporter of the FLN and a violently hostile critic of colonialism. Expelled from Algeria in 1957 Fanon travelled widely in support of the FLN and survived an assassination attempt in Italy and a land mine on the Algerian border. In 1961 Fanon became gravely ill. The CIA arranged for him to be given medical treatment in Washington where he died of leukaemia.

Fanon's work is difficult to classify. Sometimes both his admirers on the left and detractors on the right categorise him as a primarily non-western theorist, but this is misleading. It is true that Fanon is black not white, and anti-western in the sense of being a critic of western colonialism, but he is not thereby, non-western. His first and most brilliant work, *Black Skin White Masks* is deeply influenced by the work of western political theorists, most notably Hegel. Fanon adapts the Hegelian idea that is sometimes labelled the 'master–slave relationship' in which humanity's movement towards freedom depends upon people, including masters and their servants, entering into the mutual recognition of the freedom and humanity of others. For blacks to be free, says Fanon, they must gain recognition of their humanity by whites. Fanon's obscure statement at the outset of his work that his project is to liberate the black man 'from himself' also takes its cue from Hegelian reasoning.

Other western theorists drawn on by Fanon include **Marx**, Jaspers and particularly Sartre, whose *Anti-Semite and Jew* provides Fanon with a point of comparison between racism and anti-semitism. Far from being a non-western thinker, therefore, Fanon is immersed in the western tradition of political philosophy. To call Fanon a western political theorist, however, does not convey a sense of the full range of his writing. He applies insights of continental philosophy to the social difficulties and dilemmas faced by black subjects in white colonial regimes, but this analysis is interwoven with poetic language, extracts of poetry by Césaire and others, and accounts of dreams. At one stage the narrative itself takes on a dreamlike quality. The work is also semi-autobiographical; Fanon uses insights gained from his professional experience as a psychiatrist as well as his personal experience as a black man involved in relationships with whites.

In *Black Skin* Fanon rejects three different ways of affirming self-worth as a black. He rejects the path of reasoning with whites to overcome racial prejudice on the grounds that reason is associated with science, which includes eugenics, which promotes racism. From reason Fanon turns to what he terms the irrational; the idea that blacks have their own unique cultural contribution to make to humanity in their sense of rhythm, their magic, their earthiness. However, this position is also repudiated by Fanon who explains that such irrationalism is not in fact unique to blacks; whites also used to be similarly irrational until white civilisation moved on. Fanon then asks if the achievements of past black civilisations before the ruination of Africa at the hands of European colonisers can provide a sense of black self-worth. His answer rejects this third stance for his final position which follows Marx's observation that an oppressed working class looks forward rather than back for its inspiration. Fanon similarly argues that the humanity of blacks is not dependent on their achievements in the past, but on their potential in the future. This future is envisaged as one in which black people are defined by themselves and others not as black but as human and this is what Fanon means when he says that blacks need to be freed from themselves.

A second strand of *Black Skin* describes how the persistence of colonial exploitation and racism, distorts sexual and marital relationships between blacks and whites. White men who have sex with black women do so in a position of power. Black women who avoid black men and seek relationships with white men do so to increase their social status by 'whitening' their children and, through marriage, themselves. Black men who have sex with white women do so as an act of revenge upon the white race that has subordinated them. White women who seek relationships with black men (as well as white women who avoid them) are absorbed by the myth of black 'genital potency', part of the bestial image of blacks promoted by colonialism.

When *Black Skin* was published in 1952, Fanon stood at a crossroads; newly married to Josie, a white French woman, he had to choose between remaining in France or moving to one of its colonies. After a brief spell in Ponterson, Normandy, the Fanons moved to Algeria. This fateful step may have had a decisive radicalising influence on Fanon's intellectual development.

There were at least two directions in which Fanon's thought could have developed. He might have built on the humanist elements in *Black Skin* to advocate the path of non-violent resistance to colonialism and racism that was followed by Gandhi and Martin Luther King. But instead, Fanon chose a second path; increasingly turning to Marx for his inspiration he became an advocate of revolutionary violence. For the coloured population of the world to gain their future as human beings, Fanon argued, they had first to overcome the violence of their colonial oppressors. In Fanon's rather chilling phrase, this colonial violence 'will only yield when confronted with greater violence'. Fanon's adoption of this position is perhaps made more understandable when it is realised that with the start of the campaign for Algerian independence, the psychiatric hospital in which he worked became filled with the victims of police torture – as well as some of their torturers who were also suffering mental difficulties. Staff at the hospital were under threat; a fellow doctor with FLN sympathies was tortured and hospital nurses suspected of involvement with the FLN were killed. Harrowing descriptions of the sufferings of torture victims appear in Fanon's writings on the Algerian war, including *L'An cinq de la révolution algérienne*.

Fanon built upon his experiences in Algeria to provide a broad account of decolonisation in *Les Damnés de la terre* (The Wretched of the Earth), to which Sartre contributed a bloodthirsty preface. In this work, Fanon combines a Marxist analysis of resistance to colonialism in Africa, practical and moral justifications for anti-colonial violence, and FLN propaganda. In his analysis of the social situation in the colonies, Fanon distinguishes three broad economic groups: the European settlers, the native elite and the masses. Settlers, the 'colonialist bourgeoisie' are in an economically powerful position having expropriated native lands. The native elite are 'bourgeois nationalists' – comparatively wealthy, well-educated individuals who are liable to be co-opted and corrupted by the colonial administration into pursuing what Fanon sees as the reprehensible path of negotiation, compromise and non-violent reforms. The third group, the 'masses', are the revolutionaries who will rise up against the exploitation and oppression of the settlers. Fanon identifies the masses not with the urban working class but with the impoverished peasantry who formed the great majority of subjects in colonial countries.

Although Fanon describes methods of torture used by the colonialist forces in some detail, he is much more circumspect in his descriptions of FLN violence. He does, however, justify this violence, in part on the grounds that its victims, such as brutal policemen, deserved it. But what of its victims who are not brutal policemen? In his preface to *Les Damnés*, Sartre states that *all* Europeans are 'executioners', and all are legitimate targets. Fanon is more ambiguous on this issue, but does offer a general justification of revolutionary violence by explaining that its perpetrators develop 'positive and creative qualities' of character and gain a sense of unity with other violent revolutionaries until the whole becomes a single 'great organism of violence'.

We will never know what further developments Fanon may have made to this fascinating train of thought because he died tragically early at the age of thirty-six. *Les Damnés* was his last work, although a collection of essays *Toward the African Revolution* was published posthumously.

In the turbulent years of the 1960s Fanon's later works were widely read by campus revolutionaries throughout the west and black radicals in the United States. However, it is his first work *Black Skin* that has best stood the test of time. The book is widely quoted by academics and professionals with an interest in race issues, although it must be said that these quotes are often used to embellish arguments quite at variance with Fanon's conclusion that perceived race differences must be superseded by the recognition of common humanity. The book is particularly popular amongst social workers.

Fanon's supporters often suggest that he would have been disappointed by Algeria's post-colonial history whose future he painted in glowing colours. Perhaps this is partly because Fanon used his intellect to conjure away potential problems and sources of tension outside the anti-colonial war rather than confront them. For example, Fanon proves that by wearing a veil Algerian women paradoxically make themselves free. But although this argument is brilliantly constructed with an impeccable dialectical logic, one is left wondering if there is nonetheless something a little wishful about the analysis. Certainly the current civil war in Algeria with its torture and killing is not the legacy that Fanon would have wished for his adopted homeland. Whether Fanon's intellectual legacy to the Algerians has helped matters is another question.

Main works

The Wretched of the Earth (Les Damnés de la terre), trans. Constance Farrington, Harmondsworth: Penguin, 1967.

A Dying Colonialism (L'An cinq de la révolution algérienne), trans. Haakon Chevalier, London: Writers and Readers Publishing Co-operative, 1980.

Toward the African Revolution, trans. Haakon Chevalier, London: Writers and Readers Publishing Co-operative, 1980.

Black Skin White Masks, trans. Charles Lam Markham, London: Pluto, 1986.

Further reading

Bulham, Hussein A., *Frantz Fanon and the Psychology of Oppression*, New York: Plenum, 1985.

Caute, David, *Fanon*, London: Fontana and Collins, 1970.

Geismar, Peter, *Fanon*, New York: Dial, 1971.

Gendzier, Irene, *Frantz Fanon: A critical study*, New York: Random House, 1973.

Worsley, Peter, 'Frantz Fanon and the "Lumpenproletariat"', in Ralph Miliband and John Savile (eds), *The Socialist Register 1972*, London: Merlin, 1972.

Zahar, Renate, *Frantz Fanon: Colonialism and alienation*, trans. Willfried F. Fevser, New York: Monthly Review Press, 1986.

Foucault, Michel (1926–1984)

Born in Poitiers, Michel Foucault quickly rose to prominence within Parisian intellectual circles after the publication of his Doctorate d'Etat in 1961, *Madness and Civilisation: A history of insanity in the age of reason*. With this work and the series of investigations into mental and physical illness, penal theory and sexuality that followed through the 1960, 1970s and 1980s, Foucault clearly proved himself to be one of France's leading theorists, and certainly its most renowned post-structuralist. His ideas are both of a first- and second-order nature, contributing not only to our empirical knowledge of the historical development of medical and social scientific discourse, but also to major advances in thinking about the methodology of these sciences and the metatheoretical issues surrounding them. Along with service at the Institut Français and the University of Clermont-Ferrand, from 1970 Foucault was Professor of the 'History of Systems of Thought' at the Collège de France. His accession to such a position within the French educational establishment did not, however, diminish his capacity for controversy nor his outspoken defence of unpopular causes. He was a prime example of the politically engaged thinker right up until his death in 1984.

The development of Foucault's ideas is generally thought to straddle an early (impure) structuralist phase and a later post-structuralist or 'genealogical' one. *Madness and Civilisation*, his first major work, certainly utilises the language of structuralism with its distinction between surface and depth within the discourse of mental illness. It is the job of what Foucault calls 'archaeology' to decode the surface level of such discursive practices in order to expose the structures beneath. Similarly, his emphasis in this period on the statements of the human sciences in isolation from the questions of truth, falsity, or sense, are typically structuralist moves.

In *The Order of Things*, Foucault's major metatheoretical work as a structuralist, he argues that the history of discourse is mutative, going through a series of epistemic jumps that consequently efface the possibility of any linear, causal analysis. History is composed of discrete periods which are defined as such by possession of a characteristic 'episteme'. An episteme is the total set of relations uniting the discursive practices which condition the epistemological axioms and sciences of a particular era. It is that set of rules dictating which discourses can and cannot be taken seriously and how the sciences of any one epoch define their subject-matter, develop their methodologies, and construct their theories. Moreover, such epistemes or codes of knowledge do not replace one another smoothly by gradual transition but by wholly discontinuous rupture. Discontinuity marks the archaeology of madness, for instance. Whereas madness was regarded in the pre-Classical era as an intimation of divinity, by the Classical age it was considered to be a criminal threat and remained so up until the nineteenth century when it came to be understood as a medical condition. Each of these interpretations of madness stands free of any causal explanation linking it with the others. That is why such linear analyses are impossible. The task of the archaeologist is simply to decode these unwritten rules of knowledge and chart their mutations by conducting a cross-disciplinary comparison between the statements made by each of the sciences concerning their subject-matter with what was said about *words* in general in that particular episteme. *The Order of Things* examines three fundamental epistemes in varying degrees of depth: that of the Renaissance (which saw words as things), the Classical age (which saw words as representations of things) and the Modern (which sees words as autonomous, self-referring entities with no external relations whatsoever).

Foucault's inaugural lecture at the Collège de France, 'Nietzsche, genealogy, and history', represents a turning point in his work whereby the method of decoding discursive practices is no longer paramount but now serves larger genealogical questions concerning their individual beginnings and general social functions. Practice and technology are now deemed more fundamental than theory and discourse. Rather than their own statements or subtending rules, the human sciences find their intelligibility in a larger set of social practices dominated by the theme of *power*. Genealogy, Foucault explains, attempts to reveal the various forms of subjection at work in what he terms the 'hazardous play' of dominations. *Discipline and Punish*, Foucault's first fully Nietzschean work, discovers that the *raison d'être* of its own subject-matter, penal reform, is the discovery of new techniques for regulating, universalising and economising punishment: it is not about rehabilitating the criminal or any other such humanitarian aims. Penal art in the various disciplinary institutions where it is found works by comparing, differentiating, hierarchising, homogenising, excluding and, in short, *normalising*.

Foucault's turn to Nietzschean genealogy brings with it a hermeneutics of suspicion that sees the workings of power become ubiquitous. These are not forms of a *will* to power, however, because there is no willing subject in Foucault's thought. Power *simpliciter* is Foucault's theme. Indeed, the willing subject and subjectivity in general is but one more creation formed in the interests of subjugation. Foucault calls this 'subjectification': the practice of tying the subject to a particular identity; it stands alongside what he understands as the three other primary practices of power: the technologies of the body, sexuality and surveillance. A word then on each of these

In *Discipline and Punish* the modern usage of power is analysed as it works through 'discipline' which Foucault explains in terms of tiny, everyday, physical mechanisms. Discipline propels itself via asymmetrical and non-egalitarian systems of micro-power working directly on the body. This was not always so. Only since the eighteenth century has discipline been localised on the body through a political technology of the body and a micro physics of power.

The contemporary era, however, is marked less by any interest in the body as such than by an explosion in discourse and practice concerning physical sexuality. Control over sexuality and sexual activity is deployed not only in technologies of the body, but also by a disciplining of the self, the latter peculiarly through *therapeutic confession*. The more the subject talks, the more science knows. With this knowledge, deviance from the norm is psychiatrised such that a whole life can become a case-study (a 'pervert') requiring complete and constant surveillance. Indeed, it is finally through the advancing technologies of *surveillance* that power no longer needs to be personally exercised at all: it becomes, or reveals itself to be, ubiquitous, automatic and anonymous.

In the course of these Foucauldian exposés of body-technology, sexuality, subjectification and surveillance, the intimate relationship between power – in both its broadly political and micro-technological forms – and knowledge is revealed. Certain practices of knowledge are legitimated by suppressing and outlawing others. Power, however, is never fully identified with knowledge, so much as deemed indissociable from it in practice.

Nevertheless, Foucault also believes that the very ubiquity of power ought to lead us to a positive understanding of it as well:

> We must cease once and for all to describe the effects of power in negative terms: it 'excludes', it 'represses', it 'censors', it 'abstracts', it 'masks', it 'conceals'. In fact, power produces; it produces reality; it produces domains of objects and rituals of truth. (*Discipline and Punish*)

Foucault's influence is almost too wide-ranging to specify in detail here. The strength of his impact on philosophy and the social sciences lies less in any particularly important disciples than in a whole reorientation of thought within these fields. Amongst literary theorists, Foucault's genealogical methods have generated a taste for historicist interpretations adding new focus to the various sociological, political and micro-technological contexts in which literature is produced. Amongst sociologists, on the other hand, a large part of its current interest in the body and technologies of the body can be traced back to *Discipline and Punish*. Likewise, the three volumes of *The History of Sexuality* have spawned renewed vibrancy for such studies in their own wake. Even where he has relatively little to say, such as on the matter of feminism, Foucault's thought has gained itself increasing interest. Feminists, happy to find an eminent theorist finally prioritising sex and power in his writing, are nonetheless concerned to see these twin issues pursued in isolation from feminist theory itself. While making up for that perceived deficiency, they also, however, see the relevance that the Foucauldian perspective has for their own ideas, especially concerning the image of woman as victim of power.

Main works

Madness and Civilisation: A history of insanity in the age of reason (1961), trans. Richard Howard, New York: Random House, 1973.

The Birth of the Clinic: An archaeology of medical perception (1963), trans. A. M. Sheridan-Smith, New York: Random House, 1975.

The Order of Things: An archaeology of the human sciences (1966), trans. A. M. Sheridan-Smith, London: Tavistock, 1970.

The Archaeology of Knowledge (1969), trans. A. M. Sheridan-Smith, London: Tavistock, 1974.

Discipline and Punish: The birth of the prison (1975), trans. Alan Sheridan, London: Allen Lane, 1977.

The History of Sexuality, Vol. I: *An Introduction* (1976), trans. Robert Hurley, London: Allen Lane, 1979.

The History of Sexuality, Vol. II: *The Use of Pleasure* (1984), trans. Robert Hurley, New York: Pantheon, 1985.

The History of Sexuality, Vol. III: *The Care of the Self* (1984), trans. Robert Hurley, New York: Pantheon, 1986.

Further reading

Cousins, Mark and Althar Hussain, *Michel Foucault*, London: Macmillan, 1984.

Dreyfus, Hubert L. and Paul Rabinow, *Michel Foucault: Beyond structuralism and hermeneutics*, Brighton: Harvester Wheatsheaf, 1982.

Gutting, Gary (ed.), *The Cambridge Companion to Foucault*, Cambridge: Cambridge University Press, 1994.

McNay, Lois, *Foucault: A critical introduction*, Cambridge: Polity, 1994.

Ramazanoglu, Caroline (ed.), *Up against Foucault: Explorations of some tensions between Foucault and feminism*, London: Routledge, 1993.

Smart, Barry, *Michel Foucault*, London: Routledge, 1985.

Glossary

Genealogy A Nietzschean term which, in Foucault's work, describes his approach to history as a discontinuous process without any underlying essence, teleology or law. Furthermore, the genealogist is not a disinterested investigator but a pragmatist who recognises the selective influence of his or her own social, cultural and personal milieu when forming a historical interpretation.

Freud, Sigmund (1856–1939)

Sigmund Freud was born to a Jewish family in Freiburg, which is today Pribor in the Czech Republic. When he was three years old Freud's family moved to Vienna where he remained for most of the rest of his life. In 1938 when compelled to flee from the threat of Hitler he reluctantly left Vienna for London where he died on 23 September 1939. Initially as a neurologist but ultimately as a psychologist Freud studied human motivation and the unconscious. His psychoanalytic writings apply not only to neurotic behaviour but to all human endeavours. As a result of the ongoing application of his ideas to various dimensions of modern culture Freud has become, in the words of Peter Gay, 'a life of our times'.

Gay's words intimate something about the relationship between the character of Freud's life and the ambivalent nature of life in contemporary societies. Characterised as a representative theorist of our times Freud personifies uncertainty: self-contradiction is apparent in the precarious connection of the content of his living and writing. His living epitomised the autonomous individual of Enlightenment science, while his revolutionary writing on the unconscious decisively challenged the autonomy of reason, the idea of an undivided subject and the positivism of modern science. In developing ideas which would undermine the intellectual basis of rationalism Freud was, unwittingly, destroying the credentials of the very social order of liberal ideals, of truth and justice, in which he himself lived. Moreover, when his psychoanalytic writings were taken up – however differently – by Herbert **Marcuse**, Theodor **Adorno**, Paul Ricoeur, Jürgen **Habermas**, Jacques **Lacan** and Jean LaPlanche, the dimensions of Freud's ideas grew to constitute a many pronged challenge to modern social and political theory. The ambivalences both in his personal history and in the mixed interpretations of his theory render impossible any neat distinction between the man and the times of fragmentation and uncertainty.

Freud has left us a legacy of concepts which continue to take on lives of their own in being developed by a variety of social and political theorists. But Freud's personal changes constitute a complex catalyst for the reception of his various ideas. Even during his lifetime, the central concepts of psychoanalysis metamorphosed. Most central is the specific development of his concept of the unconscious, which continued to change along with his metapsychology. The core concern of his metapsychology was the model or models used for interpretation of the unconscious and of repression.

Freud's concept of the unconscious distinguishes his psychoanalysis decisively from other psychologies. The unconscious develops an energy, logic and ethics of its own, radically heterogeneous to the contents of consciousness. The unconscious is said to be rooted fundamentally in unavowable and unavowed desires which have undergone repression such that their content remains cut off from consciousness; and consciousness expends energy to bar knowledge and memory of such desires from itself. Yet the full complexity of his concept only becomes manifest in a study of Freud's first and second topographies. These topographies are the metatheories used to interpret the unconscious and repression in terms of spatial and temporal divisions. A division running through both topographies is between, on the one hand, consciousness and what it is permitted to know and, on the other hand, the unconscious.

In 1895 Freud developed the first spatial topography, which appeared posthumously in *Project for a Scientific Psychology*. It contains three systems: the conscious, the preconscious and the unconscious. A censorship exists between the unconscious and the preconscious and conscious; this censorship – as that which represses – works to prevent ideas of one system from moving to another or both others. In 1923 Freud introduced the second topography as a model of intrasubjective relations within the psychical apparatus: the ego, id and superego enter into relations with each other. The superego becomes the force of repression; the id the place of repressed desires; and the ego attempts to balance the demands of the other two, as well as its responsibility to external reality.

Both topographies are marked by the censorship which represses and so constitutes the barrier to the unconscious. Freud maintains that an initial repression of the child's incestuous desires has the crucial role of constituting the unconscious. This primal repression has as its object the Oedipus complex; derivative repressions are all in some sense based upon the images and desires of the primal, explaining the infantile nature of the unconscious. For both topographies the repressed is an idea which is charged with an amount of energy; the act of repression cuts the energy off from the idea. Yet in the second topography, with its personal tripartite structure of ego–id–superego, Freud is more explicit about the link between the individual and the cultural, in the scene of primal repression.

Freud's first topography employs an early model of interpretation which has been called an 'energetics' as opposed to the 'hermeneutics' of the second topography. The energetics names his use of an anatomical, quantitative model, while his later hermeneutics is built upon a symbolic, qualitative model of interpretation. Giving Freud's project its scientific distinctiveness, the energetics employs a naturalistic language of energies or organic forces. In contrast the later topographical model of interpretation analyses a symbolic language of double meanings. To understand Freud's accounts of desire and sexuality it is necessary to recognise when he treats language in *naturalistic* terms and when *symbolic*. If the former terms, then expressions of sexual desire should be read according to the positivism of a hypothetical physics, which refers directly to psychical forces. If the latter terms, then the analysand's statements conceal unconscious meanings; so the analyst works to interpret symbols, uncovering the duplicity of desire. These models of interpretation establish that the unconscious cannot be equated with the latent meaning of consciousness.

Freud does not simply replace his energetics with a hermeneutics, despite the importance associated with the interpretation of symbols. The energetics provides the terms to explain the strength of any affect, of rage, envy, love, hate. Even with his hermeneutics of double meaning, Freud continued to discuss these affects employing a hypothetical physics, but now placing energies on a separate, economic level of psychical organisation. The first topography appears in Freud's *The Interpretation of Dreams*, but this equally informs his second topography on the formation of individual and cultural symbolism. The continuing employment of an energetics suggests that psychical reality remains linked with the material reality of energies and forces. But this important link is often missed.

Building upon this link, Drucilla Cornell argues that psychoanalysis can play a role in imagining differences, in the intersection of race and gender within our own culture. Psychoanalysis aims to reveal what takes place in the dark. Post-Freudian psycholinguistics adds to understanding what gets called dark and how dark is itself symbolised through who gets identified as coloured and signified as black. In this light, the political struggle against racism would attempt to change reality through shifting the meaning of our shared symbols. Politics is, then, not just about power but about the basis of what can become real and thus accessible to consciousness and change. Freudian psychoanalysis implies that our political obligations cannot be separated from our dreams and fantasies.

During and since his life Freud's influence became immeasurable, even though there exists no agreement on any Freudian discovery. Feminism as a political movement illustrates both the impact of Freud on contemporary theory (uncertainty) and the disagreement concerning the significance of his ideas (fragmentation). Femininity remains a dark continent – a riddle – in Freud's writings. But these same writings have played a formative role in the social and political development of feminism. Notwithstanding disagreements and ambivalences, Freud's belief in and theories about the unconscious and sexual difference continue to have a fundamental influence upon social and political theorising, upon ideological accounts of patriarchy and upon revolutionary debates about male and female sexualities.

Major works

Standard Edition of the Complete Psychological Works of Sigmund Freud, 24 vols, trans. under the general editorship of James Strachey in collaboration with Anna Freud, with assistance by Alix Strachey and Alan Tyson, London: Hogarth, 1953–74.

Further reading

Brennan, Teresa, *The Interpretation of the Flesh: Freud and femininity*, London: Routledge, 1992.

Cornell, Drucilla, 'What takes place in the dark' *Differences: A journal of feminist cultural studies*, 4 (1992), pp. 45–71.

Gay, Peter, *Freud: A life for our time*, London: Dent, 1988.

Laplanche, Jean and J.-B. Pontalis, *The Language of Psychoanalysis*, trans. D. Nicholson-Smith, London: Hogarth and the Institute of Psychoanalysis, 1983.

Ricoeur, Paul, *Freud and Philosophy: An essay on interpretation*, trans. Denis Savage. New Haven, CT: Yale University Press, 1970.

Storr, Anthony, *Freud* (Past Masters, general ed. Keith Thomas), Oxford: Oxford University Press, 1989.

Glossary

Oedipus complex   The configuration around which Freud's theory revolves, accounting for the infant's negotiation of incestuous drives, including erotic and destructive desires for the parent as well as the associated feelings of guilt and fear of punishment.

Friedan, Betty (1921–)

Betty Friedan gained a degree in psychology from Smith University in 1942, and held a research fellowship in psychology at the University of California in Berkeley. After her marriage, she worked as a journalist before being fired from her newspaper job for being pregnant, an event which she later described as crucial in bringing her to feminism. In 1963, her first book, *The Feminine Mystique*, was published, immediately placing her at the forefront of the increasingly active feminist movement in America. In 1966, Friedan was one of the dominant figures in the founding of the National Organisation of Women (NOW), which grew to be the largest feminist organisation in the United States, and campaigned in support of such issues as abortion, increased access to childcare, and the Equal Rights Amendment to the US constitution. Throughout the 1960s and 1970s, Friedan was a high-profile feminist activist, speaker and writer, and her follow-up to *The Feminine Mystique, The Second Stage*, was published in 1982. However, in her most recent book, *Fountain of Age* (1993), Friedan has turned her attention away from feminist issues to study the social situation of the elderly.

In *The Feminine Mystique*, Friedan drew on her training as a psychologist, her experience as a writer for women's magazines and the personal testimony of housewives themselves, in order to argue that both women specifically and society in general were being damaged by a 'feminine mystique', which only envisaged female fulfilment in terms of an extremely limited concept of the female role, founded on early marriage, motherhood and a retreat into the home.

This 'mystique', claimed Friedan, has its origins in popularised misreadings of Freud, which ignored the fact that his theories concerning women – which essentially defined femininity as a passive state – were shaped by his particular personal and cultural perspective, and not necessarily applicable to women in twentieth-century America. These ideas, however, were reinforced by 'functional' sociologists, who argued in support of women's *fundamental* difference from men, which therefore required different social and educational goals. Consequently, although more American women than ever before were going to college, female students were channelled away from more intellectually rigorous academic subjects towards 'a potpourri of liberal-arts courses, suitable only for a wifely veneer, or narrow programmes such as "institutional dialectics", well beneath their abilities and suitable only for a "stop-gap" job between college and marriage' (*The Feminine Mystique*). Young women's view of their potential was therefore limited to striving to attain to the kind of idealised images promoted by the media, which defined the feminine ideal as 'young and frivolous, amost childlike; fluffy and feminine; passive; gaily content in a world of bedroom and kitchen, sex, babies, and home' (*ibid.*). The result for such women, however, was not fulfilment, but entrapment within a 'comfortable concentration camp' (*ibid.*), having lost all sense of an autonomous self in the face of constant demands made upon them by husband, home and children.

The answer according to Friedan, however, was simple. Increased access to education would not only train women for a career outside the home, but also allow them to regain their lost sense of self. The end result would be the revitalisation of the institution of marriage itself; it would not be regarded as an 'escape but a commitment shared by two people that becomes part of their commitment to themselves and society' (*ibid.*). Nor should responsibility for children hold women back – instead, they should campaign for maternity leave and professionally run nurseries. Housework should no longer be regarded as a full-time occupation, but as something that must be done as quickly and efficiently as possible.

The Feminine Mystique was hugely popular with the very housewives whom Friedan identified as being confined by the mystique. However, it has also been the target of extensive criticism from within the women's movement, which tends to focus on the unacknowledged limitations of the text's middle-class, innately conservative, perspective. The black feminist bell hooks, for example, draws attention to the fact that Friedan 'made her plight and the plight of white women like herself synonymous with a condition affecting all American women' (*Feminist Theory*). And hooks is echoed by Zillah R. Eisenstein:

> Friedan presents this problem, which is particular and specific to the suburban middle-class woman's identity as though it is woman's problem in general . . . Friedan misses the point that in actuality it applies differently to women of different economic classes and races, and that the way one relates to it is not a matter of individual choice. (*Radical Future*)

Indeed, Friedan's relationship with the women's movement has always been somewhat uneasy. Although one of its principal popularisers, she has clearly grown uncomfortable with the concept of radical political or ideological activism, in spite of her involvement with NOW, which used marches and sit-ins as some of its primary campaign tactics. In the book that followed *The Feminine Mystique, It Changed my Life: Writings on the women's movement* (1977), she speaks disparagingly of 'women's libbers' whose radicalism, she fears, will alienate mainstream support. This unease was finally fully voiced in *The Second Stage* (1983), in which she accuses radical feminism of having gone too far, denying 'the importance of family, of women's own needs to give and get love and nurture, tender loving care'. The feminine mystique, she claims, has been replaced by a *feminist* mystique which forces women into the workplace and denies them the opportunity of finding fulfilment within a home and family.

Although *The Second Stage* might be seen as a refutation of the argument put forward by Friedan in *The Feminine Mystique* (Susan Faludi, for example, accuses Friedan of 'yanking out the stitches in her own handiwork' (*Backlash*)), it is possible to read it more charitably as representing an advancement of her thought. One of the main criticisms that can be levelled at *The Feminine Mystique* is that, although Friedan argued for women's right to find fulfilment outside the home, she also appeared to believe that, with a few minor changes to their lives, women could slot into the existing social structure more or less as it stood. In *The Second Stage*, Friedan at least begins to place the movement towards female autonomy within a larger framework, arguing for, among other things, the necessity of restructuring the domestic space in order to free women from housework and childcare.

However, Friedan is perhaps better served when approached as a liberal humanist rather than a feminist, since the consistent basis of her argument is that women cannot, and should not, be regarded as separate from the other half of humanity. If feminism is to achieve anything at all, it must take into account the needs of men as well; for '[how] can we evade the final fact that our humanity is *ours* as male and female if we are to truly realize ourselves?' (*It Changed my Life*).

The Feminine Mystique is one of the most famous texts of twentieth-century feminism, whose sales total approximately 2·5 million copies worldwide. Friedan remains one of the most immediately identifiable names of the movement, and her writing, which is a readable mixture of personal anecdote, sociology and psychology, is still an accessible introduction to the kind of social debates that initiated second-stage liberal feminism. In addition, Friedan's campaigning on behalf of the feminist cause spanned over two decades, and should not be underestimated.

However, the theoretical weaknesses of Friedan's work are nowhere more apparent than in the relentlessly optimistic ending of *The Second Stage*, in which she looks forward to an America on the verge of being transformed both socially and politically by a 'new male–female, second-stage mode . . . defined by a fluidity, flexibility and pragmatism demanding more individual responsibility and voluntary pooling of community resources'. As this has conspicuously failed to happen, such a conclusion rings somewhat hollow to a contemporary reader, indicating the limitations of Friedan's vision: her naïve adherence to both an idealistic notion of 'American' individualism and an uncomplicated conception of subjectivity. The fact that she obviously does not condone the revolutionary restructuring of either society itself or the ideologies which underpin it probably accounts for both her mainstream popularity and her problematic reputation within the feminist movement.

Main works

The Feminine Mystique, Harmondsworth: Penguin, 1965.

It Changed my Life: Writings on the women's movement, London: Victor Gollancz, 1977.

The Second Stage, London: Sphere, 1983.

The Fountain of Age, London: Jonathan Cape, 1993.

Further reading

Eistenstein, Zillah R., *The Radical Future of Liberal Feminism*, rev. edn, Boston, MA: Northeastern University Press, 1993.

Faludi, Susan, *Backlash: The undeclared war against women*, London: Vintage, 1992.

hooks, bell, *Feminist Theory: From margin to center*, Boston, MA: South End, 1984.

Spender, Dale, *For the Record: The making and meaning of feminist knowledge*, London: Women's Press, 1985.

Tong, Rosemarie, *Feminist Thought: A comprehensive introduction*, London: Unwin Hyman, 1989.

Friedman, Milton (1912–)

Milton Friedman is perhaps the world's best-known 'monetarist' economist. He was born in Brooklyn, New York. In 1933 he took an MA from Chicago University and in 1936 a Ph.D. from Columbia University in

New York. He returned to Chicago in 1946, and remained there as one of its most illustrious members of staff until his formal retirement in 1979. Chicago became the home of the modern American *laissez-faire* movement, stressing a neo-liberal approach to economic analysis and policy-making. Friedman was the key figure in this development at Chicago.

Friedman was trained as a statistical economist and his first efforts in economic analysis were directed towards empirically grounded investigations. He established himself as an outstanding applied economist, working on patterns of income and consumption, and during the War on sampling techniques for munitions production. These early explorations in statistical and empirical matters convinced Friedman that economics is an empirical science, one absolutely dependent upon its testing and verification procedures. He set out this position in *Essays in Positive Economics* (1953), which became a classic in the methodology of economics and set the tone for a large part of the debate about economic methodology in the post-war period. His reinterpretation of the Keynesian consumption function to think of it in relation to lifetime income (or 'permanent income', as he termed it) rather than just to current income, remains standard fare in economics teaching, and established him as an eminent theorist as well as econometrician (*A Theory of the Consumption Function*, 1957). For the professional economist, this work on the consumption function probably remains his crowning achievement. During the late 1940s and early 1950s Friedman also made significant advances in the theory of demand, the pure theory of choice and in decision-making.

It is in respect to his monetary theory and associated empirical work, and – though to a lesser extent – in connection with the idea of a 'natural rate of unemployment', that the popular perception of Friedman's importance lies. Friedman began his long association with work on monetary matters in 1951. He published an initial jointly authored book in 1956 (*Studies in the Quantity Theory of Money*), another in 1963 (*A Monetary History of the United States*) and a final one in 1982 (*Monetary Trends in the United States and the United Kingdom*). It is fair to say that these studies changed the professional attitude amongst mainstream economists towards monetary issues, and a good deal of public policy-making as well.

The prevailing Keynesian approach in the 1950s and 1960s was said to be that 'money did not matter'. (Actually, this is a misconception of Keynes's own position, but that is another issue.) In early Keynesian models of the economy the level of output was determined by the level of aggregate demand – and manipulation of aggregate demand by the government (in the form of interventionary fiscal policy) was sufficient to manipulate aggregate output. The role of money was 'neutral' in these models. Monetary policy was there to support fiscal policy moves. Aggregate supply simply adapted to changes in demand, and the level of inflation could be controlled by adjusting aggregate demand, which affected the level of employment, which in turn affected the inflation rate. (The relationship between unemployment and inflation was expressed through the so-called 'Phillips curve' mechanism.)

Friedman began by tackling these models obliquely. He undertook typically painstaking investigation into the history of US monetary conditions and the role of the Federal Reserve Bank in conducting monetary policy. He first resurrected the quantity theory of money by suggesting that the *demand* for money was stable; thus fluctuations in monetary conditions were the result of changes in the money-*supply* process. In re-examining the effects of monetary variations on nominal money incomes, prices and output, he suggested that any increase in the government's fiscal deficit (whether the result of active policy or notion) had only a limited impact on nominal incomes in the short run. Any effect soon wore off as the implied increase in the money stock needed to finance the increased deficit permanently augmented the rate of inflation. Thus the long-run addition to the monetary growth affected only the rate of inflation and had virtually no effect on either the level of output or its growth rate. What is more, in a final *coup de grace*, he put forward the startling suggestion that the Great Depression in the United States was not the result of either business decisions or changes in real variables, but occurred primarily because of the incorrect monetary policies of the Federal Reserve System. It was 'the government machine' that was responsible for the Great Depression, not changes in the underlying real economy.

Here, then, by the mid 1960s were firmly in place all the main ingredients of the monetarist position. Interventionary fiscal policy had no permanent impact on output levels; it was changes in the money supply that caused inflation – the link between them being provided by the quantity theory of money. Broadly speaking Friedman continued to refine these propositions for the rest of his professional life as an economist. And it is in regard to this project that his other main claim to popular fame – the 'natural rate of employment' – was invented.

One of the problems identified in respect of the monetarist story just outlined was the connection between the labour market and the money supply process. The traditional Keynesian view linked this via the Phillips curve, which suggested a genuine empirical trade-off between unemployment and inflation – the system could be managed to produce either higher unemployment with lower inflation or lower unemployment with higher inflation. Friedman rejected this because it was not theoretically grounded. Instead he took the 'classical' position: there was no trade-off. The Phillips curve was illusory because it did not take account of workers' expectations. Once workers had come to expect a rise in the general price level, the attempt by the government to reduce unemployment by expansionary fiscal policy would fail because this would simply lead workers to demand higher nominal money wages (to compensate for the anticipated increase in the price level). The net effect on employment and output would be nil, while the fiscal expansion would just create more inflation ('The role of monetary theory'). There was nothing the government could do on the demand side about the long-run equilibrium level of unemployment; this was determined by 'real' structural factors like the conventions of wage contracts (restrictions on lay-offs, impediments to occupational entry, restrictions on mobility and flexibility of labour use), the levels of unemployment benefits, the degree of technological development, the quantity and quality of capital, and the like. The level of employment determined by these elements was termed the 'natural rate' (sometimes designated as the 'non-accelerating inflation rate of unemployment', or NAIRU, in some later formulations). These 'supply-side' impediments to labour use – not the fiscal policy of the government –were what controlled the levels of unemployment.

When this package of arguments was put together with the monetarist account of inflation previously outlined, a neat and seemingly coherent explanation was provided for the growing problem of first 'stagflation' (stagnation in employment and output existing alongside continued inflation), and then for 'slumpflation' (a slump in employment and output with continued increases in the rate of inflation). And it won Friedman the Nobel Prize in Economics in 1977.

Alongside his economic work Friedman developed a formidable polemical style of popular argumentation. He combined his economic analysis with a strong advocacy of free enterprise, and a defence of economic freedom and liberty from the ever-present encroachment on these by government actions. The market mechanism and free trade offered the solution to all outstanding economic and social problems. In *Capitalism and Freedom* (1962) and *Free to Choose* (1980, written with his wife Rose Friedman) amongst other books, these populist themes were eloquently elaborated into a doctrinal defence of individualistic competition and the primacy of the price system and market exchange. These issues were eagerly embraced by the new political forces of the Right, particularly in Anglo-American political cultures. They undoubtedly contributed to the dramatic policy changes experienced in these countries during the 1980s.

But finally there remains a question over their adequacy and effectiveness. The money supply and inflation story came up against the formidable obstacles of actually controlling the money supply in financially sophisticated and internationally integrated economies. The success here was mixed at best. The labour market and 'natural rate of employment' story has proved equally problematical. The theory has not tracked the actual course of labour market adjustments well, particularly in Europe, though in the mid 1990s it was still animating a good deal of public policy. What these approaches did, however, was to give a credence to the highly 'adventurous' macro-economic policy making experienced since 1980. The full consequences of these have not yet been appreciated.

Main works

Essays in Positive Economics, Chicago: Chicago University Press, 1953.

Studies in the Quantity Theory of Money (ed.), Chicago: Chicago University Press, 1956.

Capitalism and Freedom, Chicago: Chicago University Press, 1962.

A Monetary History of the United States, 1867–1960 (with Anna J. Schwartz), Princeton: Princeton University Press, 1963.

'The role of monetary theory', *American Economic Review*, 58 (March 1968), pp. 1–17.

Free to Choose (with Rose Friedman), New York: Harcourt Brace Jovanovich, 1980.

Monetary Trends in the United States and the United Kingdom, their Relation to Income, Prices and Interest Rates, 1867–1975 (with Anna J. Schwartz), Chicago: Chicago University Press, 1982.

Further reading

Butler, Eamonn, *Milton Friedman: A guide to his economic thought*, London: Gower/Maurice Temple Smith, 1985.

Hirsch, Abraham, *Milton Friedman: Economics in theory and practice*, Hemel Hempstead: Harvester, 1990.

Wood, J. C. (ed.), *Milton Friedman: Critical assessments*, London: Routledge, 1990.

Fuller, Richard Buckminster (1895–1983)

In 1960 Buckminster Fuller donated a 'Chronofile' to Southern Illinois University Library consisting of some 250 volumes and 80,000 letters. He also compiled an obsessive statistical record of references to himself in books, newspapers and periodicals. This archive grew exponentially from the 1960s onwards, when his name became for a time a household word.

Fuller claimed he wanted to transform his life into a documentary project, and there are perhaps traces of megalomania in this degree of self-regard. His biographical dateline, for instance, compiled by himself in the sixties, includes world events alongside more intimate details. We learn that he was born in 1895, the year x-rays were invented. Ten years later, whilst Einstein published his theory of relativity, Fuller's family took up residence in Bear Island off the coast of Maine. 1914 is notable not just for the outbreak of the First World War, but because Fuller was expelled from Harvard. And in 1917, the year of the Russian Revolution, Bucky married Anne Hewlett.

After several failed enterprises in the 1920s, Fuller then had three decades in which he pioneered many radical design projects in transport, accommodation and storage. In the 1930s, he focused upon a pilot-project for an experimental car built on aircraft principles and cheap to produce. In the 1940s, he turned his attention to a form of housing which would be affordable by all and rapidly assembled. From the 1950s onwards, his energies were absorbed by the production of geodesic domes, his most influential undertaking. By the time of his death in 1983, he had circum-navigated the globe almost sixty times, spreading his belief that 'the most important fact about Spaceship Earth [is that an] instruction book didn't come with it'.

Richard Buckminster Fuller once declared that 'Whenever I draw a circle, I immediately want to step out of it', and in both his life and work he was a highly unconventional figure. As *Fortune* magazine wrote in 1946, he had 'a mind that functions like a cross between a roll-top desk and a jet-propulsion motor'. On leaving university he took up a series of unsuccessful business ventures, culminating in the crash of the Stockade Company in 1927. The crucial turning-point in Fuller's life came in 1928, the so-called 'Year of Silence', when he refused to speak to anybody, including his wife, but instead immersed himself in mathematical and architectural volumes. He emerged from this prolonged self-isolation with a fully formed philosophy, which he called 4-D thinking. The phrase indicated that his concern as an inventor was not just with the length, breadth and height of the materials he used, but also with the consequences of his constructions through time – a concern which demonstrates his social conscience.

After the 'Year of Silence' the inventions came thick and fast. First there was the Dymaxion car, of which three different versions were produced by Fuller and Starling Burgess between 1932 and 1934. The public relations section of the Marshall Field department store invented the term 'Dymaxion'. It is an acrostic, formed from three of Fuller's most frequently used words: *DYnamic*, *MAXimum*, and *IONs*. The word was unusual, and so was the car. It had a front-wheel drive, a rear-engine and a chassis so streamlined it looked like something from a science-fiction movie. Little wonder that when Fuller took his creation for a spin along Fifth Avenue he was stopped by a traffic cop exclaiming 'What the hell is this?' Fuller, born in the year that the automobile was first introduced into the United States, never fulfilled his ambition of becoming the Henry Ford of his generation. A fatal accident involving the car at the 1933 Chicago World Fair revealed some fundamental design faults.

Undeterred, Fuller scrapped the car but kept the name: he was fond of striking nomenclature. A house was not a home to him, it was a Dymaxion Dwelling Machine. The DDM was intended to provide a prefabricated, factory-built house which was easy to transport and assemble, and cheap to purchase and maintain. There was tremendous interest in this idea from the American government, as the house would use materials and techniques from aircraft factories, thus ensuring that aviation workers would still be guaranteed employment at the end of the Second World War. The prototype for this ready-made accommodation was displayed in Wichita in 1946. Despite looking from the outside like a glorified tin-shed, it was an instant success with the wives of the aviation workers themselves, who were impressed by the fact that it took only half an hour to clean. It took almost the same amount of time for the entire project to come to grief, thanks to some marketing problems and Fuller's reluctance to relinquish total control of his project. Fuller refused to accept that these setbacks were failures, even though his Dymaxion bathroom of 1937 and Dymaxion map of 1942 were dreams also destined to be discarded.

His next venture was to prove rather more successful. In the late 1940s, he began experimenting with designs for a geodesic dome at Black Mountain College in North Carolina. This was the right place to be at this time. It was a fertile ground for experimentalists of all kinds: John Cage in music, Merce Cunningham in dance, Robert Rauschenberg in the visual arts. The geodesic dome was a lightweight self-supporting hemispherical structure made up out of triangular components. Like the Dymaxion concepts, it strives to achieve 'more for less' (a variation of the *Bauhaus* principle that 'less is more'). The success of the dome was phenomenal. Over 300,000 were erected between 1954 and Fuller's death in 1983. The military were enthusiastic patrons, and constructed domes in both the Arctic and Antarctic polar regions, and many points in-between. The most famous domes were the 1959 gold anodised aluminium construction exhibited in Moscow in 1959 and acclaimed by Kruschev, and the seven-tenths spherical dome erected as a pavilion at the Montreal Expo Fair of 1967, but devastated by fire during renovations in 1976. The futuristic appearance of the domes tells us a great deal about their forward-thinking, non-conforming creator.

The significance of Buckminster Fuller is not simply limited to his creations. Indeed, in most histories of architecture or engineering he merits a footnote at best. Most of Fuller's designs were self-consciously ephemeral, disposable stages in the ongoing evolution of technology. His importance lies rather in what we might call his transcendentalist vision. His work was never conceived merely as problems of housing or design, but projected into the widest possible context. The Emersonian insight preventing him from committing suicide back in 1928 was, 'You do not belong to you. You belong to the universe.' By reintroducing terms such as 'synergy' and 'ecological patterning' into the architectural vocabulary, Fuller showed an environmental sensibility which was ahead of his time. Whether his other ideas for 'floating tetrahedronal cities, air-deliverable skyscrapers, submarine islands' and the like were ever meant to be anything other than provocations is irrelevant. A visionary must be allowed to have visions, after all, and Fuller's visions chimed perfectly with the utopianism of post-war America.

By proclaiming 'I am not a . . . noun. I seem to be a verb', Fuller wrote his own epitaph, one which emphasises his intransigence and transitivity. It is ironic, therefore, that his everlasting fame should be assured precisely because his name has become a noun. In 1985, researchers at the University of Texas discovered that the smallest atoms in carbon had shapes which were similar to geodesic domes, and so called them 'Buckminster-fullerenes'.

Main works

Nine Chains to the Moon, Philadelphia and New York: Lippincott, 1938.

No More Secondhand God and Other Writings, Carbondale: Southern Illinois University Press, 1963.

The Buckminster Fuller Reader, ed. James Mellor, London: Jonathan Cape, 1970.

I Seem to Be a Verb (with Jerome Agel and Quentin Fiore), New York: Bantam, 1970.

4-D Timelock, Albuquerque, NM: Biotechnic, 1972.

Operating Manual for Spaceship Earth, New York: E. P. Dutton, 1978.

Further reading

Harris, Mary Emma, *The Arts at Black Mountain College*, Cambridge, MA: MIT Press, 1987.

McHale, John, *R. Buckminster Fuller*, Brighton: Prentice Hall, 1962.

Marks, Robert W., *The Dymaxion World of Buckminster Fuller*, Carbondale: Southern Illinois University Press, 1966.

Pawley, Martin, *Buckminster Fuller*, London: Trefoil, 1990.

Potter, Robert, *Buckminster Fuller*, Morristown, NJ: Silver Burdett, 1990.

Sieden, Lloyd Sieven, *Buckminster Fuller's Universe: An appreciation*, New York: Plenum, 1989.

G

Galbraith, John Kenneth (1908–)

A mercurial figure, Galbraith is difficult to categorise, except perhaps as controversial. Brought up in a Scottish–Canadian farming community dominated by a Calvinist work ethic and puritan hostility to luxury – a background not dissimilar to Thorstein **Veblen**, the original Institutionalist – Galbraith was to become the best known of post-war Institutionalists with his critique of capitalist systems and advocacy of intervention to combat their failings. But it is his celebrity status as one-time editor of *Fortune* magazine, speech writer and advisor to President Kennedy (for whom he served as American Ambassador to India), and as best-selling author across a range of topics, that sets Galbraith apart from his contemporary economists. Whilst being one of the most controversial economic, social and political critics of his time, Galbraith has held coveted academic appointments; notably, Paul M. Warburg Professor of Economics at Harvard and President of the American Economic Association.

Ephemeral pieces aside, such as *The Great Crash, 1929, Ambassador's Journal, How to Control the Military, How to Get Out of Vietnam* and the novel *The Triumph . . .* , Galbraith's most controversial literary productions are *American Capitalism* (1952), *The Affluent Society* (1958), *The New Industrial State* (1967) and *Economics and the Public Purpose* (1973). At least two recurrent themes from these works can be identified as distinctly Galbraithian: (1) counter-vailing power and (2) private affluence and public poverty.

Galbraith never supported neo-classical micro-economics or the 'neo-classical synthesis' interpretation of Keynes. For such mainstream orthodox economics was not about the search for 'truth', but instead about the preservation of a belief system supporting existing power structures. Mainstream economists, for Galbraith, were merely the 'high priests' of a capitalist belief system. In *American Capitalism* Galbraith argued that the perfect competition model, the lynch-pin of orthodox economics, which assumes a built-in regulatory force that sees the economy function smoothly and efficiently, had been displaced in sector after sector. Competition had broken down in the face of concentration and monopoly power. However, Galbraith called into question the orthodox view that large organisations are exploitative. On the contrary, because power inevitably develops in pairs, countervailing power can grow to negate exploitative potential and lead to the creation of large productive organisations. For example, the powerful corporation begets the countervailing power of a trade union, keen to acquire some of the profits of the strong and to defend the interests of the weak. Thus the defence of the consuming public at large does not depend on anti-trust legislation, which would damage the productive (efficient) capacity of the producer and hinder sophisticated organisational relationships that facilitate fast technological progress and development. Policy-makers should abandon anti-trust legislation in pursuit of the fictitious goals of the perfect competition model, and confine their attention to the reinforcement of policies that encourage the development of countervailing power amongst consumers, so as to check monopoly power.

The Affluent Society, the book that more than any other catapulted its author into world fame by striking a chord with the general public, undoubtedly played some political part in the rise of the Kennedy administration, with its commitment to increased provision of public goods. The book contrasts 'private affluence' and 'public poverty'. As regards private affluence, Galbraith argues that the basic wants, for food, shelter and clothing, have so extensively been achieved in the modern industrial society that our wants are now for 'unnecessary' goods. Yet orthodox economics, worked out in times when wants chased goods, does not distinguish necessary from unnecessary goods. For Galbraith, consumer sovereignty is a myth. The chain of causation in the affluent society runs from production to consumption: producers manufacture tastes and preferences by means of advertising and salesmanship. The cost of manipulating wants for new consumer goods ('trinkets and baubles' as they are often referred to, to emphasise their unnecessary nature) is a lack of public, social goods which could improve the quality of life. To correct the social imbalance and public squalor created by an 'inappropriate' value system, such as the view that the private sector is the only producer of wealth or that progressive taxation destroys economic incentives, Galbraith proposes increased taxation and a redirection of government expenditure: in other words, social intervention.

In *The New Industrial State*, the advanced industrial economy and its social imbalances are given a more systematic treatment, and the reader is treated to a rhetorically rich and striking set of phrases such as the 'Techno-structure', the 'Educational and Scientific Estate', and the 'Revised Sequence'. Again, it is a picture of the modern economic environment dominated by big business – the large industrial organisation. But, by internally generating investment funds, these large organisations are not subservient to market pressures and the disciplines of the capital market. They are instead controlled by the Technostructure, groups of professionals and specialists whose skills provide the necessary know-how for key, strategic decision-making. Such decisions are, however, based on the Technostructure's goals, notably the company's and its own stability. Thus, the company's resources are not used to pursue profit maximisation, but instead to promote growth and stability. This is achieved by planning. The 'market' as an entity controlled by the consumers is replaced by producer sovereignty and planning: the 'Revised Sequence', large corporations *creating* markets and determining consumer behaviour to retain a productive rhythm.

The New Industrial State, and the supplementary afterthought volume, *Economics and the Public Purpose*, emphasise the success of the planning within the large organisation, even though it represses individual creativity not serving the industrial organisation. This is particularly reminiscent of Veblen in *The Theory of Business Enterprise* (1904) and *Absentee Ownership* (1923), and extends the symmetry between the two thinkers beyond their similar backgrounds. Galbraith did not pass judgement on the process or the outcome of the power relationships which he revealed in *The New Industrial Estate*. He acknowledged the degree of efficiency with which the process performed its tasks in the pursuit of its goals, questioning instead the purposes such a process served.

In *The Culture of Contentment*, his most recent significant book, Galbraith identifies how society, particularly American society, has come to be dominated by the 'contented constituency' – the comfortable class, which, having become 'secure', is less dependent on government. As it forms the majority of voters, and dominates political opinion, this class generates an impetus for lower taxes and less government. The result is that the underclass (the minority), with little or no political voice, is increasingly disenfranchised and marginalised. Galbraith warns that this is a case of the self-serving Western majority sowing the seeds of its own destruction. His solution, one recalling the 1930s vision ever present in his work of the state as provider and healer, is a strong affirmative role for the state.

Galbraith's ideas have been subject to much criticism, for being loosely formulated, intuitive rather than factually supported, and theatrical and exaggerated in style. However, much of this criticism ignores what he intended to achieve overall with his economics. Rather than gain the support of his professional colleagues, Galbraith was concerned to influence the literate masses, and through them the politicians. The overstatement, the theatrical style, the omission of laborious qualifications are indeed present, and some criticism is thus inevitable. The criticism his work faces also reflects a reaction against the Institutionalists' methodology. Like Veblen, Galbraith uses an institutional approach to provide a theory of unifying process and the consequences of modern industrial capitalism. Thus, whilst he became probably one of the best-known economists of his generation, and influenced public and political opinion, primarily in the 1960s, his fate lay with that of the Institutionalist school. Although strong in the 1960s, and still at the fringe, this school did not turn the tide against orthodox economics. In the long term the western world's core belief system returned, to be fully behind the market system.

Main works

American Capitalism, Harmondsworth: Penguin, 1963.

The Affluent Society, Harmondsworth: Penguin, 1969.

The New Industrial State, Harmondsworth: Penguin, 1969.

Economics and the Public Purpose, Harmondsworth: Penguin, 1975.

The Culture of Contentment, Harmondsworth: Penguin, 1993.

Further reading

Breit, W. and R. L. Ranson (eds), *The Academic Scribblers: American economists*, London: Dryden, 1982.

MacFadzean, F., *The Economics of John Kenneth Galbraith: A study in fantasy*, London: Centre for Policy Studies, 1977.

Reisman, D., 'The dissenting economist: J. K. Galbraith', in J. R. Shackleton and G. Locksley (eds), *Twelve Contemporary Economists*, London: Macmillan, 1981.

Reisman, D., *State and Welfare: Tawney, Galbraith, and Adam Smith*, London: Macmillan, 1982.

Reisman, D., 'Galbraith on ideas and events', *Journal of Economic Issues*, 24 (1990), pp. 733–60.

Sobel, R., *The Worldly Economists*, New York: Free Press, 1980.

Geertz, Clifford (1926–)

Clifford Geertz trained as an anthropologist, completing a doctoral dissertation under the supervision of Talcott **Parsons** at Harvard University. After extensive fieldwork studies in Indonesia, notably Bali, he taught Anthropology at the University of Chicago before joining Princeton's Institution for Advanced Study in 1970, where he holds the position of Professor of Social Sciences.

Geertz can be seen as the founder and instigator of a distinct cultural anthropology, and as responsible for the introduction of an interpretive anthropology, based upon hermeneutic principles, to investigate symbols and meanings in human societies. Geertz's extensive field work, carried out in Indonesia and North Africa, whilst influential in its own right, is in many ways overshadowed by his contribution to discussions concerning the nature and possible course of the human sciences, where his strong anti-universalist project distinguishes him from recent trends in anthropology, in particular structuralism and functionalism.

The fieldwork studies, based on excursions carried out in the 1950s and 1960s, and exemplified by publications such as *The Religion of Java*, *Agricultural Involution*, *Peddlers and Princes*, *The Social History of an Indonesian Town* and *Islam Observed*, are wide-ranging analyses of particular aspects of, primarily, the relationship between culture and social system. Geertz's early work, modifying functionalist analyses, evolves into a form of cultural analysis that relies on local understanding of conditions and life to suggest that it is the construction of cultural paradigms that become a force in social action and meaning. The functionalist approach is rejected, as collapsing the cultural into the categories of social system and social action does not adequately explain the range of phenomena identified in the field work. Geertz offers a differentiation of culture from the social, such that social action cannot be predicted from analysis of culture, and social action must be understood with reference to culture, and this becomes a main theme of his theoretical anthropological essays. However, Geertz has a particular conception of culture, a semiotic one that is broadly in line with **Weber**'s interpretive approach. Weber sees man as an animal suspended in webs of significance he himself has spun: 'I take culture to be those webs, and analysis of it therefore not an experimental science in search of law but an interpretive one in search of meaning' (Geertz, *The Interpretation of Cultures*).

The Interpretation of Cultures, published in 1973, collected fifteen of Geertz's essays together and was enormously influential, touching as it does on the nature of interpretive understanding for all the human sciences. Geertz's introduction to this book, 'Thick description: towards an interpretive theory of culture', describes the ways in which ethnographers carry out their studies, through an emphasising of context in which human acts take place in an attempt to capture the meanings associated with such acts. A strong Weberian influence is visible here, although previous concerns with cultural significance as a generator of human action and a pattern created by human action is the emphasis that Geertz offers. The implicit challenge to non-interpretive approaches, in other words 'thin descriptions', is a rejection of forms of analysis that focus on purely 'objective' categories of description – the physical, behavioural, documentary. Ethnography in this account is an attempt to understand other cultures, not simply an attempt to describe these other cultures. The further challenge Geertz presents is against ethnocentrism, both of the overt, cultural superiority type, and the covert, where the culture of others is explained with reference to the cultural concepts and structures of the observer. It is the construction of meaning and the incorporation of the observer into the cultural and social spheres of those being observed that becomes a crucial methodological point for successful cultural anthropology.

The famous study of a Balinese cockfight (*Interpretation of Cultures*) is used to illustrate this. Geertz, attending an illegal cockfight, has to flee from a police raid with the villagers he is observing, allowing him to establish rapport through a shared experience of danger. Geertz's analysis of the cockfight as a component of the articulation of Balinese status hierarchy can only be apprehended through experience and involvement, not through observation alone. Extending this metaphorically, Geertz suggests that the key anthropological analogies of 'dissecting an organism, diagnosing a symptom, deciphering a code, or ordering a system' (*ibid.*) need to be replaced with 'penetrating a literary text' (*ibid.*). The focus of the anthropologist shifts from being concerned with social dynamics to a concern with social semantics: culture can be seen as an assemblage of texts, and our analysis of culture must reflect this textual nature.

This shift, away from structural analysis and towards hermeneutic analysis, remains the central theme of Geertz's later work, collected in *Local Knowledge* (1983). The introduction to this collection of essays notes that the controversy surrounding *The Interpretation of Cultures* and its challenge to 'grand theory' are waning, as cultural anthropology moves towards a more pluralistic form, witnessed by universalistic modes of explanation taking on the challenges of relativism to contextualise their analyses. However, the project of interpretive anthropology is still in its theoretical infancy, and Geertz attempts in *Local Knowledge* to provide some theoretical frameworks to orient the discipline. Notable here is the uptake of the work of Wittgenstein, particularly in the essay 'Common sense as a cultural system'. Our understanding of common sense as a cultural system is essential for an understanding of the ways in which culture is 'jointed and put together' (*Local Knowledge*), but this is by no means a simple project, given that common sense, which surrounds our thoughts and action, is practically invisible. Common sense can be understood in a number of different ways, but a straightforward cataloguing of content is not sufficient, nor is the analysis of its logical structure (as it has none). Geertz's analysis is an attempt to uncover the nature of Wittgenstein's analysis of a 'form of life' – from this perspective, an interpretive analysis of experience rather than a description of experience.

However, it is the essay 'From the native's point of view' that provides the clearest statement of the project of interpretive anthropology. The starting point for this essay, the debunking of the myth of the ideal–typical anthropologist in the field provided by the publication of Malinowski's diaries, leads Geertz to question the ways in which knowledge of others is attained by anthropologists. The anthropologist is incapable of perceiving what those he observes can perceive, but he can, and should, observe what people are perceiving with, or through, that is 'their symbolic forms – words, institutions, behaviors – in terms of which, in each place, people actually represented themselves to themselves and to one another' (*Local Knowledge*). Understanding can be achieved by locating modes of expression in a larger whole, thus allowing the observer to make a distinction between experience-near and experience-distant concepts, immediacies and abstractions, in an overall context.

Geertz's interpretive anthropology provides both methodological foundations for field work and a standpoint from which to launch a critique of non-interpretive anthropological strategies.

Geertz's delineation and advocacy of cultural hermeneutics has had a wide-ranging influence, extending from anthropology to the human sciences as a whole. This influence has changed over the years: cultural anthropology created itself as a separate discipline in the 1960s and 1970s and coalesced around Geertz's methodological precepts to generate a new subdiscipline. However, it is Geertz's wider critical and theoretical writings that have had most impact on the human sciences. The conception of the cultural 'event' as text allows Geertz to suggest a new perspective from which to interpret and understand other cultures. However, the cultural event as 'text' marks the entry of deconstructionism into the field of anthropology and has prompted other anthropologists to radicalise this project far beyond Geertz's original horizons; see in particular Clifford and Marcus (*Writing Culture*). The turning of anthropology onto itself, such that it investigates and analyses its own texts as cultural forms produces a textualist meta-anthropology which rapidly moves towards a postmodern perspective. Geertz nods in the direction of this self-referentiality, but never fully accepts its consequences.

Geertz shifts our notions of anthropological understanding away from the description of the social structures of other cultures, through a linguistic turn, to attempts to understand the meanings embodied in cultural patterns and events. That these objects for understanding may be located in 'alien' cultures or in our own society further extends the range and applicability of anthropology.

Main works

The Religion of Java, Chicago: Chicago University Press, 1960.

Agricultural Involution: The processes of ecological change in Indonesia, Berkeley: University of California Press, 1963.

Peddlers and Princes: Social change and economic modernization in two Indonesian towns, Chicago: University of Chicago Press, 1963.

The Social History of an Indonesian Town, Cambridge, MA: MIT Press, 1965.

Person, Time and Conduct in Bali: An essay in cultural analysis, New Haven, CT: Yale University Southeast Asia Studies, 1966.

Islam Observed: Religious development in Morocco and Indonesia, New Haven, CT: Yale University Press, 1968.

The Interpretation of Cultures, New York: Basic Books, 1973.

Local Knowledge, New York: Basic Books, 1983.

'History and anthropology', *New Literary History*, 21 (1990), pp. 321–35.

Further reading

Clifford, J. and G. E. Marcus (eds), *Writing Culture: The poetics and politics of ethnography*, Berkeley: University of California Press, 1986.

Rice, K. A., *Geertz and Culture*, Ann Arbor: University of Michigan Press, 1980.

Ricoeur, Paul, *Lectures on Ideology and Utopia*, New York: Columbia University Press, 1986.

Gellner, Ernest (1925–1995)

Gellner went to the London School of Economics in 1949 and was to stay there until 1984. In 1962, he was appointed Professor of Philosophy with special reference to Sociology and despite changes of title and department, he would remain at the LSE until 1984 when he took up the post of William Wyse Professor of Social Anthropology at the University of Cambridge. From 1993 until his death in November 1995, he was both a Fellow of King's College, Cambridge and Director of the Centre for the Study of Nationalism (which he had been instrumental in founding) at the Central European University in Prague, a post which reflected his long-term interest in nationalism, and his commitment to the creation of new liberal societies in the post-communist world. In spite of a serious illness in the late 1960s, he was not only a prolific writer producing a range of books on nationalism, Islam and contemporary theoretical issues in the social sciences but he was also a regular speaker at conferences and an acerbic critic of postmodernism. His background was cosmopolitan, born in Paris, he was educated in both Prague and Britain.

Central to all of Ernest Gellner's work whether in philosophy, sociology or social anthropology is a preoccupation with epistemological issues. His first major published work *Words and Things* (1959) was a critique of the dominance of Linguistic Philosophy at Oxford where he had studied as an undergraduate at Balliol, and all his subsequent writing, including the most concrete of them, *Saints of the Atlas* (1969), have epistemological concerns. Whilst issues of epistemology are present in all his writing, his work can be further divided into three broad areas: Islam, nationalism and work concerned with the nature of society and the impact of industrial society on social formations. This last concern is the base upon which he built his most recent work focusing on the concept and meaning of civil society. Hence much of the content of his work is characterised by a high level of abstraction. However, this is mediated by short, pithy and often allusive book titles, e.g. *Plough, Sword and Book* (1988); and chapter headings, e.g. 'Modular man' (*Conditions of Modernity*), 'How did mankind acquire its essence?' or 'The palaeolithic October' or 'The Marxist book of Genesis' (*State and Society*). Such allusions and use of irony are intended to convey to the reader some sense of the content and meaning of the idea which Gellner intends to explore. However, they also require that the reader is in some ways familiar with a broad European intellectual tradition and culture which Gellner pinpoints as the necessary base for the development of nationalism. His own definition of this is as 'a shared *high* culture (i.e. one whose members have been trained by an educational system to formulate and understand context-free messages in a shared idiom' (*Encounters*). Nowhere is this more apparent than in his work on nationalism, begun with the chapter on 'Nationalism' in *Thought and Change* (1964), then expanded in *Nations and Nationalism* (1983) and reviewed in *Encounters with Nationalism* (1994). Gellner argued that nationalism was a temporary if necessary social phenomenon which was created out of the same conditions that saw the rise of capitalism and the dominance of western European states in world affairs. The starting point for this work was the chapter, 'Nationalism' in *Thought and Change*, where he critiques both the Marxist view that nationalism is a bourgeois phenomenon and is therefore doomed and those who argued that nationalism expresses man's deepest passions and therefore will always be with us. He characterises this conflict over the role that nationalism plays as falling within a Kantian dualistic framework of 'a tug of war between reason and passion' (*Thought and Change*). For Gellner, nationalism is essentially contingent, and this notion of contingency is neatly expressed in the definition of nationalism as 'primarily a political principle, which holds that the political and the national unit should be congruent' which opens *Nations and Nationalism* (1983).

Although Gellner's initial intellectual foundation was in philosophy and it was his critique of the linguistic philosophical tradition derived from Wittgenstein which first brought him notice, in the formulation of his sociological thinking, it is Emile **Durkheim** and an array of primarily French authors who wrote in the late nineteenth and early part of the twentieth century on societal formation in North Africa (amongst them Fustel de Coulanges, Emile Masqueray and Robert Montagne together with the fourteenth century North African historian, Ibn Khaldoun), who appear to have had a formative influence on the construction of his view of the nature of society in not only North Africa and the Muslim world but in all societies. However, it is Durkheim's concept of 'organic solidarity' and the effect which this has on the formation of social structures, particularly that of the segmentary society, which is at the core of his writing on nationalism and civil society as well as Islam.

Gellner's work has ranged across a wide variety of subject areas and he has been a prolific writer. It is therefore difficult to find works which can introduce the new reader to the full range of his interests. However, the twenty-nine short reflective chapters published in 1994 under the title *Conditions of Liberty: Civil society and its rivals* do cover many of the themes which have been explored in more detail in other works. These chapters are both an examination of the epistemological roots of the use and new meaning which has been given in the post-communist world to the term 'civil society' and an exploration of why the fullest development of civil society, that is a pluralistic range of self-regulating institutions, has been in western capitalist societies. One can also see his discussion of the nature of civil society as an extension of his discussion of industrial society in *Thought and Change* (1964). The discussion of the nature and origins of civil society provides Gellner with the opportunity to review and critique other societal structures and to revisit old battlegrounds. The failure of Marxism he attributes to its attempt to live in the here and now and to place the good of the community above the possibility of individual redemption. However, he also argues that it is the very absence of civil society in Eastern Europe which allows for the clearest articulation of what it consists of. In looking at the world of Islam, he utilises the key concept of the *umma* but argues that this has been achieved in the west where a compromise was reached in which individuals might express religious extremism within private space, but in public space tolerance of differing views became the backdrop for the development of the successful capitalist economy and society. Gellner thus explicitly locates progressiveness in north-west Europe and it is this absolute commitment to the notion of progression in the development of human society which made him such a critic of what he saw as the relativist stance of the postmodernist theorists. It also means that while he sees much to admire in the Muslim world and in Islam and has extensively utilised the Muslim world in the development of his thinking, he does not see it as being able to achieve unilaterally the development of civil society which he would argue is necessary for progress to occur.

Gellner has been a controversial and challenging intellectual figure in a number of academic fields, most notably philosophy, sociology and social anthropology where his rejection of postmodernity's relativist stance reflects what he saw as the replacement of one social sciences orthodoxy (Marxism) by a new orthodoxy (postmodernism). His commitment to the value of the Enlightenment project and in particular its view that there are universal values which transcend the specificities of individual cultures has been an obvious critical site. His view of society as a combination of the universal and the particular, his 'modular man' or in the words of Homi K. Bhabha in *The Location of Culture* (1994), 'the diversity of man in a unitary world' illustrates, Bhabha argues, Gellner's inability to resolve the issue of difference. Another writer, Bryan S. Turner, in *Orientalism, Postmodernism and Globalism* (1994) suggests that Gellner's complete rejection of relativism means that in his work on Islam, he is more concerned with problems 'at the level of priests and other intellectual leaders of religious systems' than he is with the interrelationship between them and the popular. Similarly Eric Hobsbawm in *Nations and Nationalism since 1780* (1990) argues that despite providing a useful definition of nationalism, his top–down approach is ultimately too restrictive.

Main works

Words and Things: An examination and an attack on linguistic philosophy, London: Gollancz, 1959. Revised as *Words and Things: An examination of, and an attack on, linguistic philosophy*, London: Routledge and Kegan Paul, 1979.

Thought and Change, London: Weidenfeld and Nicolson, 1964.

Saints of the Atlas, London: Weidenfeld and Nicolson, 1969.

Cause and Meaning in the Social Sciences, London: Routledge and Kegan Paul, 1973. Revised as *The Concept of Kinship and other Essays on Anthropological Method and Explanation*, Oxford: Basil Blackwell, 1987.

Contemporary Thought and Politics, London: Routledge and Kegan Paul, 1974.

The Devil in Modern Philosophy, London: Routledge and Kegan Paul, 1974.

Legitimation of Belief, Cambridge: Cambridge University Press, 1974.

Spectacles and Predicaments, Cambridge: Cambridge University Press, 1979.

Soviet and Western Anthropology, London: Duckworth, 1980.

Muslim Society, Cambridge: Cambridge University Press, 1981.

Nations and Nationalism, Oxford: Basil Blackwell, 1983.

The Psychoanalytic Movement or the Cunning of Unreason, London: Paladin, 1985.

Relativism and the Social Sciences, Cambridge: Cambridge University Press, 1985.

Culture, Identity and Politics, Cambridge: Cambridge University Press, 1987.

Plough, Sword and Book: The structure of human history, London: Paladin Grafton, 1988.

State and Society in Soviet Thought, Oxford: Basil Blackwell, 1988.

Postmodernism, Reason and Religion, London: Routledge, 1992.

Reason and Culture: The historic role of rationality and rationalism, Oxford: Basil Blackwell, 1992.

Conditions of Liberty: Civil society and its rivals, London: Hamish Hamilton, 1994.

Encounters with Nationalism, Oxford: Basil Blackwell, 1994.

Further reading

Bhabha, Homi K., *The Location of Culture*, London: Routledge, 1994.

Hobsbawm, Eric, *Nations and Nationalism since 1780*, London: Canto, 1990.

Turner, Bryan S., *Orientalism, Postmodernism and Globalism*, London: Routledge, 1994.

Glossary

Organic solidarity Concerns links which exist between individuals involving the free exchange of rights and obligations.

Giddens, Anthony (1938–)

Giddens graduated from Hull in 1959, and, after an MA at the London School of Economics, was appointed lecturer at Leicester in 1961. He also taught at Simon Fraser University, Vancouver, and UCLA, before going to

King's College, Cambridge, in 1969 where he took a Ph.D. He was lecturer and senior lecturer at Cambridge University before becoming Professor of Sociology. In 1997 he took up the post of Director at the LSE.

Giddens has always been sceptical about epistemological certainties, whether traditional or postmodern. His approach is essentially ontological, developing an image of the social world incorporating both ordered relations and conscious actors, that is, elements of both structure and action. His key concept, *structuration*, is a deliberate attempt to combine the two words and their associated sociologies which once fought for supremacy in sociological theory. Giddens fundamentally envisages actors, not as passive, programmed objects of structure but as possessing knowledge and choice. He therefore rejects the supposed abolition of the subject in many forms of contemporary social and cultural theory. *Structure* is defined as comprising intelligible practices and actions undertaken by actors in society. Because structures are both the *medium* and the *outcome* of actions (the 'duality of structure'), people both act within pre-existing understandable situations and by their actions produce new ones. As structures – the collection of individually reciprocal relationships and forms of action – are reproduced in time and space they take on a greater permanence, becoming elements of a social *system*, forming relationships between groups or collectivities.

This model appears highly voluntaristic but Giddens's view of social reproduction is subtle. For structures to last, they must have 'time–space distanciation', that is, extension over geographic or social distance for more than a moment or generation. This is possible because resources of power, which are both enabling and constraining, stretch relationships in time and space. His distinction between authoritative (moral or political) and allocative (economic) resources of power stresses the way that social reproduction can depend on both normative authority and economic force. Yet these could act independently. Ideological influences in particular possess extensive authoritative impact whatever their economic base (the Papacy, or modern science, for example). Giddens has therefore moved away from the Marxist model of power derived from class domination to one closer to, but literally more grounded, than **Foucault**'s. The geographic reach of authoritative forms of power depends mainly on the extension of surveillance and control and storage of information. In pre-industrial societies, no matter how absolutist their state system, power was limited by primitive surveillance, information and communication systems, but modern organisations can operate globally. In our society information storage generates enormous power.

Giddens's sociology therefore attempts to replace some of the theoretical simplicities of previous perspectives, while continuing the analysis of the present within an historical context. This is most apparent in his three-volume critique of historical materialism which ends (in *Beyond Left and Right*) with a review of the prospects for radical politics today. He aims to replace Marxist teleological history, in which industrial capitalism is the culmination of preceding stages, with a 'discontinuist' one viewing it as unique. In previous periods 'class divided' societies integrated the economic with other areas of social life; consequently they were not driven by their class conflicts. In industrial capitalism the economic is clearly a separate, dominant, sector of social life, and the commodification of labour (the labour market) is the key element in increasing production. This unique class character of modern society, together with its geographic spread and its 'detraditionalising' destruction of local cultures, creates difficulties of personal and collective identity. The 'dialectic of control', of power and resistance, becomes increasingly uncertain. Fundamentalism – the defence of tradition by traditional means – is one response, though less plausible in a self-reflexive society which compels everyone to be self-consciously explanatory. Dogmatism has no common language. But what alternative forms of identity and social solidarity are possible in a globalising world?

Giddens explores these issues in his most recent works which attempt to meet the challenge presented by the theorists of the postmodern who stress the impact of advanced capitalist processes upon ideas of the self, identity and the subject. Yet he rejects the basic contradiction in proclaiming a new historical (postmodern) epoch while simultaneously pronouncing the end of history. However, he does agree that fundamental changes have occurred which have developed modernity to a 'high' or 'late' stage. In *Modernity and Self-Identity* he argues that this period is distinguished by 'separation of time and space', 'disembedding mechanisms' and 'institutional reflexivity'. Reflexivity here is extended beyond actors' self-monitoring to become, through constant 'chronic revision' of contemporary experience, constitutive of all modern institutions. Reflexivity thus provides the link in structuration theory between personal identity and social structure: everyone, and every institution, becomes capable of reflecting on the nature of reflection itself. In presenting this antifoundationalist argument Giddens characterises the experience of living in late modernity as one of doubt and uncertainty which are 'existentially troubling for ordinary individuals'. Consequently the self becomes a 'reflexive project' in marked contrast to the constancy of identity associated with traditional society or indeed with the aspirations and expectations of Enlightenment thought itself.

If in traditional society ontological security was found through continuity, then the paradox of late modernity is that chronic uncertainty is the only source of security. Our identities are inescapably tied to a constant questioning of the basis of identity itself. This development of Giddens's ideas demonstrates his attempt to address the criticisms of structuration theory which suggested that although he has shown the interdependence of agency and structure, he has failed to provide an adequate account of the individual. This criticism is made more powerful by the late twentieth-century dominance of political and economic ideologies proclaiming both the death of collectivism and the necessity of individual interest as the prime movers of human activity. Giddens presents a multiple, non-essentialist version of the self as a counter to the prevailing image of atomistic individuals driven by market competition.

In *The Transformation of Intimacy* Giddens explores the nature of intimate relationships in the late twentieth century, describing the shift from the 'forever and one and only' belief of romantic love to that of 'pure relationships' and 'plastic sexuality'. In both these forms, he argues, human relations are moving from external legitimations based in reproduction and family towards 'unhooked', individually centred interaction undertaken to satisfy the needs of each person or for reasons defined entirely within the relationship itself rather than according to society's old rules. Consequently these relationships may be terminated if a partner no longer feels that her or his needs are met. The central tenet of identity-making in an age of corporate capitalism is to avoid becoming fixed.

Giddens's intellectual career has demonstrated an extraordinary continuity of theoretical concerns that have made him the most well-known sociologist in the English-speaking world. He has consistently pursued the classical themes of sociology, of modern society and its ills, but with none of the classical overconfidence. His current focus on the individual builds upon his central theme of structuration. As he continues to explore the mutuality of structure, by stressing the twin strands of 'security and danger' and 'trust and risk' in modern society, he defines the central problem of life under late modernity as a fragile existence based on the acceptance of constitutive uncertainty. By exploring the structures of this insecure life he provides the main counter to the theoretical helplessness and nihilism of extreme postmodernism.

Main works

New Rules of Sociological Method: A positive critique of interpretative sociologies, London: Hutchinson, 1976.

Central Problems in Social Theory: Action, structure and contradiction in social analysis, London: Macmillan, 1979.

The Class Structure of the Advanced Societies (1979), London: Hutchinson, 1981.

A Contemporary Critique of Historical Materialism, Vol. I: *Power, Property and the State* (1981), 2nd edn, London: Macmillan, 1995.

Profiles and Critiques in Social Theory, London: Macmillan, 1982.

The Constitution of Society: Outline of a theory of structuration, Cambridge: Polity, 1984.

A Contemporary Critique of Historical Materialism, Vol. ɪɪ: *The Nation-State and Violence* (1985), Cambridge: Polity and Basil Blackwell, 1992.

The Consequences of Modernity, Cambridge: Polity, 1990.

Modernity and Self-Identity: Self and society in the late modern age, Cambridge: Polity, 1991.

The Transformation of Intimacy: Sexuality, love and eroticism in modern societies, Cambridge: Polity, 1992.

Beyond Left and Right: The future of radical politics, Cambridge: Polity, 1994.

Reflexive Modernisation: Politics, tradition and aesthetics in the modern order (with Ulrich Beck and Scott Lash), Cambridge: Polity, 1994.

Further reading

Bryant, C. G. A. and D. Jary (eds), *Giddens' Theory of Structuration: A critical appreciation*, London: Routledge, 1991.

Cassel, Philip (ed.), *The Giddens Reader*, London: Macmillan, 1993.

Clark, J., C. Modgil and S. Modgil (eds), *Anthony Giddens: Consensus and controversy*, Brighton: Falmer, 1990.

Held, D. and J. B. Thompson (eds), *Social Theory of Modern Societies: Anthony Giddens and his critics*, Cambridge: Cambridge University Press, 1989.

Cohen, I. J., *Structuration Theory: Anthony Giddens and the constitution of social life*, London: Macmillan, 1989.

Craib, I., *Anthony Giddens*, London: Routledge, 1992.

Goffman, Erving (1922–1982)

Erving Goffman was a Canadian who came from a family of Ukrainian Jews. He worked briefly in the film industry before completing his first degree in sociology and anthropology at the University of Toronto. He went on to doctoral research, completed in 1953, at Chicago, with field research in the Shetland Isles. This research informed his first book, *The Presentation of Self in Everyday Life*, published in 1956. It was reissued by Penguin three years later and became a bestseller. Between 1954 and 1957 he was a research fellow at the National Institute for Mental Health in

Bethesda, where his participant observation in mental wards led to the hugely influential essays on mental illness and 'total institutions', which was later published as *Asylums: Essays on the social situation of mental patients and other inmates*. He was a professor in the Department of Sociology at Berkeley from 1957 to 1968, and then the University of Pennsylvania until his death in 1982.

Goffman can be thought of as the inheritor of the Chicago tradition of 'symbolic interractionism', the approach of George Mead and others, who, through close participation in the day-to-day lives of their research subjects, described how members of a social group interact to sustain a common social environment. Goffman's practice, too, was to evaluate face-to-face interaction and show how tiny, apparently insignificant, aspects of individual behaviour function to maintain and structure it. Influenced by Chomsky's work on linguistics, he looked at how gestures, facial expressions, the direction of gaze or inclinations of the head and body form a kind of grammatical structure of social interaction. For instance, a hand laid lightly and briefly on someones arm or shoulder is used to convey the sincerity of condolences or apologies. Leaning slightly forward and nodding at appropriate intervals will convey a listener's interest and attention.

These micro-elements of interaction are both an important contribution to the meaning of encounters, and to the syntax we use for constructing social order. Goffman showed how sequences of behaviour, or 'interaction rituals', such as those seen in greetings and farewells, are universally used to control interaction. The style of greetings and farewells (whether there is a handshake or a bow, how long eye contact is maintained, how close people stand to each other) will vary from culture to culture; but there is always some kind of predictable sequence that characterises the interaction. The extent to which interaction is governed by rules can be seen by examining what Goffman called a 'remedial sequence': the action taken by participants to restore normal social interaction after a breach of social conduct. If a person steps on another's toe, he immediately apologises and perhaps offers an excuse. The other then accepts the apology. The transgressor may ensure no offence is taken by thanking the other and checking his reaction – 'Are you sure you're alright?' – and the other may reassure the transgressor by playing down the injury. Joint participation of this kind in very detailed and subtle patterns of behaviour is needed to maintain order.

This analysis now sounds much like common sense and it is easy to forget Goffman's contribution to our knowledge. However, he did more than simply describe the technicalities of interaction. He argued that in addition to our conscious determination of what we wish to achieve in interaction with others, we employ tacit or unconscious knowledge to control the interaction – what **Giddens** later called 'practical consciousness'. Take behaviour in lifts for example. We stare at the numbers of the floors or posters on the walls, anything to avoid staring at the other passengers. This 'civil inattention', as Goffman called it, protects the privacy of other passengers. It is learned behaviour – look at the way young children innocently stare – but not something we have to think about.

In this way Goffman opened up a new area of sociological enquiry: how the unconsciously patterned interaction of individuals produces and maintains social order. He showed how social interaction creates the world as a predictable place. He drew some links between social order and social structure – for instance, in his observation that patterns of self-disclosure in interaction relate to the social status of participants – but made little attempt to address the way in which social interaction might constitute society. Social institutions, such as factories and families, and social structures, such as class, figure in his thinking mainly as important influences on interaction rather than as the outcome of social order. Because his work concentrated on a detailed analysis of social interaction and the norms governing encounters, Goffman is certainly a 'micro-sociologist'. But beyond that he is more difficult to categorise. He was more than an ethnomethodologist, who confined himself on principle to the forms and meanings which agents' own common sense gives to their own acts and gestures. Ethnomethodology would be concerned exclusively with *what* people do to perform social acts like greeting or apologising. Yet, whilst Goffman was certainly interested in *what* people do, he was more preoccupied by the *why*: the principles that underly their performances. He interpreted the act of apologising, for example, as a 'remedial sequence', an act undertaken to restore a particular social interaction which has been disrupted. Similarly, he saw mental illness as a number of 'situational improprieties', acts which refuse to consider the normal rules that govern behaviour. Throughout Goffman's work, then, there is a search for the underlying rules of conduct which enable people to protect and maintain the broader social order.

In his first and most popular book, *The Presentation of Self in Everyday Life*, Goffman made extensive use of the metaphor of the theatre. Social life, he argued, was always a performance, and all our public dealings an effort to present an appropriate impression. Individuals present a 'front' whenever they interact with others. By making use of props, such as clothes or material possessions, as well as posture, gestures and facial expressions, they create the desired impression in others. Furthermore, life and even the individual can be divided into front- and back-stage. In a restaurant, for example, the dining room is front-stage, where the waiters must perform their professional role; while the kitchen is a back room, in which they can drop pretences and gossip about the customers. Goffman was fascinated by the way in which performances in the 'front room' serve to maintain normative standards.

One of the most creative aspects of Goffman's work was his focus on unusual situations and individuals. He recognised that one way to understand normative behaviour was to look at what happens when normal assumptions are disrupted. In *Stigma* he looked at how people manage impressions of themselves when they deviate in some way from approved standards of behaviour or appearance. They usually protect their identities through concealment, covering or disclosure. For instance, a man might never reveal that he has a criminal record, or cover a stay in prison as a period spent abroad, or disclose and excuse the blemish on his character as a youthful indiscretion.

In *Asylums*, Goffman investigated the influence of an extreme situation – the experience of being incarcerated in a mental hospital. In doing so, he presented one of the most influential analyses of 'total institutions'. He argued that total institutions, such as prisons, hospitals and army camps share common structural features: all inmates are treated alike, all behaviour is regulated and all activities are subsumed to the aims and will of a single authority. Consequently, these institutions have a huge impact on patterns of interaction. Yet Goffman observed that, despite this, the patients in the mental hospital in Bethesda found ways of 'making out', or redefining their roles so as to offer an alternative meaning of self to that laid down by the institution. Thus two forms of social order, the formal and the informal, can co-exist in institutions; indeed both are needed to make sense of behaviour such as mental illness.

Goffman used an eclectic range of data. Observations from his daily life, his field notes from periods of ethnographic study, newspaper stories and books on etiquette all provided source material for him. He used metaphors or 'ideal types' to make sense of this material. Such an approach was contrary to the objective, experimental research of the times and drew criticism. But in Goffman's view, it was precisely subjective analysis that was needed to make sense of the complexity of social interaction.

Goffman's books were witty and entertaining. They caught the public imagination and brought his ideas to a wide audience. This is one reason for the continuing influence of his work. Its academic reception was more muted. Inconsistencies in his theories and his neglect of social institutions made him peripheral to the mainstream sociology of his time. Since then his academic importance has increased, perhaps mainly because of the growing interest in discursive behaviour amongst social scientists influenced by postmodernism. Paradigmatic shifts in sociology and social psychology, from asking why we want to achieve things to asking how we do so, have also focused interest on theories of action, such as Goffman provided. Consequently, he is probably more cited today than when he was alive. A number of contemporary writers have used Goffman's ideas to examine the relationship between individual behaviour and the reproduction of social systems. Most notable perhaps is Giddens's structuration theory, which affords a central place to 'practical consciousness' in the form of the tacit knowledge that enables us to function as social actors.

Main works

The Presentation of Self in Everyday Life, Harmondsworth: Penguin, 1956.

Asylums: Essays on the social situation of mental patients and other inmates, Harmondsworth: Penguin, 1961.

Encounters: Two essays on the sociology of interaction, Harmondsworth: Penguin, 1961.

Stigma: Notes on the management of spoiled identity, Harmondsworth: Penguin, 1963.

Interaction Ritual: Essays on face-to-face behaviour, New York: Anchor and Doubleday, 1967.

Relations in Public, London: Penguin, 1971.

Frame Analysis: An essay on the organization of experience, New York: Harper and Row, 1974.

Further reading

Berger, P. L. and T. Luckman, *The Social Construction of Reality, a Treatise in the Sociology of Knowledge*, New York: Anchor Books, 1967.

Burns, T., *Erving Goffman*, London: Routledge, 1992.

Manning, P., *Erving Goffman and Modern Sociology*, Cambridge: Polity, 1992.

Perry, N., 'The two cultures and the total institution', *British Journal of Sociology*, 24 (1974), pp. 345–55.

Psathos, G. and C. Waksler, 'The essential features of face-to-face interaction', in G. Psathos (ed.), *Phenomenological Sociology: Issues and implications*, New York and Chichester: Wiley, 1973.

Gorz, Andre (1924–)

Born in Austria of a Jewish father and Catholic mother, Andre Gorz moved to Switzerland during the war, and then to Paris in 1948, where he became involved with the existentialist movement. He was an editor of *Les Temps modernes*, and subsequently a founder of *Le Nouvel Observateur*, for whom he wrote under the pseudonym of Michel Bosquet for twenty years. Neither an academic nor a member of the French Communist Party, Gorz worked as a journalist and with the labour movement, for example in the campaigns for workers' control in the 1960s and to reduce workers' hours in the 1980s.

While he has been called 'an iconoclastic marxist', Gorz has been as influenced by existentialism and psychoanalysis as by orthodox Marxism, and is cited as a key thinker in the development of the Green movement. While his most influential works are political and sociological, he has referred to himself as 'a failed philosopher', in the Sartrean tradition. In a series of provocative and highly original works, he has sought to develop a socialist response to contemporary developments in political economy and society, for example the impact of new technology and the rise of new social movements. His influences include the 'limits to growth' economists, and the work of **Illich** and other social critics, and he is one of the key post-industrialists. Never afraid to be utopian, his work draws on the spirit of early **Marx** in order to construct a conception of a post-capitalist society in which human beings can achieve their creative potential and attain a better quality of life. As he himself says, 'In the present phase, we must dare to ask questions we cannot answer and to raise problems whose solution remains to be found' (*Farewell to the Working Class*).

Gorz's early work, which seeks to develop a Marxist analysis of the labour process and the possibilities for class struggle, now seems dated in its assumptions, while innovative in its approach. His autobiographical novel, *The Traitor*, is the best source for a fuller picture of his existentialist philosophy of life and his various personal crises. His most important works, certainly for English language audiences, are the quartet of social critiques, *Ecology as Politics, Farewell to the Working Class, Paths to Paradise* and *Critique of Economic Reason*, all of which intersect and the last of which restates positions adopted earlier.

For Gorz, ecological politics is part of the broader socialist project. He is interested in the human costs of capitalist accumulation, as much as in the environmental impact. He argues that socialists and environmentalists need to recognise these connections and work together. All his work attacks the market rationality which is based on the desirability of economic growth, involving the production of unnecessary consumer items, and leading to waste and inequality. Modern production makes possible the planning of a system where a minimum of goods are centrally produced, and basic needs are easily satisfied. Use of automation results in the erosion of work, which necessitates work rationing: rather than mass unemployment, work is shared amongst the population and everyone enjoys a shortened working week. Non-essentials can be produced by citizens for themselves, outside the market economy.

In *Farewell to the Working Class*, Gorz develops his theme of the transformation of production, based on the separation of income from labour and the sharing of work. Human beings can then devote themselves to 'autonomous production'. This account is his response to two structural developments: the erosion of the industrial working class and the increase in mass unemployment in western societies. In a sense, then, Gorz has applied the socialism of early Marx to the post-industrial reality of the contemporary world. However, several critiques can be levelled at this inspiring account: first, Gorz's analysis is very much based on the western experience, and fails to confront the international division of labour, and the growth of proletarianisation in the developing world. Second, while usefully demolishing the traditional Marxist conception of working-class agency, Gorz is unable to substitute any other motor of change: his appealing vision of the potential future lacks an effective idea of how to get there. This is linked to the wider critique of his work as utopian and failing to offer a practical political strategy for change.

Paths to Paradise continues the analysis, and pays particular attention to the crisis of capitalism, based on the failure of Keynesianism and falling profits. Gorz looks at the role of state welfare, the social costs of which act as a break on capital accumulation, but the social benefits of which are essential to the capitalist order. He sees two alternative solutions to this impasse: either a leftist socialisation of welfare, with an egalitarian reorientation of medicine towards public health and generalisable treatments, or a capitalist move to use new technology in order to create opportunities for profit within the welfare sector: a commodification of welfare services, which would turn welfare from a cost into a market. While Gorz is sceptical about this possibility, events have proved, in Britain at least, the relevance of his suggestions. For Gorz, the socialist way forward is again based on the abolition of work and the development of a guaranteed income for life, in a vision owing much to Marx's *The German Ideology*:

> Life, like society itself, will become multi-centred. A wide range of forms of production and of rhythms and styles of life will co-exist, each person moving in several different spheres and finding their own balance in the passage from one to the other. Waged work will cease to be the primary activity but, through the guaranteed income for life which it provides for all, it will remain the economic basis for a limitless variety of possible activities without economic objectives or economic logic. (*Paths to Paradise*, p. 41)

While *Critique of Economic Reason* restates many of themes from the earlier works, it is a more developed account, also exploring the philosophical foundations of Gorz's approach, and engaging with other contemporary thinkers such as **Habermas**. Again, the critique of the work ethic and contemporary social organisation is at the heart of the project, and Gorz highlights the social and environmental costs of new technology and industrial development. As in earlier works, Gorz argues for socialist emancipation and human creativity, against the market and economic rationality: here, as throughout his career, the Marxist concept of alienation remains central.

Andre Gorz is an extremely useful, if somewhat neglected, social critic and philosopher. While his work has been published and discussed in British leftist journals such as *New Left Review* and *Marxism Today*, it is difficult to see much direct influence on other thinkers. His books are extremely accessible: brief, clearly written, and straightforwardly argued, they have contributed to discussions on the margins of the left, and especially within the Green movement. For example, manifestos of the British Green Party share very similar concerns and priorities to those of Gorz. However, his work has possibly failed to reach other English-speaking audiences, although he has had more impact in France and Germany. German trades unions, for example, have taken up the campaign for a shorter working week, and he has been associated with the French Confédération Française Démocratique du Travail (CFDT) trades union. His concern with economics and social relations renders him marginalised in circles where cultural, psychoanalytical and literary theories are more fashionable, and his utopianism limits his appeal to the labour movement and mainstream social democratic parties. Much of his work is engaged and topical to the extent that it dates quickly, although the substance of his analysis certainly retains its relevance. For those looking for stimulating, controversial and imaginative accounts of contemporary social developments and possibilities, Gorz remains essential.

Main works

Strategy for Labour, trans. A. Nicolaus and V. Ortiz, Boston, MA: Beacon, 1967.

Socialism and Revolution, trans. Norman Denny, London: Allen Lane, 1975.

The Division of Labour, Brighton: Harvester Wheatsheaf, 1976.

Ecology as Politics, trans. Jonathan Cloud and Patsy Vigderman, Boston, MA: South End Press, 1980.

Farewell to the Working Class, trans. Mike Sonnenscher, London: Pluto, 1982.

Paths to Paradise, trans. Malcolm Imrie, London: Pluto, 1985.

Critique of Economic Reason, trans. Gillian Handyside and Chris Turner, London: Verso, 1989.

The Traitor, trans. Richard Howard, London: Verso, 1989.

Further reading

Frankel, B., *The Post Industrial Utopians*, Cambridge: Polity, 1987.

Giddens, A., 'The perils of punditry: Gorz and the end of the working class', in A. Giddens, *Social Theory and Modern Society*, Cambridge: Polity, 1987

Goldblatt, D., *Social Theory and the Environment*, Cambridge: Polity, 1996.

Paehlke, R.C., *Environmentalism and the Future of Progressive Politics*, New Haven, CT: Yale University Press, 1989.

Gramsci, Antonio (1891–1937)

Antonio Gramsci was born in Arles, Sardinia, into the impoverished household of a disgraced petty official. He won a scholarship that enabled him to study philology in Turin, the 'red centre' of Italy, joined the Socialist Party (PSI) in 1913, and became involved in the militant workers' movement. In 1919 he and Palmiro Togliatti founded the *L'ordine nuovo*, a socialist weekly newspaper. In 1921 Gramsci participated in the foundation of the Italian Communist Party (PCI). From 1923, under the shadow of the victory of fascism, Gramsci served for three years as its leader.

Despite his immunity as a Member of Parliament, Gramsci was arrested in 1926 by the fascist government and sentenced to twenty years' imprisonment. He spent the last ten years of his life in prison, under Mussolini's personal supervision, yet succeeded in filling thirty-two notebooks (over 2,350 printed pages) which have come to be regarded as an unfinished classic of Marxist thought. Gramsci's *Prison Notebooks* offer some of the most important Marxist studies of culture, ideology and politics. Gramsci died in 1937, but the publication of his thoughtful and moving *Letters from Prison* in 1946 made the Italian public aware of this forgotten figure and ensured his continued influence on politics and on political and cultural theory.

Like many intellectuals of his generation, Gramsci began his intellectual development under the influence of the neo-Hegelian idealism of Benedetto Croce, who had made the 'ethico-political' into a driving force in history. In the *Prison Notebooks* Gramsci involves himself in an extended wrestling match with Croce (which Gramsci himself saw as a parallel to Marx's struggle with Hegel). In Italy the liberal Marxist philosopher Antonio Labriola had also established a tradition of the 'philosophy of praxis', opposed to the orthodoxy of 'scientific' Marxism of the Second international with its concommitant economic determinism. In this sense, Gramsci's thought is also a 'philosophy of praxis', stressing the active, and voluntary, even the spiritual, aspects of revolution.

Gramsci made a genuinely original contribution in his treatment of the relationship between 'structure' and 'superstructure'. He was a thorough-going Marxist in seeing the mode of production (the 'structure') as the ultimately determing force in society. But more consistently than any other Marxist thinker, he shifted the focus of Marxist practice into the realm of the 'superstructure': the world of ideologies, culture, religion and politics, to which, at least in his political writings, Marx had granted a significant degree of autonomy. By creating a 'national–popular will', the Communist Party would bring about the liberating dictatorship of the proletariat and effect a transformation of civilisation as total as the emergence of Christianity.

There is in the Marxist tradition an understandable concern with ideology in the sense of false consciousness. Gramsci's treatment of ideology in the *Prison Notebooks* goes much further, to embrace 'the terrain where men become conscious of themselves and of their tasks'. He attributes to the Communist Party a role in giving moral and intellectual direction, to shaping values and defining the general interests of society. Gramsci modelled the revolutionary activity of the Communist Party on the activities of *The Prince* as analysed by Machiavelli. As a kind of collective Machiavelli, the Communist Party would apply a Marxist political science to modern complex society. The socialist revolution, therefore, should not simply be pursued through a frontal attack on the state (in a 'war of movement'). Such a final stage of revolutionary struggle must be prepared for by a long struggle and the 'war of position', during which the working class would undermine the ideas and values of the ruling classes and prepare a new national–popular collective will, in which it will be the hegemonic force.

The concept of hegemony is crucial to Gramsci's thinking and embodies his most important legacy. By 'ideological hegemony' he means the process whereby a dominant class contrives to retain political power by manipulating popular opinion, creating what Gramsci refers to as the 'popular consensus'. Through its exploitation of religion, education and elements of popular national culture, a ruling class can impose its world-view and come to have it accepted as common sense. So total is the 'hegemony' established by bourgeois society over mind and spirit that it is almost never perceived as such at all. It strikes the mind as 'normality'. To counter this, Gramsci proposes that ideological struggle is a vital element in political struggle. In such struggles for hegemony, for the minds and hearts of the people, intellectuals clearly have a vital role. Gramsci conceived of his major work, the *Prison Notebooks* as an enquiry into the contemporary role of intellectuals in the wake of the Russian revolution, the defeat of the workers' movement in Western Europe (and in particular, in Turin), the rise of fascism and the general reorganisation of capitalism in advanced industrial countries (typified by 'Fordism'). He vastly extended the concept of 'intellectuals', until it seems to embrace anyone who exercises an organising function in society. And he evolved the suggestive idea of 'organic intellectuals' to describe those who expressed and defined the ideas and the will of a class or group as it enters into historical existence and comes to self-consciousness. He contrasts these with 'traditional intellectuals': those whose role is that of maintaining traditions and supporting an existing hegemony. He supports his analysis with minute and suggestive explorations of Italian and European history being obsessed, in particular, with the political and historical role of the Catholic Church.

Gramsci was pre-eminently a revolutionary leader in a non-revolutionary situation. He distinguished between the 'epoch' (which was revolutionary) and the 'situation' (which was not). His *Prison Notebooks* are a sustained effort to understand not only the military triumph of fascism but its ubiquitous 'hegemony'. The writing is episodic, uneven, sometimes contradictory. The notebooks were constantly being reworked and were subject to at least three major revisions. They expand from the problems of great political urgency to embrace a perspective that is consistently long-term and allows Gramsci to explore a huge diversity of human experience.

After 1945 Gramsci was taken up as a hero by the Italian Communist Party committed to the democracy which the historical Gramsci had despised. Because of his stress on the long-term nature of the 'war of position', and the struggle for hegemony, he was considered a theoretical forerunner by the new ideologues of 'Eurocommuninism' in Italy and other countries of Western Europe. When his works were comprehensively translated in the 1960s and 1970s Gramsci's work proved attractive across the whole spectrum of the New Left movement. The discussions of ideology by the French neo-structuralist Marxist, Louis **Althusser** owed a huge (largely unacknowledged) debt to Gramsci. Gramsci's concept of hegemony has been a key concept in the development of cultural studies, especially in the influential work which emerged from the Birmingham Centre for Contemporary Studies in the 1970s. Gramsci continues to have an enormous influence on cultural studies in Britain. Despite his own suspicion of the social sciences, he is today an integral part of the sociological establishment.

Main works

Selections from the Prison Notebooks, ed. and trans. Q. Hoare and G. Nowell-Smith, London: Lawrence and Wishart, 1971.

Letters from Prison, trans. Lynne Lawner, London: Jonathan Cape, 1975.

Selections from the Political Writings 1910–1920, ed. Q. Hoare, tra. Matthews, London: Lawrence and Wishart, 1978.

Selections from the Political Writings 1921–1926, ed. and trans. Q. Hoare, London: Lawrence and Wishart, 1979.

Selections from the Cultural Writings 1921–1926, ed. D. Forgacs and G. Nowell-Smith, trans. W. Boelhower, London: Lawrence and Wishart, 1985.

A Gramsci Reader, ed. D. Forgacs, London: Lawrence and Wishart, 1988.

Further reading

Fiori, G., *Antonio Gramsci: Life of a revolutionary*, trans. Tom Nairn, London: New Left, 1970.

Joll, J., *Gramsci*, London: Fontana, 1979.

Mouffe, C. (ed.), *Gramsci and Marxist Theory*, London: Routledge, 1979.

Ransome, Paul, *Antonio Gramsci: A new introduction*, Hemel Hempstead: Harvester Wheatsheaf, 1992.

Sassoon, Ann Showstack (ed.), *Approaches to Gramsci*, London: Writers and Readers, 1982.

Simon, Roger, *Gramsci's Political Thought: An introduction*, London: Lawrence and Wishart, 1982.

Glossary

Praxis   Human action with the capacity to transform the real world, the idea of such action.

H

Habermas, Jürgen (1929–)

Jürgen Habermas was born in Düsseldorf, Germany. From 1956–9 he was assistant to Theodor **Adorno** in Frankfurt. As a second generation member of the Frankfurt School, Habermas was influenced by, but also took issue with, Adorno. From 1961–4 Habermas taught philosophy in Heidelberg. In 1964 he was appointed Professor of Philosophy and Sociology at Frankfurt University. Subsequently he has been Professor of Philosophy and Director of the Max Planck Institute in Starberg. Throughout these years Habermas has dedicated his intellectual life to continuing, while revising, the Frankfurt School project of Enlightenment critique. This project has constituted his philosophical discourse of modernity.

Habermas's project departs from Adorno's mode of negative dialectics which had resisted any idea of rational consensus. Instead Habermas returns to Immanuel Kant in orientating thought towards a regulative notion of truth – as consensus – as the critical goal of inquiry. From the beginning of his critical theory he also incorporates aspects of both Hegel's critique of Kant and **Marx**'s critique of modernity.

In the 1960s Habermas develops a post-Kantian and Marxist-derived reconstruction of the genealogy of the natural and human sciences by enquiring back into their social, historical and epistemological conditions. In *Knowledge and Human Interests* he argues that despite positivist claims to the contrary, the modern sciences are not built upon value-free principles, but have been shot through with distinctive interests. These interests need to be acknowledged in order to restore just relations between theory and practice. According to Habermas, reason and rational consensus had been Enlightenment weapons against superstition, falsehood, evil and tyranny; but with the beginning of the bureaucratic organisation of industrial societies, science and rationality took on a purely instrumental form; and so reason lost its emancipatory role. Following the early Marx's emancipatory concerns Habermas sought to reverse this situation.

Habermas uses the early Marx to develop a strategy of critique which would be emancipatory. While Marx had stressed the formative role of practical labour, Habermas demonstrates the achievements of the German hermeneutic tradition, including the interpretative work of **Freud**, in opening the way for an emphasis upon symbolic forms of interaction. Habermas turns Marx's early work into a more effective critique of industrial society by emphasising the greater potential in its hermeneutic aspect. Following Marx, Habermas maintained that science, technology and instrumental rationality in modern capitalist societies had been turned *against* humankind. But another form of rationality could be used *for* humankind. The critical theory of the early Frankfurt School offered a means to turn the negative form of positivist knowledge into an emancipatory form of activity concerned with political and social reform. In its positivist form the instrumental use of reason is ideological in denying the hermeneutic component of knowledge. But this could be reversed; hermeneutically mediated knowledge and symbolic forms of interaction could subvert the positivism of scientific reason as ideology. Habermas's anti-positivism included the positivism of Marx's later writings.

After the 1970s Habermas published his monumental *Theory of Communicative Action*, Vol. I: *Reason and the Rationalization of Society*, and Vol. II: *Lifeworld and System: A critique of functionalist reason*. While retaining his commitment to truth, critique and rational consensus, Habermas reformulates the Enlightenment epistemological project. Instead of a subject-centred epistemology Habermas introduces a transcendental pragmatics which depends upon a regulative principle of the ideal-speech situation, i.e. the ideal of uncoerced debate in a public sphere. To make good the emancipatory claims of Enlightenment reason Habermas derives a theory of communicative action from speech-act philosophy, sociolinguistics and, in particular, from the Gricean idea of conversational implicature. The anti-positivism of the latter idea, originating in ordinary language philosophy, reinforces both his pragmatic concern with the rich context of meaning, of beliefs and goals, from which individuals speak, and his Kantian concern with universal rules. In addition, while the early Frankfurt School had not distinguished between system rationality and action rationality, Habermas insists that the Marxian concept of system should be replaced with a Husserlian notion of the lifeworld (of action), i.e. the world of lived experiences mediated by the symbolic discourse of social agents. Habermas saw the dangers in the inner colonisation of the lifeworld by the money and power of the economic system. Colonisation occurs when money and power, as imperatives of the system, take over the lifeworld of action and the structures of rationality, which were accessible communicatively, recasting them in instrumental and strategic forms. But the decisive issue is whether the success of communicative action is at the expense of the concrete other and the heterogeneity of the public realm of discourse.

Habermas has become one of the most influential yet controversial philosophers of social and political theory alive today. He is a central figure in debates concerning modernity and postmodernity; reason, truth and subjectivity; and meaning and meaninglessness. Postmodern philosophers have presented sustained criticisms of Habermas's philosophical discourse of modernity, while Habermas claims to expose the inadequacies of the radical critique of reason by postmodern theorists.

His translator Thomas McCarthy has made possible and kept alive much of Habermas's influence on Anglo-American intellectuals. McCarthy's positive view of Habermas's critical theory is especially relevant for debates about the postmodern. McCarthy defends the continuity and validity of Habermas's project, seeing the critical theory of Max Horkheimer as a crucial foundation which remains important for his theory of communicative action. McCarthy argues that one of the advantages of Habermas's critical theory, for our postmodern world, lies in making possible a critique of reason as transparently grounded in the nature of things, while his later intersubjective conception of rationality offers a critique of unreason. The great achievement of Habermas's project is in demonstrating that the obligations implicit in communicative action demand – universally – inclusion of and openness to the other.

However, other contemporary philosophers are not so positive. Although calling Habermas's project remarkable, J. M. Bernstein argues that Habermas failed to overcome meaninglessness and ethical dislocation. Bernstein adds that this failure signals a need for social and political theorists to return to Adorno's earlier Frankfurt School critique of Enlightenment philosophy. Critical theory may be unique in engaging with both injustices and nihilism yet, Bernstein argues, Habermas's communicative rationality increases nihilism by relying upon abstract moral reason. Bernstein puts Habermas's fundamental idea of rational consensus – instead of Adorno's negative dialectics – into question: has Habermas missed an opportunity, with his reliance on the abstract reason of morality, to use the resources of a concrete ethical life in need of transfiguration?

A parallel question emerges in the context of feminist debates about rationality and the postmodern. Two feminist political philosophers influenced by Habermas's critical theory, Seyla Benhabib and Iris Marion **Young**, take opposing sides, for and against his modern project. While Young takes issue with Habermas's failure to address a heterogeneous public and the concrete Other, Benhabib takes direction from Habermas, remaining circumspect about claims concerning the end of Enlightenment philosophy. From such debates we can conclude that in an age of postmodern irrationality, Habermas's project remains one to be reckoned with.

Main works

Knowledge and Human Interests, trans. Jeremy J. Shapiro, Boston, MA: Beacon, 1971; London: Heinemann, 1992.

Legitimation Crisis, trans. Thomas McCarthy, Boston, MA: Beacon, 1975.

Communication and the Evolution of Society, trans. Thomas McCarthy, London: Heinemann, 1979.

Justification and Application: Remarks on discourse ethics, trans. Ciaran P. Cronin, Cambridge: Polity, 1983.

The Theory of Communicative Action, Vol. I: *Reason and the Rationalization of Society*, trans. Thomas McCarthy, Boston, MA: Beacon; London: Heinemann, 1984.

'Philosophy as stand-in and interpreter', in Kenneth Baynes, James Bohman and Thomas McCarthy (eds), *After Philosophy: End or transformation*, Cambridge, MA: MIT Press, 1987.

The Theory of Communicative Action, Vol. II: *Lifeworld and System: A critique of functionalist reason*, trans. Thomas McCarthy, Boston, MA: Beacon; Cambridge: Polity, 1987.

The Philosophical Discourse of Modernity, trans. Frederick Lawrence, Cambridge: Polity, 1992.

Further reading

Benhabib, Seyla, *Critique, Norm and Utopia: A study of the foundations of critical theory*, New York: Columbia University Press, 1986.

Bernstein, J. M. *Recovering Ethical Life: Jürgen Habermas and the future of critical theory*, London: Routledge, 1995.

Hoy, David Couzens and Thomas McCarthy, *Critical Theory*, Oxford: Basil Blackwell, 1994.

McCarthy, Thomas, *Critical Theory of Jürgen Habermas*, Cambridge, MA: MIT Press, 1978; Cambridge: Polity, 1984.

Meehan, Johanna (ed.), *Feminists Read Habermas: Gendering the subject of discourse*, London: Routledge, 1995.

Rasmussen, David M., *Reading Habermas*, Oxford: Basil Blackwell, 1990.

Glossary

Communicative action   A form of interaction where the success of the interaction depends on the hearer responding with a 'yes' or 'no' to the validity claim raised with a given utterance.

Conversational implicature   The concept, developed by Paul Grice and taken up by other twentieth-century philosophers of language, is used for what the speaker implies as opposed to what her words in a sentence might logically imply. Here what is implied by the rich context of speaker meaning cannot be ignored by or replaced with abstract rules of logical implication.

Hart, H. L. A. (1907–1992)

Hart spent most of his life in the context of Oxford University, apart from the years in MI5 during the Second World War. He was Professor of Jurisprudence in Oxford from 1952, resigned in 1968, and was then research fellow at University College, and Principal of Brasenose College 1973–8. He remained active in supporting the Labour Party, as well as in disputes over law and punishment, and serving on the monopolies commission.

Hart's importance for sociolegal studies was in his consistent and thoughtful engagement with philosophical questions within jurisprudence. His distinctive approach lay in his skilled combination of modern analytical philosophy with the classic debates in British legal theory on the need for law, the potential for rational models of laws and punishment and the ideal of individual freedom. He is usually classified with the legal positivists who distinguished themselves from other schools by holding that law is essentially a social phenomenon but one whose relationship to society needs careful exploration.

Hart's first major work, *The Concept of Law*, contained both his areas of interest, namely analytical linguistic philosophy and what he termed 'descriptive sociology' of law. He defined law essentially as a set of rules of limited scope independent of, and analytically distinguishable from, society's wider range of moral rules and obligations. With moral standards viewed as a separate sphere outside law, the legitimacy of the law can be rendered questionable, for there should be no assumption that it embodies (or ought to embody) an everyday morality. Laws (particularly repressive statutes) require both analysis and social justification, possessing no inherent quality which makes them right. Hart distinguished *positive* from *critical* morality, that is the real mores practised in society, contrasted with the general moral principles we use to evaluate that consensus, and justify why certain of its moral rules should be embodied in law. Critical morality, following Bentham, sees repression and painful punishment as necessary evils, so reasons for the criminalisation of behaviour have to be very good.

The idea that law requires legitimation, that is, justification, is central to Hart's perspective, because law needs rules to govern its processes of recognition, adjudication and change. These principles, which Hart called *secondary* rules, have provided practising lawyers and theorists with great problems, but highlighted the fact that each legal system has its own way of evolutionary innovation, including both external processes such as parliamentary statute and internal decisions in individual legal actions. In the English tradition it is often held that common law changes as much by internal debate and precedent (judge-made law) as by parliamentary statutes. For Hart both are part of law's secondary rules. Inside the law are embodied specific values, *primary* rules, possessing far greater obligatory character than the secondary, for they limit the freedom of ordinary life.

It was Hart's concern to set limits to this legal constriction on freedom that led him to debate famously with Lord Patrick Devlin. In *Law, Liberty and Morality* (1963), which introduced Hart to an audience outside the law schools, his purpose was to challenge the self-adopted role of the courts as guardians of morality, and undermine what he called *legal moralism*, that is, the intrusive use of law to enforce standards of private (particularly sexual) morality. His chosen means was to reintroduce the debate between J. S. Mill and the utilitarians concerning the idea of a 'measure of morality'. Utilitarianism had proposed a strict measure of damage by which actions would only be criminalised if they harm individuals: outrage or moral indignation do not provide sufficient justification for suppression. Activities which cause shock but no damage to people are therefore no business of the law. Mill, by contrast, could see some benefit in the law's attempt to reflect current moral values in society, particularly where people needed to be protected from themselves. In renewing this debate Hart did battle with judges such as Devlin who, sensitive to changing morality and anxious about the declining respect with which traditional laws were being regarded, wished to preserve a moral role for law and the courts in a rapidly changing society. Writing in the aftermath of the Wolfenden Report (1957) on sexual laws, but before the reforms were introduced, Devlin proposed that laws must embody a consensus (if it exists) condemning a practice, but, equally importantly, legislation and the courts should have a role in proclaiming new standards of behaviour. So laws can both reflect *and* change society, literally for the good (*The Enforcement of Morals*, Oxford: Oxford University Press, 1965). The Wolfenden Report had defined an area of private morality into which the law should not intrude, thus allowing minorities to be different. Although Hart saw Devlin as a moderate moralist, when compared with his extremist Victorian predecessors such as James Fitzjames Stephens, both hold the social fact of a shared morality as proof that an arena of private morality is an impossibility: all actions are subject to moral and legal evaluation. For Hart this is a dangerous argument: laws require more than moral justification if they are to inflict loss of freedom and miseries of punishment on people. Otherwise, by using democratic procedures a majority may tyrannise minorities with their moral disgust: worse, this may enshrine dominant values in law long after they have been abandoned by people in society. The legal moralist argument is based on the unproven thesis (like that in **Durkheim**'s sociology) that societies need common values in order to survive. Despite deep-felt misgivings Hart suspected, like Mill, that law should contain some shared moral values, but always held this should be a minimum: legal moralists, by contrast, were always attempting to maximise this quota.

Hart's later work, *Punishment and Responsibility*, shows the same scepticism and analytical search for justification of legal penalties. 'General interest in the topic of punishment has never been greater than it is at present and I doubt if the public discussion of it has ever been more confused', he wrote in 1968, though it could equally be said today. Hart trod a path between the utilitarians who demanded a careful scale of deterrent penalties to protect society, and the retributivists who demanded punishments proportionate to the seriousness of the criminal's guilt. In some ways he was among the most convincing of the compromise theorists, conceding that there might have to be different justifications for different punishments. He followed both the utilitarians in demanding careful rational assessment of punishment's consequences, and the retributivists who emphasise that serious offenders must be punished. But his key criticism of the first was that they neglect the problems of establishing the guilt of the punished, so eager are they to see beneficial social effects in punishment. As for retribution, he wrote, in *Punishments and Responsibilities* (1968) that the death penalty, the most extreme form of judicial vengeance, was no longer in the 'true interests of a civilized society'. Yet he conceded that it was impossible to measure the full social impact of any punishment, as Bentham had thought. In effect, Hart's compromises between utility and 'just deserts' ironically drew close to Patrick Devlin's ideas (*The Judge*, 1979), for in the end he concedes that a single justifying principle for punishment is impossible.

In his later work he participated in the revival of interest in classical eighteenth-century penology, editing Bentham's legal texts. At the same time, his basic concepts and philosophy were kept alive through the works of his critics, notable among whom were Ronald Dworkin, Lon Fuller and Joseph Raz.

Hart's importance is that he consistently maintained a critical distance from careless and vengeful moralism which still characterises the politics of punishment today. A dose of minimalist, rational assessment of both the scope of the law and the severity of punishment is precisely what might refresh current debates. Hart's was among the most trenchant defences of civil liberties within legal philosophy. By demanding justification while retaining sceptical attitudes to all easy moralising, he made law and its decisions a matter of everyday relevance and social debate.

Main works

Causation in the Law (with A. M. Honoré), Oxford: Clarendon, 1959.

The Concept of Law, Oxford: Clarendon, 1961.

Law, Liberty and Morality, London: Oxford University Press, 1963.

The Morality of the Criminal Law, Jerusalem: Magnes, 1965.

Punishment and Responsibility: Essays in the philosophy of law, Oxford: Clarendon, 1968.

Jeremy Bentham: Introduction to the principles of morals and legislation, London: Athlone, 1970.

Essays on Bentham: Studies on jurisprudence and political theory, Oxford: Oxford University Press, 1982.

Essays in Jurisprudence and Philosophy, Oxford: Clarendon, 1983.

Jeremy Bentham, A Fragment on Government, Cambridge: Cambridge University Press, 1988.

Further reading

Gavison, Ruth (ed.), *Issues in Contemporary Legal Philosophy: The influence of H. L. A. Hart*, Oxford: Clarendon, 1987.

Hacker, P. M. S. and J. Raz, *Law, Morality and Society: Essays in honour of H. L. A. Hart*, Oxford: Clarendon, 1977.

Harris, J. W., *Legal Philosophies*, London: Butterworths, 1980.

Leith, Philip and Peter Ingram (eds), *The Jurisprudence of Orthodoxy: Queen's University essays on H. L. A. Hart*, London: Routledge, 1988.

Mitchell, Barry, *Law, Morality and Religion in a Secular Society*, Oxford: Oxford University Press, 1970.

Hayek, Friedrich von (1899–1992)

Hayek gained two doctorates from the University of Vienna, and then from 1927–31 was the Director of the Austrian Institute for Economic Research. In 1931 he became a lecturer at the London School of Economics, where he delivered a series of lectures which was published as *Prices and Production*. This publication brought him to prominence in the discussion concerning the causes of the great depression. Later that same year he was appointed Tooke Professor of Economic Science and Statistics at the University of London. In 1950 Hayek joined the University of Chicago as Professor of Social and Moral Science, and in 1962 he accepted the position of Professor of Economic Policy at the University of Freiburg. He was awarded the Nobel Prize in 1974.

Throughout his long academic career Hayek applied his formidable intellect to a broad range of issues across a number of disciplines, although his most substantial and original contribution was to economics. His most influential and widely read work was, however, in the field of political philosophy, and *The Road to Serfdom* played a significant role in strengthening the intellectual credentials of the forces which would coalesce into the 'New Right' in the 1970s, as well as providing inspiration to democrats seeking to dismantle the communist regimes in Eastern Europe. He was to live to see the reunification of Germany, an event that marked the start of the collapse of the socialist experiment in Europe.

Hayek's first major work was his highly original account of the nature of the trade cycle, which appeared as *Prices and Production*. This was later revised as a long essay in *Profits, Interest and Investment* (1939). Hayek outlined what was later to become known as the 'Austrian trade cycle theory', and in *Profits, Interest and Investment* set out to dissolve the confusion between 'rate of interest' and 'rate of profit'. This was important because Hayek ascribed fluctuations in trade cycles to the natural action of the banking system. Hayek's business cycle theory is a mixture of the Austrian theories of capital, prices and money. In essence, if a monetary disturbance (for example, an increase in the money stock) causes a fall in interest rates below an equilibrium level, encouraging investment in capital and a diversion of production away from consumer goods towards capital goods, then the prices of capital goods rise and the prices of consumption goods fall. This modification in relative prices alters the structure of production. Because of the longer time element involved in producing capital, such an alteration leads to overinvestment in these methods of production. This causes a disruption in the co-ordination of plans between consumers and producers, and also between savers and investors, which Hayek felt in turn explained the cyclical alterations in the pace of economic growth. The policy conclusion advocated by Hayek, to 'do nothing', must, in part, answer the question as to why he lost out to **Keynes** in the debate over macro-economic theory. Hayek's conclusion proved to be politically unacceptable amidst the widespread suffering caused by the great depression.

Next, Hayek turned his attention to a subject which became a recurrent theme in his later work – the futlity of attempts to adapt or abolish the price mechanism. He developed the theme in a pithy essay, 'Economics and Knowledge' (1937). Here he argued that the price mechanism is so sophisticated an antenna of people's needs, with such an innately superior ability to handle information, that it reduces the task of governments with regard to the economy.

During the Second World War, Hayek developed the ideas which would appear in his most influential and widely read publication, *The Road to Serfdom* (1944). This classic critique of the dangers of 'creeping socialism' was written at a time when the United Kingdom, for the purposes of the war effort, was virtually a planned economy, and when Keynesian ideas were gaining an ascendancy within both academic and government economic circles. It cannot be said, therefore, that Hayek was advancing a viewpoint that was in step with majority intellectual opinion of the day. By the time that he lecture-toured the United States in the late 1940s, however, the ideas of *The Road to Serfdom* were absolutely in step with the deepening mood of anti-communism arising from the west's fear of the Soviet Union.

The main thesis put forward in *The Road to Serfdom* is that there is little to distinguish the essential characteristics of fascism or communism, since both creeds are collectivist and anti-individualist in character. More controversially, Hayek cast doubt on whether social democracy and extreme collectivism differed significantly from each other, and suggested that even moderate planning, such as Keynesian demand management or a welfare state, could produce outcomes which were not foreseen by the planners. A 'road to serfdom' could be embarked upon, because intervention in the evolution of the economy could initiate developments that would stifle spontaneity. Creeping totalitarianism was a likely outcome of economic intervention. Hayek knew that the case he argued in *The Road to Serfdom* would never find a hearing amongst the intelligentsia to whom it was really addressed, so he took his case to the people. *The Road to Serfdom* is his most accessible publication, and in 1945 it made the best-sellers' list in the United Kingdom: a remarkable achievement for a book of political philosophy. It was even more successful in the United States, provoking an enormous amount of media and popular interest. In fact it was possibly this very success which led to a decline in Hayek's credibility amongst his peers in the world of economics, given that some of them believed he was a scholar turned propagandist.

Hayek's major publication whilst in the United States was *The Constitution of Liberty* (1960), where he developed his ideas on liberty and justice. What is unique about Hayek's approach to the concept of liberty is his insistence on the priority of freedom over other ideals, and his intellectual unease at the appeal of other values – especially equality and social equity. Freedom was at the very centre of his social thought, and informed his perspective on the welfare state. For Hayek, welfare had done much to undermine people's personal responsibility, which in itself was essential for liberty. Furthermore, the 'welfare' extended to the needy was not genuine altruism, since it was carried forward in a framework of compulsion. We have no right, for example, not to pay the taxes which go towards welfare expenditure. The social responsibility which collectivists believe individuals ought to possess, has in the end been imposed by the state.

Receiving the Nobel Prize marked a revival in Hayek's fortunes. By the early 1970s, the fiscal burden of maintaining the welfare state was beginning to cause severe economic difficulties, and Hayek's warnings of the economic and social dangers of creeping socialism were looking increasingly credible. Many right-wing thinkers turned to Hayek's pure and logical defence of the free market in an attempt to find a new intellectual framework, as an alternative to the failed model which had arisen from the years of post-war 'consensus'. In the United Kingdom, a number of intellectuals on the right were influenced by Hayek's insights, notably the late Sir Keith Joseph, who was in turn a major influence on Margaret Thatcher.

Hayek offered a cogent defence of the free market as a foundation for a free society, insisting that the market will prevail, no matter how far underground it goes. Life in all its multitudinous forms is, in Hayek's view, far too complex for the human mind to regulate and control. Hayek attacked the constructivist ideal of controlling society by demonstrating the impossibility of ever achieving this goal without restricting human liberty, and therefore human development. He argued that the evolution of spontaneous systems such as the free market, was the only way to ensure that flexible adaptation to change occurs.

Hayek's ideas have undoubtedly been influential, and his status as one of the great thinkers of the twentieth century is unquestioned. Ultimately, every economy and society is forced to prioritise the key value which shapes it, and for Hayek the choice had to be liberty above all else. Many critics of this view have expressed the fear that this unlimited and unregulated society would display such vast inequalities of opportunity and wealth that 'freedom' would only be achieved by the 'winners', and that the fate of the majority of 'losers' would merely be the 'freedom' to remain poor, exploited and powerless.

Main works

Prices and Production, London: Routledge, 1931.

Monetary Theory and the Trade Cycle, London: Routledge, 1933.

'Economics and knowledge', *Economica*, 4 (1937), pp. 33–54.

Profits, Interest and Investment, London: Routledge, 1939.

The Pure Theory of Capital, London: Routledge, 1941.

The Road to Serfdom (1944), London: Routledge, 1952.

The Sensory Order, Chicago: University of Chicago Press, 1952.

The Constitution of Liberty, London: Routledge, 1960.

Further reading

Barry, Norman P., *Hayek's Social and Economic Philosophy,* London: Macmillan, 1979.

Kresge, Stephen and Leif Wenar (eds), *Hayek on Hayek: An autobiographical dialogue,* London: Routledge, 1994.

Bartley, W. W., *The Fatal Conceit: The errors of socialism,* London: Routledge, 1988.

Klein, Peter G., *The Fortunes of Liberalism,* London: Routledge, 1992.

Heidegger, Martin (1889–1976)

Martin Heidegger was born in the south-western German town of Messkirchen and educated in a Jesuit school. He studied at the University of Freiburg, theology at first, then philosophy, finishing his studies with a Ph.D. in 1913 and starting to lecture at the University of Freiburg in 1916. After having fought in the First World War, he was eventually made Professor of Philosophy at the University of Marburg, where he taught from 1923–8. In 1928 he accepted a call to a Professorship at the University of Freiburg, where he also became its 'Rektor' after the Nazis had come to power in 1933. Disillusioned by what he perceived to be happening, he resigned from this position early in 1934, but continued lecturing at Freiburg nevertheless. This came to an end in 1945, when the French occupation government prohibited his teaching, a prohibition which lasted until 1951. A year later, he became an emeritus professor and continued his writing and lecturing up until his death in 1976. His writings are so numerous that his works have still not been completely published, even in German.

Heidegger's early masterpiece, *Being and Time* (1927) attempted to continue and also shift the ground of the study of phenomenology, a new 'science' begun by Heidegger's teacher, Edmund Husserl. By disregarding all that was particular in perceptions or ideas, phenomenology tried to describe, and extrapolate from, the underlying, given forms in *all* perception and knowledge. In this massive text, Heidegger goes beyond the subjective tendency of Husserl's philosophy and pursues an ontological inquiry about human existence as such. In their fundamental condition of 'thrown-ness into the world', argues Heidegger, humans easily forget *Being* and what it actually signifies for them. He attempts to retrace a path to Being from the standpoint within the world and its temporality: beginning with finite 'being-there' (*Dasein*), which he also calls the 'ontical', and moving from that to Being as it is *understood*, the 'ontological'. However, he stresses that it is *Dasein*, its temporality and ultimate finitude, which will always determine life as we experience it. Only when *Dasein* is threatened, does Being make itself known and is able to be momentarily glimpsed. In short, we cannot encounter unadulterated Being and really 'know' the real world systematically or logically. (He reveals some of his Kantian roots here with the question of the form of our knowledge of the world as against its reality.)

While *Being and Time* was a formidable exercise in phenomenological thinking, it remained fragmentary and it appears that Heidegger already realised that his mode of enquiry would not yield the results he had envisaged. Accordingly, his philosophy changed exceptionally, an event he described as 'turn-about' (*Kehre*). If his earlier philosophy – especially his negation of the possibility of knowing the world or objects with any degree of certainty – had been eyed suspiciously by colleagues, things became even more problematic after the *Kehre*. Given that, as Heidegger had argued, the direct way to knowledge about Being was blocked, one had to attempt to fulfil the function of knowledge by circumventing this elusive term 'knowledge' altogether, using other means than the merely epistemological or logical. So, Heidegger's mode of inquiry moved on to the arts and to the philosophy of technology. These areas, where knowledge and singular truth were not in any case the ultimate goal, became for him the path by which humans might be able to come closer to Being. This solidly anti-systemic thinking brought him into close proximity with Nietzsche, the one philosopher to whom he devoted, over several decades, an enormous labour of reflection, which was published in a monumental two volumes in 1961.

Already in the 1930s, Heidegger had begun his study of art with the poetry of Hölderlin, alleging that art was at once allegory and a symbol of Being. He viewed all art as poetry (*Dichtung*). The 'unconcealing' of art brought it close to *aletheia*, truth itself. Art, as he described it, performs the work of revealing 'the Open of the world', creating a clearing (*Lichtung*) for Being to be glimpsed. If Cartesian quests for knowledge were in vain (in fact Heidegger traced this quest back to the very beginnings of philosophy as a science, in Aristotle), then it fell to the artist to provide a different device for charting the world into which humans are 'thrown'.

From there Heidegger's thinking moved on to language itself. If poetry, because it defamiliarised the world to the reader, was the pinnacle of language, then language itself must be capable of holding the key to Being. As in the case of Nietzsche, Heidegger's philosophy is inconceivable without his style, his creation of language. Mostly through inventive etymology, Heidegger moved away from rational discourse and allowed language to speak for itself. The fragmentary and illogical character of language hinted at the impossibility of coming to rational terms with reality. In his later seminal essay, *Identity and Difference* (1957), Heidegger returns to pre-Socratic philosophy and, following Parmenides, denies the possibility of the sameness with self that is implied in the copula, 'is', in a statement such as 'A is A'. He demands that the relationship contained in 'is' should be viewed as more than mere equivalence. He thereby launched an attack on all 'tautological' systems: that is, those, such as mathematics, the sciences and technology, based on logical identity between a thing and itself. In preference to the presuppositions of technology, Heidegger introduced the notion of release/patience/calmness (*Gelassenheit*), that which would help humans to recognise and deal with their 'thrown-ness' into the world.

This essay, together with Heidegger's 'letter on Humanism', would eventually become the launching pad for post-structuralism: Jacques Derrida took from it his cue for his conceptions of 'differance' and deconstruction (another idea on loan from Heidegger, although the latter had stopped at 'destruction').

Heidegger cannot be thought of without discussing his dealings with the National Socialists in Germany. For many years after the Second World War, he was viewed as a philosopher *non grata* in Germany and abroad. And, indeed, in an interview given to the German *Spiegel* magazine in 1967 (though only printed after his death), he strenuously refused to recant his, albeit short-lived, support for the Nazis in 1933 and 1934. As with Nietzsche, who had suffered a similar political and social ostracism, it would take (French) post-structuralism to rehabilitate him as an original and highly innovative thinker.

Heidegger personifies one of the two important and longest-lasting strands of German philosophy in the twentieth century (the other being the neo-Marxist negative dialectics of **Adorno** and the Frankfurt School): the pursuit of a 'fundamental ontology'. While much of Heidegger's thinking remained idiosyncratically (and dangerously) mired in a certain post-metaphysical neo-Romanticism, his insights spurred philosophy on to look for new ways, styles and methods to describe (and thereby change) the world that humans inhabit.

The social in general, since he viewed it as a symptom rather a moving cause, was never central to Heidegger's thinking. Yet, his phenomenological route to undermine the solidity of the social has had a profound

impact on late twentieth-century social theory. If human life is fundamentally foredoomed to the pursuit of an unattainable fixity in knowledge
and system, then the social world has no substance, and no fundamental
social laws can be discovered for it (after the manner of **Durkheim**). The
late-twentieth-century interest in the social *construction* of our consciousness of time (**Elias**), in 'postmodern' conditions of unfixed identity, or in
the sociology of risk and uncertainty (**Giddens**), can be ascribed in part to
the rejection by German philosophy, in the form of Heidegger's thought,
of earlier certainties about the social world.

Main works

Being and Time (1927), trans. J. Macquarrie and E. Robinson, London: SCM,
1962.

What is Called Thinking? (1954), trans. J. Glenn Gray, New York: Harper
and Row, 1968.

Essays in Metaphysics: Identity and difference (1957), trans. J. Stambaugh, New
York: Harper and Row, 1969.

On the Way to Language (1959), trans. P. D. Herz, New York: Harper and
Row, 1971.

Nietzsche (1961), trans. J. Stambaugh, London: Routledge, 1981.

The Question concerning Technology and Other Essays (1962), trans. W. Lovitt,
New York: Harper and Row, 1977.

On Time and Being (1969), trans. J. Stambaugh, New York: Harper and Row,
1972.

Poetry, Language, Thought, trans. A. Hofstadter, New York: Harper and Row,
1971.

Basic Writings, ed. David Farell Krell, London: Routledge, 1993.

Further reading

Derrida, Jacques. *Of Spirit: Heidegger and the question*, Chicago: University
of Chicago Press, 1989.

Franzen, Winfried, *Martin Heidegger*, Stuttgart: Sammlung Metzler, 1976.

Lacoue-Labarthe, Philippe, *Heidegger, Art and Politics*, Oxford: Basil Blackwell, 1990.

Lyotard, Jean-François, *Heidegger and 'the jews'*, trans. Andreas Michel and
Mark Roberts, Minneapolis: University of Minnesota Press, 1990.

Sheehan, Thomas. *Heidegger – The Man and Thinker*, Chicago: Precedent, 1981.

Wolin, Richard (ed.), *The Heidegger Controversy: A critical reader*, Cambridge, MA: MIT Press, 1991.

Glossary

Being-there   A literal translation of the German expression Dasein, being-there refers to the normal *general* attributes of personhood: physical and temporal location, vulnerability to mood and states of mind, personal characteristics, awareness of being susceptible to the world, identity, etc.

Ontical/ontological   'Ontology' is the philosophy of the general character of that which does, or might, exist in the real world. The 'ontical' features of a being are therefore a substratum by virtue of which the being in question is actually able to exist in the real world, amongst the beings that are adumbrated in an ontology.

Thrown-ness   The necessity of existing *within* certain categories, such as time, space, intelligibility of meaning and discourse, which obscure the underlying nature of Being.

Hobson, John Atkinson (1858–1940)

As a radical economist, journalist and social theorist Hobson sustained a prolific output of books, pamphlets and articles over half a century. The range of his political and intellectual interests makes him difficult to categorise although he is best known for his economic theories of under-consumption and imperialism and his contribution to the reformulation of liberal ideology. In 1897 Hobson's embryonic academic career was effectively ended by the critical response of professional economists to his challenges to established economic theory. Subsequently devoting himself to journalism and writing he became a leading theorist of new liberalism. Hobson's life-long work for progressive causes was augmented by direct participation in a variety of British reform movements involving both national and international affairs. In politics an advanced Liberal he left the party in 1916. After standing unsuccessfully as an independent parliamentary candidate in 1918 he became closely associated with the Independent Labour Party and joined the Labour Party in 1924.

In his autobiographical *Confessions of an Economic Heretic* (1938) Hobson identified a humanist interpretation of economics and a revolt against *laissez-faire* as the core of his heresy. In the development of his economic and social philosophy he was profoundly influenced by Ruskin's qualitative conception of wealth ('there is no wealth but life'), by the Darwinist revolution which informed his distinctive organic conception of society and by his perspective as a social reformer primarily concerned with the 'condition of England' question. The most creative period of Hobson's life came with his move to London in 1887 and his association with a brilliant group of like-minded writers and politicians including L. T. Hobhouse and Ramsay MacDonald. Two organisations were of particular importance to Hobson's development: the South Place Ethical Society, which represented the radical wing of a movement dedicated to the propagation of a rationalist, humanist ethic: and the Rainbow Circle, a political discussion group which he helped found in 1893. In responding to the crisis of late nineteenth-century liberalism the group was committed to the creation of a progressive political ideology allied to a radical and comprehensive programme of social reform. The key to this new liberal philosophy was to be found in its rejection of the anti-statism of orthodox liberalism in favour of the positive and enabling role of a reformed and enlarged state, a position powerfully endorsed in Hobson's *The Crisis of Liberalism* (1909).

The fusion of the theoretical and the empirical which characterised Hobson's writing was already in evidence in his first book, *The Physiology of Industry* (1889). In large part the creation of its co-author, the businessman A. F. Mummery, it expounded the theory of under-consumption which provided a recurrent theme of Hobson's work and formed the basis of his reputation as a pioneer of economic thought. Identifying thrift (oversaving) as a primary cause of economic depressions it rejected the doctrine that supply creates its own demand (Say's Law of Markets) thus challenging the belief that capitalism was a self-equilibriating system. Hobson continued to challenge economic orthodoxy, with respect to both doctrine and method, in a wide range of studies which addressed contemporary social and economic problems.

Hobson's most famous work, *Imperialism: A study* (1902), was a tract for the times which became a classic of modern political literature. Drawing on his experience as a correspondent in South Africa on the eve of the Boer War he identified imperialism as the external manifestation of a malfunctioning capitalist system. Applying his theory of underconsumption he saw finance (surplus capital) as the governor of the imperial engine. In Hobson's view investors from Britain's plutocracy conspired to manipulate patriotic forces and shape external policy in their own interests. Drawing on the liberal Cobdenite tradition he argued that imperialism not only stimulated militarism and international conflict but also threatened domestic political liberties. His remedy for the ills attendant upon imperialism was a reform of the capitalist system through a more democratic distribution of wealth and power. In its exploration of the social, political, cultural and economic dimensions of the imperial process

Imperialism was a remarkable work of synthesis. It provides the best example of Hobson's insistence on seeing problems as a unified whole and of his willingness to cross conventional disciplinary boundaries in order to analyse them.

In the field of international relations, to which he was increasingly drawn and on which he wrote extensively, Hobson was essentially an idealist. Appreciative of the interrelationship of national and international politics he drew on his new liberal ideology in a search for solutions to the destructive competitiveness which characterised contemporary inter-state relations. His political actions reflected the reforms which he saw as essential for the attainment of his ideal of a pacific internationalism. He was a leading member of the International Arbitration League, a founder member and subsequently chairman of the Union of Democratic Control (of foreign policy) and a campaigner for the establishment of the League of Nations whose mandate system he had foreshadowed in his analysis of imperialism. In both a national and an international context Hobson advocated the intervention of representative institutions to progress the interests of the organic whole and to counter what he saw as the anarchic tendencies inherent in the unfettered individualism of *laissez-faire*.

Traditional assessments of Hobson's influence have focused on his reputation as an economist and on his linked theories of underconsumption and imperialism in particular. As **Keynes** acknowledged in *The General Theory of Employment Interest and Money* (1936) the former marked an epoch in economic thought. It was instrumental in breaking the stranglehold of *laissez-faire* on economic theory thus paving the way for the Keynesian revolution. Hobson's theory of capitalist imperialism, adapted to Marxist purposes in **Lenin**'s *Imperialism, the Highest Stage of Capitalism* (1916), was to dominate interpretations of the new imperialism of the late nineteenth century until the revisionist challenges of the 1960s. In establishing the concept of economic imperialism Hobson's study provides the starting point of and has profoundly shaped, the twentieth-century discourse on the nature of modern imperialism. Subsequent analysis of Hobson's work has focused on his seminal contribution to social democratic thought and the progressive political tradition. He has been described as the most original of English social reformers and as one of the last great liberal intellectual system builders. In searching for solutions to the social and economic problems of industrial Britain Hobson rejected both the minimalist state of classical liberalism and the degree of centralisation associated with state socialism. Drawing on his belief in the organic nature of society he formulated as an alternative a liberal socialist synthesis which reconciled individualism and collectivism. The philosophical framework which he helped to construct provided the intellectual foundations of welfare politics in modern Britain and remains relevant to the continuing debate on the role of the state in a modern democracy.

Main works

The Physiology of Industry (with A. F. Mummery), London: Murray, 1889.

Problems of Poverty, London: Methuen, 1891.

The Evolution of Modern Capitalism, London: Walter Scott, 1894.

The Problem of the Unemployed, London: Methuen, 1896.

The Psychology of Jingoism, London: Grant Richards, 1901.

The Social Problem, London: Nisbet, 1901.

Imperialism: A study, London: Nisbet, 1902.

The Crisis of Liberalism, London: P. S. King, 1909.

The Industrial System, London: Longmans, 1909.

Work and Wealth, London: Macmillan, 1914.

Towards International Government, London: Macmillan, 1915.

The Science of Wealth: A human valuation, London: Macmillan, 1922.

The Economics of Unemployment, London: Macmillan, 1922.

Wealth and Life, London: Macmillan, 1929.

Rationalism and Humanism, London: Watts, 1933.

Confessions of an Economic Heretic, London: Allen and Unwin, 1938.

Further reading

Allett, John, *New Liberalism: The political economy of J. A. Hobson*, Toronto: University of Toronto Press, 1981.

Brailsford, Henry Noel, *The Life-Work of J. A. Hobson*, Oxford: Oxford University Press, 1948.

Clarke, Peter, *Liberals and Social Democrats*, Cambridge: Cambridge University Press, 1978.

Freeden, Michael, *The New Liberalism: An ideology of social reform*, Oxford: Clarendon, 1978.

Freeden, Michael, *J. A. Hobson: A reader*, London: Unwin Hyman, 1988.

Townshend, Jules, *J. A. Hobson*, Manchester: Manchester University Press, 1990.

I

Illich, Ivan (1926–)

As an undergraduate at the Gregorian University in Rome Illich studied theology and philosophy. He obtained a doctorate in history from the University of Salzburg. In 1951, he went to the United States and served as an assistant pastor in an Irish/Puerto Rican parish in New York City. From 1956–60 he was vice-rector of the Catholic University of Puerto Rico. Illich was a co-founder of the Center for Intercultural Documentation (CIDOC) in Cuernavaca, Mexico, where he directed research seminars which explored the effects of industrialised society, particularly on Latin America, until 1976.

Illich's writings have concerned a wide variety of matters. Although he is probably most widely known for his vehement critique of schooling and the medical profession, he has also written on topics such as gender, social ecology, social justice, personal freedom and consumerism. However, underpinning all of his writings is a concern to chart the damaging consequences of industrialisation and to offer solutions to the problems he identifies. In this sense, his work runs parallel to, and occasionally connects with, the work of radical or Marxist theorists and social scientists. We can illustrate Illich's broad concerns by examining his critique of schooling and medicine.

Illich's critique of schooling has had a significant impact upon educationists and sociologists of education. Put bluntly, Illich argues that schools are repressive institutions which operate with a hidden curriculum. Because pupils have no control over what they learn, nor any say in the ways in which they are taught, schools are able to indoctrinate young people into conformity, and to ensure that individual creativity and judgement are repressed. Success in education is a matter of demonstrating the capacity for conformity and acceptance. These characteristics are rewarded with academic qualifications. Qualifications therefore index a passive and unthinking individual. However, these are precisely the kinds of personality traits required by modern industrialised society. Consequently, a person who has gained success in education is a good risk for the established order. Conformity breeds success at school and in adult life.

It is here that Illich's damning analysis of schooling merges with his sustained critique of industrialisation and consumerism. He claims that schooling does not merely perform a disservice to pupils, but that it is fertile soil for, and an integral part of, a wider social malaise.

Through indoctrination by the hidden curriculum, schools are able to produce citizens who are accepting and easily manipulated. These citizens are passive consumers, inculcated at school with the expectation that they should consume the varied outpourings of modern society and its 'experts'. They are led to believe that they require the services of professionals, trained to accept the authority of 'those who know', and encouraged to become dependent on the directives of those in authority.

Schooling, then, produces a society of individuals whose initiative and judgement have atrophied, and who have become increasingly dependent upon the goods and services provided by industrialised society. This malaise is compounded by the fact that a common individual response to personal problems which stem from the organisation of industrialised society is to consume more of its products: to purchase more goods and commodities, to consult therapists, social workers and doctors, and to obtain more educational qualifications. However, Illich argues that a reliance on precisely these kinds of services is at the root of contemporary social problems. Moreover, dependence upon the services of modern society ensures that individuals are increasingly less likely to seek support from the help and compassion of their fellow citizens.

Illich's solution is quite simple: 'deschool' society and establish radical new ways of learning and education which facilitate and cultivate people's own skills, judgments and initiative. As an alternative to traditional schooling Illich makes two proposals. First, he calls for 'skill exchanges' in which people would teach other talents they use in their everyday life, such as foreign languages, manual crafts, computing and word processing. Second, he calls for the establishment of learning webs in which people could collaborate with others with similar interests in tackling a common problem or pursuing a shared goal. Skill exchanges and learning webs would constitute 'a new style of educational relationship between man [sic] and his environment' (*Deschooling Society*) in which personal development and real learning could flourish.

Given that he is arguing for the abolition of the school, it is not surprising that Illich's suggestions have met with strong opposition from professional educationists. And even those who are sympathetic to his critique of schooling may be perplexed that he provides no detailed account of how to deal with the practical difficulties of implementing an entirely new system of education. However, Illich has also been criticised for missing the point. For example, Bowles and Gintis (*Schooling*) claim that the system of schooling is not a causal agent in the emergence of societal problems:

the organisation of schooling in contemporary society has evolved to meet the demands of the underlying capitalist economy mode of production.

Illich has not only upset the teachers and educationists, but he has also upset doctors. His critique of the medical profession is, if anything, even more contentious than his demolition of contemporary schooling. Illich dismisses claims that advances in medical science have led to a decline of life-threatening illness, and increased the quality of life for the average citizen. He does not deny that there have been improvements in the health of the population; but he attributes these to the availability of better quality food, greater awareness of the importance of hygiene, better working conditions, advances in housing and public sanitation systems and so on. Indeed, Illich argues that the main life-threatening diseases such as cholera and typhoid were in decline before the emergence of professional medicine.

Much of Illich's analysis of the organisation of contemporary medical care revolves around the concept of 'iatrogenesis', or medical problems created by doctors in particular, and the medical profession in general. He argues that medicine is damaging individuals and society on three levels. First there is clinical iatrogenesis. This consists of 'all clinical conditions for which remedies, physicians or hospitals are the pathogens, or "sickening agents"' (*Limits to Medicine*) – he cites, for example, inappropriate treatment, unnecessary surgery and addiction to prescribed drugs. Secondly, social iatrogenesis is a consequence of the power of the medical profession and its ability to create a need for medical intervention when common sense and ordinary compassion would suffice. In this sense the medical profession undermines human independence by depriving the social environment of 'those conditions which endow individuals, families and neighbourhoods with control over their own internal states' (*Limits to Medicine*).

Perhaps Illich's most controversial claim concerns his analysis of cultural iatrogensis (sometimes referred to as structural iatrogenesis). This is the way the relationship of the lay person to ill health and suffering has been changed through dependence on the medical profession. Initially, this seems to be a reprise of his argument about social iatrogenesis; the common focus on the way that medicine fosters a dependence on its outpourings certainly can lead to confusion, and at least one critic has remarked that the two forms of iatrogenesis are not clearly demarcated in Illich's writings (Horrobin, *Medical Hubris*). However, we can think of the difference in this way. Social iatrogenesis is the way that the medical profession undermines the organisational fabric through which the lay population would deal with ill health in its midst. So that, for example, no longer do we find that ill people are cared for by the family, except as an auxiliary to conventional medical treatment. However, cultural iatrogenesis refers more to the way that the bond between the medical profession and the individual consumer of medicine has altered the basic premise of the relationship between an individual and his or her body and its malfunctions. For Illich, pain and suffering are part of everyday reality; living with them is dignified and empowering. However, the medical profession is ostensibly dedicated to the eradication of pain and suffering. The responsibility for dealing with these integral episodes of human existence are removed from the individual, and devolved to doctors. The medical profession allows people to abnegate their responsibility to reality. In this sense, then, Illich is using the concept of cultural iatrogenesis to identify a corrosion of the entire mind-set of the population.

As on schooling, Illich's critique of the medical profession resonates with his primary concern: to expose the damaging consequences of industrialisation. He argues that many medical problems are a consequence of the organisation of contemporary society. So, for example, people get ill because of the tedious nature of their work, their poor working conditions, a lack of freedom, a dependence upon powerful institutions and, most significantly, a desire to acquire and consume material possessions and the services of professions such as medicine. By virtue of the fact that doctors treat the individual as a physical organism in need of repair, medicine generally ignores the social origin of many physical problems. Moreover, the fact that doctors are generally perceived as being able to offer cures or treatments fosters individual dependence upon the medical profession. Yet it is precisely this kind of deference to professional authority which Illich cites as a cause of medical problems. So, by turning to medicine, people merely reproduce one of the primary conditions which, in the first instance, actually give rise to ill health.

How are we to assess the impact of Illich's writings? Practically, he has had little effect on the organisation of western society: children still receive the same kinds of formal education in schools that they did prior to his critique of schooling, and the medicalisation of health and illness continues. His intellectual impact, however, has been considerable. Debates about educational reform in Europe during the 1970s were deeply indebted to Illich. Similarly, *Deschooling Society* is routinely discussed as a core text in undergraduate courses in the sociology of education. Furthermore, his analysis of schooling and the medical profession have provided radical alternatives to more conventional Marxist-inspired discussions of contemporary society.

It is tempting to see Illich's work as being a series of critiques of disparate segments of contemporary society. This is compounded by the fact that many of his critics only address those parts of his arguments which directly concern their own area of expertise. However, it is important to recognise that Illich's specific concern with, for example, medicine, schooling, the division of gender in society, and modern day transport systems are discrete contributions to his overarching goal of documenting the psychological, moral and social consequences of industrialised society. His radical critiques remain as classic statements of today's much more widely voiced scepticism, about industrialisation and the institutions of industrialised society.

Main works

Celebration of Awareness, London: Calder and Boyars, 1971.

Deschooling Society, London: Calder and Boyars, 1971.

Tools for Conviviality, London: Calder and Boyars, 1973.

Energy and Equity, London: Calder and Boyars, 1974.

Limits to Medicine: Medical nemesis – the expropriation of health, London: Marion Boyars, 1976 and London: Penguin, 1981.

Disabling Professions (with I. K. Zola, J. McKnight, J. Caplan and H. Shaiken), London: Marion Boyars, 1977.

The Right to Useful Unemployment, London: Marion Boyars, 1978.

Gender, London and New York: Marion Boyars, 1983.

Further reading

Bowles, S. and H. Gintis, *Schooling in Capitalist America*, London: Routledge and Kegan Paul, 1976.

Horrobin, D. F., *Medical Hubris: A reply to Ivan Illich*, Edinburgh, London and New York: Churchill Livingstone, 1978.

Jones, A. 'The violence of materialism in advanced industrial society: an eco-sociological approach', *Sociological Review*, 35 (1987), pp. 19–47.

Luke, T. W., 'Social ecology and critical political economy', *Social Science Journal*, 24 (1987), pp. 303–15.

Morrow, R. A. and C. A. Torres, 'The deschooling thesis: a reassessment of Illich's proposals two decades after', *New Education*, 12 (1990), pp. 3–16.

Navarro, V., 'The industrialization of fetishism or the fetishism of industrialization: a critique of Ivan Illich', *Social Science and Medicine*, 9 (1975), pp. 351–63.

J

Jung, Carl Gustav (1875–1961)

Carl Gustav Jung was born in Switzerland in 1875, the son of a pastor. He studied medicine at Basel and practised as a psychiatrist at institutions in Zurich between 1900 and 1909. Jung became widely known abroad after publishing a number of papers outlining a new interpretative psychology, which confirmed the findings of **Freud**. The two men met in 1907 and exchanged ideas for several years. They disagreed, however, about the importance of sexuality in the psychoanalytic process. This breakdown led to the formation of a Jungian school of analytical psychology.

Jung's subsequent career was distinguished by the conferral of numerous awards (honorary degrees from Harvard, Oxford, Geneva and elsewhere), and the publication of many influential papers and treatises. He sustained his intellectual curiosity through visits to Africa and the Pueblo Indians of New Mexico in the 1920s, and by collaborating with thinkers from many different fields. He remained intellectually active until his death in 1961.

Carl Jung recounts many dreams in his autobiography *Memories, Dreams, Reflections*. One of the most striking takes place on a dark, wintry night in Liverpool. A number of Swiss march through symmetrical streets until they come to the radial heart of the city. At the centre of the square is a round pool, and in the middle of the pool they see a small island, on which flourishes a magnolia tree. The beauty of the tree against the backdrop of the dirty metropolis furnished Jung with visionary materials for his own personal myth of the centrality of the self. 'Through this dream', he wrote, 'I understood that the self is the principle and archetype of orientation and meaning. Therein lies its healing function.'

Initially Jung was a staunch advocate of Freudian ideas, but in *Complete Works* he later diverged from his mentor with the publication of his book *The Theory of the Unconscious* in 1912. They differed markedly about the role of the sexual drive within human affairs. In a letter Freud had asked Jung, somewhat indiscreetly, to 'promise me never to abandon the sexual theory. That is the most essential thing of all. You see, we must make a dogma of it, an unshakeable bulwark.' Jung, upset by this seeming collapse of scientific judgement, asserted that Eros was only one factor influencing the economy of the self, and coined the term 'libido' to refer to the cohort of energies impelling human behaviour. He wanted to accommodate 'all those psychic contents which could find no room, no breathing space in the constricting atmosphere of Freudianism and its narrow outlook'. Jungian libertarianism therefore acts as a necessary corrective to Freudian dogma. Without devaluing the impact that sexual disturbance can have upon a person, Jung stresses that the individual continually moves toward wholeness and integration. In this light we might therefore say that analytical psychology is, paradoxically, synthetic. It does not dwell unduly upon the fragmenting mechanisms of repression, like Freud, but prioritises the religious and spiritual potentialities of the psyche.

Partly because of this 'open church' approach, Jungian psychoanalysis has moved in and out of fashion. It was out of favour in the 1950s, for instance, when harder-edged conceptions of therapeutic intervention were formulated. Jung's rhetorical flourishes about eastern philosophy, the occult and methods of divination did not square with the new emphasis placed upon the patient collection of data and scrupulous experimental verification. Time plays peculiar tricks, however, and it was precisely because of these more recondite aspects of Jung's work that, thanks to the counter-cultural rediscovery of myth and magic, his ideas were revived in the 1960s.

Jung was a figure of immense learning. He was a classical scholar, and collaborated with, amongst others, the sinologist Wilhelm, the indologist Zimmer and the mythologist Kereny. It is this syncretism which makes Jung relevant to so many different twentieth-century social and political concerns. His theory of types, for example, introduced the terms 'introvert' and 'extrovert' into the lexicon to distinguish between two different types of inward and outward personality. This twofold distinction maps rather neatly on to the old Renaissance theory of humours, with the melancholic and sanguine on one side of the spectrum, and the phlegmatic and choleric on the other. The same synthesising tendencies can be detected in Jung's attempts to connect the contemporary clinician with the medieval alchemist, in terms of their transformative functions.

The human imagination, according to Jung, is not imprisoned within any one individual, but is a reservoir of ideas and representations that are communally owned. From this springs his notion of the collective unconscious. The unconscious is not just that penumbra of things inaccessible to any one individual, but a network of memories and intuitions common to all people in all circumstances. Jung's anthropological excursions with African tribes and the Pueblo Indians convinced him that there are certain tendencies towards representing patterns of experience which cut across all cultures. He called these elemental images – of mothers, fathers, tricksters, wise old men – 'archetypes'. As Jung explains in *Memories, Dreams, Reflections*:

> An archetype is like an old watercourse along which the water of life has flowed for centuries, digging a deep channel for itself. The longer it has flowed in this channel the more likely it is that sooner or later the water will return to its old bed.

Water flows throughout Jung's writings. One of his earliest childhood memories was of a visit to Lake Constance with his mother, which convinced him that without water nobody could live at all. It is the most Chinese of elements, always changing yet always the same. Commenting on the dream of the magnolia tree, Jung pointed out the significance of its watery setting: 'Liverpool is the pool of life.'

Jung, like Freud, has had a profound influence on Anglo-American culture, both high and low. We should remember that the Beatles placed Jung on the cover of the *Sgt. Pepper* album, alongside their other heroes. There he is, peeking out between the shoulders of W. C. Fields and Edgar Allan Poe, justly poised between comedy and tragedy. It is as good an indication as any of the sway Jung has exerted upon all manner of artists. The novels of Herman Hesse, the paintings of Max Ernst and the music of Michael Tippett clearly testify to the impact Jungian ideas have had upon the creative temperament in the twentieth century.

Main works

The Collected Works of C. G. Jung, 20 vols, ed. Herbert Read, Michael Fordham and Gerhard Adler, trans. R. F. C. Hull, London: Routledge and Kegan Paul, 1953–78.

Memories, Dreams, Reflections, trans. Richard Winston and Clara Winston, London: Routledge and Kegan Paul, 1963.

Man and His Symbols, ed. Carl Jung, London: Aldus, 1964.

Further reading

Fordham, Frieda, *An Introduction to Jung's Psychology*, London: Penguin, 1953.

Hall, Calvin S. and Vernon J. Nordby, *A Primer of Jungian Psychology*, New York: Taplinger, 1973.

Hannah, Barbara, *Jung: His life and work*, London: Michael Joseph, 1976.

Homans, Peter, *Jung in Context: Modernity and the making of a psychology*, Chicago: Chicago University Press, 1979.

Jaffé, Aniel (ed.), *C. G. Jung: Word and image*, Princeton, NJ: Princeton University Press, 1979.

Serrano, M. C., *Jung and Herman Hesse*, London: Routledge and Kegan Paul, 1966.

K

Keynes, John Maynard (1883–1946)

J. M. Keynes was the son of J. N. Keynes, the eminent logician and essayist on the methodology of economics. He was educated in the classic late Victorian 'Mandarin' style: Eton followed by King's College, Cambridge, and then on to the India Office in 1906 at the age of twenty-three. As a young scholar at King's Keynes developed a variety of academic interests in mathematics, literature and, later, monetary theory. On his return to Cambridge, Keynes was given the editorship of the prestigious *Economic Journal*, a position he kept for thirty-three years. His colleagues at Cambridge and the India Office, and his obvious talent, assisted Keynes in joining the British Treasury in 1915 as an expert on monetary affairs. He became a key figure representing Britain at the Versailles Peace Conference in 1919, and in that year he published *The Economic Consequences of Peace* a thoroughgoing attack on, and condemnation of, the Versailles Treaty. This polemical tract brought him international recognition.

In the 1920s Keynes's interest focused increasingly on the theory and practice of macro-economics. His published output was prodigious in the 1930s, major works of the period including *A Treatise on Money* (1930), *Essays in Persuasion* (1931), *Essays in Biography* (1933) and the work for which he is most famous, *The General Theory of Employment, Interest and Money* (1936). In the latter Keynes basically rejected the classical idea of automatic adjustment in the economy and argued that public policy and government spending are required for the elimination of economic stagnation and mass unemployment. The watershed in Keynes's thinking between the *Treatise* and the *General Theory* was marked by two fundamental changes of position in monetary theory. First, in *General Theory* Keynes focused on real output as the crucial variable to be explained, rather than prices. Second, he propounded the truly original idea that it is variations in aggregate economic output rather than variations in the rate of interest that work to equate savings with investment in a market economy. Alongside these notions Keynes proposed an equally revolutionary idea, namely that it is investments and not savings that trigger changes in income. Whereas earlier theorists had always started with the public's propensity to save and then showed how investment adapts itself to saving via the rate of interest, Keynes argued that at any given point in time investment was autonomous. He then showed how savings will be generated through the multiplier to satisfy the level of investment.

Such theoretical innovations would not have been sufficient to create the famous 'Keynesian Revolution' without the crucial proposition that, in a capitalist economy, the equilibrium level of output which equates saving to investment is not necessarily the level of income which produces full employment. The proposition that a competitive market economy inherently gravitates to a steady state of full employment whenever it falls below full utilisation of the capital stock, pervaded all macro-economics theory and policy before Keynes. The profoundly new thinking in *General Theory* was Keynes's deliberate attack on the conventional faith in the inherent self-recuperative powers of the free market mechanism. For this Keynes faced stern criticism in theoretical terms from both British and continental economists. Leading the Cambridge critics at the time were A. C. Pigou and Sir Dennis Robertson, while on the continent Joseph **Schumpeter** and Frederick von Hayek denied the logical consistency of the entire Keynesian schema. Others argued that Keynes had failed to make a theoretical case, but agreed that he had made his point in practice. In any event, the 'Keynesian Revolution' marked an end to the conventional wisdom of *laissez-faire*.

The content of *General Theory* provided much material for theoretical controversy about what Keynes 'really' meant. Like the famous treatises of Ricardo, Marx, Walras and Marshall, *General Theory* is an ambiguous and tortuous text replete with digressions and difficult definitions.

For Keynes a 'classical' economist was any writer who defended Say's 'Law of Markets', the proposition that incremental increases in output automatically generated equivalent increases in expenditure and income so as to keep the capitalist economy at full employment. Since the dominant orthodoxy in mainstream economic thought had not abandoned Say's Law, any orthodox economist from Ricardo to Pigou was condemned as guilty of the sins ascribed to the classical economists. To attack such a broad target meant that Keynes stimulated a debate in macro-economic theory and policy which continues unabated today.

The high point of Keynesian influence on government macro-economic policy was reached in the late 1960s, when Richard Nixon could claim 'we're all Keynesians now'. In the 1970s, however, Keynes's grip on governmental attitudes started to wane. Thus in his Nobel Memorial Lecture in 1976, Milton Friedman stated that 'stagflation' had recently given way to 'slumpflation', the simultaneous occurrence of rising unemployment and rising rates of inflation. These phenomena were difficult for extreme Keynesian economists to explain. At the same time in the United States, R. E. Lucas, Jr, T. J. Sargent and N. Wallace started to use the idea first advanced by J. F. Muth (1961) regarding the rational expectations of all economic agents. Lucas and others argued that economic agents form their expectations on the basis of exactly the same data as policy-makers, and hence act to neutralise every systematic governmental attempt to intervene in the economy. This is the so-called 'new classical' view of the economy, and it is fundamentally anti-Keynesian in so far as the economy is viewed as a composition of rational maximising agents who use all 'available' data to optimise economic decisions. Hence all markets clear instantaneously and yield aggregate full employment equilibrium. The new classical school, which has been influential in policy circles in both the United Kingdom and the United States for some years, views the economy as basically stable and operating at near full employment, with the consequence that government intervention will be neutralised in the long run. This school received much attention recently, when R. E. Lucas, Jr received the Nobel Prize in Economics in 1995.

The debate triggered by the publication of *General Theory* in 1936 eventually created new schools of thought and factions in macro-economic theory, so that today a stylised picture of competing views would include extreme Keynesians, new Keynesians, eclectic Keynesians, monetarists and new classicals. Interestingly, in 1992 the British government decided to appoint a team of seven 'wise men' to advise the Chancellor on macro-economic policy, and this team represented all the competing schools outlined above.

Keynes's contribution to macro-economics theory was therefore monumental, because for the first time political parties and governments were forced to include unemployment, inflation and growth variables as paramount issues on economic policy agendas and election manifestos. Hence the political impact of Keynes's work has been as far-reaching as its impact on economic theory over the course of the last fifty years.

Main works

Collected Writings of John Maynard Keynes, 30 vols, ed. Sir A. Robinson and Donald Moggridge, London: Macmillan, 1971–89.

Key volumes include:

I   *Indian Currency and Finance* (1907).

II   *The Economic Consequences of Peace* (1919).

III *A Revision of the Treaty* (1921).

IV   *A Tract on Monetary Reform* (1928).

V   *A Treatise on Money: I, The pure theory of money* (1930).

VI   *A Treatise of Money: II, The applied theory of money* (1930).

VII   *The General Theory of Employment, Interest and Money* (1936).

VIII *A Treatise on Probability* (1922).

IX   *Essays in Persuasion* (1931).

X   *Essays in Biography* (1933).

XIII *The General Theory and After: Part II, defence and development* (1937).

XXIX *The General Theory and After: A supplement to vols. XIII and XIV*, ed. D. Moggridge.

Further reading

Leijonhufvud, A., *Information and Coordination*, New York: Oxford University Press, 1981.

Moggridge, D. E., *Maynard Keynes: An economist's biography*, London: Routledge, 1995.

Schumpeter, J. A., *Ten Great Economists: From Marx to Keynes*, London: Allen and Unwin, 1952.

Skidelsky, Robert, *John Maynard Keynes*, Vol. I: *Hopes Betrayed 1883–1920*, New York: Viking, 1985.

Skidelsky, Robert, 'Keynes's political legacy', in O. F. Hamouda and J. N. Smithin (eds), *Keynes and Public Policy after Fifty Years*, Vol. I: *Economics and Policy*, Aldershot: Edward Elgar, 1988.

Glossary

Eclectic Keynesians   A group who believe that active short-run government intervention is always necessary.

Extreme Keynesians   A group who believe that government intervention is always necessary to remove mass unemployment.

Macroeconomics   A top-down perspective of the economy, focusing on aggregate characteristics like inflation, unemployment and investment trends.

Market clearing   A situation which occurs when supply equals demand, so that excess supply and demand do not exist.

Monetarists   Economists who argue that an appropriate monetary policy is all the economy needs from government, so market forces will then solve all macroeconomic problems.

Multiplier The factor by which a change in a component of aggregate demand, like investment or government expenditure, is multiplied to lead to a greater change in equilibrium national output.

New Keynesians: A group who in the 1980s focused attention on unemployment, seeking explanations for the failure of wages and prices to adjust to make labour markets clear.

Klein, Melanie (1882–1960)

Melanie Klein was born Melanie Reizes in Vienna and died in London. After her marriage to Arthur Klein in 1913, Melanie lived in Budapest where she was analysed in 1914 by Sandor Ferenczi and later in Berlin, by Karl Abraham. During that time she studied the work of **Freud**. Subsequently she pioneered her own work on child analysis and became a highly influential psychoanalyst. Klein's psychoanalytic study of childhood affected profoundly her later analysis of adults. After her divorce in 1926 she moved to London, and in 1931 was naturalised as a British citizen. She became a member of the British Psychoanalytical Society and, although provoking controversy within and beyond the society, she had a formative impact upon the practice of psychoanalysis in Britain.

Freud's theory of unconscious drives became the ground for Klein's new theories. She posited and explored a pre-oedipal phase – arguably of femininity – for both sexes. Her work on early mental processes led to new understanding of psychosis and borderline states of mind in adults, having implications for psychological and social theory.

Klein used a descriptive phenomenology to elucidate the fluid and mobile experiences of non-verbal affect discovered in her experience of analysis. Instead of theorising about developmental stages, Klein described mental states or positions which appear in the experiences of the adult as well as the child. Klein's distinctive theory of mental processes made the life and death drives central to understanding the positions taken by the ego.

Klein's theorising of the ego's positions assumes that the infant splits its objects into good and bad categories under the pressure of the death drive operating within psychical reality. This splitting depends upon the further assumption that the infant fantasises. In fantasy the infant creates a good and bad breast, a good and bad mother. The mother and her breast are real, but are constructed as good and bad objects in a psychical reality. The psychical reality may or may not be reinforced by material reality.

Klein maintains that if the infant splits its object into good and bad categories, it is only because the infant's ego is also split into good and bad parts. On a most fundamental level, this splitting presupposes that the infant is aggressive.

The key positions in Klein's psychoanalytic theory are the depressive and paranoid–schizoid. The depressive position is the result of recognising that good and bad co-exist in the same object *and* in the same subject. The position denotes the transition of the infant from seeing the mother as a part-object to seeing her as a whole object. The infant becomes aware of the co-presence of feelings of love and hate directed at the same person and – implicitly – at its own self, experiencing depression at its own destructiveness. At the same time these feelings become the condition for reparation and creative action.

Klein's concept of the depressive position constitutes a significant advance on Freud: it alters the dating and dominance of Freud's Oedipus complex. Klein gives an earlier dating to the Oedipus complex, noting the emergence of both an early and a later superego. For her, the Oedipus complex, and so an early superego, begin with the end of breastfeeding. The depressive position then reflects the change from the early to the later superego. Klein and Freud do agree upon the significant impact of (the superego's) repression on the ego but, after Klein, the question seems to be *what* form of the superego dominates when. Klein's understanding of the depressive position opens up the possibility of working out women's early and later relationships with the mother. And this possibility for women challenges the dominance of Freud's Oedipus complex. Klein maintains that when the child recognises her feelings of hatred are directed against the loved mother, she feels guilt and loss, and so need for reparation; these feelings continue into her later life. Reparation can be creative work. Thus bringing good and bad together is the condition and the consequence of reparation.

The other position in Klein's psychoanalytic theory is the paranoid–schizoid. Similar to the depressive position, it is important for understanding the infant's earliest relationship to part-objects, e.g. the mother's breast. While fear of death leads to the fragmentation which splits the breast into good and bad categories, the death drive also leads to fear of retaliation. The paranoid aspect of this position results from the infant projecting its own aggression on to the object and hence the retaliation it fears mirrors its own desires. The schizoid aspect means that the paranoid projection involves a splitting both of the ego and the other. Because the badness the infant fears begins with its own self the splitting of the object presupposes and perpetuates a splitting of the ego. And the repression that this entails constitutes a denial of the ego's own aggression.

The ego can only recover its wholeness from this position of fragmentation by recognising that the projected badness lies within itself. Such recognition could again lead to depression, but this can culminate in reparation and so creativeness. Here Klein introduces an ethic related to the ego's realisation of wholeness. The paranoid–schizoid position is characterised by experiences of fear and fragmentation; but the mental processes of defence – i.e. splitting and projection – seek to organise the internal chaos of the primitive self. The best outcome is an ethical wholeness. But in assuming fundamentally aggressive and destructive sexual drives, Klein's account challenges popular ethics of woman as essentially caring and self-sacrificing.

Klein's followers formed one of three schools of British psychoanalysis, the other schools are the Anna Freudians and the Middle School. Klein and those who took up object relations theory altered British psychoanalysis, in theorising the relation between the mother and the infant during the first year of life. The Kleinian assumption is that from birth, the infant has formative relations with objects, i.e. entities separate from the self, either whole persons or parts of the body. Yet social and political theorists have not labelled Klein a feminist, since she did not engage with the social structures which oppress women. Nevertheless Klein's analyses of young children, especially those of the infant's phantasy about the mother's body, provide the groundwork for various feminist accounts of the mother–child relationship.

On the one hand, Klein seems to have had an indirect influence upon contemporary feminist work on object relations theory. Feminist object relations theorists focus on the formative relations of the mother and infant in the first year of life. They privilege the relations with the maternal object in the development of the self, finding an alternative to the Freudian focus on the father. At least some feminist object relations theorists build on Klein's study of childhood to interpret behaviour and social reality itself in terms of gender differences. On the other hand, Klein's studies of unconscious and non-verbal processes, especially the constitution of depressive and paranoid–schizoid positions, directly informed the Bulgarian psychoanalyst and semiotician Julia Kristeva. This is clearly evident in Kristeva's highly significant work *Black Sun: Depression and melancholy*.

Disagreement exists over Klein's influence. In Europe Klein has been considered, notably by Jean LaPlanche, to be the founder of object relations theory. However, in America prominent feminist Nancy Chodorow insists that Klein is an instinct theorist, influencing feminists such as Dorothy Dinnerstein, but definitely not a feminist object relations theorist. In her feminist account of mother–child relations Chodorow focuses on the social reality of gender relations, while virtually denying psychical reality. In contrast the significance of psychical reality is central to Klein. So an object relations theorist who followed Klein would criticise feminist object relations theorists who, like Chodorow, develop strictly social interpretations of the formation of gender. Such feminists fail to appreciate the crucial importance of the power of the unconscious, for psychoanalysis, which is preserved by Klein.

Main works

The Psychoanalysis of Children and Other Works (1931), London: Virago, 1989.

Narrative of A Child Analysis (1961), London: Virago, 1989.

Love, Guilt and Reparation, and Other Works 1921–1945, London: Virago, 1988.

Envy and Gratitude and Other Works 1946–1963, London: Virago, 1988.

Further reading

Brennan, Teresa, *The Interpretation of the Flesh: Freud and femininity*. London: Routledge, 1992.

Chodorow, Nancy, *The Reproduction of Mothering: Psychoanalysis and the sociology of gender*, Berkeley: University of California, 1978.

Dinnerstein, Dorothy, *The Rocking of the Cradle and the Ruling of the World*, London: Souvenir Press, 1978; published in the USA, *The Mermaid and the Minotaur: Sexual arrangements and human malaise*, New York: Harper Colophon, 1977.

Kristeva, Julia, *Black Sun: Depression and melancholy* (1987), trans. Leon Roudiez, New York: Columbia University Press, 1989.

LaPlanche, Jean and J.-B. Pontalis, *The Language of Psychoanalysis*, trans. D. Nicholson-Smith, London: Hogarth and the Institute of Psychoanalysis, 1983.

Glossary

Psychical reality   The result of a discovery by Freud not of a 'real event', not something *that is*, but of an event which has the effect of a real event, *as if* it occurred. For Klein this means that the fantasies an infant had but repressed (e.g. desire for the mother), and the reactions to those fantasies (e.g. guilt over the desire) can have the same effects on behaviour and feelings as if they had both been real events.

Kuhn, Thomas (1922–)

Thomas Kuhn is one of the leading figures of his generation in the history and philosophy of science, and the author of several highly influential books, most notably *The Structure of Scientific Revolutions*, a work whose impact has extended well beyond the boundaries of his subjects. In particular, the concept of 'paradigm' that Kuhn outlines in his writings of the 1950s and 1960s has passed into general cultural usage. By training, a physicist, Kuhn has since worked at various American institutions such as Harvard University, the University of California at Berkeley, Princeton University and the Massachusetts Institute of Technology.

Kuhn provides a very different picture of scientific history from the popular conception of it as the steady accumulation of knowledge towards an ever greater understanding of the world around us: a conception which has also been something of an orthodoxy in the teaching of the history of science for most of the twentieth century. For Kuhn, science should not be regarded as an inexorable progression towards ever more truthful theories about the nature of reality, but instead as a series of 'paradigms', where one theory or set of theories holds sway, punctuated by dramatic crises and revolutions where new theories sweep away the old to become new paradigms in their turn. It is a much more dramatic picture of the history of science than is generally found in textbooks, which, as Kuhn points out, tend to imply that 'scientists have striven for the particular objectives that are embodied in today's paradigms' (*The Structure of Scientific Revolutions*). Kuhn rejects such a teleological view of the scientific enterprise, and indeed this anti-teleological bias constitutes an important part of his popular appeal.

Kuhn's best-known book is *The Structure of Scientific Revolutions* (*SSR*), where the notion of paradigm is given its most sustained treatment. A paradigm is simply those 'universally recognized scientific achievements that for a time provide model problems and solutions to a community of practitioners', and in so doing constitute 'particular coherent traditions of scientific research' (*SSR*) which can guide each new generation of scientists. Kuhn's critics have complained about the imprecision of the term paradigm, and have claimed that it is used in a bewildering variety of ways in *The Structure of Scientific Revolutions*; the author's response (see 'Second thoughts on paradigms', in *The Essential Tension*) has been to refine the notion into two separate terms, 'disciplinary matrix' and 'exemplar' (the general and narrow sense of paradigm respectively), but the original term has tended to stick.

While a paradigm is unproblematically in operation, what Kuhn calls 'normal science' takes place. Normal science consists of the systematic clearing up of all those problems left in the wake of the paradigm, and as Kuhn points out, such 'mopping up' operations are what most scientific careers consist of. Science from this perspective is concerned primarily with 'puzzle-solving', that is, applying the theory in vogue to new phenomena. When the theory fails to explain such phenomena, adjustments are made to ensure that it does, but when this happens repeatedly and anomalies become, in effect, the normal state of affairs, then the theory's validity can come to be doubted. Eventually, some new explanation of the phenomena, generally incommensurable with the last, emerges and a new paradigm is proclaimed.

The process of paradigm-creation can be a tortuous one – the old paradigm almost inevitably rejects the claims of the new – and involves a characteristic pattern described by Kuhn as follows: 'the previous awareness of anomaly, the gradual and simultaneous emergence of both observational and conceptual recognition, and the consequent change of paradigm categories and procedures often accompanied by resistance' (*SSR*). The collision between the two competing paradigms projects scientific practice into a state of crisis, and it is often the case that defenders of the older paradigm never can be persuaded of the virtues of the new, given that this involves a radical conceptual shift, indeed a change in world-view, which most scientists are temperamentally unable to manage. In fact the new paradigm often only achieves total professional dominance when defenders of the old die out and a new generation can be trained in the new orthodoxy.

Revolution is taken to be a necessary part of scientific history, no less than it is of political history, and Kuhn emphasises the parallels between the two very strongly. In each case the objective is to correct anomalies that can no longer be hidden away. 'Political revolutions', Kuhn notes, 'aim to change political institutions in ways that those institutions themselves prohibit' (*SSR*), in much the same fashion that a new scientific paradigm finds itself prohibited from operating by the old; there is an incommensurability in world-view in each instance that cannot be resolved by any kind of compromise. No doubt the commitment to revolution contributed to the popular success enjoyed by *The Structure of Scientific Revolutions*, being much in keeping with the anti-establishment temper of the 1960s.

Kuhn provides various examples of paradigm change in *The Structure of Scientific Revolutions* (the shift from Newtonian to Einsteinian physics, for example), but an earlier work of his, *The Copernican Revolution*, is in many ways an even better illustration of his paradigm concept. *The Copernican Revolution* traces the shift from Ptolemaic to Copernican astronomy in Western culture, and is a textbook example of how paradigms come into collision; although Kuhn makes it clear that the process can be a long-winded one, in which advocates persevere with a dominant theory even in the face of a considerable body of evidence to the contrary. In the case of the Ptolemaic astronomical model, which placed the Earth at the centre of the universe, modifications in the form of epicycles were made to the circular motion of planets to account for their failure to appear when predicted. Eventually epicycles had to be added to epicycles, with the resultant model becoming ever more cumbersome over time. The Copernican model resolved many of the residual problems of the Ptolemaic one by means of a radical shift of perspective: the sun became the centre of the universe. This was essentially incompatible with the Ptolemaic world-view, and led ultimately to the establishment of a new astronomical paradigm.

Kuhn's ideas have come under attack from various quarters, most famously perhaps from Karl **Popper**, whose falsification principle implies a very different picture of scientific method than the notion of paradigm suggests. Falsification demands that theories be continually subject to testing and that they are only ever provisional in nature; that is, acceptable and usable only until such time as they are falsified. Kuhn and his followers tend to point out that this is rarely what happens in the history of science, and that defenders of a theory usually try to save it in the face of falsifying anomalies (as in the case of the Ptolemaic astronomical model). One could see this difference between the two thinkers as indicative of the clash between history of science and philosophy of science, with the Kuhnians basing their theories on empirical evidence, and the Popperians putting forth an ideal of how scientific practice ought to be conducted.

The debate between Kuhn and Popper, and their respective followers, became a staple element of philosophy of science courses throughout the 1970s and 1980s. There are few areas of western discourse that have not made use of the notion of paradigm at some point or other in the last few decades, and Kuhn's influence has extended deep into fields such as the social sciences and the arts. Paradigm now looks an increasingly dated notion, however, and Kuhn's influence has waned in recent years, especially given the much more chaotic picture of science and scientific method that has emerged from chaos theory and complexity theory.

Main works

The Copernican Revolution: Planetary astronomy in the development of western thought, Cambridge, MA and London: Harvard University Press, 1957.

The Structure of Scientific Revolutions (1962), Chicago: Chicago University Press, 1970.

The Essential Tension: Selected studies in scientific tradition and change, Chicago and London: Chicago University Press, 1977.

Black-Body Theory and the Quantum Discontinuity, 1894–1912, Oxford: Oxford University Press, 1978.

Further reading

Bloor, D., 'Two paradigms of scientific knowledge', *Science Studies,* 1 (1971), pp. 101–15.

Chalmers, A. F., *What is this Thing Called Science?*, rev. edn, Milton Keynes and Philadelphia: Open University Press, 1982.

Lakatos, Imre, *The Methodology of Scientific Research Programmes: Philosophical Papers,* Vol. ɪ, ed. John Worrall and Gregory Currie, Cambridge: Cambridge University Press, 1978.

Lakatos, Imre and Alan Musgrave (eds), *Criticism and the Growth of Knowledge,* Cambridge: Cambridge University Press, 1970.

Newton-Smith, W. H., *The Rationality of Science,* London, Boston, MA and Henley: Routledge and Kegan Paul, 1981.

Shapere, Dudley, 'The structure of scientific revolutions', *Philosophical Review,* 73 (1964), pp. 383–94.

L

Lacan, Jacques (1901–1981)

The writing of Jacques Lacan continues the psychoanalytic tradition after **Freud**. After qualifying he joined the International Psychoanalytic Association in 1934 but when the French psychoanalytic institution divided in 1953, he founded a new society. From 1953 he gave a fortnightly seminar, which at first was attended mainly by other practising analysts but gradually attracted an audience from the whole of intellectual Paris.

The work of Lacan continues to have impact outside psychoanalysis because of the novel terms in which he attempted to describe a relation between subjectivity and human discourse. His teaching is open to many readings, and what follows here is a brief account of the later Lacan very much within the commonsensical interpretation standard in the Anglo-Saxon world.

Saussure showed that signifiers in the form of phonemes, the smallest units of sound systematised in a language, are defined only by their differences. Taking the measure of this Lacan rejects the conventional view that one subject simply uses the signifier as a means to communicate meaning to another, asserting instead that subjectivity and discourse cannot be separated. When he repeats that 'a signifier is that which represents the subject for another signifier' Lacan is insisting that to be a subject means I am always entrammeled in a pre-existing system in which signifiers relate to *each other*. In every sentence the subject is in address to the signifier since to utter it I must have an idea of who I am and who I am talking to before I ever try to say something to someone.

To represent the three-dimensional process of subjectivity Lacan frequently experimented with mathematical expressions. One of these is:

$$\frac{S}{s}$$

Capital S stands for the signifier, lower case s for the signified, the diagram as a whole indicating the priority of the signifier over the signified as well as the bar between them. For Lacan this bar corresponds to the split between conscious and unconscious in Freud's account since, arguably, we are conscious in terms of meaning and the signifier while the process of the signifiers, linked to each other, is unconscious. Apparently present in the signified, the subject is lacking (or barred) in the signifier.

Another set of terms in which Lacan explores this notion of the subject barred by the ontological difference between signifier and signified is through a distinction between meaning and being, which he illustrates as:

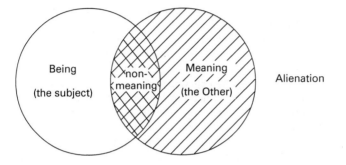

In approaching this opposition between Being and Meaning it is helpful to remember how babies develop. A new-born infant is completely at one, ignorant of any difference between itself and the surrounding world. As the subject grows into language, however, it enters the world of meaning which, of course, is the possession of other people (Lacan refers to it as the Other). The either/or between Being and Meaning poses the subject with an option (it is not an actual choice). If I choose Being I remain completely myself but my life has no meaning; choose Meaning and I get it, but only because my Being is eclipsed by its disappearance into the field of the signifier. As a speaking subject I can only say things that *anyone* could say (there is no private language); though I try to appropriate language to my very own Being it can never belong just to me.

In his essay on 'The mirror stage' Lacan suggests why the infant aspires towards an identity within the Other of language. At an age between six and eighteen months the toddler becomes caught between two correlative fantasies – one of its body in pieces, one of itself as stable and enduring ideal. Mirrored back to the child by others ('Who's a good little girl, then?') the second image is internalised to become the substance of the I, an identity which is misrecognised, not real. In this process the subject begins to desire to be what the Other desires of it.

In the Being/Meaning distinction Lacan implies there is a pre-linguistic self. Freud proposed that after the Oedipal transition the subject aimed to refind what it had most enjoyed beforehand; Lacan suggests that the speaking subject tries to refind within Meaning what it imagines it first experienced as Being. That structure is explained in his terms need, demand, and desire. Need is simply the level of biological necessity, at which the infant cries for milk in a way no different from a kitten. Demand, however, witnesses the birth of the signifier for in it the subject 'constitutes the Other as already possessing the "privilege" of satisfying needs' (*Ecrits*); the infant, to continue the example, cries for milk as symbolic proof that it is loved by a special someone and hates them if they seem to withhold it.

The intense world of demand contains its own undoing. The infant wants to address its particular needs to a particular Other but since it has already begun to enter symbolisation that particularity is abolished. What is now a speaking subject can only seek its particularity at the level of desire, within the universality of language (the signifier is only available to any one person because it's available to everyone).

Lacan contrasts the orders of the real, the symbolic and the imaginary. The symbolic refers again to the Other of language, the historically specific organisation of signifiers which pre-exist the subject. For Lacan reality can only be known as it becomes represented in the signifiers of the symbolic order but the real is the real as it is for me, what gets lost when I enter discourse and am set the task of refinding a trace of my Being within Meaning. Since that particularity is different for everyone Lacan signifies it algebraically as 'object *little o*'. In the imaginary the subject appears to be a knowing, conscious ego, directing itself at signified meaning while overlooking the process of the signifier. Within the imaginary the subject fantasises that it can indeed retrieve object *little o* even though this is impossible because it has to be won from the big Other of the shared symbolic order.

Lacan sees subjectivity as both impossible and inescapable – I simply have no where else to go (except death). A certain vibrant and erotic pessimism carries over into his discussion of sexuality. He re-reads the phallus as a signifier, the signifier which promises to indicate object *little o*; then, in a traditional patriarchal scenario, he proposes that men may seem to have the magic signifier if women seem to be it by being an object of desire.

He represents the situation as follows:

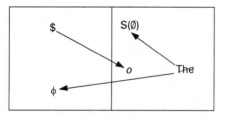

The left-hand side displays masculinity, a barred subject (one who lacks) who seeks object *little o* in the direction of T̶h̶e̶ (that is, T̶h̶e̶ Woman, appearing under erasure because this masculine, universalised ideal of woman does not exist). Femininity appears on the right-hand side but pulled in two directions: between a desire to be what man wants (ϕ, the phallus) and a desire for a transcendental *jouissance* (S($\emptyset$)) of her own. The diagram suggests that, along the arrow pointing up the vector of the feminine, men all want the same thing; that women are all different since they are defined by a double imperative, one line crossing on to the other side of the divide but one remaining separate as something for themselves alone. Although sexual intercourse obviously does take place, as Lacan insists more than once, there can be no sexual relation in the sense of a reciprocal dyad in which A loves B as B loves A.

With its wide range of anthropological, linguistic, scientific and philosophic reference Lacan's teaching has been taken up in many directions. Essentially he offers a materialist theory of the subject. If most previous accounts had assumed that individual identity was in some way inborn (like the soul in Christianity) Lacan would demonstrate how the subject comes about as an effect of language; yet, through the notion of object *little o*, he remains able to answer the question of how the subject desires to identify itself in a particular set of signifiers. A notable adaptation of this was made by **Althusser**.

Because Lacan's views displace sexuality from its dependence on the body, his ideas have been taken up (not uncritically) by feminists including Irigaray and Kristeva. And his view that we all desire but can never find object *little o* has been drawn on to analyse the effect of the aesthetic text as an object of endlessly unsatisfied fantasy.

Main works

Ecrits, trans. Alan Sheridan, London: Tavistock, 1977.

The Four Fundamental Concepts of Psychoanalysis, trans. Alan Sheridan, Harmondsworth: Penguin, 1977.

The Seminar of Jacques Lacan, Book I: *Freud's Papers on Technique, 1953–1954*, trans. John Forrester, Cambridge: Cambridge University Press, 1988.

The Seminar of Jacques Lacan, Book II: *The Ego in Freud's Theory and in the Technique of Psychoanalysis, 1954–1955*, trans. Sylvana Tomaselli, Cambridge: Cambridge University Press, 1988.

The Ethics of Psychoanalysis. 1959–1960, Book VII: *The seminar of Jacques Lacan*, trans. Dennis Porter, London: Routledge, 1992.

The Psychoses: The seminar of Jacques Lacan, Book III: *1955–1956*, trans. Russell Grigg, London: Routledge, 1993.

Further reading

Derrida, Jacques, 'Le facteur de la vérité', in *The Post Card: From Socrates to Freud and beyond*, trans. Alan Bass, Chicago: Chicago University Press, 1987.

Grosz, Elisabeth, *Jacques Lacan: A feminist introduction*, London: Routledge, 1990.

Juranville, Alain, *Lacan et la philosophie*, Paris: Presses Universitaires de France, 1984.

Mitchell, Juliet and Jacqueline Rose (eds), *Feminine Sexuality: Jacques Lacan and the Ecole Freudienne*, London: Macmillan, 1982.

Nancy, Jean-Luc and Philippe Lacoue-Labarthe, *The Title of the Letter: A reading of Jacques Lacan*, trans. François Raffoul and David Pettigrew, New York: SUNY Press, 1992.

Žižek, Slavoj, *Everything you Always Wanted to Know about Lacan but were Afraid to Ask Hitchcock*, London: Verso, 1992.

Laclau, Ernesto (1935–) and Mouffe, Chantal (19??–)

Ernesto Laclau is a political theorist who was born and educated in Buenos Aires. He worked in several Argentinian universities before settling in Britain, where he has lectured at Essex University as well as being visiting professor at the universities of Toronto, Chicago and various Latin American universities. Chantal Mouffe is a political philosopher who studied at the universities of Louvain, Paris, Essex and London. She has taught at the National University of Colombia in Bogota, City University, London, and Westfield College, London.

Although they have both published singly (and continue to do so), Laclau and Mouffe are best known for their collaborative work, which has established them at the forefront of debate about post-Marxism, of which they can be considered amongst the most prominent theoretical voices. Post-Marxism is a term used in a variety of ways, often very loosely. Laclau and Mouffe provide a useful guide to the range of the term when they distinguish between *post*-Marxism and post-*Marxism*. In the former camp we have those who have become disenchanted with Marxism and have ultimately rejected its doctrines, and in the latter those whose concern it is to graft elements of more recent theoretical developments on to a Marxist theoretical base. In this respect Laclau and Mouffe present themselves to us as post-*Marxists*, whose brief is to reorient Marxist theory for a new, we might say postmodern, set of cultural conditions that can no longer be comprehended by the doctrines of classical Marxism. They identify a crisis which they argue makes it necessary 'to go beyond the theoretical and political horizon of Marxism' ('Post-Marxism without apologies').

The idea of a 'crisis' in Marxist theory is hardly new: as Laclau and Mouffe note it was first introduced as long ago as 1898 by the Czech politician Thomas Masaryk. But events of the last couple of decades – the collapse of the Soviet Empire and its satellite states, the highly symbolic destruction of the Berlin Wall, the rise of a democracy movement in China and its brutal suppression in the massacre of Tiananmen Square, to name but the most obvious – have seemed to many to deal a death blow to Marxism as a serious political movement on an international scale. *Post*-Marxists such as Jean-François **Lyotard** and Jean Baudrillard have made their disenchantment with Marxist theory very plain (in Lyotard's case to the extent of declaring loftily, in *The Postmodern Condition*, that we no longer have any need for such outmoded 'grand narratives'); post-*Marxists* such as Laclau and Mouffe, on the other hand, have set themselves the objective of bringing Marxism into dialogue with various new theoretical imperatives in order to prevent the theory, as they see it, from ossifying. This has required a critical re-examination of all aspects of Marxist theory, including some of its most sacred cows (the notion of a universal class, for example), that has not always been well received by the older guard of the Marxist movement, who are prone to see such dialogue less as a reorientation to take account of changed cultural conditions, than as a case of selling out to the enemy which destroys Marxism's credibility.

Hegemony and Socialist Strategy is probably the most provocative work of Laclau and Mouffe in the way that it takes issue with classical Marxist thought. It starts with the claim that the left now stands at a historic crossroads where the need for change has become paramount, and the 'evident truths' of classical Marxism 'have been seriously challenged by an avalanche of historical mutations which have riven the ground on which those truths were constituted'. They proceed to argue that it is now time to revise Marxism to take account of a whole new wave of protest movements that have arisen in late twentieth-century society – for example, the new feminism, the greens, and various ethnic, national and sexual minorities. What is required to achieve such an objective, it is claimed, is a thoroughgoing deconstruction of Marxism, which seeks to recover the 'plurality' of classic Marxist texts (anathema in itself to the older guard) so that what is still useful in them can be incorporated into a new, self-consciously pluralist, emancipatory discourse. Laclau and Mouffe's analysis of the central Marxist concept of hegemony, for example, reveals it to be not so much complementary to the basic categories of Marxist theory as incompatible to them in a way which calls into question such other Marxist 'evident truths' as historical necessity. Their aim is to go beyond the

Gramscian conception of hegemony (hitherto probably the most flexible idea in the Marxist canon) in order to construct a new form of leftist politics based on the notion of radical democracy.

Radical democracy is a state where 'the plurality and indeterminacy of the social' is acknowledged (Laclau and Mouffe reject the notion of homogeneous universal classes, or even national 'social formations'). A radically libertarian political practice can be constructed, however, concerned with creating the conditions for collective action against social inequalities and structures of dominance which keep individuals in a subordinate position. Although they find the term itself unsatisfactory in many ways, Laclau and Mouffe applaud the role played in contemporary society by the 'new social movements'. These latter represent a diversity of struggles – 'urban, ecological, anti-authoritarian, anti-institutional, feminist, anti-racist, ethnic, regional or sexual minorities' – taking place around the globe, and are seen to extend the boundaries of the 'democratic revolution' Laclau and Mouffe wish to promote. Plurality is the key to the successful prosecution of the democratic revolution by the left. Rather than, as in the past, imposing a unified theory and political practice on them, the left should be forging as many links as it can between the various struggles against oppression being waged by the 'new social movements'.

The extent of the break with classical Marxist thought becomes evident when Laclau and Mouffe announce that 'The task of the Left therefore cannot be to renounce liberal–democratic ideology, but on the contrary, to deepen and expand it in the direction of a radical and plural democracy.' Sentiments such as these appear little short of heresy to the Marxist establishment, whose criticism has been dismissed by Laclau and Mouffe as the predictable reflex response from 'the fading epigones of Marxist orthodoxy' ('Post-Marxism without apologies'). The latter article, an attack on one of their many critics, Norman Geras, finds them in unrepentant mood, insisting that the historical reality faced by the socialist project has changed irrevocably in the last few decades and that the 'reformulation of socialism . . . is a challenge to the imagination and to political creativity'. It should be said, however, that Laclau and Mouffe are rather better at polemic than political practicalities, and that the exact details of post-*Marxism* as a form of political action remain irritatingly vague after reading *Hegemony and Socialist Strategy*, or their subsequent defence of the book against its critics.

Post-Marxism has been a significant trend in recent cultural theory, and the work of Laclau and Mouffe has certainly been very influential in its development. How successful it will be in the longer term it is more difficult to say. Whether post-Marxism, in the positive sense championed by Laclau and Mouffe, can continue to maintain itself in the volatile cultural climate of the postmodern world, where 'isms' of any kind are generally viewed with suspicion is very much an open question. And it would have to be said that in the decade since *Hegemony and Socialist Strategy* was written Marxism of any kind has come to seem progressively more marginal to political debate. It remains to be seen whether Laclau and Mouffe-style post-Marxism is anything other than the prolonged death throes of Marxism in general, and whether the term itself will continue to have any meaningful theoretical content and to inspire debate in the wider cultural arena.

Main works

Politics and Ideology in Marxist Theory: Capitalism – fascism – populism (Laclau), London: NLB, 1977.

Gramsci and Marxist Theory (Mouffe, ed.), London, Boston, MA and Henley: Routledge and Kegan Paul, 1979.

Hegemony and Socialist Strategy: Towards a radical democratic politics (jointly), London: Verso, 1985.

'Post-Marxism without apologies' (jointly), *New Left Review*, 166 (1987), pp. 79–106.

'Politics and the limits of modernity' (Laclau), in A. Ross (ed.), *Universal Abandon? The politics of postmodernism*, Minneapolis: University of Minnesota Press, 1988.

The Making of Political Identities (Laclau), London and New York: Verso, 1994.

Further reading

Aronowitz, Stanley, 'Theory and socialist strategy', *Social Text* (Winter, 1986–7).

Forgacs, David, 'Dethroning the working class', *Marxism Today* (May, 1985).

Geras, Norman, 'Post-Marxism?', *New Left Review*, 163 (1987), pp. 40–82.

Smart, Barry, *Modern Conditions: Postmodern controversies*, London and New York: Routledge, 1992.

Laing, R. D. (1927–1989)

R. D. Laing was born in Glasgow. Although a gifted pianist, who initially considered a career in music (he was offered a scholarship to the Royal Academy of Music at the age of twelve), Laing decided to study medicine, graduating from Glasgow University in 1951. After a brief period as an intern in neurosurgery, Laing became interested in psychiatry while serving his compulsory period of military service in the Royal Army Medical Corps. After leaving the army, he worked in the psychiatric departments of hospitals in Glasgow, during which period he began to question established assumptions concerning the causes and treatment of schizophrenia.

In 1956 Laing joined the staff of the Tavistock Clinic in London, where he quickly became established as a radical psychotherapist; his first, and still, perhaps, best-known book, *The Divided Self* (1960), became one of the best-sellers of the decade. He put his ideas concerning so-called 'anti-psychiatry' (the term is one coined by David Cooper, a colleague of Laing's) into practice in 1965, where, along with other psychiatrists, he set up a therapeutic community at Kingsley Hall in East London.

The project terminated in 1971, and although Laing continued to publish until his death in 1989, and retained a devoted (though somewhat reduced) following, in this last two decades of his life he 'moved with the conservative spirit, making quiet appearances in books of conversations with his children or sonnets to his second wife, as the advocate of yoga, a vegetable diet, and the Leboyer obstetric method' (Showalter, *The Female Malady*).

Laing is primarily remembered for his radical critique of traditional psychiatric methods. From the very beginning of his career, he was concerned with the repressive techniques used to treat psychiatric illness, which included not only routine incarceration, but also electro-convulsive shock therapy and lobotomies. In his 1964 introduction to *The Divided Self*, Laing argued that 'psychiatry can so easily be a technique of brainwashing, of inducing behaviour that is adjusted by (preferably) non-injurious torture'. Consequently, his work was concerned with challenging the accepted view of schizophrenia as an illness capable of being 'cured', and thus, by extension, deconstructing the hierarchical nature of the doctor–patient relationship, in which the patient is objectified as an object of study. Take, for example, his claim in *The Divided Self* that '[d]epersonalisation in a theory that is intended to be a theory of persons is as false as schizoid depersonalization of others . . . Although conducted in the name of science, such reification yields false "knowledge".'

For Laing, schizophrenia was essentially an ontological crisis whereby the individual 'may feel more unreal than real; in a literal sense, more dead than alive; precariously differentiated from the rest of the world, so that his identity and autonomy are always in question' (Laing, *The Divided Self*). He believed that this state was frequently a response to unresolveable familial pressures; a view which motivated his third book, *Sanity, Madness and the Family*, which he co-authored with fellow psychiatrist Aaron Esterson. They analysed the case studies of eleven young women in order to demonstrate that it was the parents' attempts to thwart their daughters' developing independence that led to the onset of psychiatric illness. At the end of their final study (of a girl they name 'Agnes Lawson') Laing and Esterson concluded that, while:

> Agnes and the other patients we have studied have all come to be regarded as suffering from some meaningless pathological process. By building up a picture, however, of the actual situation in which Agnes has been living for years, we begin to see that she is struggling to make sense of a senseless situation – senseless at any rate from her position within it.

Psychiatric illness, in other words, can only be understood when examined in the context of the family, and, indeed, of the larger society within which the family unit is constituted. From this perspective, psychiatrists become the agents of a society which is itself repressive and alienating, and extensions of the very pressures from which the patient is striving to withdraw. What is conventionally considered a 'cure' is actually a process which consists of inducing the patient to conform to a consensus view of reality which their 'antisocial' behaviour threatens to undermine. The result is, according to Laing, that traditional psychiatric treatment only alienates the patient further, both from self and from others.

With each subsequent publication, therefore, Laing can be observed moving further away from a strictly clinical analysis of mental illness towards a tendency to view it as representative of the human condition as a whole. As a Marxist, he regarded schizophrenia as an inevitable symptom of the depersonalising pressures of capitalism, and from *The Divided Self* onwards he drew on the work of existentialist philosophers such as Sartre to convey his belief that the schizophrenic experience of isolation and alienation within an uncertain universe is an understandable reaction to a social structure which itself isolates and alienates.

The Politics of Experience, published in 1967, took Laing's already radical theories further away from accepted scientific method. He now believed that the division between 'madness' and 'sanity' was purely relative. Indeed, in a world which appeared to be actively celebrating its own potential for nuclear self-destruction, the truly mad were those who appeared to be the best adjusted to such a situation. Schizoprenia, therefore, should not be treated by clinical methods, for it constituted a kind of psychic quest for transcendence which the individual should be encouraged to complete. The Kingsley Hall community, founded by Laing and other members of the Philadelphia Association – a group set up to reform the treatment of mental illness – strove to put these ideas into practice. Here, the mentally ill lived on equal terms with those who cared for them, and were encouraged to display, rather than suppress, their symptoms. In Laing's words, it was 'a free-for-all: freedom to think, see, feel in any way whatever' (*Wisdom, Madness and Folly*). It evolved into a thriving, though eccentric, artistic community centred on Laing as countercultural prophet or guru.

Much of Laing's fame rests on the way in which his ideas chimed perfectly with the radical utopianism of the 1960s; its fascination with the mystical and the transcendental, and its dissatisfaction with conventional political and social structures. As the euphoria of this era waned, however, so did Laing's career. The Kingsley Hall community broke up when the lease on the property expired in 1971, by which time its founding members were already at odds. Laing retreated from many of his more radical opinions, and his subsequent publications do not constitute any real development of his thought. Texts such as *Conversations with Children* (1978), *Sonnets* (1979) and *Madness, Wisdom and Folly* (1985) are instead concerned with the personal and the anecdotal, and bear little relationship to the vigorous scientific iconoclasm of his earlier work.

As a psychiatrist, Laing's insistence on respect for the schizophrenic patient remains valid. The anti-psychiatric movement, in which he played a prominent part, helped to change the institution's view of the people they treated. His views on the social origins of schizophrenia, however, were seriously compromised by research carried out from the mid-1970s onwards, which show that the illness is caused by biochemical imbalances in the brains of genetically predisposed individuals. However, as Laing recognised, environmental factors also play a vital part in the development of the condition.

Laing's readable style and ecclectic approach to his subject have made him widely read outside professional psychiatric circles, and this is, perhaps, his most enduring achievement. *The Divided Self*, for example, has sold 385,000 copies in the Penguin edition alone. He consistently drew on sources other than the strictly scientific for the development of his ideas: the influence of not only philosophy, but also of myth, religion and literature on his thought are openly acknowledged in his work. Laingian ideas have also been perpetuated though the work of writers who encountered his ideas during the Kingsley Hall period in the 1960s.

One particularly well-known exponent of his theories within a fictional setting is Doris Lessing, whose novels *The Golden Notebook* (1962), *The Four-Gated City* (1969) and *Briefing for a Descent into Hell* (1971), are all clearly inflenced by Laingian theories concerning the schizophrenic experience as quest and social protest. Although Lessing herself became reluctant to continue to endorse Laing's ideas, these texts, which constitute some of her best-known work, continue to provide a platform for discussion of his philosophies.

Main works

The Divided Self: An existential study in sanity and madness (1960), London: Penguin, 1965.

Sanity, Madness and the Family (1964) (with Aaron Esterton), London: Penguin, 1970.

The Politics of Experience and the Bird of Paradise (1967), London: Penguin, 1990.

Knots, London: Tavistock, 1970.

The Politics of the Family, London: Tavistock, 1971.

Reason and Violence: A decade of Sartre's philosophy 1950–1960 (with Dr G. Cooper), London: Tavistock, 1971.

The Self and Others, rev. edn, Harmondsworth: Penguin, 1971.

Wisdom, Madness and Folly, London: Macmillan, 1985.

Further reading

Collier, Andrew, *R. D. Laing: The philosophy and politics of psychotherapy*, Brighton: Harvester Wheatsheaf, 1977.

Friedenberg, Edgar Z., *R. D. Laing*, New York: Viking, 1973.

Mitchell, Juliet, *Psychoanalysis and Feminism*, Harmondsworth: Penguin, 1975.

Showalter, Elaine, *The Female Malady: Women, madness and English culture, 1830–1980*, London: Virago, 1987.

Laski, Harold James (1893–1950)

As well as a prolific writer and lecturer on political philosophy, Laski was also a left-wing activist. Precociously intellectual, he published his first essay (on eugenics) at seventeen, took a first-class degree in history at Oxford in 1914 and in the autumn of that year travelled to Canada to take up a lectureship at McGill University. He subsequently moved to Harvard University in 1916, where, developing an interest in law and politics, he remained until 1920, when he accepted a post at the London School of Economics. He taught at the LSE, from 1926 as Professor of Political Science, until his death. With G. D. H. Cole and R. H. **Tawney**, Harold Laski became known as one of the 'Red Professors' of the British labour movement.

Critics of Laski have particularly emphasised the inconsistencies that occur in his writings, which, it is charged, arise from the greater interest he took in immediate issues than in the formulation of a philosophical system. It is true that he always sought to engage with, and find answers to, the questions of his day. At first, while still a pupil at Manchester Grammar School, he was drawn to the possibilities offered by Darwinian biology. An article in the *Westminster Review*, 'The scope of eugenics', led to meetings with Sir Francis Galton and Sir Karl Pearson; however, at university he switched to the study of history, without abandoning what he believed to be a scientific approach to the pursuit of knowledge. His rationalism also extended to the rejection of the Jewish faith with which he had been raised.

Laski claimed that he had been a socialist from his earliest years, although the writers who most influenced him in his twenties – including F. W. Maitland, Otto Gierke, J. N. Figgis, Ernest Barker and Léon Duguit – were from liberal and pluralist traditions and often concerned to identify the legal and other bases of the sovereignty of the state. From Figgis, an Anglican clergyman who was exercised by the relationship between church and state, he drew ideas about the institutional structures within which individuals and organisations could pursue their interests. Rejecting the view that the state was supreme, Laski, particularly in *Authority in the Modern State* (1919) and in a series of essays reprinted in *The Foundations of Sovereignty* (1922), argued the case for political pluralism. Up to the early 1920s at least, he was mistrustful of statist, Fabian Society, approaches to social reform and more inclined to sympathise with guild socialists who stressed decentralised and participatory forms of democracy. He was unhesitating in relating his ideas to current issues; in 1919 his support for a strike of Boston policemen provoked the propertied classes into an outcry, the anti-semitic tone of which was a factor in his return to England.

As early as 1925, when he published what is probably his best-known and most enduring book, *A Grammar of Politics*, the eclipse of his pluralism was under way. The working-class unrest of the immediate post-war period had shown that the principal struggles within the modern state were between capital and labour. He attempted to set out the theoretical principles by which a democratic programme of economic, social and political reform could be realised. The working out of these ideas placed a greater emphasis on the state's role, though he did not depart from his position that while the state should not claim absolute sovereignty, it could be 'the fundamental instrument of society'. As such, it would organise the satisfaction of the wants of society, with some checks – such as measures of decentralisation – placed on its activities. However, under the circumstances of the time, the balance of power within the state was held by a relatively small number of wealthy and influential people; change could, he believed, be brought about by a democratic form of socialism.

Laski's socialism retained a libertarian element, one expression of which was his belief that social conflict resulted in the loss of individual freedom. He therefore hoped that capitalists would accede to democratic schemes of economic reform, although he was not optimistic that they would go along with peaceful change. In this approach he differed from Marxists, who regarded capitalism as incapable of changing its exploitative character. Though Laski was sympathetic to much of **Marx**'s ideology – so much so that in the 1930s he referred to himself as a Marxist – he stopped short of accepting the predictive element: the idea of inevitable laws arose, in his view, because Marx was a child of the eighteenth-century Enlightenment. While Laski would not be drawn into the chorus of anti-Soviet propaganda, and he sometimes favourably mentioned the ideals of the communist system, the emergence of a small ruling elite in the Soviet Union offended his democratic beliefs.

Some commentators on Laski's writings believe he shifted his position towards accepting that capitalism was facing an unavoidable crisis in the 1930s. Mass unemployment was one reason for this, together with recent political events in Britain and the United States (where he had spent four months in 1931). Beginning with *Democracy in Crisis* (1933) his writings developed a more pessimistic tone, particularly arising from a fear that change would result in less rather than more individual freedom. Fascism's increasing impact in the 1930s deepened his belief in the precariousness of democratic institutions, though he remained untiring in his public and academic work. During 1938–9 he taught at the University of Washington and took the opportunity to warn President Roosevelt, with whom he was on friendly terms, of the futility of attempting to appease the fascist powers.

The onset of war led to Laski taking up the position that the Labour Party (which was part of the coalition government from May 1940) should insist that military victory be followed by an extensive programme of social and economic reforms. Wartime unity could be used to ensure 'a revolution by consent', as vested interests yielded to the will of the majority. He developed these and related ideas in several essays and in his books *Reflections on the Revolution of Our Time* (1943) and *Faith, Reason and Civilisation: An essay in historical analysis* (1944). In 1943 overwork led to a nervous breakdown, but by the general election of 1945 he was able to campaign vigorously – so much so that on one occasion opponents accused him of calling for a violent revolution (his subsequent loss of a libel action demoralised him greatly).

His interest in US society and politics, developed as a young lecturer at Harvard, was continuous and resulted in his longest book, *The American*

Democracy (1949). Some welcomed it as a magisterial analysis in the tradition of Tocqueville's *Democracy in America* and Bryce's *The American Common-wealth*; others criticised its theme that the interests of business and commerce had shaped all aspects of American life and found it *doctrinaire* and *passé*. Another visit to lecture in the United States in 1949 led to *Trade Unions in the New Society* (1949) in which he made the case for the formation of a political party of labour by American trade unions. Laski poured out writings until the end of his life – he died suddenly at the age of fifty-six – but he never completed the study of early French political thought for which he had amassed a large collection of books and pamphlets. His presence had given the LSE a reputation as a centre of left-wing politics; that this was somewhat false is partly indicated by the appointment as successor to the chair he had held of Michael **Oakeshott**.

Some commentators, such as Deane, have dismissed Laski's work as of no major philosophical significance. The most that can be claimed for his reputation in the opinion of such critics is that Laski was a gifted teacher who influenced several generations of students (and many of those he taught rose to influential positions), and that he was also a political activist who had access to many of the leading politicians of his day. Others, including Greenleaf and more recently Newman, have found in Laski's eclectic and seemingly inconsistent approach to political theory the free play of intellectual integrity. Moreover, as Hirst maintains, Laski wished to influence the political process and accordingly he adapted his interests to engage with the changing events of his lifetime. The reassertion of state sovereignty during and after the First World War, for example, impacted on the concept of pluralism, while the advent of the Labour Party to government, and the collapse of 1931, brought forward the need for a formula that incorporated the case for statist remedies. Laski's importance lay in his understanding of these changes and in his attempts to explain them.

Main works

Studies in the Problem of Sovereignty, London: Humphrey Milford and Oxford University Press, 1917.

Authority in the Modern State, London: Oxford University Press, 1919.

The Foundations of Sovereignty and Other Essays, London: Allen and Unwin, 1922.

A Grammar of Politics (1925), London: Allen andUnwin, 1938.

Liberty in the Modern State, London: Faber, 1930.

Democracy in Crisis, London: Allen and Unwin, 1933.

The State in Theory and Practice, London: Allen and Unwin, 1935.

Parliamentary Government in England, London: Allen and Unwin, 1938.

The American Presidency, London: Allen and Unwin, 1940.

Reflections on the Revolution of our Time, London: Allen and Unwin, 1943.

Faith, Reason and Civilisation: An essay in historical analysis, London: Victor Gollancz, 1944.

The American Democracy, London: Allen and Unwin, 1949.

Further reading

Deane, Herbert A., *The Political Ideas of Harold J. Laski*, New York: Columbia University Press, 1955.

Greenleaf, W. H., 'Laski and British socialism', *History of Political Thought*, 2 (1981), pp. 573–91.

Hirst, Paul Q. (ed.), *The Pluralist Theory of the State: Selected writings of G. D. H. Cole, J. N. Figgis and H. J. Laski*, London and New York: Routledge, 1989.

Kramnick, Isaac and Barry Sheerman, *Harold Laski: A life on the left*, London: Hamish Hamilton, 1993.

Newman, Michael, *Harold Laski: A political biography*, London: Macmillan, 1993.

Zylstra, Bernard, *From Pluralism to Collectivism: The development of Harold Laski's political thought*, Assen: Van Gorcum, 1968.

Le Corbusier (Charles-Edouard Jeanneret) (1887–1965)

Le Corbusier was born as Charles-Edouard Jeanneret in 1887 at La Chaux-de-Fonds, the centre of the Swiss watch and clock-making industry. At thirteen he was apprenticed as a watchmaker, but switched to architecture at seventeen after losing the sight of his left eye through too much study. The precision associated with his watchmaking origins would influence his later work as one of the foremost architectural theoreticians of the twentieth century. Le Corbusier published several manifestos, such as *Towards a New Architecture* (1923) and *Almanac of Modern Architecture* (1926), which established the basic principles of modern building. His own early designs included commissions for wealthy clients; for example, the villa

La Roche, the villa Savoye at Poissy and the Maison Stein (built for Gertrude's brother). After the war, the task of reconstruction across Europe was simplified by Le Corbusier's ready-made projects for high-rise, low-cost communal dwellings. The Unité d'Habitation (1947–52) in Marseilles is crucial in this regard, as this large tower block fused Le Corbusier's twin obsessions with concrete and collectivity. Other triumphs in the 1950s included the monastery at Ronchamp, the Philip's Pavilion at the 1958 Brussels World Fair, and the city of Chandigarh in the Punjab. Le Corbusier drowned in 1965 near some Mediterranean huts which he himself had built.

Go to the inner suburbs of almost any large European or American city, and you will see serried ranks of high-rise apartments, sentinels of decay and squalor. Decorating the grey is the aerosol delirium of disaffected youth, graffiti and vandalism their only forms of expression. Mothers fear for their safety as they scurry over windy walkways, or gaze through cracked windows at their toddlers playing many storeys below. Ironically, this grim scenario is the unforeseen result of some of the twentieth century's staunchest visionaries, architects who wished to create a truly modern architecture which would encompass the purity of basic forms and the desire for a new form of communal habitation. Le Corbusier, a name derived from his crow-like appearance, was one such visionary, inspired by the glories of Ancient Greece to design buildings of cleanliness and grace; yet his legacy is an environment made dirty and ugly by the concrete equivalent of crows' nests. In his youth he travelled widely, inspecting architecture in Budapest, Vienna, Berlin and Athens. Le Corbusier concluded that the Parthenon was a 'terrible machine', a hymn to function and rationality. In this perception lay the seed for his most famous proclamation, made many years later, that 'a house was a machine for living in'.

In 1913 Jeanneret set up a practice with his cousin, Pierre, in Paris, the epicentre of the new *avant-gardism*. A friend of the family had earlier introduced him to Amedée Ozenfant, a polemicist who founded the movement of Purism, which married the basic forms of the cube, the sphere and the cylinder with mass-produced industrial materials. Together, they propounded an aesthetic of asceticism in their journal *L'Esprit Nouveau*, first published in 1920. They celebrated the rigour of the right angle, the integrity of the straight line and the mathematical beauty of the modern city. It was at this time that Jeanneret adopted the pseudonym 'Le Corbusier', which was one of several aliases: Paul Boulet and the enigmatic ****! were others. Both Ozenfant and Jeanneret were convinced about the objectivity of their endeavours, boasting that, 'The spirit which dominates this review is that which animates scientific research. We are a few designers who believe that art has laws, just as physics and physiology.'

This spirit also governed Le Corbusier's manifesto *Almanac of Modern Architecture*, in which he outlined five fresh principles for the new architect to follow. The first idea was free supports, so that a building could be raised off the ground on legs, creating extra space beneath. The second idea was to create space at the top of a building by using a flat roof as a garden or viewing platform. Thirdly, open planning arrangements made the mobilisation of interior space more efficient by dispensing with walls or doors. Similarly, stairs could be placed outside the building altogether in the form of ramps, promoting the free design of façades. Lastly, the wrapping of large horizontal bands of glass around buildings divided the window into its component parts: one strip to let light in, one strip to see out of, and so on.

These five principles formed the blueprint for modern architecture, and in their utility and simplicity we can see the Cartesian side of Le Corbusier, laying down the laws of art like a philosopher describing the fundamental laws of thought. This rationalism extended to Le Corbusier's schemes to revolutionise town planning. In many ways he attempted to become a kind of social engineer, believing that man could be conditioned by his architectural environment. As a reaction to the untidy sprawl of European capitals such as Paris and London, Le Corbusier posited a city of the future which would be ordered and rational, organised by rectangular grids, co-ordinated streets whose beauty could only properly be appreciated from an aerial view.

Throughout the 1930s Le Corbusier worked feverishly on plans for reordering the cities of Paris, Barcelona and Stockholm, none of which were accepted or executed. In fact the only time his urban ambitions were given free rein was in the design of the city of Chandigarh. This was to be the new administrative capital of the Punjab and a showpiece for the modern, industrialised nation of India. Le Corbusier had a blank canvas to work with as the surrounding landscape was flat, so he planned everything round a proportional grid, citing Sir Edwin Lutyens' success with New Delhi as an exemplar. The High Court and General Assembly buildings are particularly satisfactory solutions to the problems he set himself.

The Second World War marked a dividing line in Le Corbusier's ideas. Before it, he was a staunch advocate of rationality and rectitude, a tendency too readily absorbed by the rhetoric of fascism. Rumour has it that he even approached Mussolini with a view to implementing his plans for a new style of architecture to accompany the new state. Whatever the truth of this, it is certain that during the war he collaborated with the Vichy government in France. After the war, however, he abandoned many of the tenets of the Machine Age. Harsh angularity and geometric conformity were replaced by serendipitous curves and Klee-like ornaments.

The new style, known as brutalism because of its use of raw materials and its distrust of 'finish', is best exemplified in Le Corbusier's design for the Ronchamp chapel near Belfort. Unlike Chandigarh, Le Corbusier was working on a wavy, hilly canvas, and the building he devised rhymes with these gradients. The roof is a shell-like construction which tilts upwards like a pair of praying hands or a nun's wimple. He was keen to deny a religious reference, though, and in true pseudo-scientific style claimed that 'the form was an answer to a psychophysiology of the feelings'. Nevertheless, the bulbous supporting towers and Swiss-cheese frontage have more to do with feelings than psychophysiology.

A similar project is the Dominican monastery at La Tourette, built in 1960 at Eveux outside Lyons. As Colin Rowe notes (quoted in K. Frampton, *Modern Architecture*, London: Thames and Hudson, 1980), here 'architecture and landscape, lucid and separate experiences, are like rural protagonists of a debate who progressively contradict and clarify each other's meaning'. Le Corbusier himself did not demur from describing the retreat in spiritual terms, when he called it a 'vase of silence, of sweetness'. A far cry from the high-rise flats and office buildings with which his name is now associated.

Le Corbusier, alongside Walter Gropius, of the Bauhaus school, and Mies van der Rohe, was one of the heroes of the so-called Heroic Period of the International Style of architecture, a style defining the high watermark of modernism between the years 1917 and 1928. As such, his influence has been immense, although it has not always been positive: 'a pitiable creature working in reinforced concrete', was Salvador Dali's verdict. His switch from espousing the virtues of geometry to championing organic forms invites analogies with Wittgenstein, who also moved 360 degrees within his chosen field.

Main works

Towards a New Architecture (1923), trans. Frederick Etchells, Oxford: Butterworth, 1989.

The City of Tomorrow and its Planning (1929), trans. Frederick Etchells, London: Architectural Press, 1971.

When the Cathedrals Were White (1937), trans. Francis E. Hyslop, Jr, New York: Reynal and Hitchcock, 1947.

The Modulor (1949), trans. Peter de Francia and Anne Bostock, London: Faber and Faber, 1954.

Modulor 2 (1955), trans. Peter de Francia and Anne Bostock, London: Faber and Faber, 1958.

L'Esprit nouveau (ed., with Amadée Ozenfant), 8 vols, New York: Da Capo, 1968.

Further reading

Blake, Peter, *The Master Builders: Le Corbusier, Mies Van der Rohe, Frank Lloyd Wright*, New York: Norton, 1976.

Curtis, William, *Le Corbusier: Ideas and forms*, New York: Rizzoli, 1992.

Gans, Deborah, *The Le Corbusier Guide*, New York: Princeton University Press, 1987.

Guiton, Jacques, *The Ideas of Le Corbusier: On architecture and town planning*, New York: George Braziller, 1981.

Hitchcock, Henry-Russell and Philip Johnson, *The International Style*, New York: Norton, 1966.

Jencks, Charles, *Le Corbusier and the Tragic View of Architecture*, Cambridge, MA: Harvard University Press, 1974.

Lenin, Vladimir Ilyich (1870–1924)

Lenin was born V. I. Ulyanov in Simbirsk, in Eastern Russia but spent most of his life in exile writing and organising a political party that he hoped would lead a socialist revolution in Russia. After leading a fairly bloodless insurrection in October 1917, he became head of the first professedly Marxist state in the largest country in the world, whose future he attempted to secure against appalling odds. The following four years saw civil war, invasion by fourteen foreign armies, famine and pestilence that left five million dead, leaving the new communist state isolated and the class that had made the revolution decimated. Lenin survived the revolution by seven years and towards the end of his life became critical of the state he was central in creating.

Although Lenin published voluminously on the history, theory and practice of revolution, his major work, as Christopher Hill suggests, is the Russian Revolution itself, of which he was chief architect. Lenin is the twentieth century's greatest exemplar of **Marx**'s famous directive about changing as well as interpreting the world. But, whilst his greatest influence was as a political activist and leader, his political theory, a close reading of Marx and Engels developed for a Russian context, was central to his life and led his practice. His early work is a Marxist response to the Russian Populists, who believed that a utopian society could be built around the existing peasant commune. Despite their name, they had no real base amongst the peasants and their terrorism merely brought about severe state repression. Lenin sought to show how a mass movement of the urban proletariat aligned with the poorest peasants could bring about revolutionary change. The theory underpinning these ideas is the bedrock of his first major work and it formed the basis of his politics until the First World War.

His massively researched *The Development of Capitalism in Russia* (1899) argues that capitalist relations of production had made serious inroads in late nineteenth-century Russia. Many Marxists felt that revolution would only happen in an advanced capitalist country. The Russian Revolution, however, took place where the overwhelming majority of the population were peasants. Lenin explains why by establishing that 'the peasantry' was not homogeneous; while the rich peasants (Kulaks) owned a third of the land, they were only 10 per cent of the peasantry. Over 80 per cent were poor peasants who owned little or nothing and who relied on wage labour to survive. Most were involved in forms of collective exploitation. For Lenin, this meant that the majority of peasants would be far more radical than the small and underdeveloped Russian bourgeoisie, who were politically bound to the tsarist autocracy. Citing Marx, Lenin wrote that revolution could succeed in a relatively underindustrialised country, provided it was spread to the leading industrial nations of Europe.

In *What is to Be Done?* (1902) Lenin suggests that workers will not go beyond narrow 'economistic' demands for better pay and conditions. 'Socialist consciousness' would have to be introduced from without by a tightly knit group of dedicated and disciplined revolutionaries, who could lead the best class fighters as part of a 'vanguard party'. Lenin would modify this view of class consciousness in the light of the spontaneous emergence of soviets during the revolution of 1905, but not the need for the vanguard party. This proved crucial in 1917, when the timing of the insurrection determined its success or failure.

The need for a socialist revolution in Russia was borne in Lenin by his study of the causes and economic roots of the First World War, *Imperialism: The highest stage of capitalism* (1916). World war was the logic of the inherent contradictions of 'imperialism', Lenin's term for worldwide monopoly capitalism. He argued that the capitalist war should be turned into a civil war: one international class against the other. Imperialism itself, a decaying system, both necessitated, and provided the conditions for revolution. Lenin's book notes a number of features about this new stage of capitalism in the most advanced industrial nations: the merging of bank and finance capital to form unprecedented concentrations of economic power; the growth of monopolies supported by the armed might of their governments; the export of capital to high-yielding markets in the colonies where labour and raw materials are cheap; and a global scramble – the final but unequal division of the world by the colonialist powers. For Lenin, this last feature of imperialism made war inevitable.

But if imperialism brought military devastation on an international scale, it also created the objective conditions for revolution through the rationalisation of labour and production; the bringing together of the proletariat in immense numbers – the 'grave diggers of capitalism' in Marx's words. A key element in a successful socialist revolution would be a properly Marxist understanding of the state which would presage its final overthrow. This was Lenin's next theoretical task.

Written in the months before the revolution, *The State and Revolution* (1917) meditates on the nature of government under capitalism and communism. Returning to Marx's experience of the Paris Commune of 1871, Lenin contends that the bourgeois state is organised for the oppression of the majority and cannot be reformed. Its coercive aspects – the military, the police and certain forms of bureaucracy – must be smashed, while national administrative structures would be turned over to the people. He argues that the responsibility of running the state should devolve to *soviets*, democratic workers' councils, which were, for Lenin, models for participatory democracy and the form of future proletarian power. The 1905 revolution made Lenin rethink his earlier position on workers' consciousness. He now felt that workers' self-activity through the spontaneous generation of soviets showed that people could develop a political consciousness.

In the appalling years following the revolution, Lenin and the Bolsheviks attempted to put into practice what had previously been a theory of the socialist state. The state's survival was predicated upon the spreading of the revolution. When it became clear that this was not going to happen, the Bolsheviks set about shoring up a state in which famine demanded the forced expropriation of peasants' surplus grain. This led to a revolt and then to the retreat of the state through the establishment of forms of capitalist trade in grain and other products.

The civil war years required a highly centralised state. Nationalisation replaced worker's control, postponed until, as Lenin put it, 'our grandchildren's time'. The war also brought about a dramatic increase in the centralised state bureaucracy which led Lenin to ask, 'who is directing whom?'. He argued that the new state had become 'a workers' state with a bureaucratic twist'. The civil war had killed off the most militant members of the working class. By its end in 1921, Lenin believed that the proletariat had all but ceased to exist in Russia. Stalin became general secretary of the workers' state against Lenin's express (but little-publicised) wishes. Lenin did not lead to Stalin, but 'war communism' made Stalin's unscrupulous rise all the easier. The tragedy and sign of both Lenin's and his state's isolation lies largely in the fact that the fate of the first attempt at a workers' democracy should hang on the word of its dying leader. There were massive gains in rights for workers (legalised abortion, divorce for both parties on demand, the end to discrimination on the basis of race, religion or gender), but much was clawed back later.

Lenin resisted the term 'Leninism', claiming only to be an orthodox Marxist. However, until recently many millions have lived under regimes that claimed to be 'Leninist', meaning that they followed his post-revolutionary political practice. This practice was deeply (and often necessarily) distorted by war communism. However, Lenin's theory and practice have been influential on modern revolutionaries in a number of ways: his understanding of the revolutionary potential of the peasantry, of imperialism and his support for national liberation struggles have made his work central to many anti-colonialist struggles. As far back as 1893 Lenin argued for national self-determination, seeing that *any* oppressed group fighting against the state should have unconditional support against the common enemy: a position that still has a resonance today.

His writings on the need for a vanguard party (what has become known as 'democratic centralism'), for the necessity, in times of political reaction, to argue against 'ultra-leftist' refusals to participate in 'reformist' structures of power (trade unions and parliaments, for example), have also been widely influential and hotly debated by political activists. This is unsurprising, for the system he dedicated his life to fighting is still with us.

Main works

Collected Works, Moscow: Progress House, 1960–1970. These include:

> *The Development of Capitalism in Russia* (1899).

> *What is to Be Done?* (1902), Harmondsworth: Penguin, 1986.

> *Imperialism: The highest stage of capitalism* (1916), Harmondsworth: Penguin, 1984.

> *The State and Revolution* (1917), Harmondsworth: Penguin, 1985.

> *Left-Wing Communism: An infantile disorder* (1920), London: Bookmarks, 1992.

Further reading

Cliff, Tony, *Lenin: A political biography*, 4 vols, London: Pluto, 1975–9.

Harding, Neil, *Lenin's Political Thought*, 2 vols, London: Macmillan, 1977, 1981.

Hill, Christopher, *Lenin and the Bolshevik Party*, Harmondsworth: Penguin, 1970.

McLellan, David, *Marxism after Marx*, London: Macmillan, 1970.

Reed, John, *Ten Days that Shook the World*, Harmondsworth: Penguin, 1993.

Service, Robert, *Lenin: A political life*, 3 vols, London: Macmillan, 1985–95.

Lévi-Strauss, Claude (1908–)

Claude Lévi-Strauss was born in Brussels, but was educated and has spent the greater part of his career in France. The author of a string of highly influential books in the field of social anthropology, he studied law and philosophy at the University of Paris, and then for several years in the 1930s taught sociology at the University of Sao Paolo in Brazil. While in Brazil Lévi-Strauss undertook some anthropological fieldwork amongst Indian tribes in the interior. After brief military service in France in 1939–40, Lévi-Strauss spent the remainder of the war years in America working at the New York School for Social Research. A post-war spell as French cultural attaché to the United States was followed by appointment as Director of Studies at the Ecole pratique des hautes etudes at the University of Paris in 1950, and then as Chair of Social Anthropology at the Collège de France in 1959. In 1973 Lévi-Strauss became a member of the French Academy, and in 1991 he was awarded the Legion of Honour.

Lévi-Strauss is one of the leading figures in the structuralist movement, and, like most structuralists, his major concern has been to locate underlying patterns to human behaviour. In this respect his anthropological studies, structural anthropology so-called, have been very much theory-led, less concerned with the steady accumulation of empirical detail than with establishing deep structures of discourse. Indeed, he has often been criticised, particularly by the Anglo-American school of social anthropology, for the relative paucity of empirical research in his career – a paucity which could be considered to cast doubt on many of the conclusions of his anthropological studies. Structural anthropology is to be distinguished from social anthropology by its reliance on models drawn from the discipline of linguistics (Saussure or Jakobson, for example) to analyse cultural phenomena, rather than on fieldwork by individual anthropologists. Like Saussure, Lévi-Strauss's interest lies in *langue*, the system, rather than in *parole*, the individual utterances of that system; in the case of anthropology, from such a perspective the findings of long-term fieldwork equal *parole*.

Lévi-Strauss's primary concern throughout his many cultural analyses is to reveal 'the unconscious nature of collective phenomena' (*Structural*

Anthropology). Whether he is dealing with kinship systems, culinary habits or tribal myths, he is always striving to identify common features and universal patterns within the system in question. All systems are considered to be structured like a language, on the structural linguistic model. *The Raw and the Cooked* provides an excellent example of Lévi-Straussian methodology in action, particularly his firm commitment to deep structure. His famous analysis of a group of South American Indian myths, drawn from various tribes such as the Bororo and the Ge, reveals a common deep structural pattern which undergoes a series of transformations as it moves from one myth to another. Thus fire in one myth can be considered as transformed into 'anti-fire' (rain and wind) in another, such that the basic structure of the myth remains intact. The basic structure, plus its set of transformations, can even be notated in a semi-algebraic form by Lévi-Strauss, lending a scientific (some would say pseudo-scientific) air to the proceedings. Ultimately, all the stories are held to be variations on a theme and it is claimed that in real terms we are confronted by the same one each time around: 'in all these instances we are dealing with the same myth', Lévi-Strauss insists, and thus 'the apparent divergences between the versions are to be treated as the result of transformations occurring within a set' (*The Raw and the Cooked*). Any myth, western as well as Third World, is susceptible to such a structural analysis, as in Lévi-Strauss's treatment elsewhere in his work of the Oedipus myth.

Predictably enough, many critics find such conclusions just too neat to be acceptable; as the English social anthropologist Edmund Leach has remarked:

> Lévi-Strauss on Myth has much the same fascination as Freud on the Interpretation of Dreams, and the same kind of weaknesses too. A first encounter with Freud is usually persuasive: it is all so neat, it simply must be right. But then you begin to wonder . . . Lévi-Strauss' discussions about the structure of myth are certainly very clever talk; whether they are really any more than that still remains to be seen. (*Lévi-Strauss*)

The clear implication of such criticism is that Lévi-Strauss is more of an artist than a scientifically minded anthropologist, and indeed, that this is where the main virtue of his work must be considered to lie. The musical analogy that Lévi-Strauss himself sets up in *The Raw and the Cooked*, where the analysis of myth is presented in the form of a composition-like theme and variations, can only help to encourage such a view of his work.

In recent years attacks on structural anthropology have come from the theoretical direction as well. Lévi-Strauss's analytical method is heavily dependent on the notion of binary opposition – raw versus cooked, for example, which is taken to be a distinction universally operative throughout culture – and this has made him very vulnerable to attack by post-structuralist critics eager to demolish the validity of the notion. Jacques Derrida, as a case in point, has been harshly critical of Lévi-Strauss on this issue, arguing in 'Structure, sign and play in the discourse of the human sciences' that the nature/culture opposition, which looms so large in Lévi-Strauss's analyses, is internally self-contradictory, since, as Lévi-Strauss himself admits in *The Elementary Structures of Kinship*, it cannot capture the incest prohibition. This latter proves to be *both* natural *and* cultural, thus escaping the framework of binary opposition and signalling the presence of difference rather than unity. As Derrida points out, one need only regard this as the 'scandal' Lévi-Strauss claims it is, if one insists on the universal efficacy of binary opposition. Whether one agrees with Derrida's critique or not, the suspicion remains that, as was the case with myth, such oppositions are just rather too neat for the messy world that most of us inhabit.

Lévi-Strauss's reputation has been very much tied up with that of structuralism. During the heyday of the structuralist movement in the 1950s and 1960s he was a much-admired, and much-quoted, figure, and his influence was felt in a whole range of areas, such as anthropology, sociology, aesthetics and literary studies (narratology, for example, drew extensively on Lévi-Straussian method). Post-structuralism, with its emphasis on difference at the expense of unity, has dealt a severe blow to the system-building and universalising sides of structuralism, and the decline of structuralism has meant a corresponding decline in the reputation of such perceived 'high structuralists' as Lévi-Strauss. His anthropological studies were always viewed with a certain amount of suspicion, and even disdain, outside France anyway, given their low fieldwork content and excessive reliance, as social anthropologists saw it, on theory rather than painstakingly collected data. (Leach noted that Lévi-Strauss hardly ever stayed in any one place in his travels throughout the Brazilian interior for more than a few weeks at a time.) Whatever his ultimate anthropological reputation might be, Lévi-Strauss is at the very least likely to be remembered for the sheer ingenuity of his cultural analyses, as well as their aesthetically elegant quality.

Main works

Structural Anthropology. trans. Claire Jacobson and Brooke Grundfest Schoepf, New York: Basic Books, 1963.

Totemism, trans. Rodney Needham, London: Merlin, 1964.

The Savage Mind, London: Weidenfeld and Nicholson, 1966.

The Elementary Structures of Kinship, trans. James Harle Bell, John Richard von Sturner and Rodney Needham, London: Eyre and Spottiswoode, 1969.

Introduction to a Science of Mythology, trans. John Weightman and Doreen Weightman, Vol. I: *The Raw and the Cooked* (1970), Vol. II: *From Honey to Ashes* (1972), Vol. III: *The Origin of Table Manners* (1978), Vol. IV: *The Naked Man* (1980), New York: Harper and Row.

Tristes Tropiques, trans. John Weightman and Doreen Weightman, London: Jonathan Cape, 1973.

Anthropology and Myth: Lectures 1957–82, Oxford: Basil Blackwell, 1987.

The Jealous Potter, trans. Benedicte Chorier, Chicago: Chicago University Press, 1988.

The Way of the Masks, trans. Sylvia Modelski, Seattle: University of Washington Press, 1988.

Further reading

Clark, Simon, *Foundations of Structuralism: A critique of Lévi-Strauss and the structuralist movement*, Brighton: Harvester Wheatsheaf, 1981.

Derrida, Jacques, 'Structure, sign and play in the discourse of the human sciences', in *Writing and Difference*, trans. Alan Bass, Chicago: Chicago University Press, 1978.

Gardner, Howard, *The Quest for Mind: Piaget. Lévi-Strauss and the structuralist movement*, New York: Alfred A. Knopf, 1972.

Kurzweil, Edith, *The Age of Structuralism: Lévi-Strauss to Foucault*, New York and Guildford: Columbia University Press, 1980.

Leach, Edmund, *Lévi-Strauss*, London: Collins, 1974.

Paz, Octavio, *Claude Lévi-Strauss: An introduction*, Ithaca, NY, and London: Cornell University Press, 1970.

Glossary

Structuralism   A method of analysis which treats all cultural phenomena as systems of signs based on the model of language (Saussure's linguistics being a major point of reference). Each system is seen to have its own 'grammar' which the analyst can map out.

Lukács, Georg (1885–1971)

Lukács was born György Bernát Löwinger on 13 April 1885 in Budapest. His father's success as director of a leading bank had led to him being ennobled by the Hapsburgs. After studying law, Lukács went to Berlin to study philosophy and social science. Lukács welcomed the Russian Revolution of 1917, believing it offered a new beginning for Western civilisation. In 1918 he joined the Communist Party of Hungary. During Béla Kun's shortlived Hungarian Soviet Republic in that year, he served as a Deputy People's Commissar for Education. He then went into exile in Austria, Germany and later the Soviet Union. Despite his own difficulties with the later Stalinist regime, he was to remain committed to the Marxist cause for the rest of his life.

Beginning with his hugely influential collection of essays, *History and Class Consciousness* (1923) Lukács established himself as one of the most important Marxist thinkers of this century. As well as contributing to the philosophical renewal of Marxism, he was a formidable literary historian and critic. His defence of a notion of critical realism had a profound impact on Marxist aesthetics. Lukács returned to Budapest and gave spirited support to the Hungarian uprising in 1956–7, serving as a Minister of Culture in the reform cabinet. As a consequence he was removed from his chair at the University of Budapest and was expelled from the Communist Party and deported (briefly) to Rumania. He was only readmitted to the Party in 1967, four years before his death in 1971.

During studies in Germany, Lukács came under the influence of the aesthetes in the circle around the poet, Stefan George and of neo-Kantian philosophers. Like his friend, Ernst Bloch, he studied for a while under Georg **Simmel**. He was also influenced by personal acquaintance with Emil Lask and Max **Weber**.

Lukács first came to prominence in Hungarian and German intellectual circles as an essayist on aesthetics and literary matters in the pre-1914 period. His first two works, *The History of the Evolution of the Modern Drama* and *Soul and Form*, were both written in Hungarian and published in 1911. By the end of the First World War, he had become an enthusiastic convert to communism, and joined the Hungarian Communist Party within a week of its foundation. But he had not yet begun a direct engagement with Marxism.

In *The Theory of the Novel* (1920), Lukács effected what he later described as a transition from the 'subjective idealism' (of his neo-Kantian contemporaries and the Romantics) to the 'objective idealism' of Hegelian phenomenology. The historical development of the novel is shown to emerge out of the dialectic between the urge for totality and man's alienated situation. The novel is 'the epic of a world from which God has departed'. Lukács is drawing on a notion of irony derived from Friedrich Schlegel, from Hegel and especially from their contemporary, Solgar. Irony is the freedom of the poet in relation to the divine. By means of irony, we can perceive divine presence in a world forsaken by God. On this basis, the historical development of literary forms expresses a species of historical self-conciousness. From this point on, Lukács dropped any explicit reference to his early visionary perspective; but he spent his life developing and refining his sense of the relationship between history and the historical development of literary form.

Between 1919 and 1922, Lukacs wrote the eight essays which make up *History and Class Consciousness* (published in 1923). This became a seminal work of 'Western' or 'Hegelian' Marxism partly because it broke definitively with the idea of 'dialectic' as some sort of objective process, evident (as Engels had argued) even in nature. For Lukács, the dialectic is essentially a methodological notion. In Lukács's view, to be faithful to the inspiration of **Marx** involves not a body of doctrine, to be dogmatically defended, but a method: the dialectic. This implies awareness of the importance of the relation of theory to practice, which introduced into Marxism a new grasp of the importance of, and responsibility for, theory. Lukács subscribed to the Hegelian idea that the understanding of the world is itself a function of world, that it belongs to reality, as an active and shaping ingredient. Conversely, it meant that theory could not be merely contemplative, but was intimately bound up with practice.

Furthermore, dialectical thought as method involved not only a self-conscious (or ironic) grasp of its own relation to the world but also the aspiration towards a Hegelian sense of 'totality': that one's understanding of each part is related to a sense of the whole and that whole, again in a Hegelian sense, is thoroughly historical. Lukács reworks the key ideas of Marx in this Hegelian language. The working class is seen as the true creator (or subject) of the world, but at the same time workers under capitilalist economic relations are reduced to objects. If it can be made (by the revolutionary party or *avant-garde*) to grasp its true historical mission, then it can become the 'identical subject–object' of history: a social class which can both penetrate social reality (analytically, theoretically) and, at the same time, change it.

Lukács wrote *History and Class Consciousness* before Marx's unpublished *1844 Manuscripts* had become available. The central role of reification in Lukács's early work is a generalisation, at the cultural level, of Marx's concept of commodity fetishism as expounded in *Capital*. The *1844 Manuscripts* showed that a concern with 'alienation' was central to Marx's economic and philosophical studies during his Paris years. Yet, at the 1924 Congress of the Comintern, *History and Class Consciousness* was condemned for its Hegelian abstraction. Lukács disowned the work (and later expressed his annoyance when it acquired renewed popularity amongst the student activists of the New Left in the 1960s). In a much later study of *The Young Hegel*, however, he sought to show how far Hegel had anticipated the concerns of the young Marx. Despite opposition, he continued to regard a grounding in Hegel as vital for any serious Marxist theorist.

Lukács spent the next half a century providing the foundations of a Marxist theory of art and culture. From *The Historical Novel* (1936) to *The Meaning of Contemporary Realism* (1958) he was always primarily concerned with the novel as the paradigmatic literary vehicle. He developed a profound sense of the relationship between narrative form and socio-economic development. In this aspect of his life's work Lukács showed his continued indebtedness to the aesthetics of Hegel and of Friedriech Schlegel. It is what most influenced literary scholars such as Lucien Goldmann and Fredric Jameson.

As a literary critic, Lukács was at the centre of aesthetic and literary debates among the German-speaking exiles during the 1930s. In particular, he was ranged against Bertolt Brecht and other Marxist champions of modernism. As a Marxist poet and dramatist speaking from the perspective of literary practice, Brecht emphasised the need for modernism to respond positively to the development of new methods and techniques by the artists. As a Marxist literary critic, Lukács interpreted modernism as a symptom of Western, capitalist decadence. He demanded that authors aspire towards the perspective of 'totality', offering as his paradigm of this virtue the 'critical realism' of Thomas Mann. (Thomas Mann, for his part, paid Lukács the dubious compliment of portraying him as the Jesuitical communist Naphta in *The Magic Mountain*.) Lukács pushed the debate to a stark choice between the narrative methods of Kafka or Thomas Mann.

Drawing on the models of Scott, Balzac, Stendhal, Tolstoy, Gorki and Mann, Lukács develops a concept of 'realism' in which the leading characters live lives shaped by historical forces. Enthusiastic about the great tradition of realism in the novel, Lukács was therefore deeply ambivalent about the emergence of socialist realism as the aesthetic dominant in the Soviet sphere from the 1930s on. He attacked its romanticised (and uncritical) picture of reality. A guarded critic of Stalin's cultural policy during the dictator's lifetime, he was openly hostile to it after Stalin's death in 1953. He hailed Solzhenitsyn's novels as exemplars of a revitalised realism. But towards the end of his life Lukács was also ready to admit that in his own way Kafka had also been a realist.

During his lifetime, Lukács was pressured into issuing various self-criticisms and denounced his early works. Nevertheless, his life's work reveals an amazing consistency of concept and political orientation. A 'survivor', his life provides the paradigm case of the difficulties faced by critical faculties within the Marxist movement of this century.

Lukács's early work had an enormous impact on the development of an aesthetic and critical Marxism. Ernst Bloch, Walter Benjamin, Herbert **Marcuse** and Theodor W. **Adorno** testified to this impact on their development. Lukács's adversaries, such as Bertolt Brecht, were also crucially influenced by the process of engagement with the ideas of Lukács and his disciples in Moscow. Lucien Goldmann and Fredric Jameson have developed a Lukácsian approach to literary and cultural history. Lukács's treatment of the concepts of realism and of modernism remains of vital importance to anyone concerned with these notions.

Main works

Soul and Form (1911), trans. Anna Bostock, London: Merlin, 1974.

The Theory of the Novel (1920), trans. Anna Bostock, London: Merlin, 1980.

History and Class Consciousness: Studies in Marxist dialectics (1923), trans. Rodney Livingstone, London: Merlin, 1971.

Lenin: A study on the unity of his thought (1924), London: Nicholas Jacobs, 1970.

The Historical Novel (1936), trans. Stanley Mitchell, London: Penguin, 1969.

Essays on Thomas Mann (1947), trans. Stanley Mitchell, London: Merlin, 1964.

Goethe and his Age (1947), trans. Robert Anchor, London: Merlin, 1968.

Essays on Realism (1948), trans. David Fernbach, London: Lawrence and Wishart, 1980.

The Young Hegel (1948), trans. Rodney Livingstone, London: Merlin, 1975.

Studies in European Realism (1950), trans. Edith Bone, London: Merlin, 1972.

The Destruction of Reason (1954), trans. Peter Palmer, London: Merlin, 1980.

The Meaning of Contemporary Realism (1958), trans. John Mander and Necke Mander, London: Merlin, 1963.

Die Eigenart des Asthetischen (The Specificity of the Aesthetic), Neuweid: Luchterhand, 1963.

The Ontology of Social Being, 2 vols, trans. David Fernbach, London: Merlin, 1978.

Further reading

Arato, Andrew and Paul Brienes, *The Young Lukács and the Origin of Western Marxism*, New York: Seabury, 1979.

Heller, Agnes (ed.), *Lukács Revalued*, Oxford: Basil Blackwell, 1983.

Kadarky, Arpad, *Georg Lukács: Life, thought and politics*, Oxford and Cambridge, MA: Basil Blackwell, 1991.

Lichtheim, George, *Lukács*, London: Fontana and Collins, 1970.

Löwy, Michael, *Georg Lukács: From Romanticism to Bolshevism*, trans. Patrick Camiller, London: New Left, 1979.

Sim, Stuart, *Georg Lukács*, Hemel Hempstead: Harvester Wheatsheaf, 1994.

Glossary

Reification The process whereby human activities or relations take on the character of things, and are hence seen as unquestionable. This concept in Lukács's early work parallels the 'tragedy of culture' which so concerned Georg **Simmel**.

Luxemburg, Rosa (1871–1919)

Polish Marxist Rosa Luxemburg was born in 1871 and from her early teens involved herself with the clandestine socialist groups growing up at that time. These illegal activities, along with a desire to grasp political and economic theory, made her escape from Poland a necessity. In 1889 she began to study law and philosophy at the progressive University of Zurich. Here she came into contact with some of the leading Marxists of her day, including Plekhanov and **Lenin**. She finally settled in Germany in 1896 and joined the Social Democratic Party (SDP), at that time the largest working class party in Europe. It was from the left of its ranks that she wrote the majority of her work and carried out her political activity. She quickly became an influential member of the party and made lasting contributions to the debates on imperialism, nationalism and war, the use of the mass strike, the necessity of the revolutionary overthrow of the state and the nature of socialist democracy. One of the founders of the German Communist Party (KDP) and imprisoned for anti-war activities, she was murdered in 1919 by Prussian soldiers after the suppression of the German revolution.

Rosa Luxemburg gave her life fighting for the revolutionary overthrow of capitalism. All her work was produced to this end. While her major work of theoretical economics, *The Accumulation of Capital*, did not appear until

1913, its controversial central thesis underpins her other writings. In it Luxemburg suggests that while capitalism depends upon increasing output, production of commodities will outstrip the demand for them in the home market and so other, pre-capitalist markets must be found. Expansion is therefore essential to capitalism, the political expression of which is imperialism. The scramble for markets amongst the major imperialist powers will finally manifest itself in war. Once capitalism becomes a fully global system, its internal logic will result in a series of crises and a final collapse.

While for Luxemburg this collapse was inevitable, she did not believe that it would necessarily usher in socialism. In one of her most famous passages, she quotes Engels on the choice that faced humanity: 'either to an advance to socialism or a reversion to barbarism', while capitalism, with its massive development of productive forces, is a pre-condition for socialism, 'without conscious interference it will never come about'. Any attempts to reform capitalism so as to bring about a gradual development towards socialism are doomed by the internal logic of capital itself. Just such a reformist (or 'revisionist') argument became popular in the SDP towards the end of the nineteenth century, and it was Luxemburg's implacably hostile reply to this position that marked the beginning of her rise to prominence in the party.

In 1898 Eduard Bernstein published an elaborated series of articles as a book, whose English title, *Evolutionary Socialism*, sums up its content. A leading theorist in the SDP, Bernstein argued that after a twenty-year period of rising wages and economic stability, the development of cartels, a complex and flexible system of credit and the growth of small-scale but successful firms, capitalism had begun to solve its internal problems and to regulate itself, thus alleviating the need for social revolution. This line of argument was anathema to Luxemburg, whose response was a series of formidable articles which still form the basis of the revolutionary position against reformism.

In these articles, collected as *Social Reform or Revolution?* (1899), Luxemburg persuasively argued firstly that Bernstein was wrong about capitalism's internal contradictions: credit, cartels and a plurality of small capitalists would not produce stability in the long run, but quite the reverse. Secondly, Bernstein abandons the theory of capitalist crisis central to Marxism. Through forms of regulation and trade union support, Bernstein saw the state as an agent of change. For Luxemburg, the state itself could never bring about socialism; it was not (as it appeared to be for Bernstein) a class-neutral institution. Through the use of the judiciary and the police, it was a class weapon used against the majority in the interests of a minority.

Luxemburg saw Bernstein's argument as fundamentally flawed because capitalism's inevitable collapse into barbarity meant that revolution was absolutely essential: Bernstein 'was not choosing a more tranquil [road] but a different goal . . . not the realisation of socialism, but the reform of capitalism'. Reformism could never bring about the liberating self-emancipation and revolutionary change of consciousness in the working class that would then allow them to change the world. How then might this 'realisation of socialism' be achieved?

Luxemburg's answer came in *The Mass Strike* (1906), her exhilarating study of the mass action that erupted towards the end of the nineteenth century and culminated in the Russian Revolution of 1905. Containing memorable descriptions of the spontaneous release of the creative energy of ordinary people it suggests that 'for the first time awoke class consciousness in millions upon millions as if by electric shock'. The SDP and the trade unions were suspicious of the mass strike and saw it both as a defensive measure and as a threat to their reformist aims, for Luxemburg it was a political strategy that was 'the spontaneous form of every great revolutionary proletarian action' developing the class as a fighting force in the framework of the widest possible forms of participatory democracy.

The mass strike might occur over a wage cut or over a demand for the change of an employment law; for Luxemburg it was impossible to separate economic and political demands: 'cause and effect continually change places' and therein lay its revolutionary potential. Luxemburg saw the role of the revolutionary in all this as one of leadership; directing the struggle, offering slogans and developing tactics for the spread of the strike. However, the mass strike is only *potentially* revolutionary. Tempering Luxemburg's account, Trotsky later wrote 'whatever its mass character, the general strike does not settle the question of power; it only poses it'. This question was answered by the Russian revolution of October 1917 and it was the increasing restrictions on democracy by the Bolsheviks that engaged Luxemburg.

In *The Russian Revolution* (1918), Luxemburg produced a critique of the Bolsheviks' centralisation of power that has been read by anarchists, liberals and non-Marxists of the left and right as a rejection of Bolshevism and of Leninism in particular. The work is, however, supportive of Bolshevism, but her criticisms were nevertheless important and prophetic. Luxemburg criticises the way that virtues have been made of the necessary restrictions on democracy made by an embattled government during a civil war. She is clear, however, about the cause: the isolation produced by the failure of the revolution to spread, in particular to Germany. Luxemburg saw that Bolshevik democracy was becoming increasingly circumscribed, moving centripetally from workers' councils to party itself and then to higher echelons of the party: 'without freedom of expression and assembly . . . life dies out of every public institution in which the bureaucracy remains the only active element'. Her solution, of no comfort to non-Marxists, was the spread of Bolshevism, not its rejection.

Luxemburg had disagreed with Lenin about the need for a vanguard party of professional revolutionaries and argued for a much broader based organisation, yet when revolutionary struggle exploded in Germany,

Luxemburg's fledgling revolutionary party had little influence and few roots in the German working class. Luxemburg had made two related errors; she had underestimated the influence of reformism and therefore the unevenness of class consciousness amongst the working class and had failed to build a revolutionary party that could have won a significant number of workers to those politics with, in Luxemburg's case, tragic consequences.

Luxemburg's life encompassed the most radical period in recent history and both shaped and was shaped by it. Her impassioned writings on the need for revolutionary change and the most open forms of democratic participation have influenced anarchists, socialists and left liberals throughout the century. While her writings have been used to attack notions of the tightly organised revolutionary party, Luxemburg's work is finally a critique of Leninism, not an alternative to it. She herself was always a member of a political party and was hostile to anarchism, left liberalism and bourgeois feminism. Luxemburg organised an international women's anti-war conference but believed, true to her Marxism, women's liberation could only come about with socialist revolution. In a time when left reformist parties across Europe offer little even in the way of reforms, Luxemburg's uncompromisingly revolutionary writings may seem to come from a past world, but continue the small but visionary current that speaks of a very different future one.

Main works

Social Reform or Revolution (1899), London: Bookmarks, 1989.

The Mass Strike (1906), London: Bookmarks, 1986.

The Accumulation of Capital (1913), trans. Agnes Shwarzchild, London: Routledge and Kegan Paul, 1971.

The Russian Revolution (1918) and *Leninism or Marxism?* (1904), ed. B. D. Wolfe, Ann Arbor: University of Michigan Press, 1961.

The Junius Pamphlet (1916), London: Merlin, 1979.

Rosa Luxemburg Speaks, ed. and trans. Mary-Alice Waters, New York: Pathfinder, 1970. Contains all of the above.

The Letters of Rosa Luxemburg, ed. Stephen Bronner, Boulder, CO: Westview, 1978.

Further reading

Cliff, Tony, *Rosa Luxemburg*, London: Bookmarks, 1986.

Dunayevskaya, Raya, *Rosa Luxemburg, Women's Liberation and Marx's Philosophy of Revolution*, Atlantic Islands, NJ: Humanities Press, 1981.

Frolich, Paul, *Rosa Luxemburg: Ideas in action*, London: Bookmarks, 1994.

Geras, Norman, *The Legacy of Rosa Luxemburg*, London: Verso, 1983.

Geras, Norman, 'Rosa Luxemburg and democracy', *New Left Review*, 203 (1994), pp. 92–106.

Nettl, J. P., *Rosa Luxemburg*, Oxford: Oxford University Press, 1966.

Lyotard, Jean-François (1924–)

Jean-François Lyotard has had a long and distinguished academic career, having taught in various universities in both France and North America as well as being one of the founders, along with Jacques Derrida, of the prestigious Collège Internationale de Philosophie in Paris. Lyotard spent some time teaching in Algeria in the early 1950s, experience which was later to stand him in good stead when he became the spokesman on Algerian affairs for the *Socialisme ou barbarie* group during the Algerian war of liberation. *Socialisme ou barbarie*'s objective was to conduct a critique of Marxism from within, and Lyotard remained with the group (and its accompanying journal of the same name) for several years, until leaving to join the splinter *Pouvoir ouvrier* group in the 1960s. Active in the 1968 *événements* in Paris, Lyotard became increasingly disenchanted with Marxism as a political doctrine, and in his later career has become a trenchant critic of Marxist theory and a proponent of postmodernism.

Lyotard is undoubtedly best known for his book *The Postmodern Condition: A report on knowledge*, which established his reputation as one of the most influential theorists of the postmodern, but in his long career (his publications now span half a century) he has produced several important works of philosophy and cultural theory whose ultimate impact may well outlast that of his most popular book (a book which many of his followers insist is amongst his least representative anyway). Works such as *Libidinal Economy*, *The Differend*, *Just Gaming* and *The Inhuman* all contain important reflections on our current cultural situation, and show Lyotard to be one of the most provocative and penetrating thinkers of his generation. Regardless of the

l, his thought, as various commentators have pointed
lly oriented, and thus provides an important fund of
orists.

ording to his followers, unrepresentative and in fact
terms of Lyotard's general oeuvre, *The Postmodern*
considerable impression on contemporary thought.
re, delivered in a somewhat magisterial tone, is that
we have now outgrown our need for 'grand narratives' (that is, universal
theories or ideologies) and that 'little narratives' are the most appropriate
way of dealing with social and political problems. Little narratives function
somewhat like the American notion of 'issue politics' in that they address
specific cultural problems in the name of specific, often quite short-term,
objectives. The 1968 *événements* in Paris, with their tactical alliances between
students and unions, represent something of a model of how the process
should work. Lyotard also argues that little narratives constitute the driving
force behind what he calls 'postmodern science', where the interest lies in
discontinuity rather than continuity (the influence of both catastrophe
theory and chaos theory can be noted at this point). Continuity comes to
stand for something like the forces of tradition, or received wisdom, which
the 'discontinuous' little narrative must constantly interrupt. Overall,
the impact of *The Postmodern Condition* is to promote scepticism about
universalising theories (of which Marxism, or the Enlightenment project,
would be outstanding examples). Lyotard can be considered one of the
great sceptics of modern cultural thought.

The Differend introduces one of Lyotard's most important critical
concepts. Differends occur when the rules of one genre of discourse are
illicitly applied to another; or when one dominating genre prevents other
genres from stating their case (or, in Lyotard's terminology, putting it 'into
phrases'). Thus an exploited employee cannot really put the fact of her
exploitation by her employer into phrases, because the economic system
in which she works has institutionalised the sale of one's labour power on
the open market as the normal state of affairs. What she sees as exploitation,
her employer sees as a contract freely entered into. The only way to
overcome such situations is by the development of what Lyotard calls a
'philosophical politics', whose concern is to seek out and create idioms
(that is, new discourses) where differends *can* be put into phrases (or as it
is sometimes translated, 'sentences').

It is now becoming clear that Lyotard is one of the most important critics
of Marxism, and works such as *Libidinal Economy* offer a devastating critique
of Marxist thought, particularly of the notion of false consciousness. The
chapter entitled 'The desire called Marx' argues that false consciousness is
one of the great delusions of Marxist thought, and claims, provocatively
enough, that the nineteenth-century working-class *enjoyed* being part of
the process of industrialisation – that they were willingly swept along by
the sheer energy of it all rather than tricked into it under false pretences.

Lyotard argues that Marxism cannot cope with the notion of libidinal energy, which cuts across its rational world-view.

Lyotard's early political writings on Algeria for *Socialisme ou barbarie* (1955–63) reveal that he was even then a less than orthodox Marxist, and well aware of the possibility of cultural imperialism within western leftist thought. He argues that a Marxist scheme that is totally inappropriate to the nation's cultural heritage is being imposed on the Algerian war of liberation. We can see here the seeds of the scepticism regarding 'grand narratives' for which Lyotard has become so famous.

Lyotard is also very critical of the figure of the intellectual, whom he invariably compares unfavourably to the philosopher. He regards intellectuals as figures who collude with the authorities to disguise the existence of differends and thus help to prop up outmoded grand narratives; 'philosophers', on the other hand, consistently draw our attention to differends ('philosophical politics'), and indeed that is both their duty and their principal function. The artist can be as effective as the philosopher in revealing differends, and art is a subject to which Lyotard continually returns over the course of his writings (he is the author of numerous exhibition catalogues, for example).

The later work of Lyotard has an increasingly apocalyptic tone. *The Inhuman* pictures a world in which technology (or 'techno-science' as Lyotard refers to it) has taken over and is preparing contingency plans, as the author rather startlingly proclaims in chapters like 'Can thought go on without a body?', for the extinction of life on earth some 4.5 billion years into the future. Although he holds out little hope of ultimate success, Lyotard considers it important for individuals to offer resistance to this 'inhuman' techno-scientific programme, by constantly foregrounding differends and the fact of difference. Once again we can see the faith in the little narrative at the expense of all-embracing theories or ideologies. That may well constitute one of Lyotard's most enduring legacies to social theory, even if it is a somewhat idealistic one in the current world order.

Lyotard is one of the major intellectual presences of the later twentieth century, and his status as one of the gurus of postmodernism is unassailable: *The Postmodern Condition* continues to be one of the most widely quoted, and pored-over, books of its time. Lyotard's general cultural reputation is growing as more of his works are translated, and the bleak picture he paints of mankind's future in *The Inhuman* captures a mood of apocalyptic millenarianism that is increasingly fashionable in the 1990s. The differend is also an increasingly fashionable concept in the way it enables us to pinpoint what it is that resists resolution in sociopolitical dilemmas (Northern Ireland, the former Yugoslavia and the Middle East all provide classic examples of the differend in action). It would have to be said, however, that its practical value is very low. Lyotard's desire for the differend to be recognised rather than forced into a false resolution, while laudable, is more than a little out of touch, it could be argued, with contemporary sociopolitical realities and the harsh world of global power politics.

Main works

Phenomenology (1954), trans. Brian Beakley, Albany: State University of New York Press, 1991.

Discours, figure, Paris: Klinckseick, 1971.

Libidinal Economy (1974), trans. Iain Hamilton Grant, London: Athlone, 1993.

The Postmodern Condition: A report on knowledge (1979), trans. Geoffrey Bennington and Brian Massumi, Manchester: Manchester University Press, 1984.

Just Gaming (with Jean-Loup Thebaud, 1979), trans. Wlad Godzich, Manchester: Manchester University Press, 1985.

The Differend: Phrases in dispute (1983), trans. George Van Den Abbeele, Manchester: Manchester University Press, 1988.

Heidegger and 'the Jews' (1988), trans. Andreas Michel and Mark Roberts, Minneapolis: University of Minnesota Press, 1990.

The Inhuman: Reflections on time (1988), trans. Geoffrey Bennington and Rachel Bowlby, Oxford: Basil Blackwell, 1991.

Peregrinations: Law, event, form, New York: Columbia University Press, 1988.

Lessons on the Analytic of the Sublime (1991), trans. Elizabeth Rottenberg, Stanford, CA: Stanford University Press, 1994.

Political Writings, trans. Bill Readings and Kevin Paul Geiman, London: University College London Press, 1993.

Further reading

Benjamin, Andrew (ed.), *Judging Lyotard*, London and New York: Routledge, 1992.

Bennington, Geoffrey, *Lyotard: Writing the event*, Manchester: Manchester University Press, 1988.

Callinicos, Alex, *Against Postmodernism: A Marxist perspective*, Cambridge: Polity, 1989.

Carroll, David, *Paraesthetics: Foucault, Lyotard, Derrida*, London: Methuen, 1987.

Readings, Bill, *Introducing Lyotard: Art and politics*, London and New York: Routledge, 1991.

Sim, Stuart, *Jean-François Lyotard*, Hemel Hempstead: Harvester Wheatsheaf, 1996.

Glossary

Differend A disagreement between two parties which cannot be resolved, owing to the lack of a principle of judgement common to each party's genre of discourse. The respective genres of discourse are, in fact, to be seen as incommensurable.

M

MacIntyre, Alasdair (1929–)

Born in Glasgow, Alasdair Chalmers MacIntyre was educated at the universities of London, Manchester and Oxford. His subsequent career as an academic philosopher has been even more varied, with posts held at ten institutions including Leeds University and Oxford in Britain, as well as Princeton, Vanderbilt and Notre Dame in the United States. In tandem with his migratory path as a teacher, his own ideas have assumed a number of guises, travelling along the way through Marxist, Aristotelian and, most recently, Thomist incarnations.

The one major theme that bridges the various phases of MacIntyre's ideas, early and late, is the view that moral philosophy is not an abstract mental exercise but one which requires an extensive knowledge of history and anthropology. That moral concepts are not timeless, that they change, is not insignificant for MacIntyre: he proposes that morality can only be examined and fully understood in connection with its history. Moreover, what this recommended moral historicism reveals, according to MacIntyre, is that our contemporary age of morality is one of unprecedented chaos. MacIntyre believes that this disorder has arisen by virtue of the fact that we use moral terms like 'good', 'justice' or 'duty' without any genuine comprehension of the historical practices from which they emerged. These words today are mere 'simulacra' of morality, 'linguistic survivals' from the various long-dead traditions which would have originally provided them with their necessary context.

Of further significance is that such moral notions of rights, desert, virtue or character, come from *different* traditions of morality stemming from Classical, Kantian, Utilitarian and other backgrounds. Yet, in ignorance of their diverse origins, we moderns foist these terms together in homogenising and dehistoricising debate. Our endless arguments over morality are symptomatic of the disparate and fragmented roots of the concepts we use. MacIntyre illustrates this interminability with examples of the current debates over social justice, just war and abortion. Each side is perfectly able to argue rationally for its own point of view on the matter, be it a liberal, conservative or relativist position. But each can only argue in its own terms and from its own premises, which, because they are so diverse in origin, are also wholly incommensurable. Hence, though everyone argues as if the debate could be resolved, it is actually interminable precisely because each side is arguing according to different and incomparable models of morality.

Not that the general public are alone culpable for the current disarray within the moral sphere. Philosophers are as much if not more to blame. Public debate is matched in its fragmentation and inconclusiveness only by the ethical debates in philosophy. What MacIntyre finds objectionable in the modern philosophical treatment of morality is not its abstract nature so much as the predication of *one* type of rationality and *one* type of morality that underpins its abstract disputation. For MacIntyre, on the other hand, there are rationalities rather than rationality . . . justices rather than justice' (*Whose Justice? Which Rationality?*). A singular, wholly disinterested and autonomous rationality is unintelligible, he asserts, yet it is this very conception which is the starting point for most modern moral philosophies in their common assumption of a pure, impersonal and abstract moral perspective.

MacIntyre objects in particular to what he regards as the root cause of this modern morality: the 'Enlightenment project'. Part of this eighteenth-century enterprise was to view morality in terms of its own guiding principles: its pan-rationalism, voluntarism, universalism and anti-teleologicalism, as well as its espousal of the commensurability of all forms of value. MacIntyre traces this developing vision, in all its mutations, from Hume, Diderot and Kant in the eighteenth century, through Kierkegaard in the nineteenth century and G. E. Moore, A. J. Ayer and C. L. Stevenson in the twentieth.

The contemporary vestige of this Enlightenment revision of morality is grounded in a latent 'emotivism' – whereby morality is viewed as the expression of a personal approval or disapproval of certain acts – tied to an instrumental rationality: the modern (unspoken) metaethical understanding is that morality amounts to no more than the attempt to get (instrumentalism) what we want (emotivism). Even deontologists, failing to realise that their notions of absolute rights and duties are arbitrary constructions, must themselves, though again without realising it, resort to these basic moral prejudices. MacIntyre sees it as his own task to turn this project upside down, inviting a return to precisely the faith, values, authority and tradition that the *philosophes* tried to extinguish. He opposes their metaethical views with a socially embedded and practice-oriented notion of virtuous action aiming at certain real, particular and incommensurable goods. As these notions of 'tradition', 'practice' and the 'virtues' are so central to MacIntyre, they are each worth examining individually.

A tradition is the medium through which a set of practices are formed and transmitted. While there are economic or aesthetic traditions, MacIntyre focuses on religious, moral and philosophical traditions and the practices comprising them. In particular, MacIntyre forwards a traditional theory of knowledge according to which 'each particular theory or set of moral or scientific beliefs is intelligible and justifiable . . . only as a member of an historical series' (*After Virtue*). Far from the common understanding of a tradition as something dogmatic and inert, MacIntyre explains how, when vital, traditions are open and dynamic, embodying continuities of internal debate alongside creative mutation.

In tandem with this theory of knowledge, MacIntyre opposes the Enlightenment advocacy of liberal individualism with his own conception which emphasises the irreducible influence of the community on personal identity. In the pre-modern traditional societies MacIntyre favours, each individual's membership within a variety of groups – as brother, cousin, householder, tribesman and so on – is essential to his or her identity. And one's moral tradition is part and parcel of this communal identity.

This prioritisation of tradition, however, opens MacIntyre to the charge of relativism: if one's morality is formed through one's tradition, it would seem to follow that there are as many goods, be they in conflict or not, as there are traditions of morality. Yet if there is conflict, how would one adjudicate between rival traditions without some notion of a good that transcends any particular tradition? It seems impossible for MacIntyre to arbitrate between different traditions, for to do so it would appear necessary to adopt a stance outside all tradition, yet MacIntyre clearly states that '[t]he person outside all traditions lacks sufficient rational resources for enquiry and *a fortiori* for enquiry into what tradition is to be rationally preferred' (*Whose Justice? Which Rationality?*). Nevertheless, MacIntyre believes that debate and successful resolution of debate are possible both within and between traditions and it is *Whose Justice? Which Rationality?* and *Three Rival Versions of Moral Enquiry* which address this issue in most depth. *Whose Justice? Which Rationality?* in particular attempts to create a practical rationality that would arbitrate between rival traditions of moral thought. MacIntyre here relies on a view of rationality predicated on a coherence theory of truth rather than a correspondence theory: the preferred tradition of Thomism is triumphant because it is internally coherent and even explains the incoherence of its rivals. But one can always ask in reply whose model of coherence is being employed.

Practices are the elements of traditions. MacIntyre lists architecture, chess, football, fishing, farming and philosophy, but asserts that practices can also be found amongst the arts and sciences, as well as the making and sustaining of family life. Practices have no transcendental objective to fulfil, for their ends are transmuted by the history of the practice. It is no accident, therefore, that every practice has a history and that, consequently, to enter into a practice is to relate oneself to those who have preceded one in the practice as well as its current practitioners.

There are goods which are external to a practice (also called 'goods of effectiveness') and goods which are internal to it (also called 'goods of excellence'). The reward for winning at chess, for instance, would be an external good, while playing chess in the correct way would be an internal good. The latter is internal because it belongs to the practice and because it can only be recognised by participating in the practice. Practices, then, stand in stark contrast with technical skills, which have no internal goods as they are only instrumental.

Fundamentally, however, MacIntyre sees the pursuit of the internal goods of a practice as a paradigm for understanding moral development in general. What one learns through such action, he suggests, is the good of a certain kind of life. That is, whereas these activities are all immanent to life, pursuing them correctly teaches us something that transcends any one of them. The goods of a whole human life are never independent of the goods internal to practices but are integrative of and partly structured in terms of them.

A problem for MacIntyre, though, is the criticism that if goods are defined internally to practices, then many practices – torture, for example – appear able to lay claim to some moral status. Indeed, MacIntyre admits that there are activities that could never be practices – theft, betrayal, murder – and which must be outlawed. But one might respond that this is merely arbitrary and that MacIntyre's description of a practice fits torture no less than cricket. He can only outlaw some practices if he has some standard transcendent to practices – minimal human rights, for instance – which he has not. At best, he could argue that these practices are in-coherent, but that would be difficult to uphold without assuming a contentious definition of what coherence itself means.

Though MacIntyre does not believe that he is advocating a 'virtue ethics' *per se*, the virtues play a very strong role in his thinking. Modernity's distress, in fact, can be traced back to the loss of such virtues. But what are the virtues? They are dispositions to act and feel in certain ways. The virtues are related to practices in two ways: we cannot know what a virtue is in isolation from the practices through which it is displayed, and we cannot know why a virtue is virtuous unless we see how it sustains such practices. The possession and exercise of the virtues enable us to achieve the goods internal to a practice and thereby participate in the idea of a good life.

MacIntyre's influence, stemming mostly from *After Virtue*, has worked on three levels: firstly, though he has dissociated himself from their move-ment, communitarian thinkers like Michael **Walzer**, Michael Sandel and, perhaps, Charles Taylor, have found much to value in MacIntyre's ideas concerning tradition and practice. One will frequently see his ideas linked with theirs in common opposition to the views of liberals like John Rawls and Ronald **Dworkin**. A second effect of that book centres primarily on moral philosophy where the advantages of a virtue ethics are increasingly being touted in preference over the traditional dichotomy of consequentialism versus deontologism. Finally, the arguments forwarded in *After Virtue* have added great weight to the current revival of interest not only in Aristotelian ethics but also in Aristotle's philosophy in general. Likewise, the turn to Thomism in *Whose Justice? Which Rationality?* has brought a comparable rise in the fortunes of Aquinas's thought in its wake.

Main works

A Short History of Ethics, New York: Macmillan, 1966.

Against the Self-Images of the Age: Essays on ideology and philosophy, London: Duckworth, 1971.

After Virtue: A Study in Moral Theory (1981), 2nd edn, London: Duckworth, 1985.

Whose Justice? Which Rationality?, London: Duckworth, 1988.

Three Rival Versions of Moral Enquiry: Encyclopaedia, genealogy, tradition, London: Duckworth, 1990.

Further reading

French, P., T. Uehling and H. Wettstein (eds), *Ethical Theory: Character and virtue*, Vol. VIII: *Midwest Studies in Philosophy*, South Bend, IA: University of Notre Dame Press, 1988.

Horton, John and Susan Mendus (eds), *After MacIntyre: Critical perspectives on the work of Alasdair MacIntyre*, Cambridge: Polity, 1994.

Inquiry, 26 (1983).

McMylor, Peter, *Alasdair MacIntyre: Critic of modernity*, London: Routledge, 1993.

McLuhan, Marshall (1911–1980)

Marshall McLuhan was born in Alberta, Canada. He studied English Literature first at the University of Manitoba and then at the University of

Cambridge. He obtained a Ph.D. from the University of Cambridge in 1943 with a dissertation on the English pamphleteer and playwright Thomas Nashe. During his time as a student, McLuhan converted to Roman Catholicism. McLuhan taught at the University of Wisconsin, St Louis University, the Assumption University of Windsor, Ontario, and finally, the University of Toronto, where he remained until his death.

McLuhan's early work is in the field of English studies. This work is very much in the tradition of both F. R. Leavis and the conservative agrarianism of the American South, critical of modern culture from the perspective of a lost organic community. The publication of *The Mechanical Bride* (1951) marks the beginnings of a shift in McLuhan's work. Although still nostalgic and critical of modern culture, the object of study is now the mass media, comic strips, film posters, newspapers, popular periodicals, etc. Here, according to McLuhan, is a world of popular mythology and industrial folklore. To understand it requires something more than the moralism of traditional English studies. As he explains,

> the time for anger and protest is in the early stages of a new process. The present stage is extremely advanced. Moreover, it is full, not only of destructiveness but also of promises of rich new developments to which moral indignation is a very poor guide.

Despite the cultural possibilities, *The Mechanical Bride* still urges vigilance against the commercial appropriation of our desires and our dreams. Nevertheless, the book marks a considerable shift from the conservatism of Leavisism and old South agrarianism. What allows McLuhan to make this move is the shift he makes in his critical gaze from the content of the texts and practices of modern culture to their form. For example, he distinguishes between the message of an advertisement and its modernist form. He sees parallels between the 'superficial chaos' of the layout of a newspaper and the experiments of Pablo Picasso and James Joyce.

The Gutenberg Galaxy (1962) presents an attack on what McLuhan regards as the unwelcome hegemony of print. McLuhan insists that its widespread introduction, following the invention of moveable metal type in the fifteenth century, 'detribalised' the world, producing a form of individualism – 'print is the technology of individualism' – predicated on uniformity, regularity and linear perspective. Instead of the multifaceted world of oral culture, print culture insists on the single perspective of the eye, the single point of view. The advent of print is, he argues, a moment of profound cultural impoverishment, the reduction of the interplay of all the senses to the privilege of the visual. For McLuhan, this amounts to the equivalent of a second Fall. Print culture encourages the rational mapping of space and time into the calculable and the predictable. It gradually produces the disciplined men and women necessary to accept the growing uniformity of industrial society.

In *Understanding Media* (1964), the book on which McLuhan's current reputation rests, he returns to the critical field of *The Mechanical Bride*: advertisements, comics, newspapers, movies, radio, the telephone, etc. He maintains that each example of 'new technology' (including mass media) is always an extension of a particular human faculty or sense. For example, clothing is an extension of the skin, the wheel an extension of the foot, the telephone an extension of the ear. What concerns him is how the new electronic mass media restructure social and cultural relations and what he calls the 'ratio' between the senses (increased use of one sense reduces the receptivity of each of the other four). This marks a fundamental shift in his critical focus. No longer is he concerned with the meaning of media texts (already signalled in *The Mechanical Bride*). Instead, under the slogan 'the medium is the message' (first coined in 1960), McLuhan now argues that the significance of the media results from their ability to reorganise human perception and social and cultural relationships. McLuhan gives the example of how the electric light 'ended the regime of day and night, of indoors and out-of-doors'. Semiotic analysis will not reveal the 'message' of the electric light. But without doubt the electric light has had a momentous effect on modern culture, restructuring practices of work and leisure by making them available twenty-four hours a day.

According to McLuhan, the new electronic mass media hold out the promise of a 're-tribalised' world (the 'global village'). Whereas print culture promoted individualism, focused as it is on individual acts of consumption, the new media promise a culture in which 'everyone is profoundly involved with everyone else'. For example, television introduces the world into our living rooms. In much the same way, the morning newspaper, with its 'communal mosaic' of electronically gathered information, opens up the world to our critical inspection.

McLuhan also insists that the new electronic mass media have the potential to reverse the cultural Fall brought about by the hegemony of print culture. As McLuhan maintains, print crushed the integrated community of oral tradition and produced in its place a hierarchical culture of the expert, allowing a minority culture to wield intellectual power over a majority supposedly without culture. The promise of the new media is the reversal of this process, breaking down distinctions between expert minority and uncultured majority. In the brave new world of electronic media everyone is potentially an expert. In short, McLuhan claims that the new electronic media are a fundamentally more 'democratic' form of communication than print.

The transition from a culture dominated by print to the culture of electronic media is marked by a shift from what McLuhan calls 'hot' media to 'cool' media. According to McLuhan,

> speech is a cool medium of low definition, because so little is given and so much has to be filled in by the listener. On the other hand, hot media do not leave so

much to be filled in or completed by the audience. Hot media are, therefore, low in participation, and cool media are high in participation or completion by the audience.

McLuhan cites the example of the telephone as a medium which 'demands complete participation'. He also notes, with a less celebratory tone, how the telephone disturbs the distinction between private and public and extends relations of power by making users available to the commands of others.

McLuhan's later work elaborates and popularises the ideas presented in *The Mechanical Bride*, *The Gutenberg Galaxy* and in *Understanding Media*. He responded to his remarkable fame with public lectures, television appearances and a series of publications which did little more than repeat the ideas of his first three books.

For most of the 1960s, McLuhan's cultural impact was immense. His message about the potential of the new electronic media to free humankind from the prisonhouse of print found a ready and enthusiastic audience in both the media industries (where he was fêted as a media celebrity) and the American counterculture (where he was seen as endorsing the new culture). During the 1970s and 1980s, McLuhan's reputation suffered something of a decline as his work came to be increasingly characterised as driven by technological determinism. He was accused of isolating technological changes, making invisible the social, cultural and political contexts in which the changes occurred. In this way, developments in electronic media were presented as inevitable and therefore beyond rational critique. Since the late 1980s, however, his reputation has moved into the ascendant. He is once again celebrated as a media guru. There can be no doubt that the rise to prominence of the French sociologist Jean Baudrillard (who openly acknowledges the influence of McLuhan) as a pivotal figure in debates about post-modernism has helped McLuhan's own return to critical consideration in the fields of cultural and media studies.

Main works

The Mechanical Bride: Folklore of industrial man, New York: Vanguard, 1951.

Explorations in Communications: An anthology (ed. with Edmund Car-penter), Boston, MA: Beacon, 1960.

The Gutenberg Galaxy: The making of typographic man, Toronto: Toronto University Press, 1962.

Understanding Media: The extensions of man, New York: McGraw-Hill, 1964.

The Medium is the Massage: An inventory of effects (with Quentin Fiore), New York: Bantam and Random House, 1967.

The Global Village: Transformations in world life and media in the twenty-first century (with Bruce R. Powers), New York and Oxford: Oxford University Press, 1989.

Further reading

Fekete, John, *The Critical Twilight: Explorations in the ideology of Anglo-American literary theory from Eliot to McLuhan*, London and Boston, MA: Routledge and Kegan Paul, 1977.

Ferguson, Marjorie, 'Marshall McLuhan revisited: 1960s Zeitgeist victim or pioneer postmodernist?', *Media, Culture and Society*, 13 (1991), pp. 71–90.

Kroker, Arthur, *Technology and the Canadian Mind: Innis, McLuhan, Grant*, New York: St Martin's Press, 1984.

Marchand, Pierre, *Marshall McLuhan the Medium and the Messenger*, New York: Tichenor and Fields, 1989.

Miller, Jonathan, *McLuhan*, London: Fontana, 1971.

Stevenson, Nick, *Understanding Media Cultures: Social theory and mass communication*, London: Sage, 1995.

Macpherson, Crawford Brough (1911–1987)

Crawford Brough Macpherson was born in Toronto. He graduated from the University of Toronto in 1933, and went on to study for an M.Sc. at the London School of Economics before returning to his native city to take up an academic position in 1935. With the exception of a few visiting appointments he remained in Toronto for the rest of his career. He was President of the Canadian Political Science Association from 1963–4.

As a political theorist, Macpherson might be termed something of a late developer. Appointed to the faculty of the University of Toronto in 1935, his first book *Democracy in Alberta*, did not appear until eighteen years later. In its pages Macpherson sets the pattern for his subsequent books by building on the work of **Marx**, in this case by transferring Marx's analysis of social democracy in nineteenth-century France to the social credit movement in twentieth-century Alberta. Macpherson argues that to explain the support gained by the Social Credit League in Alberta one has to see it in class terms. The party was a petty bourgeois movement with an ideology that reflected the difficult economic position of small farmers in the province by making the false assumption that the adverse effects of capitalism could be mitigated while retaining a capitalist economic structure. This argument is contentious, but whether or not its thesis is accepted the book provides a superb account of the relationship between a developing political theory and practical political campaigning. At Toronto Macpherson was promoted to the rank of professor.

Although *Democracy in Alberta* was well received it hardly set the academic world alight, and it was only with the publication of *The Political Theory of Possessive Individualism* in 1962 that Macpherson achieved his international reputation. In this analysis of seventeenth-century political thought Macpherson discovers the core western ideological justification of market society (i.e. capitalism) hidden in the work of Thomas Hobbes, the author of *Leviathan*, and, less controversially, in the work of John Locke. This highly influential analysis was followed by a series of books that focused on problems Macpherson believed he had identified with contemporary liberal democracy in the west, problems whose origins lay in the emergence of capitalist society in seventeenth-century England.

Macpherson's criticism of liberalism is tempered by his acknowledgement that the liberal objective of maximising freedom is a desirable one. The problem, according to Macpherson, is that the western liberal political system and the theories built in support of it have made it impossible to realise this objective. For the aims of liberals to be achieved, the liberal system must be transformed. Liberal democracy must become more like some of the systems that challenged the West; perhaps by learning from the Soviet bloc for example, or perhaps from Sekou Touré's 'democratic dictatorship' in Guinea. It is possible that Macpherson may have been a little hazy about exactly what was going on in these places so far from Toronto, but he had a firm grip on the theories of **Lenin** and Rousseau and on this basis categorised radical non-western regimes as either a Leninist vanguard or as the embodiment of the 'general will' of the population.

Macpherson's criticism of liberalism and his suggestions for how it might change is centred on his attack on liberal concepts of power, desire and property. Macpherson argues that from Hobbes onwards liberal theorists have tended to analyse power in terms of 'zero-sum' relations between people so that in order for some people to have *more* power, others must have *less*. According to Macpherson, Hobbes and subsequent liberal thinkers have assumed that the amount of natural power held by each individual is approximately equal. For one person to become more powerful than others, therefore, he or she must 'extract' power from other people. Macpherson is highly critical of this concept of power, which he sees as underlying exploitative work contracts drawn up by employers to extract power from their employees. He argues that western society is based on this extractive form of power-seeking and does not adequately recognise a second dimension of power: the power to realise one's capacities. If power is understood as the full development of human potential, then the increase in one person's power need not take place at the expense of the power of another. It is the increase in developmental power among citizens that Macpherson sees as one of the objectives of societies that challenge western liberalism.

Macpherson combines his criticism of the liberal concept of power with criticism of the liberal understanding of desire. Starting once again with Hobbes, Macpherson contends that just as liberal theorists assume a general human desire for unlimited extractive power, so they tend to assume that human beings have an unlimited desire to consume material things. If the desire to consume is assumed to be unlimited, Macpherson says, the result is a perpetual state of scarcity as human beings can never be satisfied; however much they have they always want more. Macpherson's response to this doctrine is that the desire to consume should not be unlimited as human beings have the capacity to be more than mere consumers.

The liberal defence of privately owned property is the third idea challenged by Macpherson, who argues that liberal theorists have failed to realise that *individual* property rights are not necessarily connected with the *exclusive* right to own property. A right not to be excluded from property, for example, is just as much an individual right as the right to exclude others from property. Further, the institution of private productive property (such as a factory) allows property owners to extract power from workers, who, without property of their own, are forced to enter into contracts to devote their natural power (i.e., their labour) to the benefit of their employers. Private property also allows for unlimited acquisitive desire as there is no limit on the amount of property that can be owned. The solution, argues Macpherson, is for property to be owned by the community.

Although Macpherson's stress on the development of human capacities and his criticism of the unlimited desire to consume has Hegelian and Platonic overtones, when these ideas are added to the attack on private property, it becomes plain that the key intellectual influence on Macpherson is Marx, especially in his early humanist writings. Extractive power is Macpherson's terminology for what Marx would call bourgeois exploitation, while Macpherson's argument that unlimited desire was a necessary idea in seventeenth-century England that has now outgrown its usefulness builds on Marx's distinction between capitalism at an early stage of 'primitive accumulation' (justified by the idea of unlimited desire), and 'advanced capitalism' in which technological and industrial development can potentially provide enough for everyone if consumption is kept within limits. Similarly, Macpherson's alternative vision of human beings developing their capacities and sharing property is drawn from Marx's brief comments on communism.

As a theorist with a keen interest in the workings of democracy, Macpherson tackles one of the most perplexing questions facing Marxists: why is it that despite the democratic voting system adopted by the west the capitalist economic structure has been maintained, with only limited support going to parties advocating fundamental change? Macpherson's answer is that most westerners, whether or not they occupy a privileged position in society, have adopted the ethics and aspirations of liberalism: they see themselves as unlimited consumers and they understand power in extractive terms. Accordingly, voters maintain the market system that perpetuates their priorities as 'possessive individualists', not realising that it limits their freedom to develop their capacities. In the 1960s and early 1970s, however, Macpherson confidently predicted that all this was going to change. Advocates of student power, and black power in the west were adding to the ferment in 'much of Eastern Europe and Asia and Africa' in forcefully putting forward demands for developmental power. Life in the Soviet bloc and in developing countries provided models of alternative forms of democracy. The west could not continue in the grip of its outmoded liberal ideology for much longer. Later Macpherson became rather more cautious in his pronouncements about the future.

Although Macpherson overstated the worldwide challenge to western liberalism, his moral critique of the west remains an argument to be reckoned with. His most influential idea, however, has been in his interpretation of Hobbes as a defender of market society. This view continues to hold great sway, not least because of Macpherson's Introduction to the highly popular Penguin edition of *Leviathan*. Countless students, baffled by Hobbes's unfamiliar language and punctuation, have turned with relief to Macpherson's clear and persuasive preface for enlightenment, and – according to Macpherson's critics – have been gently led astray. Aside from his analysis of Hobbes, Macpherson's reputation has gradually begun to fade as the radical academics schooled in the 1960s, for whom his work was always the most congenial, reach retirement age. At least one of Macpherson's books, however, is indisputably of enduring value, and ultimately he may be best remembered as the author of a finely written and highly informative account of the social credit movement in Alberta.

Main works

Democracy in Alberta, Toronto: Toronto University Press, 1953.

The Political Theory of Possessive Individualism, Oxford: Oxford University Press, 1962.

The Real World of Democracy, Oxford: Clarendon, 1966.

Introduction to Thomas Hobbes, *Leviathan*, London: Penguin, 1968.

Democratic Theory, London: Oxford University Press, 1973.

The Life and Times of Liberal Democracy, Oxford: Oxford University Press, 1977.

'The meaning of property' and 'Liberal-democracy and property', in C. B. Macpherson (ed.), *Property*, Toronto: Toronto University Press, 1978.

Burke, Oxford: Oxford University Press, 1980.

Further reading

Berlin, Isaiah, 'Hobbes, Locke and Professor Macpherson', *Political Quarterly*, 35 (1964), pp. 444–68, repr. in P. King (ed.), *Thomas Hobbes: Critical assessments*, Vol. I, London: Routledge, 1993.

Carmichael, J. D. C., 'C. B. Macpherson's "Hobbes": A critique', *Canadian Journal of Political Science*, 16 (1980), pp. 61–80, repr. in P. King (ed.), *Thomas Hobbes: Critical assessments*, Vol. I, London: Routledge, 1993.

Kontos, A. (ed.), *Powers, Possessions and Freedom: Essays in honour of C. B. Macpherson*, Toronto: Toronto University Press, 1979.

Miller, David, 'The Macpherson version', *Political Studies*, 30 (1982), pp. 120–7.

Ryan, Alan, 'Hobbes and individualism', in G. A. J. Rogers and A. Ryan (eds), *Perspectives on Thomas Hobbes*, Oxford: Clarendon, 1990.

Weinstein, Michael A., 'C. B. Macpherson: The roots of democracy and liberalism', in A. de Crespigny and K. Minogue (eds), *Contemporary Political Philosophers*, New York: Dodd Mead, 1975.

Glossary

Possessive individualism The theory that the individual is the 'owner' of her person and capabilities, and that she is free only if able to dispose of that person (say, on the labour market) as she wishes. Society is seen to consist of a series of market relations between individuals.

Mandel, Ernest (1923–1995)

Marxist economist, theorist and activist Ernest Mandel was born in Frankfurt but grew up in the Belgian port of Antwerp. At seventeen he joined a Trotskyist group there and was active in the resistance against the occupying Nazis, who captured him, but from whom he escaped on a number of occasions. After the war he studied in Paris and in Brussels where he later worked for a leading trade union. All the while he was concentrating a great deal of effort on building the Fourth International, a loose collection of fissiparous Trotskyist groups. By 1946 Mandel was a leading member and remained so for the rest of his life. His career as a writer spanned over forty years, as an activist even longer. He wrote over twenty full-length books, influential works on economics, political history and analysis, as well as dozens of pamphlets of political debate with other Trotskyists.

Mandel's central insights into the nature of capitalism can be found in his most celebrated work, the epic *Late Capitalism* (1975). In his introduction to Karl Marx: *Capital*, Vol. I (1976), he explains **Marx**'s purpose is 'to lay bare the "laws of motion" of capitalism'. This is Mandel's avowed intention in the forbiddingly long and dauntingly referenced *Late Capitalism*, where he wishes to use the 'laws' discovered by Marx to explain the nature of post-war capitalism. His more specific aim is to give a Marxist account of the post-economic war boom and the slump which followed it.

Mandel begins by gamely dismissing his own *Marxist Economic Theory* (1962, a work of nearly 800 pages, credited with reviving the study of Marxist economic writing), as merely 'descriptive'. Here he has other ambitions. Mandel offers a tripartite schema for the development of capitalism: (1) competitive capitalism, usually confined within national boundaries; (2) the era of imperialism, where overseas markets were sought to absorb overproduction; (3) late capitalism, the era of the great multinational corporations of 'big capital'. Mandel gives us two warnings. Firstly, 'late capitalism' is an unsatisfactory term, for it 'in no way suggests that capitalism has changed in essence'. It is not a new epoch, but (following Lenin) merely the latest stage of imperialist monopoly capitalism: an intensification of its inherent contradictions. Secondly, the term also has chronological rather than synthesising implications; elements of late capitalism were there in capitalism's mid-nineteenth-century development.

Mandel's schema would be familiar to other economists who would label these periods competitive, monopoly and state monopoly capitalism. He would, however, resist some of the implications of the theory of monopoly capitalism as it implies that capitalism can somehow be managed and could deliver social justice. Like Rosa **Luxemburg**, Mandel believes this is impossible because capitalism is a system that is crisis-ridden, most fundamentally by a crisis of underconsumption, whereby workers cannot buy back the goods they produce. Slumps are not unfortunate accidents, but a systematic shortfall in demand, and he takes great pains to show that 'there is a dialectical unity between periods of equilibrium and disequilibrium'. Gains made in boom-times are always at risk in times of recession.

Undergirding Mandel's 'stages' theory in *Late Capitalism* is his concept of the 'long wave' of capitalist development. He derives this from an interleaving of the work of Schumpeter on business cycles with the early soviet economist Kondratieff's study of long waves. Mandel's long waves last for about twenty-five years and are judged by the ups and downs of the average rate of profit. Late capitalism, the long post-war boom from 1945 to the early 1970s, was marked by a period of accelerated accumulation, in large part made possible by arms spending, where firms are guaranteed profits. Mandel calls this period 'a long wave with an undertone of expansion'. This would be followed by 'a long wave with an undertone of stagnation'.

The economic writings that follow *Late Capitalism* are of a piece with it; *The Second Slump* (1978) is a detailed reading and comparison of the predicted 1974–5 recession and its predecessor, the slump of 1929–31. *Long Waves of Capitalist Development* (1992), first given as a series of lectures and originally published in 1980, just before a mini-boom, pursues *Late Capitalism*'s argument into the 1980s and argues forcefully once again that capitalism cannot be effectively regulated. Mandel shows this by detailing his 'long waves' theory. He shows that while downturns (signified by a tendency of the rate of profit to fall) are economically based, upturns are generated by 'extra-economic factors' such as new discoveries of minerals and precious metals, new developments in technology and, crucially, in the level of class struggle. As a revolutionary, Mandel believed that however much workers were able to squeeze out of the system, only its destruction could bring a genuine form of emancipation from want. A large proportion of his writing and activity was spent arguing about the best way to achieve this.

Trotsky was central to Mandel's politics. He and the FI (latterly the USFI, The United Secretariat of the *Fourth International*) followed Trotsky's analysis of the Soviet Union. Trotsky saw that a rising bureaucracy in the Soviet Union under the Stalinist process of consolidating 'socialism in one country' had strangled the workers' state. Because of the gains of the October Revolution, notably state ownership of the means of production, he called the Soviet Union , in a famous phrase, a 'degenerated workers' state'. Furthermore, the Stalinist bureaucracy could only play a counter-revolutionary role in the fight for socialism. Just before the outbreak of the Second World War, Trotsky had predicted that neither Stalinism nor capitalism would survive it for long. He was wrong. After the war the Red

Army extended the Soviet Union's sphere of influence by making over much of Eastern Europe in its own image. On the back of a post-war boom, liberal democracy delivered major reforms and increased standards of living. These events presented Trotskyists who adhered to the letter of Trotsky's words with a dilemma. Although critical of the regimes in the eastern bloc, after much debate they called them 'deformed workers states' on the basis of the nationalisation of private property and saw them as 'transitional to socialism'. This meant, in the end, that a counter-revolutionary force (Stalinism) had achieved (deformed) workers' states, without the intervention of workers themselves. When these regimes collapsed between 1989 and 1991, many 'orthodox' Trotskyists were thrown into confusion.

Mandel himself, true to his instincts rather than some of his clever defences of orthodox Trotskyism, condemned the anti-Gorbachev coup in the former Soviet Union and hoped that the opening up of Russian society would make it possible to argue for revolutionary politics once again. However, the logic of his political position on the 'transitional socialist states' meant that their passing must be a profoundly demoralising political step back.

Mandel's work has been much-discussed by Marxist and non-Marxist economists, but possibly his greatest influence may lie in his short primer *Introduction to Marxist Economic Theory*, beloved of students, *stolen* from most libraries and reputed to have sold over half a million copies. He was a noted orator and enthusiastic supporter of insurrections. As a seventeen-year-old Marxist Jew, he escaped sentence to a Nazi prison camp by talking the guards taking him there into releasing him. He rejoiced as his own car went up in flames on the streets of Paris in 1968. Mandel's work gained fresh readers in the mid-1980s when 'late capitalism' was cited as the economic grounding for the 'cultural logic of capital', Fredric Jameson's influential description of postmodernism. While Jameson's periodisation has been questioned, he shares with Mandel a horror of the 'colonisation of consciousness' late capitalism brings. Those, however, who wish to link postmodernism with some form of post-industrialisation would find no favour with Mandel; he saw no sign of what is now called 'post industrial' society; only a 'generalised universal industrialisation . . . standardisation now penetrates into all sectors of our life'; an *intensification* of the contradictions of capitalism, and therefore the possibility of its implosion. For this reason, he remained a revolutionary socialist until he died.

Main works

Introduction to Marxist Economic Theory (1967), 2nd edn., New York: Pathfinder, 1973.

Marxist Economic Theory (1963), London: Merlin, 1968.

The Revolutionary Student Movement (1969), 2nd. edn., New York: Pathfinder, 1971.

Europe Versus America?, London: New Left, 1970.

Formation of the Economic Thought of Karl Marx, London: New Left, 1971.

Decline of the Dollar, New York: Monad, 1972.

Late Capitalism, London: New Left, 1975.

Karl Marx: Capital, 3 vols (intr. Ernest Mandel), Harmondsworth: Penguin, 1976–81.

From Class Society to Communism, London: Ink Links, 1977.

From Stalinism to Eurocommunism, London: New Left, 1978.

The Second Slump, London: New Left, 1978.

Revolutionary Marxism Today, London: New Left, 1979.

Trotsky, London: New Left, 1979.

Long Waves of Capitalist Development (1980), 2nd edn., London: Verso, 1992.

The Meaning of the Second World War, London: Verso, 1986.

Beyond Perestroika, London: Verso, 1989.

Dictatorship and Bureaucracy in the USSR, London: Pluto, 1990.

Power and Money, London: Verso, 1992.

The Place of Marxism in History, Atlantic Islands, NJ: Humanities Press, 1993.

Further reading

Callinicos, Alex, *Trotskyism*, Milton Keynes: Open University Press, 1990.

Cliff, Tony, 'All that glitters is not gold' (1947), in *Neither Washington nor Moscow*, London: Bookmarks, 1982.

Frank, Pierre, *The Fourth International*, London: Ink Links, 1979.

Mattick, Paul, *Economic Crisis and Crisis Theory*, London: Merlin, 1981.

Molyneux, John, *Leon Trotsky's Theory of Revolution*, Brighton: Harvester Wheatsheaf, 1981.

Clarification of Mandel's position within the USFI on Stalinism and the legacy of Trotsky, along with forthright disagreements, can be found in *International Socialism*, 2:49 (Winter 1990); 2:56 (Autumn 1992); 2:57 (Winter 1992).

Mannheim, Karl (1893–1947)

Karl Mannheim was born in Budapest and studied at the universities of Budapest, Berlin, Paris and Freiburg. During the brief period of the Hungarian Soviet in 1919 he was offered a position by his friend and teacher Georg **Lukács**. After the collapse of the government Mannheim moved to Germany where he held academic posts at Heidelberg and then Frankfurt. As a recently naturalized citizen and a Jew, he was suspended from his position by one of the first National Socialist enactments in 1933. Invited to Britain by Harold **Laski**, he spent the next ten years as a lecturer at the London School of Economics. In the middle of the war he was appointed to the new professorship in the sociology of education at the University of London, where he spent his last years.

Karl Mannheim was the last and is the least appreciated of the founding fathers of classical sociology. As one of the founders of the sociology of knowledge, Mannheim developed a sophisticated analysis of the role of intellectuals and of the role and history of ideology. Although he wrote widely on sociological and political topics he returned again and again to the problems of knowledge and of ideology. His analyses are always informed by a sense of the mission of intellectuals, a mission which he saw as being that of shaping a more responsible, and more scientific, mode of politics. Like his teacher and close associate, Georg Lukács, Mannheim was strongly influenced by the philosophical ideas of Georg **Simmel**. This influence is most clear in his 1918 essay 'Soul and Culture'.

A self-conscious commitment to liberalism informed Mannheim's sociological work from his early days in Hungary. In 1925 he submitted a *Habilitationsschrift* at the University of Heidelberg on the history of conservatism. In abbreviated form, this was published as 'Conservative thought'. Although this text is often read as an empirical study of a particular pattern of political belief, the full text reveals that Mannheim had already conceived the grander ambition of a properly scientific investigation into the nature of political knowledge as well as of mere belief.

Mannheim's most influential work, *Ideology and Utopia* (1929, trans. 1936) extends the particular concerns of his study of conservatism into an ambitious programme for the study of the 'structures of knowledge' and an investigation of the relation between such structures and the social worlds with which they remained involved. Mannheim proposed a sociological perspective in which all mental structures (with the exception of the natural sciences) are context-dependent. Like **Marx** in the *German Ideology*, he wished to understand better the 'existentiality' of thought, its rootedness in social and material relations. Unlike Marx, he declared that such a perspective had to cover not only ideology, characterised by falsity, but also all forms of social knowledge. For Mannheim the *Seins-verbundenheit* (existential boundedness) of human knowledge is rooted in the social existence of competing human groups. But the nature of that connection of human knowledge to social existence is highly variable, and its exact character is to be left open to empirical research. When investigating world-views and ideologies one needs to take into account not only classes but also status groups, generations, military, cultural, political and economic elites, professions and many other groupings.

Mannheim's ambitious attempt to promote a comprehensive sociological analysis of the structures of knowledge was treated with suspicion by the Marxists and neo-Marxists of the Frankfurt Institute of Social Research, such as **Adorno**. Critical Theory viewed the rising popularity of the sociology of knowledge as a neutralisation and a betrayal of the Marxist inspiration. During his few years in Frankfurt prior to 1933 the rivalry between the two intellectual groupings – Mannheim's seminar (where Norbert **Elias** was his assistant) and Horkheimer's Institute for Social Research – was intense.

The determination to see all social knowledge in relation to material and social existence exposed Mannheim to the charge of relativism, a charge which he tirelessly rebutted. For him, the problem of relativism only arises when one takes an ahistorical viewpoint, comparing other forms of knowledge with an idealised view of the kind of knowledge produced by the (detached) natural sciences. For Mannheim the fact that the unfolding of the historical process is cognitively accessible only from various perspectives is simply an aspect of its 'truth'. Far from admitting the charge of relativism, therefore, Mannheim claimed that his brand of 'relationism' prepared the ground for a new comprehensive perspective capable of transcending heretofore fragmented and partial social and political perspectives. He conceived of sociology as a science of synthesis. Throughout his life sociology represented the 'inescapable ground of self-validation' in the modern world. It aimed at a 'complete theory of the totality of the social process'. It was 'in some sense the master science of political practice' and involved a 'total mobilisation of our intellectual and spiritual resources'.

Such a commitment entailed a critique of the 'value-free' conception of sociology of knowledge. From first to last, Mannheim proposed that intellectuals had a special responsibility and a particular mission. In *Ideology and Utopia* he indicated two main courses of political action which could be taken by intellectuals: (1) 'a largely voluntary affiliation with one or other of the various antagonistic classes'; (2) 'scrutiny of their own social moorings and the quest for the fulfilment of their mission as the predestined advocate of the intellectual interests of the whole'.

The tension between involvement and detachment is a constant theme in Mannheim's treatment of intellectuals. Although he recognised that sociology emerged at least in part as the working class came to assert its own sense of itself, he still saw a crucial role for a 'socially unattached' (free-floating) intelligentsia. He stressed the opportunities for open-mindedness, for empathy and ecumenical mediation between competing social groups. He also stressed the levelling effects of educational experience. But he did not confront the possibility that cultural participation itself, while 'loosening up' the established class structure and distancing intellectuals from their economic class moorings, may coagulate into new forms of cultural property which engender new class-like interests and novel forms of social closure and inequality.

On his arrival in Britain, Mannheim soon became enamoured of Anglo-Saxon pragmatism. This enthusiasm had been foreshadowed by more pragmatic and practical orientation already evident in his writings prior to his emigration. After the war, Mannheim became an apostle of the spirit of post-war social reconstruction. To Mannheim it seemed as if the new mood of reconstruction offered a new role for democratic social planning and hence a more central role for sociology. He also explained that education must play a central role in shaping a society free of its old, deforming conflicts. These themes had been spelt out in *Man and Society in an Age of Reconstruction* (1935), and were amplified in *Diagnosis of our Time* (1943) and in the essays posthumously published as *Freedom, Power and Democratic Planning* (1959).

In his last years Mannheim attempted to make his own work more accessible to an English-speaking audience and to make a personal adjustment to the more empirical and pragmatic temper of English and American intellectual life. But he felt constrained by the lack of self-awareness about ideology in English thinking and by the widespread inability to think in terms of comprehensive designs.

For the publishers Routledge and Kegan Paul, Mannheim founded the 'International Library of Sociology and Social Reconstruction' which aimed to foster an international community of intellectuals. Mannheim was taken up by the 'Moot' circle of (mainly) Christian socialist intellectuals formed under the initiative of Joseph H. Oldham. The circle included Michael Polany, John Middleton Murray and T. S. Eliot, who was particularly influenced by Mannheim's political ideas. Mannheim envisaged a new type of party system where the right to criticise would be as strongly developed as the individuals responsibility for the whole, and with which would go a new form of education and a new sociologically informed morality. To many a pragmatic Englishman this sounded like rather too authoritarian a form of democracy and gave rise to the misleading image of the late Mannheim as a 'utopian of the right'.

Mannheim established no school. His preferred literary form was the essay and, collectively, his works contain many inconsistencies and, in places, a certain vagueness. He himself was aware of these characteristics but appealed to his readers to see in them a sign of the provisional and experimental nature of his thinking. Of all the classical sociologists, Mannheim is the one whose biography and mode of questioning connect him most directly to the problems of our own time. Although he formulated his politics in relation to a historical situation from which we feel increasingly distant, the questions he posed in the diagnosis of conflict, on the role of the intelligentsia, on education and on democratic planning remain as pertinent as ever.

Main works

Ideology and Utopia (1929), London: Routledge and Kegan Paul, 1936.

Man and Society in an Age of Reconstruction (1935), London: Routledge and Kegan Paul, 1940.

Diagnosis of Our Time, London: Routledge and Kegan Paul, 1943.

Freedom, Power and Democratic Planning, London: Routledge and Kegan Paul, 1950.

Essays on the Sociology of Knowledge, London: Routledge and Kegan Paul, 1952.

Essays on Sociology and Social Psychology, London: Routledge and Kegan Paul, 1953.

Essays on the Sociology of Culture, London: Routledge and Kegan Paul, 1956.

Structures of Thinking, London: Routledge and Kegan Paul, 1986.

Conservatism, London: Routledge and Kegan Paul, 1986.

Further reading

Coser, Lewis, *Masters of Sociological Thought*, New York: Harcourt Brace, 1971.

Kettler, D. *et al.*, *Karl Mannheim*, London, Ellis Horwood and Tavistock, 1984.

Loader, C. *The Intellectual Development of Karl Mannheim*, Cambridge: Cambridge University Press, 1985.

Remmling, Gunter W., *The Sociology of Karl Mannheim*, London: Routledge & Kegan Paul, 1975.

Simonds, A. P., *Karl Mannheim's Sociology of Knowledge*, Oxford: Clarendon, 1978.

Wolff, Kurt H., *From Karl Mannheim*, London: Oxford University Press, 1971.

Mao Tse-tung (Mao Zhedong) (1893–1976)

Mao was born into a peasant family in the village of Shaoashan (Hunan province). Against his father's wishes, he continued his education beyond primary level, entering the teacher training school in Changsha in 1913. From Changsha he went to Beijing (1918) to work in the University Library. While there he not only began to read Marxist texts in Chinese, but also fell under the influence of the founders of the Chinese Communist Party (CCP), notably Li Ta-chao (Li Dazhao). Mao was present when, in the summer of 1921, the first meeting of the CCP took place in Shanghai, and he worked ceaselessly for the Party from that time on. For many years, the CCP was hounded and its members massacred by the Kuomintang (Guomindang) under Chiang Kai-Shek (Jiang Jieshi). It was during the fifth of Chiang's campaigns in the period 1930–5 that Mao abandoned his base in Kiangsi (Jiangxi) and set off for Northern Shensi (Shaanxi), some 6,000 miles away, on what is now known as the Long March. By January 1935, Mao had become the acknowledged leader of the CCP. The period 1936–49 was one of almost constant fighting. Initially, Mao's forces allied with the Kuomintang to fight their common enemy, the Japanese (1937–45); then, once the Japanese were defeated, two years of civil war followed (1947–9), ending with Chiang's withdrawal to Taiwan. On 1 October 1949, Mao proclaimed the People's Republic of China, and set about modernising the country on communist lines. The chief features and events of Mao's rule – the Great Leap Forward, the

Cultural Revolution, the Lin Piao (Lin Biao) affair, and relations with the superpowers – have all been widely discussed. Mao died in September 1976 in Beijing.

Mao's political philosophy is a modified version of the dialectical materialism of **Marx** and **Lenin**, and he takes over most of the main ideological pillars of this world-view. Yet Mao was no mere disciple of Marx, and he was quite ready to put forward his own thought where it seemed to him appropriate. Underlying all Mao's thought, however abstract, is a very sharp grip on political reality: he saw no reason to assume that the type of revolutionary politics and ideology which had worked in Russia would work without modification in the appreciably different circumstances of China. No two societies are quite alike, and none is static, and any politician who ignores these large facts, Mao argues, is simply courting disaster. It is this principle, a constant in Mao's thought, which made him unwilling to regard even the most fundamental Marxist–Leninist beliefs as unquestionable.

His analysis of the concept of contradiction is both central to Mao's thought and typical of the way in which he was willing to modify previous Marxist doctrine. In Mao, contradiction is in effect the most fundamental of all the properties of reality at all levels of complexity and organisation, from the laws of physics to complex social organisations, from growth in plants and animals to change in society, and is the explanation of change in both quantity and quality. Put another way, to understand the nature of any aspect of reality is to understand its internal contradictions, for these contradictions constitute the nature of the phenomenon concerned and all change of any kind is to be understood as the result of the working out of internal contradictions.

Mao next introduces the concepts of principal contradiction and the principal aspect of a contradiction. Though it is possible in theory to consider contradictions singly, in the real world situations are rarely analysable into a single tension but rather are almost invariably made up of two or more contradictions, of which one will be more important than the rest. This last is the principal contradiction, and is the one we need to identify, since it is the chief determinant of the situation in question. Again, within an individual contradiction, one of the elements will be of greater importance than the other, and this Mao calls the principal aspect of the contradiction. Once again, this principal aspect is the one we should seek to identify, since it is the major determinant of the nature of the contradiction. However, Mao stresses that change at all levels of reality is constant, and from this he draws the consequence that the role of principal and subordinate aspects of a contradiction is not fixed. The principal aspect can become the subordinate and vice versa, and when this happens, it follows from Mao's principles that the nature of the individual or situation of which the contradiction is constitutive will change also. This line of thought leads Mao to one of his most significant divergences from orthodox Marxism–Leninism. In the latter, there is one relationship which is fixed and invariant, that between the economic base (*Unterbau*) and the superstructure (*Oberbau*), i.e. the system of laws, religion, education, philosophy and so on obtaining in a given society at a given time. In classical Marxism, the superstructure is always determined by the economic base, never the other way around, and here Mao disagrees. The base–superstructure contradiction is one like any other, he argues, and it can occur that the superstructure becomes the principal aspect. When features of the superstructure (e.g. politics) obstruct economic development, then the superstructure is the dominant aspect of the contradiction.

Further, Mao draws a distinction between antagonistic and non-antagonistic contradictions. For example, contradiction between the exploiting and the exploited classes exists in all forms of society – slave-owning, feudal or capitalist – but for most of the time this contradiction is not antagonistic. However, it follows from the principle of the constancy of change that the nature of these contradictions may alter, the non-antagonistic becoming antagonistic and vice versa. Hence, at a certain point in history the tensions between exploiters and exploited will develop into open antagonism and then into revolution. Moreover, Mao accepts that contradictions will still exist under socialism, and notes their presence between different factions within the CCP, notably between those he calls 'die hards' (those unable to modify dialectical materialist dogma to suit present political circumstances) and those he calls 'Leftists' (those unable to grasp that not all desirable change can be brought about at once and who are unrealistically impatient). He stresses, however, that the contradictions within a socialist system are non-antagonistic, and should be dealt with in an appropriate way.

Another respect in which Mao, in theory at least, departs from the Russian model of communist practice is in respect of his attitude to those aspects of the superstructure which make up the culture of a society, and to science. Lenin had argued that all aspects of culture should be manipulated to serve political ends, one of the results of which was the set of aesthetic prescriptions or rules for artists known as Soviet Realism. Mao argued by contrast that in these areas differences are best settled by free discussion and debate and by practical work. He regarded administrative intervention as counterproductive to the growth of both art and science: this is the policy of 'letting a hundred flowers blossom and a hundred schools of thought contend'.

The relation of this philosophy to Mao's political practice is problematic. In many respects, the reality of Mao's China was depressingly similar to that of Stalin's Russia. Though nominally a people's democracy, Mao effectively ruled China as a dictator, using the CCP as his propaganda machine, and he made use of all the apparatus of the totalitarian state – secret police, mass arrests, forced labour, brainwashing, liquidation of all opposition and the like. Many of the 'hundred flowers', those who were dissatisfied with the way in which Chinese communism was developing and made their views known, ended their days as suicides or in the labour camps as counter-revolutionaries. Again, Mao's 'Great Proletarian Cultural Movement', the Cultural Revolution, went badly wrong, with ill-directed violence being visited on intellectuals and scientists whose gifts Mao had previously blessed as vital to the modernisation of China. On a more general level, although Mao paid lip-service to the internationalist vision of Marx, his practical politics were nationalist. Here again he resembles Stalin, who had taken care to eliminate the internationalist Trotsky.

Mao's influence on both the theory and practice of state socialism in China has been, manifestly, very great indeed, though successor regimes have found it necessary to reverse the most disastrous of his policies. As a theorist, Mao was a model for third world Marxists in states seeking to overthrow colonial rule. He showed very clearly that Marxism could be, and indeed had to be, adaptable to suit very different social conditions.

Main works

Selected Works of Mao Tse-tung, 5 vols, Beijing: Foreign Languages Press, 1965–77.

Mao's political philosophy is contained chiefly in the following works:

> *On Practice* (1937).
>
> *On Contradiction* (1937).
>
> *On New Democracy* (1940).
>
> *On the Correct Handling of Contradictions among the People* (1957).
>
> *Where do Correct Ideas Come From?* (1963).

Further reading

Chin, S. S. K., *The Thought of Mao Tse-tung: Form and content*, Hong Kong: University of Hong Kong, 1979.

Chou, E., *Mao Tse-tung: The man and the myth*, New York: Stein and Day, 1982.

Cohen, A. A., *The Communism of Mao Tse-tung*, Chicago: Chicago University Press, 1971.

Schram, S., *Mao Tse-tung*, Harmondsworth: Penguin, 1966.

Soo, F. Y. R., *Mao Tse-tung's Theory of Dialectic*, Dordrecht: Reidel, 1981.

Wylie, R. F., *The Emergence of Maoism*, Stanford: Stanford University Press, 1980.

Marcuse, Herbert (1898–1979)

A widely renowned German philosopher and social theorist, Marcuse joined the Social Democratic Party and, as a political activist, was elected to represent the Soldiers' Council in a working-class neighbourhood of Berlin during the abortive German Revolution of 1918–19. Subsequently he studied philosophy at the Universities of Berlin and Freiburg (at the latter with the German philosophers **Heidegger** and Husserl). He became a member of the interdisciplinary Frankfurt Institute for Social Research and emigrated, with other members, to the United States, following the Nazis coming to power in 1933. Marcuse continued his association with the Institute which was eventually rehoused at Columbia University. Between 1942 and 1950 he worked as a researcher for the American government with other anti-fascist intellectuals. Subsequently he held university posts at Columbia, Harvard, Brandeis and California, before returning to Germany in 1966 where he was appointed to an honorary professorship at the Free University of Berlin.

A prolific writer, Marcuse's intellectual interests covered all the current debates of his generation: the rise of psychoanalysis, phenomenology, existentialism and the legacy of classical German philosophy, art and revolution, the nature of technological change, transformation of the capitalist mode of production, the nature of the individual and the problems of socialism, Marxism and the critical theory of society. It has been argued that what gave unity to all these topics was Marcuse's dedication to the task of developing critical theory to overcome the deficiencies of traditional Marxism. Marcuse wrote one of the first reviews of **Marx**'s *Economic and Philosophical Manuscripts* when they were discovered in the 1930s. Many of Marcuse's later writings were rooted in the humanistic concerns of the 'early Marx', especially the problem of alienated labour in capitalist societies. In *Eros and Civilization*, Marcuse attempted to reconcile Freudian psychoanalysis with Marxism by revealing the linkage between economic exploitation and psychic oppression in capitalist societies. As a result, he committed himself to developing a new emancipatory political theory that would negate repressive domination.

This project continued in his famous and most influential book *One-Dimensional Man* (1964) which provided a root and branch critique of capitalism. Affluent mass technological societies, it argued, were totally controlled and manipulated. In societies based upon mass production and mass distribution, the individual worker had become merely a consumer of its commodities and the entire 'commodity way of life'. Modern capitalism had created 'false needs' and 'false consciousness' geared to consumption of commodities: it locked 'one-dimensional man' into the 'one-dimensional society' which produced these needs:

> The people recognize themselves in their commodities; they find their soul in their automobile, hi-fi set, split-level home, kitchen equipment. The very mechanism which ties the individual to his society has changed, and social control is anchored in the new needs which it has produced.

But most important of all, the pressures of consumerism had led to the total integration of the working class into the capitalist system. Its political parties and trade unions had become thoroughly bureaucratised and the power of 'negative thinking' or critical reflection had rapidly declined. The working class was no longer a potentially subversive force capable of bringing about revolutionary change. As a result, rather than looking to the workers as the revolutionary vanguard, Marcuse put his faith in an alliance between radical intellectuals and those groups not yet integrated into one-dimensional society, the socially marginalised, 'the substratum of the outcasts and outsiders, the exploited and persecuted of other races and other colours, the unemployed and the unemployable.' These were the people whose standards of living demanded the ending of 'intolerable conditions and institutions' and whose resistance to one-dimensional society would not be diverted by the system. Their opposition was revolutionary even if their consciousness was not. In Marcuse's scheme, a special place in 'the syndrome of revolutionary potential' was assigned to the 'oppositional intelligentsia', which included students.

However, with the emergence of worldwide mass protest movements in 1968, especially in France, Marcuse explicitly rejected his earlier view that the 'oppositional intelligentsia', rather than the working class, were the agents of revolutionary change. Students were at best catalysts of change: 'A real radical change is unimaginable without the reactivation of the masses.'

It was not only repressive capitalist societies that were at fault. In his *Soviet Marxism* (1958) he argued that Marxism in Stalin's Russia had been 'derevolutionised', had lost its function as the ideology of revolution and instead had become the ideological prop for the authoritarian political system and its bureaucratic ruling class. The Stalinist state was characterised by a totalitarian administration based upon terror with 'the growth of the dictatorship not of but over the proletariat and peasantry'. In fact, the Soviet Union represented a total distortion of Marx's original idea of socialism.

In May 1968 Marcuse's emphasis on the power of negative thinking, of critical thought and his vision of total human emancipation and the creation of a 'non-repressive civilisation' appealed to student radicals of the international New Left. Marcuse was regarded as their inspirational intellectual leader. One of the slogans on the banners carried by worker and student demonstrators in Paris was the 'three Ms': Marx, **Mao** and Marcuse. Marcuse enthusiastically supported the students, whom he saw as being opposed to the inhuman pressure of the system which was turning everything into a commodity.

Marcuse was not without his critics. The philosopher Alasdair **Mac-Intyre** asserted that 'almost all of Marcuse's key positions are false' and that his generalisations were based upon 'the total absence of any account of contemporary social structure' (Pippin *et al.*, 1988). Featherstone criticised his portrayal of modern consumerism: it falsely assumed that consumers were completely passive, uncritically responding to corporate advertising. But any weaknesses in Marcuse's writings should not detract from his intellectual legacy. This survived in the writings of later critical theorists, for the Frankfurt School still remains an important force in academic circles. An assessment of the continuing relevance of his political project was made by the American philosopher Douglas Kellner: 'The legacy of the 1960s, of which Marcuse was a vital part, lives on, and the Great Refusal is still practised by oppositional groups and individuals who refuse to conform to existing oppression and domination' (Kellner, 1984).

Main works

Eros and Civilization, Boston, MA: Beacon, 1955.

Reason and Revolution: Hegel and the rise of social theory, London: Routledge and Kegan Paul, 1955.

Soviet Marxism: A critical analysis, New York: Columbia University Press, 1958.

One-Dimensional Man: Studies in the ideology of advanced industrial society, Boston, MA: Beacon, 1964.

Counter-Revolution and Revolt, London: Allen Lane, 1972.

An Essay on Liberation, Harmondsworth: Pelican, 1972.

The Aesthetic Dimension, Boston: Beacon, 1978.

Further reading

Geoghegan, V., *Reason and Eros: The social theory of Herbert Marcuse*, London: Pluto, 1981.

Katz, B., *Herbert Marcuse and the Art of Liberation: An intellectual biography*, London: Verso, 1982.

Kellner, D., *Herbert Marcuse and the Crisis of Marxism*, London: Macmillan, 1984.

MacIntyre, A., *Marcuse*, London: Fontana, 1970.

Pippin, R., A. Feenberg and C. Webel (eds), *Marcuse: Critical theory and the promise of utopia*, London: Macmillan, 1988.

Wiggershaus, R., *The Frankfurt School: Its history, theories and political significance*, Cambridge, Polity, 1955.

Marshall, Thomas Humphrey (1893–1981)

T. H. Marshall was a British sociologist (professor at the London School of Economics and later on the staff of UNESCO) whose analysis of citizenship in the emergent welfare states after 1945 helped to shape and define the disciplines of social policy and social administration. His approach remains a starting point for many of those seeking to develop a broader understanding of social citizenship.

At the heart of Marshall's analysis was his identification of fundamental social tensions within capitalism, which he saw as an inherently unequal system while acknowledging that inequality was a necessary price to pay for the operation of a successful market economy. In contrast to Marxist approaches, Marshall did not identify the fundamental issue as the (necessary) emergence of conflict between classes. Instead, he stressed the gradual extension of basic rights (civil, political and social) won within states for citizens. He identified a progressive growth of what he called citizenship which paralleled the development of capitalism and the increased social divisions (class inequality) which accompanied it. Citizenship, he argued, offers the possibility of 'class abatement'.

Marshall's notion of citizenship is a powerful one. He defined it in terms which link civil, political and social rights. The first of these relates to individual freedom (and includes such aspects as freedom of speech); the second embodies the right to participation in public power (as politician, or, more frequently, as elector); the third relates to economic and social welfare. Each is linked to specific state institutions: civil rights to the courts and judiciary; political rights to government (local and parliamentary); social rights to the health service, education institutions and social services.

Marshall highlighted the way in which these rights developed over time, noting that social rights were developed later than the other two: for example, the factory codes and state elementary education only emerged in Britain at the end of the nineteenth century. Although the emphasis in Marshall's argument was placed on rights, his conception of citizenship also implies the existence of obligations. Citizens have the responsibility to obey the law, participate in democracy and contribute to the common purse; the provision of elementary education by the state was associated, as education became compulsory, with a duty on children to attend.

The particular ways that these sets of rights came together helped to define the nature of the welfare regimes which emerged in many 'western' countries in the first half of the twentieth century, and were consolidated in the twenty-five years after 1945. In contrast to neo-liberal thinkers and theorists of the New Right, who concentrate on the first two of Marshall's 'rights' (particularly the first, which may be understood as 'negative' freedom – that is, freedom from interference by others, in particular the state), Marshall himself explicitly incorporates social rights into citizenship. The key point for him is the interdependence between these aspects of social life.

Marshall himself did not like the term 'welfare state'. As an alternative, he developed the term 'welfare capitalism'. This is a rather more pluralistic conception, in which the object of consensus is a welfare *society* rather than a welfare *state*: a welfare society is one in which the achievement of social and individual welfare is given a high priority. Within such a society, 'welfare' is not defined simply in terms of providing a safety net for social and economic casualties, but implies the existence of a network of agencies and institutions embedded in the social structure to ensure that appropriate benefits and services are available to all. Marshall was committed to a mixed economy operating on the basis of economic markets (with some government oversight) alongside the provision of adequate social security, health and welfare.

It was on this basis, he argued, that modern societies are able to sustain the allegiance of their citizens, despite the inequality inherent within market capitalism. The inequality of the social class system might be acceptable provided the equality of citizenship was recognised. Marshall stressed the importance of equal rights and duties for full members of the community (citizens) existing alongside forms of economic and social inequality. Citizenship was a crucial element in helping to legitimise the existence of social inequality, since full membership of the community might be achieved through shared citizenship, rather than economic equalisation. However poor an individual citizen might be, he or she would have equal civil, political and social rights with those who were more wealthy – access to a 'universal' system of welfare services and benefits.

Marshall's approach sometimes appears to take for granted the inevitable progress of human society towards 'welfare capitalism' and social citizenship. Although the extent of the recent changes remains a matter of controversy, 1980s and 1990s approaches which have sought to reverse the commitment to a comprehensive welfare system (and seem to have encouraged the growth of a welfare underclass, i.e. one effectively excluded from the forms of citizenship Marshall identified) must call his analysis into question. Instead of flowing relatively unproblematically from the unfolding of history, Marshall's approach to citizenship has to be seen as contested.

Despite its breadth and clarity, Marshall's analysis tends to underplay two aspects of citizenship on which more recent authors (such as Maurice Roche and Raymond Plant) have placed more emphasis. His stress on citizen rights means that he pays less attention to the duties and responsibilities associated with citizenship; and his stress on 'social' aspects of citizenship also means insufficient attention to the political aspects. Citizenship becomes a remarkably uncontested concept, where each citizen has a recognised place, associated with rights but with little expectation of conflict over the ways in which the welfare systems supporting those rights are to be funded.

The approach assumes a homogeneous model of citizenship, which fails to acknowledge some important tensions and differences between citizens. 'Citizenship' itself becomes a universal category within which some groups would hardly recognise their experience. For example, the role played by many 'black' and 'Asian' people within the British welfare state is difficult to reconcile with Marshall's broad notion of citizenship, even though some of them have been employed within the welfare institutions that underpin the social rights of others. Similarly, though Marshall did highlight the significance of women's suffrage, he failed to recognise that access to social rights depended on their husbands, male partners or children. The formal structures of welfare citizenship were built around what has been called a 'male breadwinner' model, which leaves women in a secondary and subordinate role.

Main works

Citizenship and Social Class and Other Essays, Cambridge: Cambridge University Press, 1950.

'Value problems of welfare capitalism', *Journal of Social Policy*, 1 (1972) pp. 15–32.

Social Policy in the Twentieth Century (1965), 4th edn, London: Hutchinson, 1975.

The Right to Welfare and Other Essays, London: Heinemann, 1981.

Further reading

Barbalet, J. M., *Citizenship, Rights, Struggle and Class Inequality*, Buckingham: Open University Press, 1988.

Giddens, A., *Profiles and Critiques in Social Theory*, London: Macmillan, 1982.

Pateman, C., *The Disorder of Women*, Cambridge: Polity, 1989.

Pierson, C., *Beyond the Welfare State: The new political economy of welfare*, Cambridge: Polity, 1991.

Plant, R., *Citizenship, Rights and Socialism*, London: Fabian Society, 1988.

Roche, Maurice, *Rethinking Citizenship: Welfare, ideology and change in modern society*, Cambridge: Polity, 1992.

Marx, Karl (1818–1883)

Marx was born of Jewish parents in Trier, in what was then the Rhineland province of Prussia. His father was a successful liberal lawyer who had been baptised when his job was threatened by anti-Jewish laws. Marx studied philosophy, history and law at the universities of Bonn and Berlin and gained his Ph.D. from the University of Jena. Disappointed in his hopes of an academic career because of his radicalism, he turned to journalism. He was briefly editor of the *Rheinische Zeitung* until it was suppressed by the Prussian censorship. In 1843 he moved to Paris where he began a lifelong friendship and collaboration with Frederick Engels. In 1847 Marx and Engels helped found the Communist League, for which they wrote the *Communist Manifesto* (1848). During 1848, a year of revolutionary upheaval throughout Europe, Marx was in Cologne editing a radical newspaper. After the failure of the 1848 revolution, the paper was closed and Marx was expelled from Germany. He made his way eventually to London, where he settled in exile for the rest of his life.

In London he lived in poverty by occasional journalism and with financial assistance from Engels (a partner in the family cotton firm in Manchester). Using the British Museum library, he devoted himself to producing a systematic theory of capitalism, embodied in the volumes of his major work, *Capital*. The first volume was published in 1867; the remaining two volumes were assembled by Engels from notes after Marx's death. Manuscript notes for a fourth volume were later edited by Karl Kautsky and published as *Theories of Surplus Value* (1905–10). Although Marx devoted much of his later life to scholarship, he was Secretary of the International Working Men's Association (the 'First International'), in which he played a leading role up to his death in 1883.

Marx started as a member of the radical 'young Hegelian' school of social criticism which emerged after Hegel's death in 1832 and contributed to the ideas leading to the revolutions of 1848. Initially influenced by Feuerbach, Marx pursued a critique of Hegel's political philosophy from a left-Hegelian, radical humanist perspective. However, he came to appreciate that legal relations and forms of state are rooted in material and economic conditions. Engels was reaching similar conclusions from his experiences in Manchester. The two collaborated in works attacking their young Hegelian contemporaries (Feuerbach, Stirner, Ruge, Bruno Bauer) for their idealism: *The Holy Family* (1844), *The German Ideology* (1845). From this emerged the 'materialist theory of history', the theory which, Marx says, served as the 'guiding thread' for all his studies. Some writers (e.g. **Althusser**) draw a sharp distinction between Marx's early 'philosophical' work, up to 1845, and his later, materialist work, with its increasing focus on economics; but most see no radical discontinuity.

The materialist theory of history starts from the proposition that human beings are creatures of need, and hence that the material side of human life – physical needs and economic action to satisfy them – is primary and basic. This may seem obvious to the point of triviality; but it is not so. For much history and social philosophy prior to Marx had focused on the actions of states and rulers and paid virtually no attention to economic developments. According to Marx, every society is composed of certain 'forces of production' (tools, machinery and labour to operate them) with which are associated particular social 'relations of production' (property relations, division of labour). These together constitute the material 'base' of society, upon which arises a superstructure' of political and legal institutions, and ideological forms (art, religion and philosophy): 'It is not the consciousness of men that determines their being, but, on the contrary, their social beings which determines their consciousness' (Preface to the *Contribution to the Critique of Political Economy*).

Marx divides history into a number of different epochs or modes of production: the slave-based society of the ancient world, feudalism and capitalism. At any given historical period the relations of production provide the social framework for economic development. But the developing forces of production give rise to increasing conflicts which are reflected as class struggles. 'From forms of development of the productive forces, these relations turn into their fetters. Then begins an epoch of social revolution' which transforms 'the entire immense superstructure'. Economic development creates new forms of social relation and new social groups and classes. The proletariat (the industrial working class) is a product of capitalism. Marx and Engels trace its development in the brilliant opening chapter of *The Communist Manifesto*. They show how industrialisation concentrates working people in factories and cities, and how as a result the working class develops from being an unorganised and unconscious mass (a class 'in itself') to an organised and conscious political force, a class 'for itself' – a class which is destined to be the 'gravedigger' of capitalism and inaugurate a new mode of production: socialism.

For Marx, even capitalist society is not a mere collection of separate, competing individuals. All historical societies are divided into competing *classes*, defined structurally and economically by their relationship to the means of production. Thus the bourgeoisie are the owners, and the proletariat the non-owners, of the means of production. Marx believed that capitalist society was increasingly becoming polarised into 'two great opposed camps' of the bourgeoisie and proletariat. At least in the advanced industrial societies, history has not borne this out; though arguably such polarisation has occurred on an international scale. The character of the social classes of industrial society has changed considerably since Marx wrote and there has been much debate about whether they can still be understood in Marx's terms. Nevertheless, an understanding of society in terms of social class remains indispensable to modern social thought.

For Marx, the state is essentially an instrument of class rule. It does not represent the interests of 'the people' or a common 'general will' (Rousseau), nor stand above the clash of class interests (as liberal philosophers like Hobbes and Locke maintain). The state in capitalist society is a bourgeois state: 'a committee for managing the common affairs of the whole bourgeoisie'. Its standards of justice, democracy and right are bourgeois standards. Though there are forms of political democracy in which different parties represent different class interests (including the working class), liberal political institutions function within the constraints of the capitalist system. If these are radically challenged then democracy will be suspended.

Marx believed that capitalism's inherent processes of development are destined to give rise to its own dissolution: to a revolution which will result in the creation of a socialist society. The conquest of political power by the working class will lead, in the first instance, to the creation of a socialist state – where the working class is the ruling class and the interests of the working class are served. The 'dictatorship of the proletariat' will replace the 'dictatorship of the bourgeoisie'. By this Marx does not mean that such states have a dictatorial *political* form, but that they rule in the interests of a particular class. However, the 'dictatorship of the proletariat' is only the 'first phase' of post-capitalist development, which will abolish the private ownership of the means of production, the social and economic basis of class divisions, and unfetter the productive forces, leading to greater economic development. As the material basis of class divisions is dissolved, class differences will gradually disappear, and with them the need for the state as an instrument of class rule and as a distinct coercive force. In the higher stage of full communism, the state is destined to 'wither away' as Engels puts it, and 'the government of people will be replaced by the administration of things' (1884).

Marx rejects 'utopian' and ethical socialism in favour of a conception based, he claims, on an objective, 'scientific' account of historical development. Socialism, he insists, is not the expression of ethical values; it is not an ideal which merely *ought* to be brought about. It is the real, predictable tendency of capitalist development. Nevertheless, there is clearly a visionary and 'utopian' dimension to Marx's thought, which has inspired socialists ever since, and which has been one of the most potent moral ideals of the modern world.

The *Communist Manifesto* starts with the bold words, 'a spectre is haunting Europe – the spectre of communism'. Yet hardly had the *Manifesto* been published than the hopes of the revolutions of 1848 were dashed. The Communist League, for which the *Manifesto* had been written, was smashed and its members persecuted. Gradually, however, the revolutionary socialist movement reorganised and re-emerged. In 1864, the International Working Men's Association, the 'First International', was founded, with Marx as its Secretary and leading thinker. By 1883, the year of Marx's death, socialist groups had revived and his ideas were influential throughout Europe. The 'spectre' had returned. During much of the present century, history itself seemed to provide confirmation of the main element of Marx's thought: the prediction that capitalism is destined to be only a limited historical stage which will be superseded. Communism seemed to be a 'spectre' that had come to haunt not only Europe, but the whole world.

With the collapse of the regimes of Soviet and Eastern European communism in 1989, this is in doubt. Some say that Marxism is dead and its prediction of a historical stage beyond capitalism an illusion. Capitalism and liberal democracy are the 'end of history'. Given the continuing problems, crises, conflicts and contradictions in the capitalist world, that is neither a plausible nor a tenable view. No doubt Marxism needs to be fundamentally rethought in the light of historical experience. Nevertheless, it remains the most comprehensive and powerful theory for understanding and explaining the capitalist world and a continuing source of hope and inspiration for all those who believe that a better form of human life is possible.

Main works

Economic and Philosophical Manuscripts (1844), trans. Rodney Livingstone and Gregor Benton, *Early Writings*, Harmondsworth: Penguin, 1975.

The German Ideology (1845–6, with F. Engels), London: Lawrence and Wishart, 1975.

The Poverty of Philosophy (1847), London: Lawrence and Wishart, 1955.

Wage-Labour and Capital (1847), in K. Marx and F. Engels, *Selected Works*, Vol. I, Moscow: Foreign Languages Publishing, 1962.

The Communist Manifesto (1848, with F. Engels), in K. Marx and F. Engels, *Selected Works*, Vol. I, Moscow: Foreign Languages Publishing, 1962.

The Eighteenth Brumaire of Louis Napoleon (1852), in K. Marx and F. Engels, *Selected Works*, Vol. I, Moscow: Foreign Languages Publishing, 1962.

Capital, 3 vols (1867, 1885, 1894), London: Lawrence and Wishart, 1961–71.

Critique of the Gotha Programme (1875), in K. Marx and F. Engels, *Selected Works*, Vol. II, Moscow: Foreign Languages Publishing, 1962.

Further reading

Althusser, L. and E. Balibar, *Reading Capital*, trans. Ben Brewster, London: Verso, 1970.

Cohen, G. A., *Karl Marx's Theory of History: A defence*, Oxford: Oxford University Press, 1978.

Engels, F., *The Origin of the Family, Private Property and the State* (1884), in K. Marx and F. Engels, *Selected Works*, Vol. II, Moscow: Foreign Languages Publishing, 1962.

Engels, F., *Anti-Dühring*, 3rd edn, 1894, Moscow: Foreign Languages Publishing, 1962.

Kolakowski, L., *Main Currents of Marxism*, 3 Vols, Oxford: Oxford University Press, 1978.

McLellan, D., *Karl Marx: His life and thought*, London: Macmillan, 1973.

Mead, Margaret (1901–78)

Born into an academic New England family, Margaret Mead took a B.A. at Barnard College and higher degrees in psychology and anthropology at Columbia University, before leaving for field research in the islands of American Samoa. The product of this trip, *Coming of Age in Samoa* (1928), became an immediate best-seller. Over the next thirty years she was to conduct further studies of 'primitive' societies in New Guinea, Polynesia, Bali and India. She used her work on other cultures to enrich the debate in the United States and Europe on social issues, making major contributions in the areas of educational theory, race relations, sexual behaviour and the position of women.

At the time of the publication of *Coming of Age in Samoa* in 1928, a fierce academic debate was raging in North America and Europe on the respective roles of culture and biology in determining human behaviour. Mead's mentor, Franz Boas, the (German-born) father of American anthropology, was an eloquent advocate of the cultural determinist position, arguing that human personality was moulded more by the environmental forces acting on an individual than by genetic factors. Mead was to make *the* decisive intervention in this debate. Boas set Mead the task of investigating how far the rebelliousness, unsociability and sexual confusion associated with adolescence could be attributed to the biological changes of puberty and how far to the way in which children and adolescents were brought up in western societies. Clearly, if a group of people could be found in which adolescence passed without problems, in which children moved smoothly to adulthood, then a major blow would have been struck on the side of the cultural determinists.

Coming of Age seemed to provide exactly what Boas was looking for. Mead portrayed a society in which adolescence, for Samoan girls, was a period of blissful freedom, quite literally the best days of their lives. Largely free from domestic chores, and at liberty to leave the parental home for more congenial relatives if subjected to unsympathetic treatment, the Samoan teenage girl spent her days at leisure and her nights in the arms of any one of a series of lovers. It seemed that there was nothing inevitable about the traumas experienced by American teenagers, that cultural determinants out-punched biological factors. Mead was to return repeatedly to the disillusionment of the young in western societies, most notably in *Culture and Commitment: A study of the generation gap* (1970).

Mead's work in Samoa has been heavily criticised, most dramatically by Derek Freeman, whose *Margaret Mead and Samoa* (1982) severely damaged Mead's reputation as a serious anthropologist. She had left the United States as an inexperienced woman of twenty-three, unable to speak a word of Samoan. She lived with a white family and, as a woman, she was barred from the political life of the Samoan village. Although Mead's work has been defended by other anthropologists, it certainly seems that she misunderstood some aspects of Samoan life: the paradisiacal world of freedom, ease and sexual fulfilment, which so captivated her readers from the 1920s to the 1970s, seems to have been partly an invention of her young informants and partly the work of her own preconceptions. *Coming of Age*, however, retains its ability to charm. It should be read as part of a tradition of 'sexual-utopian' literature stretching back to the eighteenth century, typified by Diderot's *Supplement to the Voyage of Bougainville*, in which the South Seas (or the West Indies, or Peru) were portrayed as another Eden, at least partly in order to illuminate the problems of life in the 'civilised' world. Whatever its merits as scientific anthropology, *Coming of Age* linked Mead's name to the idea of sexual liberation, a link that was to lead to accusations that she was single-handedly responsible for the collapse of sexual morality in the 1960s.

   Growing up in New Guinea (1930), Mead's second book, depicts the less Edenic existence of the Manus people of the Admiralty Islands. Mead sees Manus society, in contrast to Samoan, as shedding a light on western culture not through its differences but through its similarities. The Manus are (or rather were) a hardworking, diligent, unimaginative people, quarrelsome, puritanical, superstitious and greedy: 'the ideal Manus man has no leisure; he is ever up and about his business turning five strings of shell money into ten.' The Manus child is left largely to its own devices, taught only to be ashamed of its body and to respect the property of others. Mead describes the children as rude and disrespectful, incapable of using their freedom for anything other than mischief-making. One of her main points is to argue that children need to be carefully tutored in their own culture, taught to respect tradition and appreciate art; it is not enough simply to allow children to follow their own whims. Neither the Manus, nor contemporary Americans, give their children what they need (by which she means a rich tradition) to grow up graciously, and in both cultures the result is the same: children envy and despise their parents. Mead returned to the Manus in 1953 and her record of the changes she found, *New Lives for Old* (1956), is perhaps her most moving work.

   Mead's assault on the idea of a fixed human nature manifesting itself in 'natural' gender roles reached its zenith in *Sex and Temperament* (1935). Mead shows how three New Guinea peoples – the Arapesh, the Mundugumor and the Tchambuli – have arranged the division of labour, and, it would seem the division of *character* between the sexes. Among the Arapesh, both men and women conform to our stereotype of the feminine: they 'unite in a common adventure that is primarily maternal, cherishing, and oriented away from the self towards the needs of the next generation'. Both the men and women of the cannibalistic Mundugomur are aggressive, violent and selfish, almost as brutal in courtship as in warfare. The Tchambuli, unlike their neighbours, have a strict division between the sexes, but, as you might guess, one which subverts the western stereotype: the men do little but adorn their bodies and rehearse ceremonial dances while the women fish and weave – two tasks which give them complete economic dominance. Mead's point is not that there are no biological distinctions between men and women, but that there are many ways in which those differences can become institutionalised, and the way in which we have done so, sending men out to work while women stay at home, is no more natural than any other.

This became the major theme of perhaps Mead's most important popular work *Male and Female* (1950). *Male and Female* is at the same time a defence of the discipline of anthropology, an argument about the nature of western society and a prescription for the reform of our oppressively limiting delineation of sex roles. She uses the full range of her investigations into other cultures to show the possibilities open to both sexes, possibilities cruelly closed, to the detriment of men and women, in North America and Europe. She accepts that there are fundamental biological differences between the sexes: men and women's bodies, roles in reproduction and, quite possibly, natural temperaments differ in important ways and this means that there are unique contributions that each sex can make to human society. It is our duty to build a society flexible enough to recognise and tap the special gifts of each sex without elevating those sex differences to the point of dogma.

From 1928, until her death in 1978, Margaret Mead was the most famous anthropologist in the world, indeed her popularising flair, her simple and lucid prose style and her focus on issues central to everyday life meant that for most people she *was* anthropology. She was an important harbinger of both the sexual revolution of the 1960s and a pioneer of the feminist movement, although her focus was always on the problems besetting humankind as a whole rather than simply women. Perhaps her greatest contribution to anthropology was her innovative use of photography as a means of cultural analysis. However, by the 1970s, her work was coming to seem theoretically naïve. The structural anthropology of Claude **Lévi-Strauss** offered anthropologists a new set of tools for analysing other cultures and Mead's field-work lacked the rigour thought desirable by most modern field researchers. Freeman's debunking was the final straw. For the first time since its publication, *Coming of Age in Samoa* is out of print. Nevertheless Mead stands out as an elegant voice advocating peace, love and understanding.

Main works

Coming of Age in Samoa, Harmondsworth: Penguin, 1928.

Growing up in New Guinea: A study of adolescence and sex in primitive societies, Harmondsworth: Penguin, 1942.

New Lives for Old: Cultural transformation – Manus, 1928–53, London: Victor Gollancz, 1956.

Balinese Character: A photographic analysis (with Gregory Bateson), New York: New York Academy of Sciences, 1962.

Male and Female: A study of the sexes in a changing world, Harmondsworth: Penguin, 1962.

Continuities in Cultural Evolution, New Haven, CT, and London: Yale University Press, 1964.

And Keep Your Powder Dry: An anthropologist looks at the American character, London: Ronald Whiting and Wheaton, 1965.

Culture and Commitment: A study of the generation gap, London: Bodley Head, 1970.

Blackberry Winter: My earlier years, New York: William Morrow, 1972.

Sex and Temperament in Three Primitive Societies, London: Routledge and Kegan Paul, 1977.

Further reading

Freeman, Derek, *Margaret Mead and Samoa: The making and unmaking of an anthropological myth*, Cambridge, MA, and London: Harvard University Press, 1983.

Howard, Jane, *Margaret Mead: A life*, London: Harvill, 1984.

Rice, Edward, *Margaret Mead: A portrait*, New York: Harper and Row, 1979.

Michels, Robert (1876–1936)

Michels was a European sociologist who was born in Germany but did much of his work in Italy. His ideas are often associated with those of the Italian elite theorists such as Mosca and **Pareto**, although he was also influenced by **Weber**, who was one of his teachers. He is famously associated with the notion of 'the iron law of oligarchy', which he developed in analysing the operation of power within political parties and (particularly) within mass parties of the left. He seeks to explain why and how 'the revolutionaries of to-day become the reactionaries of to-morrow' (*Political Parties*). Although Michels wrote extensively about other issues (including feminism), it is for 'the iron law of oligarchy' that he is remembered.

Michels initially developed his thesis (in the book entitled *Political Parties*, published in 1911) as part of an attempt to understand the distance between the radical rhetoric of the socialist parties in the early years of the twentieth century and their much more cautious political practice. He drew much of his evidence from the experience of the German Social Democratic Party (of which he was a member for a short time). In the early formulations of his argument, Michels was critical of the process and its outcomes. But in later writings its inevitability seems to have led him – wanting decisive leadership and associating that with charisma – to see oligarchical rule as not only socially beneficial but also necessary. His writings became more explicitly anti-democratic over time.

The logic of Michels's position is inexorable, and based on his view of organisational requirements rather than any psychological analysis of particular leaders or leadership types. He argues that organisation is required if the weaker groups in society are to be able to challenge the stronger and more powerful. 'Organization', he writes, is 'the weapon of the weak in their struggle with the strong' (*Political Parties*). The emergence of the mass socialist parties and the trade unions often associated with them is, therefore, a response to the power relations inherent within capitalist society. They offer workers their only chance to challenge their rulers and their employers. However, Michels goes on to argue, the danger of organisation is that it is also a fundamental source of conservatism. Organisation is required, but organisation itself ensures the emergence of an oligarchy of leaders over led.

It soon becomes necessary within organisations to delegate responsibilities to particular people. At first these may merely act as servants of the masses, but then their skills and expertise are gradually professionalised. The growth of organisations brings the need for rapid decisions, complexity and difficulties of communicating with a mass membership. As a result one begins to see the emergence of stable, professionalised leaders. This in turn leads to the construction of an elite. Growth means complexity, which implies increased specialisation of tasks. Specialism itself, argues Michels, implies authority, since it makes it difficult for the non-specialist to mount a challenge. It becomes increasingly difficult for members to have an overview of the activities of the organisation to which they belong, so that the leaders begin to have wider freedom of manoeuvre. Hierarchy, says Michels, flows from the technical needs of organisation, and becomes an essential part of the smooth operation of the party machine.

Michels stresses that the leaders themselves are not personally to blame. They have not 'sold out' as their internal opponents may claim. In becoming leaders in the first place they may well have believed in good faith that they would always act in the interests of and be directly accountable to, their members. In practice, however, they cannot do so. Increasingly, leaders come to respond to the interests of the organisation (or to the interests of their own survival within it), rather than the interests of their members, although they may not consciously make this distinction. The survival of the organisation is perceived to be essential both for the leaders themselves and for those it claims to represent, but since most members are relatively apathetic most of the time that leaves the leaders to define what the needs of the organisation are. Michels stresses the need which the masses feel for guidance and the cult of veneration for leadership which tends to develop as a consequence of this (often expressed in slogans, posters, banners and even lapel badges).

Michels argues that this process will affect even the most revolutionary of parties, because power within political parties is always conservative. Once there is a professionalised leadership (as required for effective organisation), then it will be in their interest to manipulate the membership to retain power. Michels notes that office-holders tend to be the strongest supporters of discipline within the organisation, in the interest of ensuring the survival and effectiveness of the organisation. For a party which seeks to represent the working class such an approach can be justified by the hostility of the environment within which the party finds itself (in some cases encouraging military analogies); but it also substantially limits the opportunities for opponents within the movement to challenge the leadership.

The argument is of relevance beyond the study of individual political parties or trade unions, since it directly questions the possibility of democratic politics. Michels makes this explicit. Parliamentary democracy is a fraud, he says, because delegates cease to be representative as soon as they are elected. Elected representatives, he suggests, will necessarily come to dominate those they represent – although he also acknowledges that 'the democratic party (even when subjected to oligarchical leadership) may influence the state in democratic directions'. Unfortunately, however, such parties soon just become competitors for power with bourgeois parties. New oligarchies emerge and undergo fusion with the old, ensuring that there is always oligarchical rule, never a real prospect of democratic rule. Democracy at best offers a means through which elites are renewed, allowing electorates choices between elites. Michels agrees with Mosca that socialists may win elections, but socialism (which implies that the rule by class or elite is overturned) can never be introduced. In his later writings, Michels became more and more convinced of the (necessary) power of elites and less and less sympathetic to the claims of democracy.

Much writing in political and organisational sociology continues to refer back to Michels, with *Political Parties* as one of its classic texts. Elite theory remains an important strand in debates about democratic accountability and the analysis of social and political power, even if explicit reference is not always made to Michels. To a considerable degree, Michels's arguments have become part of sociological common sense; at least to the extent that it is widely taken for granted that officals tend to dominate the mass organisations which they nominally serve. Because Michels's work highlights how much officials have interests of their own within organisations, it makes it impossible simply to accept the formal arrangements which are often spelt out in the rule books and administrative hierarchies within a range of organisations, from local authorities to civil service agencies.

That does not mean, however, that the approach adopted by Michels has been accepted uncritically. Since his arguments were developed, in large part, as a critique of Marxist approaches, not surprisingly Marxist thorists have questioned them, suggesting that he downplays the significance of social class and fails to acknowledge the extent to which power effectively remains in the hands of those who own business and property. C. **Wright Mills** makes similar points. Even those who have drawn most directly on Michels have questioned many of his assumptions, particularly since the empirical evidence on which he draws is relatively thin. Pluralists (such as Lipset) have applied Michels's approach to the analysis of trade unions, only to conclude that there are also tendencies within organisations which work against the centralisation of power. While there may be oligarchic tendencies, the mass is not so easily controlled as Michels implies, and choice between competing elites (or even the possibility of competitors entering the political process) means that the 'iron law' operates rather more flexibly than might be expected. Some (such as **Schumpeter**) have argued that democratic politics is characterised by a competition between elites, so that, even though some political elite or other is always in power, none can escape a form of accountability if it is to remain in power. This may be a very limited vision of democracy, but it also substantially limits the claims made by Michels.

However superficially attractive some of Michels' conclusions, thay are difficult to sustain as a comprehensive approach to the understanding of organisational power. Because of their starting point in the analysis of a particular form of political party at the start of the twentieth century, they fail to recognise the extent to which professional groups may have an incentive to support radical change rather than conservatism. Conservatism is not always the most appropriate response. In some circumstances (for example, because the organisation might be under threat), their survival might itself require quite innovative responses. Michels may have been accurate in his description of the way in which the mass socialist parties of Germany and Italy operated. But, even within the same movement at the same time, it does not seem to have been how the Russian Bolshevik Party operated – unless 'conservatism' includes revolutionary action and civil war. It is still less clear that it will necessarily be the way in which officials within today's rather broader party coalitions (always supposing that they qualify as 'parties' under Michels's definition) will operate.

Main works

Political Parties: A sociological study of the oligarchical tendencies of modern democracy (1915, initially published in German in 1911), New York: Dover, (1959).

Further reading

Beetham, D., *Bureaucracy*, Buckingham: Open University Press, 1987.

Bottomore, T. B., *Elites and Society*, London: C. A. Watts, 1964.

Lipset, S.M., Trow, M. and J. Coleman, *Union Democracy: The inside politics of the international typographical union*, New York: Free Press, 1956.

Schumpeter, J. A., *Capitalism, Socialism and Democracy*, London: Allen and Unwin, 1943.

Wright Mills, C., *The Power Elite*, New York: Oxford University Press, 1956.

Morgenthau, Hans J. (1904–1980)

Hans J. Morgenthau was the leading figure in the post-Second World War 'realist' (or power politics') school of international relations which dominated transatlantic international theory up to the 1960s. Born in Coburg in Germany in 1904, he studied at the universities of Berlin, Frankfurt and Munich before beginning a legal career. Having left Germany just before the rise of Hitler he spent periods in Switzerland and Spain before arriving in the United States in 1937. After a number of teaching appointments in New York and the Mid-west he began his long and fruitful association with the University of Chicago in 1943.

In Chicago Morgenthau set about a fundamental reformulation of the intellectual bases of the relatively new discipline of international relations. The academic study of the subject had begun in the post-First World War years primarily as a 'problem-solving' project. Effort was devoted to identifying and encouraging the development of alternative structures to replace the free play of aggressive foreign policies which had led to the breakdown of the international system and the trauma of 1914–18. This 'idealist' school of international relations placed great emphasis on the League of Nations and other structures of collective, rather than national, security.

To Morgenthau this idealism was dangerously misplaced, being based on a fundamental misunderstanding of human and political realities. Tracing a theoretical basis of international politics back to the harsher insights of Plato, Thucydides and Thomas Hobbes, he formulated what he claimed to be a more 'realistic' if less reassuring theory of international behaviour. The 'systematic' and 'scientific' study of international politics, according to Morgenthau, pointed to the centrality of 'power' in all international interactions. The pursuit of power as the currency of personal and national security was, in this view, the primary motivating factor on the part of both the individual in relation to other individuals and of the state in its relations with other states.

In 1946 Morgenthau published *Scientific Man versus Power Politics*, which was concerned with the limits and range of scientific method as applied to political analysis. This represented an early volley in his attack on idealist approaches to the analysis of international relations, but the definitive statement of his propositions came in 1948 with the publication of his *magnum opus, Politics among Nations: The struggle for power and peace*. For more than two decades *Politics among Nations* was the most influential international relations text in English-speaking universities.

At the heart of Morgenthau's grand theory lie 'six principles of political realism' which supposedly must underpin all contemplation of national foreign policies and their interplay in the international system:

1. International politics, like all social processes, is 'systematic' in the sense that it is governed by objective laws rooted in human nature. It is therefore amenable to 'scientific' study.

2. States interact in the international system on the basis of (national) interest. This interest is synonymous with the pursuit and accumulation of 'power'. Thus 'statesmen think and act in terms of interest defined as power, and the evidence of history bears (this) out' (*Politics among Nations*). This fundamental reality, however, is frequently at variance with the institutions and structures of the international system, such as international organisations and the protocols of diplomacy. Here, by implication, Morgenthau warns against the idealist heresy which is mistaken in regarding these co-operative structures as relevant to the 'real' world of international politics.

3. While interest defined as power is a constant in all international relations, the *nature* of interest/power will vary from time to time and from place to place: 'the kind of interest determining political action in a particular period of history depends upon the political and cultural context within which foreign policy is formulated' (*Politics*). Realism, therefore, need not involve the grim acceptance of conditions as they are in the international system; the environment of international relations is amenable to change. Nor is 'power' necessarily physical or military in nature. The pursuit of *interest* itself remains constant, but the *content* of this interest can change and can be changed.

4. Realism in international relations does not ignore the moral dimension to international action. It does, however, caution against the assumption that universal moral principles can be 'applied to the actions of states in their abstract universal formulation (rather) they must be filtered through the concrete circumstances of time and place' (*ibid.*). The state cannot allow itself the 'luxury' of universally acknowledged 'moral' behaviour; it has a higher duty to the pursuit of national interest.

5. Following on from this last point, the realist perspective 'refuses to identify the moral aspirations of a particular nation with the moral laws which govern the universe' (*ibid.*). The important point here is that the pursuit of interest (or 'security' or 'power' because all three ultimately intersect in national foreign policies) is not *immoral*, nor is it *amoral*. It is bound by *its own* moral laws which are specific to the pursuit of national interest. Indeed, Morgenthau argues, the recognition of this separate morality is a positive good as it prevents the confusion of pragmatic national interests with moral crusades which cannot be controlled and are invariably destructive. Writing in 1951 he argued that the 'choice is not between moral principles and the national interest, devoid of moral dignity, but between one set of moral principles divorced from political reality, and another set of moral principles derived from political reality' (*In Defense of the National Interest*).

6. Finally, realism concerns itself with politics as an autonomous process. While not dismissing the potency of moral, legal and economic forces affecting the making of national foreign policies, realist analysis is concerned primarily with political calculation in international relations. In this way Morgenthau separates realism from the contending claims of the other main approaches to the theory and practice of international relations in the first half of the century: the idealism of ethical and legalistic frameworks and the economic determinism of Marxism. Contingent on this emphasis on the 'political' is a highly 'state-centric' view of international activity, which sees the sovereign state as the dominant and significant actor in international relations. International organisations,

whether intergovernmental or non-governmental, whether the United Nations, pressure groups or multinational companies are, in this view, ultimately subordinate to the dictates of the states which make up the international political system.

Having identified and defined these well-springs of international behaviour Morgenthau anatomises the means by which relations between states may be regulated. Characteristically, he is dismissive of the restraining influence of public opinion, international law and collective security through international organisation. Only the careful management of an imperfect 'balance of power' can provide stability in the international system. The responsibility for this management must, in Morgenthau's view, lie with the art of diplomacy – though diplomacy itself, he felt, was in need of revivification after its depreciation in the twentieth century. In this Morgenthau looked back to a supposed pre-twentieth-century 'golden age' of international relations. His ideal was a system in which national interests were pursued by professionals who would reach pragmatic accommodations free from the populist vulgarities of public opinion and summit conference posturing. The banal certitudes of cold war bipolarity were to be regretted; the elegant complexities of the multipolar concert' of post-Napoleonic Europe were to be celebrated.

Perhaps the most striking attempt to apply Morgenthau's general theories was that of another Professor of International Relations, Henry Kissinger. As Secretary of State in the Nixon and Ford administrations in the 1970s, Kissinger sought to manage détente between the superpowers through a diplomacy which emphasised their mutual self-interest and which sought to ease the bipolarity of the post-1945 settlement towards a new global multipolarity.

In the 1960s and 1970s Morgenthau's brand of orthodox realism came under pressure from two alternative paradigms of international behaviour. Firstly, an emerging 'pluralist' school of thought challenged the centrality of both 'power' and 'politics' in international behaviour. In the pluralist view an increasingly complex international system was characterised by self-interested interdependence rather than competition while economic and other 'non-political' relations had produced a plurality of international actors and eroded the centrality of the state. Secondly, the 'world system' school argued, usually from a neo-Marxist position, that international relations could be understood only in terms of a world 'division of labour' based on the relationship between an exploiting 'core' and an exploited 'periphery'. In this perspective national interests and their management by diplomats were secondary to and dictated by fundamental, historically determined economic relations.

Finally, in the 1980s, the realist school of international relations itself underwent an internal revolution. The emergence of 'neo-realism' (or 'structural realism') coincided with the reversion from *détente* back to cold war in the 1980s. Its propositions differed from those of Morgenthau in acknowledging a greater significance for non-political relations and non-state actors. More particularly, neo-realism rejected Morgenthau's explicit connection between state behaviour and human nature, arguing instead that pursuit of power is dictated by the imperatives of the international system rather than the interior drives of decision-makers.

Despite these challenges to his basic arguments, Morgenthau's influence as an international theorist remains immense. Few contemporary debates on power in international politics are conducted without reference to his seminal contribution.

Main works

Scientific Man versus Power Politics, Chicago: Chicago University Press, 1946.

Politics Among Nations: The struggle for power and peace (1948), New York: Alfred A. Knopf and McGraw-Hill, 1993.

In Defense of the National Interest, New York: Alfred A. Knopf, 1951.

American Foreign Policy: A critical examination, London: Methuen, 1952.

Dilemmas of Politics, Chicago: Chicago University Press, 1958.

The Decline of Democratic Politics, Chicago: Chicago University Press, 1962.

The Impasse of American Foreign Policy, Chicago: Chicago University Press, 1962.

A New Foreign Policy for the United States, London: Pall Mall, 1969.

Truth and Power: Essays of a decade, 1960–70, London: Pall Mall, 1970.

Further reading

Dougherty, James E. and Robert L. Pfaltzgraff, *Contending Theories of International Relations*, New York: Harper and Row, 1990.

Nobel, Jaap W., 'Morgenthau's struggle with power: the theory of power politics and the Cold War', *Review of International Studies*, 21 (1995), pp. 61–85.

Olson, William C. and A. J. R. Groom, *International Relations Then and Now: Origins and trends in interpretation*, London: HarperCollins, 1991.

Thompson, Kenneth and Robert J. Myers, *Truth and Tragedy: A tribute to Hans J. Morgenthau*, Washington: New Republic, 1977.

Glossary

Bipolarity   The structure of the international system associated with the cold war years during which global power was concentrated around two opposing 'poles': the United States and the Soviet Union.

Multipolarity   In contrast to bipolarity, a systemic structure in which power is spread more or less equally between several states. Characteristic of the nineteenth century and the years before the Second World War.

Mumford, Lewis (1895–1990)

Educated at the City College of New York and Columbia University, Mumford originally planned a career in electrical engineering. His studies were interrupted when he enlisted in the navy during the First World War as a radio operator. After the war, Mumford embarked on his literary career, having been invited in 1920 to fill the vacant editorship of *The Sociological Review* in London. During this time Mumford contributed to numerous American periodicals, such as *The Freeman*, *The Nation* and *The New Republic*, and assumed editorial responsibilities for *The Dial* and *American Caravan*. By 1932 he was the regular architecture critic for *The New Yorker*, penning its 'Sky Line' column for over thirty years. At the same time Mumford was active in a number of groups concerned with regional planning, new towns and other urban and rural issues, most notably the Regional Planning Association of America. As a professional author, Mumford published a prodigious number of texts, nearly thirty in all, and bequeathed a monumental array of literary journalism. His output subsided after the Second World War as the death of his only son, Geddes, in the Italian campaign, and the horrendous effects of the nuclear devastation inflicted upon Japan stimulated Mumford to an increasing involvement in the campaign to prevent nuclear armageddon as the arms race developed momentum. Although never a full-time academic, Mumford taught at the universities of Stanford and Pennsylvania State, and at Massachusetts Institute of Technology as a visiting professor.

Mumford was truly a polymath and a generalist. He began his voluminous penmanship by writing a book on the history of utopias, which he categorises as either utopias of escape or utopias of reconstruction. Utopias, for Mumford, are quintessentially commentaries on their contemporaneous social, political and environmental circumstances. As such they constitute useful benchmarks for recognising future potentialities, earmarking alternative practices and appraising existing values. In so far as Mumford believed in the utility of utopias rather than their realisability (he was always concerned that a belief in the possibility of utopias would lead to an investment of faith in stagnant ideals), *The Story of Utopias* (1922) marks the beginning of his early literary phase in which he established himself as an axiologist investigating American literature and architecture. Mumford invariably argued that the values and characteristics of a community are reflected in its architectural environment. Hence he berated the design of the United Nations building for encapsulating the intemperate ideals of the western industrial world, rather than expressing supranational pacific values for a community of nations.

Conscious of the relationship between social values and the human environment, Mumford proceeded to analyse the association of technology and culture. *Technics and Civilisation* (1934), in which he explores the connections between the machine and human civilisation, brought Mumford widespread recognition both as a historian of technology and as an incisive critic of capitalist economic development. Originally planned as the first element of a trilogy of texts on the subject (which eventually became a quaternary), *Technics and Civilisation* displays Mumford's capacity for originality and his ability to synthesise the ideas of others.

Patrick Geddes, the Scottish biologist, sociologist and planner, was a major influence on Mumford. In *Technics and Civilisation*, Mumford melded Geddes's notion of technological phases to Marx's mode of production-based historical epochs. Geddes had defined two phases in the evolution of industrial society, labelling them the 'paleotechnic' (*c*. 1750–1900) and the 'neotechnic' (*c*. 1870 onwards). To this, Mumford added a third, the 'eotechnic' (*c*. 1000–1750). In describing the machine in *Technics and Civilisation*, Mumford envisaged not simply a single tool or manufacturing device, but rather a complex or matrix of tools, skills, technique, knowledge and other instruments. This is indicative of his attempt, inspired by the holistic and organic approach of Geddes, to discover a complex that envelops technology, the environment, the individual and the community. Thus the eotechnic phase is a complex of wood and water, whereas the paleotechnic age was distinguished as a coal and iron complex whilst the neotechnic bore the hallmarks of an electricity and alloy complex.

Much of Mumford's analysis of modern society is permeated by a moral critique of the dehumanising effects of capitalism that owes much to Marx. Somewhat paradoxically, it is also infused with a degree of optimism that stems from Geddes's concept of 'life insurgency'. For Mumford, no civic culture rests in complete equilibrium. Each civilisation is subject to two contrasting forces: those that tend to destroy life and those that tend to conserve it. Consequently, Mumford's technological phases are simultaneously moral phases. The eotechnic is epitomised by those organic balanced communities of eighteenth-century New England, of which Mumford was so fond; whereas the advent of the paleotechnic era ushered in a mechanically oriented culture (directly imposed without regard for internal structures or values) that threatened the very existence of life itself. The neotechnic phase holds out the prospect of a return to the organic (facilitating the internal dynamics and values of a community), to an intrinsic and coherent social morality that affords unity and purpose to life.

To accomplish this transformation Mumford rejects the Marxist methodology of political change, favouring a modification of values to ensure that technology is directed by human needs. If this can be achieved, then Mumford believes that political revolution may be redundant. Responsibility for amending values rests with the family, the church, and trade unions. Additionally, he echoes the Fabian strategy for social amelioration, by identifying architects, planners and other public figures as the motor force of change. Mumford's apolitical approach resonated across a world increasingly dominated by ideological conflict. His hope was that neotechnic developments would encourage people to cherish renewed organic values and establish decentralised (geographic but not democratic), economically self-sustaining communities that were part of a broader regional network. In this he is deeply indebted to the work of Ebenezer Howard on Garden Cities and Peter Kropotkin's anarchist vista of communities maintaining a balance between industry and agriculture.

In Mumford's later writings, particularly the double volume *The Myth of the Machine* (1967, 1970), his optimism for the future has been severely dented. Whilst adding a further two phases in his history of technology, the paleolithic and the neolithic, Mumford now regards the machine as a megamachine. Although not new, the megamachine was different in kind from the machine. It referred to the mechanical, the institutionalised, the centralised and regulated form of production that was both human and inanimate. It consolidated the power base and perpetuated the rule of an elite. Nowhere was this more true than in the military–industrial complex that had come to dominate the American neotechnic phase in the middle of the twentieth century. Subsequently, Mumford grew increasingly concerned about the social and political changes engendered by the arms race. For the megamachine, in Mumford's eyes, was charting the course of human history (rather than being directed by human needs and values), and propelling humankind to an ominous nuclear finale.

Mumford was a great synthesiser, examining a problem from all angles, including past, present and future, to perceive and understand the unity that lay hidden beneath. In this respect, his enduring legacy is the now commonplace acknowledgement that technology is an integral part of culture, and that recognising this is imperative to any appreciation of what it means to be human. *Technics and Civilisation* had a profound and lasting influence on many scholars from various disciplines. His ideas on architecture and planning were instrumental in the regeneration of post-war Britain in towns such as Harlow and Stevenage, and helped to situate the importance of architecture in the human environment. Equally, his ideas were influential in outlining the need for human scale in environmental planning, and were instrumental in establishing our contemporary cognisance of ecologically sustainable solutions for the industrial and environmental difficulties that pervade the whole of human society. Similarly, his libertarian ideals have inspired many later radical thinkers.

Main works

The Story of Utopias, New York: Boni and Liveright, 1922.

Sticks and Stones: A study of American architecture and civilisation (1924), New York: Dover, 1955.

The Golden Day: A study in American experience and culture, New York: Boni and Liveright, 1926.

Herman Melville, New York: Literary Guild, 1929.

The Brown Decades: A study of the arts in America, 1865–1895 (1931), New York: Dover, 1955.

Technics and Civilisation, London: Routledge and Kegan Paul, 1934.

The Condition of Man, London: Secker and Warburg, 1944.

The Myth of the Machine, Vol. i: *Technics and Human Development* (1967), Vol. ii: *The Pentagon of Power* (1970), New York: Harcourt Brace Jovanovich.

The Culture of Cities (1938), New York: Harcourt Brace Jovanovich, 1970.

Further reading

Hughes, Thomas P. and Agatha C. Hughes (eds), *Lewis Mumford: Public intellectual*, Oxford: Oxford University Press, 1990.

Miller, Donald (ed.), *The Lewis Mumford Reader*, New York: Pantheon, 1986.

Miller, Donald, *Lewis Mumford: A life*, New York: Weidenfield and Nicolson, 1989.

N

Nozick, Robert (1938–)

Born in Brooklyn, Nozick was educated at Columbia and Princeton before taking up his first lecturing post at Harvard in 1965. Nozick rose to prominence with the publication of his seminal *Anarchy, State, and Utopia* in 1974. Along with F. von Hayek and Milton Friedman, Nozick became something of a standard-bearer for the emergent libertarian right, although he took almost no part in the continuing controversy stirred up by the radical libertarianism of this work. After *Anarchy, State and Utopia*, Nozick turned his attention to the less controversial fields of the philosophy of mind and epistemology, publishing his conclusions in his second major work, *Philosophical Explanations*, in 1981. In 1989 he published *The Examined Life*, in which he returns to some of the questions raised in *Anarchy, State, and Utopia*.

Anarchy, State and Utopia attempts to justify what Nozick calls the 'minimal state' against, on the one side, anarchists opposed to any state interference in the life of the individual, and, on the other, the encroachments of the welfare state, determined to confiscate, through taxation, the hard-earned income of its citizens. Nozick's minimal state provides a police force and judicial system to protect personal and property rights and an army to defend the citizens against external force. It does nothing else.

Nozick's Janus-faced defence is based on his conception of rights and on the idea of liberty he founds on those rights. Like many social theorists before him, Nozick leans heavily on the concept of the 'state of nature', a hypothetical world existing before the rise of state institutions. In Nozick's state of nature we have two natural rights. The first (and less controversial) is that we have a fundamental right of ownership over our own bodies – we own ourselves. There can be no argument, no rightful claim which can override this right. It might well be the case that some system of compulsory organ donation, let us say the giving of bone marrow, would save many lives, and perhaps increase the sum of happiness in the world, but Nozick argues (and most people would agree) that we cannot compel a person to give up part of his or her body to achieve that worthwhile goal. The second natural right Nozick posits is the right to own property. We can come legitimately to own property by two means: we can appropriate it from nature and we can lawfully acquire it from others. We have these rights not through some agreement or convention, but because of our nature as free, rational agents, able to choose how our lives ought to be led.

For Nozick my rights over my body and my property are 'negative' and 'side constrained' – I have a right to be left alone and nobody has a right to interfere with me or remove my rights, even for the furthering of some desirable goal. In addition to these, I have the right to defend myself and my property and to punish those who infringe my natural rights. My rights are not positive in any sense – they do not entitle me to receive anything (food, health-care, social-security payments) from the state, or anyone else, to promote my right to life.

But if we assume that these rights are inviolable, how can even a minimal state be defended from the anarchist who resents having a police force around, which not only prevents him or her from exercising the right to punish (perhaps by lynching) a thief or the murderer, but which, adding insult to injury, has to be paid for? Nozick responds that people in the state of nature would move to the minimal state through their own, free, rational choices, without the need for compulsion, guided by an 'invisible hand'. In the state of nature we will not want to spend all of our time in the risky activity of pursuing those who have infringed our rights. Inevitably, a number of agencies will spring up to sell their services, enforcing the rights of those prepared to pay. Over time a natural monopoly will develop – a single agency, of which most people are members, will have emerged – an 'ultra-minimal state'.

So far, by voluntary actions, most people have agreed to give up some of their rights to this enforcement agency. But what if I do not want to sacrifice my right to vengeance? For Nozick, the agency can legitimately step in to prevent such vigilantes exercising their rights, but only by compensating them. That compensation is the offer of protection, even if the vigilante will not pay the fees of the agency. We now have an organisation with a monopoly on the enforcement of natural rights ('the Law'). In effect we have arrived at the minimal state.

Nozick uses these same rights over ourselves and our property to draw the line at the minimal state. Most, but not necessarily all, of us would count among the state's functions the provision of at least some of the following: free health-care, free schooling, social-security payments for the unemployed, subsidised housing for the poor, environmental protection programme, overseas aid to relieve famine. These all have to be paid for. If I have an absolute right over my property, how can the state compel me to pay for these things if I do not want to? Income tax is the obvious way in which governments raise revenue in the modern state. For Nozick, taxing people to provide for anything other than the minimal state represents forced labour: for at least some of the time we are working for somebody else against our will, to pay for things we may not want. Our rights over our bodies and our property are every day infringed by the welfare state. Justice demands that this stop.

These are the bare bones of Nozick's philosophy. Nozick's own work is distinguished by an argumentative brilliance and a clarity of expression unequalled among modern social philosophers. There are, however, major flaws and substantial gaps in his thinking. Nozick never properly grounds his conception of natural rights. He never explains where our rights come from or why we should have them. He has no effective rebuttal to those who have argued, along with Jeremy Bentham, that the idea of a *natural* right, something we have by virtue of being human, as opposed to a right given by a society, in return for some obligation, is simply 'nonsense upon stilts'.

More important, however, are the criticisms of Nozick's account of property rights and his attack on the concept of redistributive justice. Nozick argued that the only just basis for deciding who should own what in society is 'entitlement'. We become entitled to property by freely acquiring it from others – by a voluntary transfer – or by taking it directly from nature. The first of these has caused some marginal difficulties for Nozick. How do we decide what is a voluntary transfer? What if one party is mistaken or misled about the nature of a contract? The real problems begin, however, with the attempt to find how property came to be owned privately in the first place. John Locke had argued plausibly that we come to own bits of the earth by mixing something we own – our labour – with it, as long as we leave it as good or better for everybody else to do the same ('Locke's proviso'). Nozick dismisses this with one of his amusing analogies. If I pour my can of tomato juice into the ocean do I thereby come to own the ocean? Surely I have rather pointlessly wasted what I had than gained what I lacked. Unfortunately, Nozick never offers us a realistic alternative, other than clinging to a version of Locke's proviso, which in itself can do no more than act as a limit on appropriation.

Nozick is on safer ground when he attacks alternative systems, which attempt to distribute society's goods according to some pattern – according to desert, or need, or some measure of social utility. Nozick dismisses 'patterned' distributions with his most celebrated illustration. Let us say that we have distributed wealth according to our preferred pattern (D1). A sportsman (Nozick employs a basketball player, Wilt Chamberlain) has a contract whereby he receives 10 per cent of the face value of tickets sold for games in which he plays. Over the course of the season 500,000 fans go to watch him play. The sportsman has now become very wealthy, at the expense of those fans who have paid to watch him. We now have a new distribution (D2), quite different to the original pattern (D1). Yet this has come about through free choices made by people under no constraint or obligation. In order to prevent this sort of redistribution we would have to subject the population to constant supervision and intervene 'to forbid capitalist acts between consenting adults'.

Nozick claims that his minimal state, based on a respect for natural rights, would allow groups of people to set up any kind of community they chose – capitalist, communist, anarchist – as long as they allowed other groups to lead their own, different lives. The minimal state therefore offers a 'blueprint for Utopia', an inspiring alternative to the repressive, top-heavy and expensive modern state.

Nozick has gained few followers among social philosophers. His arguments, although frequently brilliant, are too often flawed to convince the sceptical. His impact has, however, been enormous. Almost every major work on social or political philosophy published since *Anarchy, State, and Utopia* has had to pay its respects to Nozick. In the wider world, the economic policies of the Reagan and Thatcher years seem to owe at least something to Nozick's arguments in favour of the minimal state. Nozick's radicalism, however, makes it difficult to accommodate his views within a traditional conservative context.

Main works

Anarchy, State, and Utopia, Oxford: Basil Blackwell, 1974.

Philosophical Explanations, Oxford: Oxford University Press, 1981.

The Examined Life, New York: Simon and Schuster, 1989.

Further reading

Paul, Jeffrey (ed.), *Reading Nozick*, Oxford: Basil Blackwell, 1982.

Rawls, John, *A Theory of Justice*, Oxford: Oxford University Press, 1972.

Ryan, Alan, *Property and Political Theory*, Oxford: Basil Blackwell, 1984.

Simmons, A. John, *Moral Principles and Political Obligations*, Princeton, NJ: Princeton University Press, 1979.

Waldron, Jeremy (ed.), *Theories of Rights*, Oxford: Oxford University Press, 1984.

O

Oakeshott, Michael Joseph (1901–1990)

Michael Oakeshott, the son of an Anglican clergyman's daughter and an agnostic civil servant (and Fabian Society sympathiser), was born and educated in Harpenden. He read history at Cambridge, then became, from 1927, a don. Apart from wartime, he stayed at Cambridge until 1951. Philosophically an outsider, faithful to the then waning idealist tradition of Bradley and McTaggart, his early activities were centred on a group (the 'D' Society) which sought to 'modernise' and personalise Anglicanism's conception of morality and the religious life. This period culminated in a book on the nature and boundaries of the human imagination, *Experience and its Modes*, which is one of the last masterpieces of English idealism. During the late 1930s and 1940s, Oakeshott pursued his life-long commitment to moral individualism. He wrote pieces on the statist pretensions of twentieth-century political thinking and published a widely read, rather aloof compendium of contemporary political doctrines from Nazism to representative democracy (whose 'simple-mindedness' 'makes it appear ... a fool amongst knaves'). Then, in 1951, this quizzical conservative was chosen to replace Harold **Laski**, London School of Economics's high-profile democratic socialist Professor of Government. Oakeshott remained at the LSE until retirement in 1969, transmitting to English and American political studies his perception of politics: not abstract formulas or quantitative social science, but a society's history, traditions and classic texts – namely, those that reflect on the meaning of civil and political life. His once unfashionable anti-statism and his eccentricity *vis-à-vis* the mainstreams of twentieth-century philosophical and political thinking have guaranteed him a place in the pantheon somewhere between the voice of an older wisdom and the postmodernism of the end of the century.

Though Oakeshott's later, urbane essays and lectures on political thought are easy to approach without reference to his earlier thought, the latter in fact supplied essential underpinnings to his anti-rationalist, apolitical conservatism. His thought begins with a commitment to the individual moral life and an associated, idealist conception that there is no access to an outside world, only versions of that world as shaped by human experience: 'Thinking . . . is a process of catching not wild birds, not what is outside experience . . . but tame birds already within the cage of the mind' *(Experience and its Modes)*. Idealism sustained Oakeshott's rejection of the talk of direct contact with the world, 'sense data' and other ideas from philosophy's rising star, logical positivism. Like Collingwood in *Speculum Mentis* (1924), Oakeshott identified a number of 'tame birds' in the human imagination, that is 'modes' shaping human experience: the scientific, the historical and the practical. Ever 'more aware of the futility of knowledge than its blessing', he finds each mode, though consistent within itself, confounded at points of 'arrest', where it is abstract by comparison with the richness of the overall human experience.

The abstractness of the scientific mode is the easiest to grasp: in analysing its material into neutral, universally communicable quantities, science renders itself self-contained at the cost of any capacity to deal meaningfully with what is particular. (This conclusion is hard on social sciences, which lack the containment of the laboratory: psychology is cut off from 'real' human character; economics cannot embrace the empirical world; sociology is doomed as a mere mixture of modes.) Though the historical mode shares the neutrality of science, it is distinguished by its preoccupation with what is contingent and particular. The historian's task is to make intelligible the complex of human intention and choice that converge in historical outcomes. This view both liberates and constrains historical thinking: to be sure, the historian's creativity is stressed; but equally claims about origins or overarching progress are outlawed, as is any history of the present, where 'practical' human interests are pursued. Finally, the 'practical mode' is that of ordinary life: constantly imbued with the pursuit of goals, interests and values integral to intersubjective social existence. Later, Oakeshott was to add poetry to the 'modes', and generally to broaden his conception of separate domains in human life, speaking of 'activities' ('being an historian', 'governing' and so on), or of 'ideal conditions' (such as 'civil association').

A characteristic Oakeshott analysis, then, lays out the integral character of some different aspects of humans' life experience and then derives critical implications from their discreteness. Whereas modes or activities may touch (or, to use a later metaphor, 'converse'), they must not mingle. Notably, the besetting error of modern political thinking is to mingle what should be kept apart, to push politics and the state beyond their proper bounds, into the private, moral life:

> politics . . . is a second-rate form of activity, neither an art nor a science, at once currupting to the soul and fatiguing to the mind, the activity either of those who cannot live without the illusion of affairs or those so fearful of being ruled by others that they will pay away their lives to prevent it.

In this fashion, the separation of forms articulated in *Experience and its Modes* recurs throughout Oakeshott's thought, paring down all modern political ambitions, be they reform liberal, democratic, socialist, marxist or merely welfarist.

Oakeshott critical strategy is pursued more widely in *Rationalism in Politics*, his most widely read collection of essays. Rationalism here has in a sense pre-figured in his 1920s essay on *The Politics of Faith and the Politics of Scepticism*: an obsession that the world is a site for solving problems through the application of reason. It also exemplifies how the scientific 'mode' exceeds its proper bounds: invading politics to grasp and change the world for the sake of political formulas which, through the state, pursue a perfect order. It is, one might add, what late-twentieth-century writers have called 'the Enlightenment Project'. In contrast to this rationalism, Oakeshott expounds a conservatism akin to his earlier 'practical mode' of experience: to eschew the pretensions of technical 'knowing what' in favour of 'knowing how' – skilful practice embedded in particularity. In this way, Oakeshott outdid other post-war critics of extended welfarism (such as Popper), and condemned the entirety of the nation-state's social or economic management as so many offspring of the modern world's 'collectivist' flirtation with goal-orientated rule – 'sovereign power out of romanticism', as he puts it, in a phrase recalling that he was also the author of two guides to horserace betting.

Esteem for the character and dignity of the free, non-political individual complements Oakeshott's critical strategy. For him, the modern, individualist political order ought to be fashioned primarily for such people. Its political theory, he argues (in *Morality and Politics in Modern Europe*), should elucidate the 'office of government' appropriate to the chief feature of the modern world: 'the appearance of subjects who desire to make choices for themselves, who find happiness in doing so and who are frustrated in having choices imposed upon them'. The purpose of politics, that is, should be to facilitate the aspirations of individuals in that particular sense. But the temptations of sovereign power and pressures from those 'incapable or unwilling to make choices for themselves' repeatedly divert modern government, away from individualism and towards the many forms of collectivism.

As the originator of the political philosophy of individualism, Hobbes figures often in Oakeshott's writings. He first commented on Hobbes's thought as interpreted, critically, in the late 1930s by Leo Strauss's conservative nostalgia for the classical ideal of civil association (sociability based upon voluntary, mutual, self-conscious commitments amongst individual citizens). A decade later, Oakeshott had traced in Hobbes's *Leviathan* a revival from Roman law of the sovereign's power to command obligation, which, for him, was the perfect, liberal complement to the individual's freedom of will. Oakeshott, that is to say, unearthed in Hobbes's reasoning a place for his own dignified kind of individual, one who chooses civil obligation out of pride rather than the fear felt by the individual *manqué*.

When, in 1975, *On Human Conduct* finally provided the comprehensive statement of Oakeshott's political philosophy, one found again the rejection of collective interference in a typical Oakeshottian analysis of idealised liberal formulations for the politico-civil order. The essence of political society is to be itself, that is *not* to pursue goals beyond its own essence as an authoritative institution to guarantee individual human freedom and moral life. The true 'civil' association, Oakeshott reasons, is one infused by non-instrumental rules, 'moral' rules bearing on the *manner* of the members' acts, not on their *content* – and hence not aimed either at the members' happiness. The 'public' manifestation of the civil association – which is the proper realm of politics – underpins the association with an unalloyed obligation to the rule of law. For Oakeshott the unrivalled authority of the law defines, in a thoroughly Hobbesian manner, the precise scope of the individual's moral freedom of choice and action.

The direction taken by political and social thought in the later decades of the century has been kind to Oakeshott. At once a survivor of nineteenth-century high-Anglican idealism and a celebrator *avant la lettre* of incommensurability between human communities, his influence can be found successively in neo-liberalism and in US communitarianism. His anti-rationalist conservatism has latterly surfaced as a point of reference as much for Rorty, the liberal American pragmatist communitarian, as for radical English post-liberal thinkers such as John Gray.

Main works

Experience and its Modes, Cambridge: Cambridge University Press, 1933.

Social and Political Doctrines of Contemporary Europe, Cambridge: Cambridge University Press, 1939.

Hobbes's Leviathan (ed., with an introduction), Oxford: Oxford University Press, 1946.

Rationalism in Politics and Other Essays, London: Methuen, 1961.

On Human Conduct, Oxford: Clarendon, 1975.

Morality and Politics in Modern Europe: The Harvard lectures, ed. Shirley Letwin, New Haven, CT, and London: Yale University Press, 1993 (lectures delivered in 1958).

Religion, Politics and the Moral Life, ed. Timothy Fuller, New Haven, CT, and London: Yale University Press, 1995 (essays from the 1920s).

Further reading

Devigne, Robert, *Recasting Conservatism: Oakeshott, Strauss and the response to post-modernism*, New Haven, CT: Yale University Press, 1994.

Franco, Paul, *The Political Philosophy of Michael Oakeshott*, New Haven, CT, and London: Yale University Press, 1990.

Grant, Robert, *Thinkers of our Time: Oakeshott*, London: Claridge, 1991.

Gray, John, *Liberalisms*, London: Routledge, 1989 (esp. ch. 8).

Greenleaf, W. H., *Oakeshott's Philosophical Politics*, London: Longman, 1966.

Norman, Jesse (ed.), *The Achievement of Michael Oakeshott*, London: Duckworth, 1993 (collection of reviews, obituaries and memoires).

Olson, Mancur (1932–)

Mancur Olson is an economist whose work is best known and discussed by political scientists and sociologists. His first book *The Logic of Collective Action* (1965) is one of those works perpetually described as 'seminal': having a dramatic effect on the study of politics and society. His later work has been less influential, though no less sought-after. He received his Bachelor's degree from North Dakota State University in 1954, and his M.A. from Oxford in 1960, getting his Ph.D. which formed the basis of *The Logic* from Harvard in 1963. He taught at Princeton University from 1963–7 when he went to work in Washington for the Federal Government, returning to academic life at the University of Maryland in 1969. He became Distinguished Professor of Economics in 1979. He was one of the founder members and former President of the Public Choice Society (1972–4).

The fundamental argument of *The Logic* can be summed up in a passage which appears on page 2:

> unless the number of individuals in a group is quite small, or unless there is coercion or some other special device to make individuals act in their common interest, *rational self-interested individuals will not act to achieve their common or group interests.*

Olson reaches this conclusion through three arguments (though he appears to think they are identical). His *algebraic* argument is that an individual will only contribute if the difference her contribution will make is worth more to her than the contribution itself. With *private* goods this happens all the time. I buy the apple because apple is worth more to me than the

20 pence I pay for it. But what difference will my £12 annual fee to Friends of the Earth make to their campaigning activities? For this reason some organisations tell you what your money will be spent on. Children in Need tell you that your £12 will provide a cataract operation for one child, and sometimes one can actually sponsor given children. Thus the difference one's contribution makes can be seen to be worth more than the contribution itself. A related, though formally different argument in Olson is that one's contribution is imperceptible. That is one cannot see the difference the contribution makes. A third argument concerns whether the good will be provided at all. Suppose that a labour union will only be recognised by management if over 50 per cent of the workforce have joined. Should you join the union even if you think it will be good for you and all the workers if one bargains on your behalf? If the union already has over 50 per cent you can gain the benefits of its bargaining without having to pay your dues; if, say, only 20 per cent are members and you join, then you pay your fees but do not get the benefits of its bargaining. If however, the union has 50 per cent of the workers signed up, then your membership can tip the balance and the union be recognised. In this sense one joins only if one is the pivotal member. The key to this latter version of the collective action problem is Samuelson's concept of public or collective goods. A collective good is one which if it is provided for one person in the collectivity it is provided for all. Thus if others pay for the good, one may still enjoy it whilst 'free-riding' upon others contributions.

Initially Olson's book did not cause much of a stir, but by the mid-1970s – and still today – many sociologists and political scientists set themselves the task of destroying Olson's argument. There is a wealth of economic, game-theoretic and political literature demonstrating that the collective action problem is really a whole host of related but different problems. Individuals overcome these problems in numerous ways which makes the formation of organisations perfectly rational. This work extends and builds upon Olson's great book. Those who try to challenge, rather than extend, Olson fail to understand that his book argues that collective action is a *problem*, not that it is an *impossibility*.

The problem as many social scientists see it is that many organisations do form ostensibly to defend their members' interests. Olson explains organisation formation by the device of 'selective incentives'. A selective incentive is any private good that is offered to tempt people to join. Thus labour unions provide individual legal advice, social clubs and so on. Coercion, such as fines for non-payment of taxes is also an example – of negative selective incentive. However, if all organisations' provision of collective goods were to be mere by-products of their selective incentives then the rationality of pluralist democracy (see the entry on **Dahl**) would disappear. This is a controversial conclusion.

Another controversial aspect of *The Logic* is Olson's methods. The public choice method assumes that individuals are self-interested maximisers:

they behave in ways which promote their own self-interest. Many object to this 'immoral' assumption about people. Of course, most people are not self-interested all the time, but the assumption is a useful device for explaining the behaviour of individuals within their social roles.

Later, in his *The Rise and Decline of Nations* (1982), Olson applied his argument to international alliances and to relative growth rates. In *The Rise* Olson argues that over time groups do overcome their respective collective action problems and form 'distributional coalitions' to defend interests. These then bargain and barter with each other and with government. This societal bargaining process has two effects. First it slows down decision-making, which makes the entrepreneurial function harder, thus slowing growth. Secondly, each group spends more time arguing over the size of the collective pie they are to receive and so fails to contribute to producing a larger pie all round. Societies which manage to co-ordinate the groups into large-scale 'encompassing organisations' manage to mitigate the effects of the second problem if not the first. Thus we can track the rise and decline of nations by the number and complexity of their distributional coalitions. The final, and strangely least discussed, chapter of that book explains stagflation, unemployment and business cycles by extending the logic, arguing that each can be analysed as collective goods suffering from lack of collective attention.

More recently, in a series of articles Olson has explained the rise of the modern state. For many public choice writers, the state is predatory. It takes from its citizens in the form of taxes, giving defence and other collective goods in return. However, the state will always want to take more than it gives back. How, then, did the state first form? Even if the state is in the interests of all, it surely poses the biggest collective action problem of them all. In Olson's account of the formation of the state, roving bandits appropriate from peasants. They arrive and remain in an area for a while until the land is ravaged and then move on. However, as the number of roving bandit groups increase, they will find that they cannot move on to terrorise others without displacing other bandits. Each group finds it better to *defend* their peasants from external attack, taking from their proto-citizens, whilst leaving just enough for them to survive and continue producing. From this the modern state develops.

Mancur Olson's work is an example of how important a simple but clear idea can be, and how simple ideas can be applied to many different areas. In many ways, *The Logic* is not a well crafted book, with three arguments posing as one, terms defined then used differently and footnotes taking away what the text gives like the small print on a package of herbal remedies. But it stands as one of the most important books in social science of the twentieth century. No-one studying democracy, political power, revolutions, institutional organisation, or virtually any subject which involves human interaction can do so without understanding the problems of collective action that Olson first popularised in the modern age.

Main works

The Logic of Collective Action (1965), 2nd edn, Cambridge, MA: Harvard University Press, 1971.

'An economic theory of alliances' (with Richard Zeckhauser), *Review of Economics and Statistics*, 47 (1966), pp. 266–79.

'Economics, sociology and the best of all possible worlds', *The Public Interest*, 12 (1968), pp. 96–118.

'The principle of fiscal equivalence', *American Economic Review*, 59 (2) (1969), pp. 479–87.

'An evolutionary approach to inflation and slagflation', in James Gapinski and Charles E. Rockwood (eds), *Essays in Post-Keynesian Inflation*, Cambridge, MA: Allinger, 1979.

The Rise and Decline of Nations, New Haven, CT: Yale University Press, 1982.

'The logic of collective action in Soviet-type societies', *Journal of Soviet Nationalities*, 1 (1990), pp. 8–33.

'Dictatorship, development and democracy', *American Political Science Review*, 87 (1993), pp. 567–76.

Further reading

Dowding, Keith, *Power*, Buckingham: Open University Press, 1996.

Dunleavy, Patrick, *Democracy, Bureaucracy and Public Choice*, Hemel Hempstead: Harvester Wheatsheaf, 1991.

Marwell, Gerald and Pamela Oliver, *The Critical Mass in Collective Action*, Cambridge: Cambridge University Press, 1993.

Mueller, Dennis C. (ed.), *The Political Economy of Growth*, New Haven, CT: Yale University Press, 1983.

Sandler, Todd, *Collective Action: Theory and applications*, Ann Arbor: University of Michigan Press, 1992.

Ward, Hugh, 'The internal balance of power and relative economic decline', in Keith Dowding and Desmond King (eds), *Preferences, Institutions and Rational Choice*, Oxford: Clarendon, 1995.

Ortega y Gasset, José (1883–1955)

José Ortega y Gasset was born in Madrid. His father, José Ortega Munilla, was a novelist and journalist, and his mother, Dolores Gasset Chinchilla, the daughter of the owner of the important daily *El Imparcial*. Ortega's undergraduate years were spent chiefly at the Central University of Madrid, and he then spent two crucial years studying at various German universities (chiefly Marburg, under the influence of the neo-Kantians Hermann Cohen and Paul Natorp). The stimulus of foreign study convinced him that the intellectual life of his native Spain needed radical overhaul and updating, and to this purpose he was to dedicate his life's work. Back in Madrid, he was appointed Professor of Metaphysics at the Central University in 1910, a post he was to occupy until 1936. After one further year in Germany (1911), Ortega spent the period up to 1936 almost entirely in Spain, his work establishing him without contest as its leading philosopher and man of letters. In addition to his own works, he founded what was to become Spain's most prestigious learned journal, the *Revista de Occidente*, and its associated publishing house (which issued Spanish translations of major European works in science and the humanities.) This period came to an end with the outbreak of the Civil War in 1936. Fearful for his life, Ortega fled with his family in August, spending a number of years in exile in Paris, Buenos Aires and Estoril. He was able to return to Spain in 1945, and in 1948 founded the Instituto de Humanidades (Madrid) with his disciple Julián Marías; but he was unable to re-establish a settled life. His final years were occupied often with appearances at major international colloquia in America and Germany.

Ortega's social and political thought rests firmly on his overall philosophical outlook, to which he gave the name 'ratio-vitalism'. The fundamental assertion in this philosophy is that the conceptual distinction taken as ultimate in most world-views, that between the self and the world, is in fact not logically ultimate. There is a more fundamental category, namely life. Life, in Ortega's sense, is composed of 'me and my circumstances'. These two co-ultimate elements, the self and the situation in which it finds itself together constitute the basic reality which is life. Life is never static, and we can never cease to be watchful of our circumstances: as Ortega very often reiterates, 'life is a task' (*La vida es quehacer*) – we are in continual danger of shipwreck, and must work ceaselessly in order to avoid it. Reason is our greatest asset in the struggle to maintain life, and by 'reason' he means not the capacity for abstract intellection but any form of thought which brings us into contact with our circumstances (i.e. the world). He argues further that human beings are not born with a constitutive identity: we create our nature by our choices. Exactly as does Sartre, Ortega regards human beings as condemned to be free. To try to duck this, not to try to face the reality of a universe of unstable mutability, Ortega regarded as moral failure. We can only live authentically if we square up to the facts and make the choices our reason suggests to us. An important consequence of these beliefs is that the development of humanity is determined by the series of human choices. The choices of beings who lack a fixed nature are not the province of science but of history, and human affairs are fully comprehensible only if viewed historically. Following Dilthey, Ortega contends that all history ineludibly involves a viewpoint or perspective: it is not possible to transcend points of view. If objectivity is made to consist in such transcendence, then it is impossible of achievement. Ortega uses this framework of beliefs as the basis for his analysis of the society in his time.

Societies are always composed, Ortega contends, of groups with differing degrees of talent: a minority which devises the social order and invents the apparatus of civilisation, and a mass or majority, whose function it is to follow the lines thus laid down, since they are too childish and too foolish to devise such institutions for themselves. Such an order of things is an aristocracy, in its original sense of 'rule of the best', and it is in this sense that Ortega's unwavering support for aristocracy should be viewed: he believed that aristocracy is natural, and further (as will be seen) that to try to overturn it would have dire consequences. He should not be taken as advocating rule by hereditary nobles, a class which, especially in Spain, he was by no means inclined to identify with the talented minority he regarded as crucial to the existence of civilisation. Aristocrats, in Ortega's usage, are those human beings who are not smug or lazy, but who make demands on themselves. They are the creative force in human history, the originators of civilisation, and can be found in all social classes.

He contrasts this minority with the type he calls the 'mass-man in a usage applicable to either sex, and (as with Ortega's aristocrats) occurring in all social classes. The mass-man is the type of individual who is entirely content to accept the circumstances in which he finds himself, and is incurious about their origin. Such persons are undemanding of themselves, make no effort to extend their capacities or develop themselves, and are devoid alike of inventive capacity and the wish to have it. Such a person, being self-satisfied, is content that everyone else should be the same. Should this class ever come to political dominance, the results would be catastrophic: there would be a suspicion of minorities and of talent, and a gradual levelling downwards of human achievement. Ortega's fear was that in the period after the First World War, this was precisely what was happening, a situation he called 'the revolt of the masses'.

The roots of this revolt lie in the advances in science and technology in nineteenth-century Europe. Prior to this period, life for members of the majority had been hard and uncertain: nature had not been subdued to human purposes, and survival was by no means easy or guaranteed. This position changed radically in the nineteenth century, the most important feature of which was progress in subduing nature and providing a secure and abundant supply of the necessities of life. The mass-man of the mid-nineteenth century found himself in an unprecedented position of security: for the first time in history there was no need to struggle. Since there was no need to struggle, there appeared to be no need to be docile to the ideas of the organising and inventive minority, and mass-man saw no reason not to impose his own, undemanding and inauthentic standards on everyone as the ideals of life.

This condition, which Ortega found around him in all the countries of Europe in the 1920s, he regarded as dangerous in the extreme. To repeat, mass-man is incurious about the circumstances in which he finds himself, and ignorant of history. He is thus crucially unaware of one huge fact: that the civilisation on which he relies and whose existence he takes for granted is fragile, delicate and will decay if not maintained. It is, as it were, a large and improbable construction located in the midst of a jungle, and if we do not take care to maintain it, the jungle will take over again. Moreover, like every other aspect of life, civilisation does not stand still: it evolves, and needs creative minds to give it direction. Again, and importantly, it is evolving in the direction of ever-greater complexity, and the number of minds equal to the task of modifying it appropriately does not show any sign of increasing. Bolshevism and fascism, relatively new elements in the political landscape when Ortega was writing, he regarded equally as retrogressive: any exfoliation of the apparatus of the state (a feature of both systems) he regarded with alarm – the more the state takes on itself, the less the individual has to think and the less we face reality authentically ourselves, the greater the risk we run of being wrecked by the circumstances around us.

For Ortega, then, the nations of Europe were all in danger of stagnation under the dead hand of the masses. This trend could only be reversed, he argues, if Europeans found a new mission, something to struggle for, which would stimulate the creative powers of the minority and restore them to their place of leadership. His suggestion (which makes interesting reading at present) is to construct a united Europe from its constituent states. The Europeans are of a common stock and, as history shows, work best when there are problems to solve in order to realise a vision. Ortega could conceive of no fitter goal to stimulate 'European genius' than the amalgamation of European states.

There can be no doubt that Ortega's influence on the intellectual life of Spain has been incalculable: there are very few cases in which one thinker has done so much to invigorate the intellectual life of a nation. Again, not unexpectedly, his influence throughout the Hispanic-language communities in Latin America was and is enormous, and Ortega studies in these countries are extensive. In the Anglophone world, he is best known in North America, where nearly all the current English translations and studies of his works originate. In Europe outside Spain, oddly, his influence has not been great, especially in the United Kingdom where he is as unjustly neglected as is **Dilthey**, to whom he owed so much.

Main works

Obras completas (12 vols), Madrid: Alianza/Revista de Occidente, 1983.

English translations of works dealing with socio-political issues:

Concord and Liberty, trans. Helene Weyl, New York: Norton, 1946.

Invertebrate Spain, trans. Mildred Adams, New York: Howard Fertig, 1974.

Man and Crisis, trans Mildred Adams, New York: Norton, 1958.

Man and People, trans. Willard B. Trask, New York: Norton, 1957.

The Revolt of the Masses, anonymous translation, 25th anniversary edition: New York: Norton, 1957.

Further reading

Diaz, J. W., *The Major Themes of Existentialism in the Work of José Ortega y Gasset*, Chapel Hill: University of North Carolina Press, 1968.

Ferrater Mora, J., *Ortega y Gasset: An outline of his philosophy*, New Haven, CT: Yale University Press (revised), 1963.

Gray, R., *The Imperative of Modernity*, Berkeley: University of California Press, 1989.

Masrias, J., *Ortega y Gasset: Circumstance and vocation*, trans. Frances Lopez-Marillas, Norman: University of Oklahoma Press, 1970.

Rayley, H. C., *Ortega y Gasset: Philosopher of European unity*, Tuscaloosa: University of Alabama Press, 1971.

P

Pareto, Vilfredo (1848–1923)

Vilfredo Pareto is a giant amongst social theorists. He was an important figure in the early development of economics, sociology and political science. He pioneered the use of formal methods, including mathematics, to model social dynamics and also the use of social indicators to try to measure variables which are not directly observable. His work spans theoretical economics, political economy, social welfare, social change, the distribution of income, political leadership and organisational change of society. He was trained as a mathematician and engineer and worked in Piedmont, Rome and Florence, before retiring in 1889 to make a living as a consultant. It was then that he began writing in earnest, at first polemically – for which he received government and police attention. He briefly replaced Walras in Lausanne, but an inheritance allowed him to live more comfortably in Switzerland with a better home life. These stable circumstances allowed him to concentrate on writing, and his major works were all completed between 1900 and 1921. His last years were plagued with a major heart problem

Pareto may be considered one of the founders of mathematical economics. His *Manual of Political Economy* (1906) formalises many aspects of economic doctrine, including relationships of supply and demand demonstrating Walras's theory of economic equilibrium. He showed that both supply and demand, are part of a single system of interdependence operating on the basis of general principles, and that price is the manifestation of that interdependence. A change in any part of the system will result in predictable adjustments throughout the system. All major components of the economic system (such as capital formation, the number and size of firms, degree of investment, employment and inflation rates) are manifestations generated by dynamic equilibrium. Working out this equilibrium solution dominated his later sociology. He sought the fundamental dynamic equilibria which determine social and political life. He hoped to provide a deductive account of society, though his failure to do more than inductively point in the directions he thought sociology should go did not depress him. Rather he believed he had provided the groundwork for later research.

There are two kinds of equilibria: stable equilibria and unstable equilibria. The first is illustrated by increases in demand resulting in price increases which then dampen demand. The latter by increasing demand leading to new firms and technological advances which can lower price stimulating yet higher demand. Demonstrating these, he saw in these models the means by which we can understand the flux of social life and yet explain why given political and social forms present at any given moment.

By the time of the *Manual*, Pareto was a positivist and argued strongly that economics was an empirical discipline that could only describe and explain the nature of trade and economic relations. He had little time for the dominant utilitarianism of the time believing that it was impossible scientifically to make interpersonal comparisons of welfare. He made a distinction between utility, which an individual maximises by pursuing his entire set of drives (his 'residues'), and 'ophelimity', which an individual maximises from market exchange. Economics itself could say nothing about how the world should be, only how it is. In the appendix to the *Manual* (and further explained in the *Treatise on General Sociology*) he introduces the only sorts of comparison that economics can make, a conception now known as 'Pareto-efficiency'. Pareto says we can only judge that state x is better than state y if *everyone* is better off in x than in y. Economists now judge x to be 'Pareto-superior' to y, if at least one person is better off in x, and no-one else worse off. This concept is Pareto's enduring gift to economics, though these days it is often abused. Pareto believed that economics could not tell us whether or not x is superior to y if some people preferred x while *others* prefer y. But most public choice and New Right economists tend to say that x is preferable to y, only if it is Pareto-superior, which is a very different claim from Pareto's. Pareto argued that there is no invisible hand guiding us to optimal solutions, and innovations to the advantage of some may quite possibly disadvantage others. He thus argued for transfers to support the disadvantaged, a radical claim for the time.

Later Pareto became frustrated by what he saw as the narrow domain of economics, and extended his research into what is now called sociology. He held a Newtonian systemic view of society and thus searched for general equilibria in social relations. *The Rise and Fall of the Elites* attempts to identify the cycles in society, and contains the initial statement of the 'circulation of the elites' for which Pareto is best known in politics. He suggests that all aspects of society – business activity, political control, mass ideology and so on – can be seen undulating cyclically. It is the dynamic equilibrium of Walras extended to all aspects of society. He suggests that everyone is motivated by 'sentiments' or subconscious beliefs by which they evaluate the world. Each person has two types of sentiment – that which leads them to try new things, 'combinations', and that which leads them to adhere to familiar modes of actions 'persistence of aggregates'. In society as a whole, one type of sentiment dominates at any one time.

Pareto believed that regimes may remain in power as new members or subordinate classes are recruited into the elite. This circulation allows for renewal, though elites usually become dominated either by radicalism ('combinations') or conservativism ('persistence of aggregates') . If the elite gets out-of-step with the masses, this may then lead to revolutionary overthrow. Pareto argued that we get a circulation of elites as one trait (the 'lions', who use force) gets replaced by another (the 'foxes' who use guile) and back again – giving cycles to politics. Similar cycles occur amongst economic elites. This rather simplistic account in *The Rise and Fall of the Elites* became much more sophisticated in *The Transformation of Democracy* (originally published in 1921). Rather than concentrating upon the circulation of elites as individual people, Pareto looked for social transformations within organisational change. He equated force with centralised power and co-option of different groups in society with decentralisation. Regimes are most powerful when they use both force and co-option. The more centralised a regime becomes, the more probable a cult around the personality of the leader. The more decentralised, the greater the co-option of other groups. In Italy by 1920, Pareto believed that co-optation had gone too far. Too many groups had made too many demands and power had been eroded. He believed that Italy had developed into a 'pluto democracy', ruled by an oligarchic capitalist elite and hence partially plutocratic, but also with elements of mass democracy. Those who suffered were small businessmen, non-unionised labour and others outside the spheres of power. He now believed that revolution was not necessary to overthrow regimes, rather gradual organisational change could create the required circulation. However, the coming to power of Mussolini in October 1922 must have seemed a proof of this theory.

In his later writings, Pareto argued that people are not rational. In this he does not mean that they do not try to maximise their aims, but rather (a) that we cannot rationally justify aims, and (b) people act in terms of how they perceive the world, not how it is. How we view the world is dominated by the sentiments and the cycling of different ideologies. He came to the conclusion that it was impossible to justify logically one system of society, such as socialism, as superior to others; rather each type of system will give way to another in a long series of cycles. In his *Treatise of General Sociology*, he identifies a small number of features of society which determine the dynamic equilibria. The generators of equilibria are public sentiments, economic interests and the circulation of elites. Each fluctuates cyclically and is correlated with movements in the others. The character of any society depends on the sets of relationships of these general features. Cyclical change is inevitable because life is never satisfactory for everyone.

Pareto's desire to discover deductively the fundamental dynamic equilibria of society was never brought to fruition, and much of his psychology now looks dated and metaphysical. However, his aim to define equilibria is still that of economists and others who study society – instance the continuing currency of the notion of 'Pareto-optimal'. Pareto would undoubtedly have approved of modern mathematical economics, notably game theory which shares the same motivation of discovering the underlying dynamics of society and sees social, political and economic institutions as the equilibria of social interactions. More broadly, elite theory and the concepts of non-logical behaviour as he developed them are still powerful influences in social and political thought.

Main works

The Ruling Class in Italy Before 1900, New York: S. F. Vanni, 1950.

The Rise and Fall of the Elites, Totowa, NJ: Bedminster, 1968.

Manual and Political Economy (2nd edn), ed. Ann Schwier and Alfred N. Page, trans. Ann Schwier, London: Macmillan, 1971.

Treatise on General Sociology, ed. Arthur Livingstone, trans. A. Bongiorno, A. Livingstone and H. H. Rogers, New York: AMS Press, 1983.

The Transformation of Democracy, ed. Charles Powers, trans. R. Girola, New Brunswick, NJ: Transaction, 1984.

Further reading

Aron, Raymond 'Vilfredo Pareto', in his *Main Currents of Sociological Thought*, Vol. II, Harmondsworth: Penguin, 1967.

Homans, G. C. and C. P. Curtis, Jr, *An Introduction to Pareto*, New York: Howard Fertig, 1970.

Powers, Charles H., *Vilfredo Pareto*, Newbury Park, CA: Sage, 1987.

Samuels, Warren J., *Pareto on Policy*, Amsterdam: Elsevier, 1974.

Schumpeter, J. A., *Ten Great Economists from Marx to Keynes*, New York: Oxford University Press, 1951.

Parsons, Talcott (1902–1979)

Born in Colorado Springs, the son of a Protestant minister, Parsons's early life was spent in the American Mid-west. As an undergraduate, Parsons commenced his academic career studying biology and philosophy, but gradually became interested in the social sciences. On graduating, Parsons spent a year at the London School of Economics, studying sociology and anthropology, which was increasingly coming under the influence of the functionalism of Radcliffe-Brown and Malinowski. Parsons moved to Heidelberg University in 1925, where he was strongly influenced by the work of Max **Weber**. On returning to America in 1927, Parsons joined Harvard University Department of Social Relations. Throughout his career, Parsons was closely associated with Harvard University, retiring as Professor of Sociology (a post he held, in the department he helped to found, from 1942) in 1970, but maintaining contact with academia until his death.

Parsons's work is based upon detailed reconstructions and reinterpretations of a number of primary influences: principally the work of sociologists Weber, **Durkheim** and **Pareto**, functionalist anthropology and economics. Parsons's eclectic approach was crucial to his overall project of producing a universal theory of social systems which would unify the human sciences. In addition to his comprehensive theoretical expositions of social action and systems theory, Parsons produced a number of empirical studies, most notable of which are those investigating the medical profession. Parsons's work can be split into three progressive stages, although we should note that it is with Structural Functionalism that Parsons will generally be associated. *The Structure of Social Action* (1937) sets out his reconstruction and synthesis of the sociology of Weber, Durkheim and Pareto, and focuses on a theory of voluntaristic social action as a way of accounting for social order. The second phase is characterised by his work on systems theory and his formulation of structural functionalism, best represented by *The Social System* (1951). Finally, Parsons begins to move away from structural functionalism by producing a cybernetic model of social systems and social change in *Societies: Evolutionary and comparative perspectives* (1966) and *The System of Modern Societies* (1971). With each stage, Parsons attempts to answer a central question for sociology: how is social order possible?

The Structure of Social Action starts from the Weberian perspective of understanding social action: all action is meaningful, thus to understand action, we need to understand meaning associated with action. However, Parsons agrees with Durkheim's analysis that a moral order regulates society. It is the fusion of these two perspectives that creates Parsons's voluntaristic theory of social action through the creation of the action frame of reference. The understanding of social action must consider the subjective nature of action, through understanding meaning, and proceed to an analysis of the ends and means surrounding action: these occur in the context of collectively held norms and values. In this 'action frame of reference' it is the normative orientation of individuals, their orientation towards beliefs, values and norms, which is the essential component of action, rather than the simple Weberian formulation of meaning as the key component of action. Parsons uses the action frame of reference as the starting point for his solution to the problem of social order: society functions through social action, and social action is inherently normative, structured as it is by the collectively held values of society. The individual is thus seen as an agent who maximises gratification through action, and action that achieves this goal becomes institutionalised into a hierarchy of status roles.

The voluntaristic theory of social action outlined above is the starting point for Parsons's main work: his systematic functionalist sociology which receives its clearest formulation in *The Social System*. Parsons shifts his focus from analysis of the individual in society to the operation of society as a system composed of functionally interdependent subsystems and intentional agents within these: essentially Parsons here combines structural and functional analysis (hence structural functionalism) to produce a sociological theory that combines both the normative rules of social action and the functional needs of society and subsystems. In the social system (as opposed to the three other systems identified by Parsons – the cultural, personality and physical) each subsystem, and the system as a whole, has four functional prerequisites that must be met. All social systems and subsystems can be seen as meeting the functional prerequisites of adaptation to the physical world, goal attainment (ways of achieving gratification), integration (attachment of system member units to each other) and latency (ways of continuing the commitment of member units), the famous AGIL scheme. From this perspective, all social processes can be seen as solving these system problems. Parsons relates this structural analysis of system needs back to the action frame of reference through his analysis of pattern variables, the modes within which action will operate and the basic preconditions to action and meaning. Pattern variables are thus the 'choices' that individuals will make prior to establishing meaning and taking action. The pattern variables delineated by Parsons are presented in the form of polar opposites: affectivity/affective neutrality; collectivity orientation/self orientation; particularism/universalism; ascription/achievement; diffuseness/specificity. The pattern variables become an exhaustive range of values, roles and needs in human society, related directly to the AGIL functional prerequisites, although the possibility that they are incomplete as a measure of the formation of meaning becomes a point of departure for a number of criticisms of Parsons's work.

The Social System combines action, structure and function to produce a grand theory describing society in terms of functional interdependence of a hierarchy of subsystems, and functional interdependence of a hierarchy of individuals. Structural functionalism is a tool that will allow sociologists to categorise structures and actions according to a common scheme of functional requirements and modes of orientation. Given the reliance of the theory on normative analysis, Parsons faced sustained criticism from commentators who identified the lack of any way for structural functionalism to explain either social conflict or social change due to its 'static bias'. Parsons attempts to rectify these criticisms in the last phase of his work, the cybernetic model of social systems.

This model still relies upon Parsons's AGIL paradigm, but moves closer to a biological model of the social system, developing a neo-evolutionist model of social change. It is the idea of cybernetic control that predominates in the later work, with information and energy generating action in systems. By adopting the cybernetic model, Parsons can retain his goal of social equilibrium through use of the analogy of homeostasis, whilst using the AGIL scheme to show the ways in which the functional dimensions are matched by the subsystems of society, personality, environment and culture. Social change can be explained through such a theory by reference to energy and information flows between subsystems creating imbalances that will be rectified through adaptation (i.e. progress, evolution). Parsons's use of biological and organic analogies is common throughout his work, but receives heavy emphasis in *Societies: Evolutionary and comparative perspectives* and *The System of Modern Societies*. Parsons produces systematic and comprehensive accounts of the progression of societies through history based upon a highly complex analysis of the differentiation of subsystems around the production of energy and information: progressive stages of societal development arise as the four subsystems of society differentiate leading to crises of integration that are solved by adaptation and integration, controlled by flows of energy from differentiated subsystems and information from the cultural subsystem, and resulting in a more balanced and enhanced society.

Parsons's work is, at times, breathtaking in its complexity of systems analysis and typologies of social action. Yet it is a coherent formulation that attempts to integrate structure and action into an overall theory of society as a whole, and a set of classifications that can categorise all aspects of social life.

Talcott Parsons was one of the most influential of all twentieth-century sociologists, providing a complex and sophisticated systemic approach to the study of social structure and action. Parsonian systems theory became almost synonymous with American sociology in the 1950s and 1960s; indeed, we could describe structural functionalism as the paradigm of American social studies in the 1950s and 1960s: it was from within this paradigm that the work of the symbolic interactionists and, in particular, the work of Erving **Goffman** emerged, as well as being the precursor of the ethnomethodology of Harold Garfinkel, one of Parsons's graduate students.

Although Parsons's work has itself been immensely influential, we should also note that Parsons was largely responsible for the introduction of the work of Max Weber to the English speaking academic community. He translated Weber's *Protestant Ethic and the Spirit of Capitalism* in 1930, and his early years at Harvard were marked by his concern to promote the work of Weber to others. However, some would claim that Parsons's association with Weberian concepts and analysis has distorted understanding of Weber's work.

In addition to providing sociologists with a general theory of the social that incorporates possibilities for empirical research and ways of contextualising social phenomena in an overarching framework, Parsons's work has provided fertile ground for a range of critical appraisals. Most notable of these is that of C. **Wright Mills**, whose 1959 attack on Parsons's 'Grand Theory' satirises the attempt to describe society as a consensual harmonious system. Wright Mills's attack heralds the end of the hegemony of structural functionalism: as American society moved away from the (supposed) consensus of the 1950s to the divided and conflict ridden society of the 1960s, Parsons's theory, with its reliance on consensus and system equilibrium and its lack of modes of explanation for social conflict, gradually fell out of favour. In the 1970s, criticisms of Parsons's theories focused on the fixity of pattern variables, and the arbitrary nature of functional prerequisites. But in recent years Parsons's work has been utilised by **Habermas** in his analysis of system rationality in contemporary society.

Ultimately, Parsons's solution to the problem of social order is a pessimistic one, suggesting, as it does, that the individual needs restraining for society to achieve equilibrium, and that this restraint comes from institutionalised norms. When social life is seen as being conservative, social change and social conflict become difficult to explain, and conformity becomes the watchword of sociological analysis.

Main works

The Structure of Social Action, New York: Free Press, 1937.

The Social System, London: Routledge and Kegan Paul, 1951.

Economy and Society (with N. Smelser), London: Routledge and Kegan Paul, 1956.

Societies: Evolutionary and comparative perspectives, Englewood Cliffs, NJ: Prentice Hall, 1966.

Sociological Theory and Modern Society, New York: Free Press, 1967.

The System of Modern Societies, Englewood Cliffs, NJ: Prentice Hall, 1971.

Further reading

Bershady, H. J., *Ideology and Social Knowledge*, Oxford: Basil Blackwell, 1973.

Black, M. (ed.), *The Social Theories of Talcott Parsons*, Englewood Cliffs, NJ: Prentice Hall, 1961.

Habermas, J., 'Talcott Parsons: problems of theory construction', *Sociological Inquiry*, 51 (1981), pp. 173–96.

Hamilton, P., *Talcott Parsons*, London: Tavistock, 1983.

Rocher, G., *Talcott Parsons and American Sociology*, London: Nelson, 1974.

Wright Mills, C., *The Sociological Imagination*, Harmondsworth: Penguin, 1970.

Pateman, Carole (1940–)

Carole Pateman read politics, philosophy and economics at Oxford University and completed her doctorate in political theory. In 1970 Pateman published her first book, *Participation and Democratic Theory*, and in 1990 was appointed to a chair in political science at the University of California at Los Angeles. Pateman continues to write and lecture as Professor of Political Science, a leading political theorist and a feminist. Feminism is more than a social and political movement accompanying her theory or informing her style of argument, it constitutes an integral part of her challenge to modern political theory.

Generally Pateman has argued for a more democratic and active form of participatory politics than the present western form which excludes *de facto* and *de jure* certain categories of person from being political subjects. But Pateman has become known especially for her feminist critique of the political theory of liberal democracy.

In *The Sexual Contract* Pateman argues that the fiction of the social contract which initiated liberal theorising, with its notion of civil society, is a deeply patriarchal construction. For the classic liberal theorist the contract begins with the individual; individuals draw up the contract. But as Pateman points out the concept itself of the individual is a patriarchal construction in necessarily excluding women. This is true in so far as the act which constitutes the social contract depends upon an essential separation of private and public life. The social contract is a public agreement concerning civil society; and the individual who agrees to this contract must be a male, since women are restricted to the private sphere of life and as such cannot be party to any public agreement.

If the citizen in a liberal democracy is always male, then to become citizens women have to be honorary men. Furthermore, like Sigmund **Freud**, Pateman sees the contract as an agreement between brothers, against the father, to ensure male sexual rights. So the social contract conceals a *sexual contract*. The agreement between men gives them access to women; and 'far from being opposed to patriarchy, contract is the means through which modern patriarchy is constituted'.

Pateman's reconstruction of the social contract theorists, including Jean-Jacques Rousseau, Thomas Hobbes, John Locke and John Stuart Mill, contributes to the political theory of liberal democracy. Pateman's revisionary account of Rousseau brings out the difficulties with liberal theorising, due to the exclusion of women from civil society. Crucial is Rousseau's separation of private and public life, ensuring that women remain non-citizens, while men become citizens. Pateman also argues that Rousseau exhibited a profound insight: women constitute a subversive force within political order. The disorder of women results from an antagonism between the conflicting virtues of love and justice. This is inevitable for patriarchal constructions: while the demands of family life and love are particular, the demands of civil life and justice are universal and so require the subordination of private interest to public.

Pateman's reading sheds light on a problem which the formal enfranchisement of women, in recent forms of liberal democracy, has not yet solved. If contemporary women naturally respond to the moral demands of love for their own family over and above the universal principles of justice, then a question remains concerning the impact of such maternal thinking on civil life. Contemporary women, within western liberal democracy, confront two contradictory impulses: there is, on the one hand, the desire to claim admission to public life on the same basis as men, leaving aside women's private identity as irrelevant and, on the other hand, the desire to challenge the private/public distinction as a patriarchal construction denying everything real about people's life, including the realities of birth, death, desire and personal relationships.

Pateman's revisionary account of Hobbes is equally significant. But she makes Rousseau a *classic* social contract theorist who would not agree with the *modern* theorist Hobbes. Hobbes stands alone within the history of political thought in the west. Yet political theorists have not paid enough attention to his views of the state of nature as mother right and of patriarchy as masculine right. Hobbes understands patriarchy as masculine right, not paternal right; and he describes the state of nature in terms of mothers – the mother is enthroned. In the natural condition, according to his

Leviathan, 'every mother that bears children becomes both *mother* and a *lord'.* Hobbes made the convention of consent to contract absolutely fundamental. Consent identifies both enforced submission and voluntary agreement. Subordination is not natural; instead overwhelming submission is given in return for protection. Hence paradoxically, women are said to be naturally free but always subordinate to men. A wife consents to her husband in the contract of marriage; but an infant also consents to being subordinate to its mother.

In Hobbes, Pateman discovers where the modern theorist departs from the classic theorist: he rejects political right as naturally linked to the father. Modern social contract theory does not disagree with classic social contract theory about political right originating in conjugal right. But Pateman maintains that modern patriarchy endorses the subordination of wives to husbands because it arises from political interest, not from the natural rights of the father. For Hobbes, mother right exists in the state of nature and is given up in the sexual contract. So the specifically modern form of patriarchy is conventional; conjugal or sex right originates in the contract. Ultimately men's right of sexual access to women is exercised as a conjugal right and a masculine right because there cannot be two masters.

Pateman's reading of Hobbes begins with the natural dominion of mothers and the absence of the natural dominion of man over woman. Next, the social contract is introduced as a convention which gives political right to men over women, since women have consented to be subordinate as wives in marriage. Finally, Hobbes's concept of the family takes on the strange character of consensual master and slave relations. So for the modern theorist Hobbes, unlike the classic theorist Rousseau, the family is not the site of nature or nurture but of political convention and subordination.

Pateman's influence is recent. But her revisionary work receives frequent mention in feminist discussions of sexuality in political theory. More generally after Pateman, liberal political theory has not been able to remain blind to the sexual inequalities which continue unabated in deeply patriarchal constructions such as the social contract. Even John **Rawls**'s 1970s theory of justice as fairness has had to be rethought in the light of feminist critiques of political theory. Debates over precise aspects of feminist revisions of Hobbes, Rousseau and other liberal theorists are certain to continue until the inequalities and injustices of patriarchy are seen and eradicated.

However, the problem with Pateman for more radical or postmodern feminists is that her feminist revisions stay within liberal political theory, with its concepts of the autonomous individual, formal equality and abstract freedom. It is, therefore, somewhat ironic that Margaret Whitford uses Pateman to read Luce Irigaray's more radical account of women' s civil rights. In one sense, Whitford correctly uses Pateman's revisionary account of the development of liberal political theory to bring out what is implicit in Irigaray, especially the idea of a sexual contract which leaves women with no civil rights of their own. In another sense, it follows that Pateman needs to be re-read with insight from Irigaray, since the former lacks the radical feminist tools for reconceiving the specificities of female embodiment and concrete freedoms.

Main works

Participation and Democratic Theory, Cambridge: Cambridge University Press, 1970.

The Problem of Political Obligation: A critique of liberal theory (1979), Cambridge: Polity, 1985.

'"The disorder of women": Women, love and the sense of justice', *Ethics,* 91 (1980), pp. 20–34.

The Sexual Contract, Cambridge: Polity, 1988.

The Disorder of Women: Democracy, feminism and political theory, Cambridge: Polity, 1989.

'"God hath ordained to man a helper": Hobbes, patriarchy and conjugal right', in Mary Shanley and Carole Pateman (eds), *Feminist Interpretations of Political Theory,* Philadelphia, PA: Pennsylvania State University, 1991.

Further reading

Irigaray, Luce, *This Sex Which is Not One,* trans. Catherine Porter, Ithaca, NY: Cornell University Press, 1985, esp. pp. 81–5.

Kennedy, Ellen and Susan Mendus (eds), *Women in Western Political Philosophy: Kant to Nietzsche,* Brighton: Harvester Wheatsheaf, 1987.

Whitford, Margaret, *Luce Irigaray: Philosophy in the feminine,* London, Routledge, 1991.

Phillips, Anne (1950–)

Anne Phillips is Professor of Politics at London Guildhall University. Her political formation took place within the 1970s libertarian left, and it was through socialism that she first came into contact with the new women's movement. A prominent voice within British socialist feminism, Phillips was involved in working through the relationship between Marxism and feminism. More recently she has been engaged in examining the limits and possibilities of liberal democracy. She has made a vital contribution to contemporary political theory and is distinctive in refusing conventional divisions within political thought such as those between representative and participatory democracy, equality and difference.

Phillips's early work centred on the relation of women to economic policies (*Hidden Hands*) and to class (*Divided Loyalties*). This was written during an intense period of feminist engagement with Marxism over the appropriate place of politics and the relationship between capitalism and patriarchy. Themes raised in these early books, such as the importance of the division between public and private life, formal versus substantive equality and the meaning and possibilities of participation, are furthered in her later work.

Phillips's main contribution to social and political theory has focused on the need to 'engender democracy'. This work can be set in the context of a broader movement in feminist and other radical politics through the 1980s, which transformed debates on the left. These debates acknowledged the necessity of re-examining ideals of participatory politics, and demonstrated a concern to develop a specifically feminist political theory capable of articulating the difference that recognition of the gendered character of society would make to political theory and practice. *Engendering Democracy* and *Democracy and Difference* make important contributions to these discussions by examining relations between public and private life and by addressing questions of participation, citizenship, democracy and difference.

In *Engendering Democracy*, Phillips draws on Carole **Pateman**'s analysis of the patriarchal character of the individual in the liberal contract tradition and on Iris Marion **Young**'s critique of the ideal of impartiality and of notions of an undifferentiated public which dominate republican traditions of thought. Taking these issues as her starting point, Phillips problematises the existing democratic traditions of liberal representation and participatory democracy. Traditionally, representative democracy has meant non-participation for most people. The anonymity of the vote, combined with the practices of legislative bodies, have excluded women and many of the concerns raised by women from the centre of political life. Phillips agrees that participatory politics has been much practised and valued within women's movements and is important in developing the capacity to find a voice, generate agendas and act politically. However, she argues that such models present problems in relation to the demands made upon people's time (especially, but not only, women's) and in their focus on the workplace as a central site for participation. Phillips suggests that neither traditional representation nor participatory ideals of politics are adequate to address concerns raised by feminists for full political inclusion. Each requires substantial reworking to combine the strengths of the other. This raises two important issues: first, how to develop and sustain a democracy which neither subsumes women beneath pre-existing, and supposedly neutral, categories nor essentialises gendered identities; second, the need to develop specific recommendations aimed at engendering the polity through recognition of group difference.

While *Engendering Democracy* demonstrates the limitations of existing traditions of democracy, *The Politics of Presence* produces positive recommendations for reconceptualising representation. It takes up contemporary concerns regarding the recognition of difference and political exclusion through a reconsideration of the meaning of representation. Phillips argues that, as currently understood, representation derives its legitimacy from a 'politics of ideas'. Taking issue with the classic defence of representation as 'what representatives do' rather than 'who they are', Phillips argues that an exclusive focus on the 'politics of ideas' cannot deal with the political exclusion of women and minorities. It fails fully to recognise the relation of ideas to experience. Arguing against both the traditional model of representation and its simple replacement with a statistical 'mirror' of the population, Phillips advocates combining the 'politics of ideas' with the 'politics of presence'.

The Politics of Presence engages extensively with recent work by Iris Marion Young and Will Kymlicka on group representation and group rights. Phillips notes that, although commencing from different premises (respectively, a critique of impartiality versus a defence of impartiality), both Young and Kymlicka see group representation as a solution to the problem of unequal political influence. Phillips takes issue with a strong version of group representation, highlighting three kinds of problems: group narrowness and closure, 'balkanisation' and the formation of exclusive identities; how to establish what constitutes a group, which groupings are relevant and how to achieve accountability in representation; the risk of encouraging self-interest against the possibility of achieving a wider vision. While recognising that the institutional criteria appropriate for securing the presence of different groups depend on the character of the group and its particular context, Phillips suggests moving beyond these problems by focusing attention on the need to develop institutions and processes through which different voices can be heard and ideas expressed. *The Politics of Presence* therefore neither provides a monistic theory of democracy nor recommends a specific 'institutional fix'; rather, it elaborates criteria for democratic judgement, a basis on which institutional reform can be both theoretically and practically articulated.

Concern with contemporary demands for political presence made by women and minority groups has led Phillips to engage with some of the long-standing questions of the left in new and provocative ways. Her critique of existing liberal democracy in terms of the 'politics of presence' neither attacks the formalism of liberal representation (on the model of traditional Marxist analysis) nor provides a justification of dominant methods of political representation. Both fail to recognise the difference made by demands for political presence by women and minorities: Marxists have regarded liberal democracy as a sham and sought the elimination of class difference; liberal theorists have perceived difference in terms of disputes over ideas and have largely excluded substantive social and economic inequalities from having political relevance. Both approaches fail fully to address the concerns raised by movements based on gender and ethnicity. This has led Phillips to focus directly on the political level: achieving 'democracy *through* difference' via a transformation of our understanding of representation, which challenges the separation of ideas and experience.

By premising her argument on the specificity of politics as an activity and demanding political equality, Phillips leaves open the vexed question of what 'difference' the full inclusion of women and minority groups might make to the polity. Instead she focuses attention on the ways in which political theory and practice are currently gendered and exclusive and argues for mechanisms to secure equal participation through which transformation may be effected by those concerned. *The Politics of Presence* thus pursues a self-consciously limited and specifically political argument, aiming to open space for change through a conception of political equality capable of recognising difference. In this, it is radically democratic and anti-paternalist.

Phillips refuses either fully to accept or to abandon liberal democracy. Instead she works to shift the debate by combining the advantages of traditional representation with those of participation. The presence of those currently excluded from political discussion is central to the development of capacities and the expression of newly emerging needs. As such, political presence is a necessary precursor to the transformation of political agendas. This concern with the transformative possibilities of politics links Phillips's work with discussions of deliberative democracy. Both present a vision of politics which is more than the aggregation of interests and regard political debate as exploratory, encouraging new areas of understanding and providing bases for developing new areas of commonality. However, where deliberative democrats such as Jürgen **Habermas** have focused on consensus as a regulative ideal and tended to produce idealised versions of deliberation, Phillips remains aware of the potentially coercive implications of aiming to achieve consensus. Instead she emphasises the practical and reformist character of her suggestions: the 'politics of presence' suggests changes that are possible to implement now.

Phillips's work has brought feminist concerns into the political–theoretical mainstream, developing themes raised by feminism to challenge and overcome a number of important divisions within political thought. This has led to a thoroughgoing interrogation of the terms of liberal democracy, not with the aim of 'giving up on' it but of achieving greater and more equitable participation, thus reasserting the transformative possibilities of political involvement. In providing a route between universalist liberal impartiality and the potential essentialism of identity politics, Phillips has made a distinct contribution to some of the dominant questions in contemporary politics. In moving this debate from a purely theoretical realm to reconnect it with political practice through concrete suggestions for change, Phillips brings political theory together with substantive social and political concerns.

Main works

Hidden Hands: Women and economic policies, London: Pluto, 1983.

Divided Loyalties: Dilemmas of sex and class, London: Virago, 1987.

Feminism and Equality (ed.), Oxford: Basil Blackwell, 1987.

The Enigma of Colonialism: British policy in West Africa, Bloomington: Indiana University Press, and London: James Correy, 1989.

Engendering Democracy, Cambridge: Polity, 1991.

Destabilizing Theory: Contemporary feminist debates (ed. with Michele Barrett), Cambridge: Polity, 1992.

Democracy and Difference, Cambridge: Polity, 1993.

The Politics of Presence, Oxford: Oxford University Press, 1995.

Further reading

Kymlicka, William, *Multicultural Citizenship: A liberal theory of minority rights*, Oxford: Oxford University Press, 1995.

Mansbridge, Jane, *Beyond Adversary Democracy*, London: Basic Books, 1980.

Pateman, Carole, *The Sexual Contract*, Cambridge: Polity, 1988.

Young, Iris Marion, *Justice and the Politics of Difference*, Princeton, NJ: Princeton University Press, 1990.

Piaget, Jean (1896–1980)

Jean Piaget was born in 1896 in Switzerland where he spent most of his life. From an early age Piaget was interested in ontological biological studies. In his early twenties he married one of his students. His detailed case studies of the early cognitive development of their three children provided Piaget with the qualitative basis for his research into how knowledge is acquired. In the late 1920s and early 1930s Piaget published his accounts of different aspects of learning and how these developed in young children. He was not interested in individual development but in the broader genesis of knowledge; genetic epistemology. In the 1960s when his work became more widely available in English translations, his ideas became very influential in educational research and in pedagogy. Jean Piaget was the Director of the International Centre of Genetic Epistemology, Geneva which he set up and where he worked until his death. He was also Professor of Experimental Psychology at the University of Geneva and co-director of the Institut J.-J. Rousseau (Institut des Sciences de L'Education).

Piaget was interested in the concepts and tactics which are employed in developing intelligent thought and he took a biological stance towards epistemology. His position was that as children matured, so they were active in adapting successfully to their environment. Children were increasingly able to engage in internal actions through which they came to understand their environment and achieve a state of 'equilibrium'. This point about action is central to Piaget's work. However, in the unstable process of cognitive growth, equilibrium does not last long as some new event disrupts and precipitates new learning. Children develop schemata, broad patterns of understandings for all of their experiences. Piaget believed that all learning was characterised in this manner. Learning, he believed, involved the development of many schemata which were modified and reworked as a constant feature of cognitive development. Piaget and his co-workers developed a wide range of experiments which, set alongside detailed and systematic observations, were designed to elucidate and chart cognitive development. In the course of his extensive and specialised work, Piaget constructed a specific language, a conceptual method for describing this process.

Piaget proposed a sequence of three main developmental stages; sensorimotor activity which characterises the first months of infancy; pre-operational thinking which is perceptual and intuitive; the operational stage which Piaget divided into concrete and formal operational development. In the first stage the child depends on material reality and lacks the capacity to de-centre. The classic example of this stage is that, when an infant cannot see an object, or it is hidden away, the object ceases to exist for the young child. In the concrete stage the child needs practical equipment in order to support the growth of knowledge; for example, in supporting mathematical understanding it is essential to provide concrete apparatus such as counters and beads. Formal operational thought is characterised by the capacity to reason in abstract terms. The young person can now deal with the world in a hypothetical–deductive manner. Piaget formalised his ideas through many famous experiments which sought to demonstrate the invariance of these stages. One experiment involved children looking at a three-dimensional model of a landscape with three houses, spaced in a line down the centre. The task was to list the order in which the flags appeared from the opposite end of the model. The children found this difficult until they were in a stage where they could de-centre. From this, and similar experiments, Piaget argued that certain intellectual functions were just not possible until new schemata had been constructed and a specific developmental stage had been attained.

Piaget wrote about a wide range of topics; learning in mathematics and science, the development of morality, the significance of play in early childhood and the role of language in learning. His work has been highly influential in a variety of specialised contexts; linguistics, specific areas of learning such as mathematics and science as well as in the field of cognitive psychology, although it has also been criticised on various grounds. Notably it has been argued that his work with middle-class children in Geneva cannot generate a model which is applicable to all children in all social settings. However, it does have to be remembered that Piaget undertook much of his pioneering work some sixty years ago. Thus it is not surprising that contemporary workers in the field of cognitive development have critiqued his contribution. However, studies have argued for the continuity and invariance of Piagetian stage theory in a wide variety of different national/social settings. It is the specificity of time and age at each stage which has been contested.

In the United Kingdom a powerful critique has been generated by the work of Bryant and Donaldson who argued that some of the questions through which Piaget elicited his data from children, were confusing and 'tricked' children into the 'wrong' answers. They demonstrated that with appropriate material support and careful questioning, children can de-centre and can perform actions at an earlier age than Piaget believed was possible. So, in the example of the three-dimensional model, if children had a teddy bear in the seat at the other end of the table they were able to tell the experimenter the correct order in which the flags appeared to the stuffed toy. Thus it was argued that development was socially located and in the right conditions, accelerated learning could be promoted.

In relation to moral development Piaget argued that children were not able to reason about moral problems in an abstract manner until a certain stage had been reached. Piaget's work in this area was amplified and refined by theorists such as Lawrence Kohlberg who charted similar stages of maturational development. Carol Gilligan, working in the United States, has extended and partially displaced the debate in relation to her work on issues of gender and patriarchy. Her point is that moral dilemmas are tackled differently by females and males and that sex and not cognitive development is a critical issue. Gender was a variable which Piaget never explored.

Piaget's work in the area of language development has been less influential and indeed, has been superseded by others in the field, notably Lev Vygotsky and Jerome Bruner. Where Piaget saw cognitive development as a process of maturation, Vygotsky and Bruner underlined the significance of culture, interaction and context in linguistic development (as well as in other aspects of cognition). In many ways, what has happened is that contemporary insights have refined and extended the work of Piaget rather than displacing his theoretical contribution.

Piaget made a significant and unique contribution to the field of cognitive psychology over a long period of time which became reinterpreted and applied to pedagogical studies. His work has been seminal in teacher education and teacher training. A major contribution has been to revolutionise the way that childhood is conceptualised. There had been a belief that children thought in the same way as adults, they just knew less. Piaget believed that children learn in qualitatively different way from adults. Perhaps his major contribution has been to place the child's activity, physical and intellectual, in the heart of the process through which knowledge is developed.

Main works

The Language and Thought of the Child, trans. M. and R. Gabain, New York: Harcourt Brace Jovanovich, 1926.

The Child's Conception of Physical Causality, trans. M. Gabain, London: Routledge and Kegan Paul, 1930.

The Moral Judgement of the Child, trans. M. Gabain, London: Routledge and Kegan Paul, 1932.

The Origins of Intelligence in Children, trans. M. Cook, London: Routledge and Kegan Paul, 1953.

The Child's Construction of Reality, trans. M. Cook, New York: Basic Books, 1954.

Science of Education and the Psychology of the Child, trans. D. Coltman, New York: Viking, 1970.

Further reading

Brown, G. and Desforges, C., *Piaget's Theory: A psychological critique*, London: Routledge and Kegan Paul, 1979.

Beard, R. M., *An Outline of Piaget's Developmental Psychology*, London: Routledge and Kegan Paul, 1969.

Bryant, P., *Perception and Understanding in Young Children*, London: Methuen, London 1974.

Donaldson, M., *Children's Minds*, Glasgow: Fontana, 1978.

Driver, R., *The Pupil as a Scientist?* Milton Keynes: Open University Press, 1983.

Sutherland, P., *Cognitive Development Today: Piaget and his critics*, London: Paul Chapman, 1992.

Popper, Karl (1902–1994)

Born into a bourgeois Viennese family, Popper's early years were enriched by the extraordinary ferment of ideas (Freudian psychoanalysis, Marxism, the new science of relativity, the revolutionary music of Mahler and Schoenberg) in what had become the intellectual heart of Europe. From the late 1920s, Popper began to be associated with the fringes of the Vienna Circle, whose interest in the methods of science he shared. His first published work, *Logik der Forschung (The Logic of Scientific Discovery)*, was welcomed by the Vienna Circle although it undermined their most sacred doctrines. Anticipating war in Europe, Popper fled to New Zealand in 1937 where he taught philosophy and wrote the two works which were to make his name in the English-speaking world: *The Poverty of Historicism* and *The Open Society and its Enemies*. Popper returned to England in 1946 where, in 1949, he became Professor of Logic and Scientific Method at the London School of Economics. He was knighted in 1972 and continued to write, lecture and publish on a variety of philosophical questions until his death in 1994.

Any discussion of Popper's social philosophy must begin with his pioneering work on the philosophy of science. Before Popper, there was something close to a consensus on the way in which science worked. Francis Bacon proposed in his *Novum Organum* (1620) that science must begin with careful observation, through which a body of established facts could be accumulated. From these singular 'observation statements' generalisations, or scientific laws, could be formulated. The logical basis of this process, known as induction, was questioned by David Hume in his *Treatise of Human Nature* (1748). Hume pointed out that we can have no *logical* reason for believing that the future will resemble the past: because we have observed a thousand (or a hundred thousand) white swans does not enable us to state, with the force of logic, that all swans are white. Nevertheless, Hume argued that people cannot help but make generalisations based on the evidence of our senses – we are all natural inductivists, and he certainly never suggested an alternative method by which knowledge might be advanced.

Inductivism was given its most coherent statement by the logical positivists of the Vienna Circle. Seeking a method to distinguish between scientific knowledge and the 'meaningless' speculations of metaphysics, they hit on the concept of verification: a proposition is scientific to the extent that it could be verified by observations. A scientific theory could be regarded as 'true' when it had been verified by a sufficiently large number of observations and experiments.

Popper's criticism of logical positivism is generally taken to have been fatal. He agrees with Hume that inductivism is logically incoherent, but goes on to argue that scientists should, and indeed do, follow a quite different methodology. Science never begins with 'pure' observations which can then be 'worked up' into general theories. For Popper, science always begins with a problem in an existing theory, for example the inability of Ptolemaic, earth-centred cosmology to account for the motions of comets or the satellites of Jupiter. A solution can then be proposed – a heliocentric universe – which explains everything the original theory explains as well as the anomaly which initiated the whole process. Popper's originality shows itself in what comes next. The new theory should be tested, predictions should be made, experiments undertaken, not in order to *verify* the theory, but to attempt to *falsify* it. No theory can ever be proved true – multiplying confirmatory observations never establishes the universality of a law. One contradictory example, however, proves that a theory is false – the first black swan we observe disproves the theory that all swans are white.

Popper argues that science progresses through bold conjectures which are rigorously tested – through trial and error. A good theory may be more true, more useful, than its predecessors, but it can never be taken to have been proved to be true in any absolute sense. All theories will eventually be disproved – even the seemingly unassailable physics of Newton was overturned by Einstein's theory of relativity.

For Popper, human beings have evolved as problem-solving organisms. All human knowledge and, beyond that, any possibility of furthering human welfare and happiness, depends on the freedom to propose new solutions to problems, on the freedom to criticise and correct. Only an 'open' society, welcoming debate and criticism, offers the opportunity to improve itself. Popper develops his view of the open society in two works which have become celebrated more for what he attacks than for what he advocates. *The Open Society and its Enemies* develops his position through a critique of the political philosophies of Plato, Hegel and **Marx**. *The Poverty of Historicism* is a more general discussion of historicism – the view that societies develop in a given direction according to laws which, in some sense, resemble the laws of science.

Plato, a 'pessimistic' historicist, believed that every change represented a decline from an ideal. His 'perfect' state, described in *The Republic*, attempts to arrest all change. In pursuit of that goal, he advocates a rigorous censorship and the use of state propaganda to keep the citizens in their allotted positions. Both Hegel and Marx saw society as moving in the opposite direction, towards a perfect future. For Hegel, human history was the story of increasing freedom, defined as the condition of living self-consciously in a rationally organised community. Society had moved from oriental despotism (where only the king was free) through the classical world (where some were free) to the modern state (where all are free). For Marx, all history was the history of class struggle, a process that was leading, inevitably, to the triumph of the proletariat and, ultimately, to the withering away of the state.

Against the historicists, Popper argues that it is impossible to foresee the way in which human knowledge will progress and therefore predict the type of society that might develop in the future, based on that knowledge. Knowledge is a human construct, not simply the discovery of what is 'out there'. Based on conjecture, on wild guesses, it develops in unforeseeable ways, and no stage of knowledge necessarily entails any other stage, and so no stage of society entails any other stage. Hegel's 'spirit of the age' and Plato's 'fall from grace' are nothing but metaphysical justifications for the rigid and repressive forms of government they advocate.

Popper's most important arguments are reserved for the real enemy – Marxism. One line of attack confronts the claim made by Marxism to be a science - the science that had revealed the 'truth', the law by which change has occurred in our social organisation. Some Marxists had based that law of change on the Darwinian concept of evolution, thereby associating their beliefs with a notably successful scientific theory. Popper argues that the Marxist attempt to uncover universal laws of development is based on a false understanding of the nature of science. Popper had shown (to his own satisfaction, at least) that science does not discover objectively true laws that hold for all time. Rather, science is a process of trial and error, in which theories are tested, utilised if they are useful and displaced when (not *if*) they are overturned. It *is* possible, Popper agrees, to formulate good, falsifiable hypotheses from Marxism. One would be the prediction that revolution can only occur in a developed capitalist economy. Unfortunately for scientific Marxism, such predictions as it has made have all been proved wrong. Marxism has therefore, Popper asserts, been falsified and should be rejected. There are no quasi-scientific laws of development, only 'trends' with immediate causes, which can be deflected or reversed as material conditions change.

For Popper, however benign the revolutionary, the revolution must fail. It must fail because as there will be those who benefit from the existing state structure, there will inevitably be opposition to change. That opposition will need to be suppressed. Suppression will then destroy freedom. Without the freedom to criticise, to correct, change will fail. Furthermore, at each stage of a revolutionary change, events will tend to have unintended and unforeseeable consequences which frustrate the plans of the revolutionaries. These unintended consequences will demand *ad hoc* policy changes and readjustments. So utopian engineering will necessarily collapse into 'piecemeal' engineering, but of a wantonly inefficient kind, both because it is unplanned, and because it takes place in an environment where it cannot be properly assessed because of the absence of free debate.

This piecemeal social engineering is exactly what Popper puts forward as an alternative to Utopian planning. Historicists tend to argue that although there are scientific laws of social development, the actual practice of science, the hypotheses, experiments and tests that characterise physics or chemistry, cannot be applied to society. Conditions change, making it impossible to repeat experiments; society is too complex to be caught by a hypothesis; human nature itself is labile. Popper answers this by returning to his conception of science as a method of problem-solving. Society is full of *technical* problems which lend themselves to *technical* solutions. We might, for example, investigate the effects of import controls on prices or an incomes policy on unemployment. It is in confronting these piecemeal, technological problems that the scientific method of hypothesis and rigorous testing becomes useful.

Popper has been claimed by democrats of the left and the right, although he is now most often cited along with F. **von Hayek** and Milton **Friedman** as a prophet of Thatcherite/Reaganite economic policy. He is certainly an individualist and an advocate of personal freedom, but he never lost sight of the fact that the greatest threat to freedom is poverty. In contrast to the work of Hayek, Friedman and Robert **Nozick**, it is clear from all of Popper's political writings that the open society has room for a democratic socialism which advocates free health care, social security and limited intervention in the market to alleviate poverty and subjects itself to the ultimate test of free elections.

Popper has exerted a profound influence on the philosophy of science and political theory. Unusually among modern philosophers, that influence has extended beyond the academic community. Practising scientists have amended their methodology to accommodate Popper's views, and in a mark of his political influence, Helmut Kohl, the least intellectual of German Chancellors, wrote a laudatory forward to Popper's autobiography, *Unended Quest*. His reputation among professional philosophers is somewhat less exalted. His work on Plato and Hegel, in particular, has been severely criticised by specialists. His arguments against Marxism remain a formidable barrier for any would-be 'scientific' socialist to overcome.

Main works

The Open Society and its Enemies (1945), 5th edn, London: Routledge and Kegan Paul, 1966.

The Poverty of Historicism, London: Routledge and Kegan Paul, 1957.

The Logic of Scientific Discovery, London: Hutchinson, 1958.

Conjectures and Refutations: The growth of scientific knowledge, London: Routledge and Kegan Paul, 1963.

Objective Knowledge, Oxford: Clarendon, 1972.

Unended Quest: An intellectual autobiography (1976), 2nd edn, London: Routledge and Kegan Paul, 1992.

A Pocket Popper, London: Fontana, 1983.

Further reading

Hayek, F. von, *The Road to Serfdom*, London: Routledge and Kegan Paul, 1944.

Magee, Brian, *Popper*, 2nd edn, London: Fontana, 1982.

O'Hear, A., *Karl Popper*, London: Routledge and Kegan Paul, 1980.

Schilpp, P. A. (ed.), *The Philosophy of Karl Popper*, New York: Open Court, 1974.

Poulantzas, Nicos (1936–1979)

Poulantzas was a Greek Marxist sociologist who in the 1960s and 1970s produced a wide-ranging literature on contemporary capitalist societies. He focused especially on their class structure, the nature and role of the state, ideology and problems of socialist transformation. Poulantzas studied at the Universities of Athens, Heidelberg and Paris where he became a student of the French Marxist philosopher Louis **Althusser**. He subsequently lectured in the department of sociology at the University of Vincennes. He was both an academic and a political activist, holding membership of the Greek Communist Party. Poulantzas returned to Greece in 1974 following the collapse of the military dictatorship and became an adviser on education to the new government. After his death in 1979, some described him as 'the most influential Marxist writer of his generation'.

During the 1960s and 1970s in western Marxist movements there was a reaction against oppressive Stalinist dogma. European Communist parties developed new strategies for the peaceful transition to socialism. This led to debates about the nature of power in general and state power in particular, the relationship between the repressive and ideological functions of the capitalist state and its class base. One of the main contributors to these discussions was Nicos Poulantzas.

A core argument of classical Marxist theory was that the state in capitalist society served the interests of the capitalist class. Poulantzas thoroughly agreed, but believed that the real world was more complex. Building on the work of the founding fathers as well as later Marxists like **Lenin**, **Gramsci** and Althusser, Poulantzas saw his task as developing a comprehensive Marxist theory of the capitalist state. Following Althusser, Poulantzas began by dividing the capitalist 'social formation' into three main subsystems: the economic, the political and the ideological, each 'relatively' independent from one another. He asserted that the capitalist state best served the capitalist class when its members did *not* participate directly in the state apparatus; that is to say when the ruling class was not the governing class. In practice the state needed to be 'relatively autonomous' from the ruling class – that is, from both the power bloc as a whole (an unstable alliance of diverse class fractions, e.g. landed, financial and industrial capital) and the hegemonic class or dominant fraction within the alliance. Only in this way could the state represent, organise and unify the long-term political interests of the ruling class as a whole in its constant struggle with the working class. As Poulantzas put it: 'The capitalist state, characterised by hegemonic class leadership, does not *directly* represent the dominant classes' economic interests, but their *political interests*: it is the dominant classes' political power centre, as the organising agent of their political struggle' (*Political Power*). The relative autonomy of the capitalist state resulted from three sets of factors: first, it allowed the state to intervene in order to arrange concessions and compromises in dealings with the dominated classes, sometimes against powerful capitalist opposition. In the long run these policies were beneficial to the economic interests of the dominant class and the different fractions comprising the power bloc. Second, it enabled the state to arbitrate between the competing economic claims of different class fractions. Sacrifices and compromises could be imposed by the state in order to guarantee the achievement of long-term common interest, involving 'global hegemony over the dominated classes'. Finally, the relative autonomy of the state enabled it to intervene ideologically in order to reproduce capitalist relations of production. Poulantzas distinguished between 'repressive state apparatuses' like the army, police and judiciary, and 'ideological state apparatuses', which included the family, schools, church and mass media. Through the ideological apparatuses the state concealed its class nature. It gave the impression that it was a neutral arbiter among the warring social classes, representing 'the general will' rather than the interests of the ruling class. This dominant ideology functioned as an 'internal cement', contributing to the cohesion or unity of the entire social system in the interests of the capitalist class. In the long run, Poulantzas emphasised, the autonomy or independence of the state was always strictly limited by the capitalist mode of production and the domination of a single ruling class.

But Poulantzas did not only analyse conventional capitalist states. He also attempted to get to grips with the distinctive features of fascism. In *Fascism and Dictatorship* he demonstrated that the states established by Italian and German fascism were 'exceptional' types of state different from parliamentary democracies. In neither Italy nor Germany could the 'normal' capitalist state provide enough protection for big business. Economic and political crises entailing the rise of strong labour movements and revolutionary political parties necessitated the creation of 'exceptional' states which emphasised their outright repressive functions. At the same time, fascist rule did not simply represent the 'dictatorship of capital'. Poulantzas stated that: 'Throughout the rise of fascism and after the conquest of power, fascism . . . *characteristically* has a relative autonomy from . . . big monopoly capital, whose hegemony it has established.' The relative autonomy between the economic and political realms guaranteed that the fascist state could play the crucial role of attempting to reconcile the different class fractions and conflicts within the power bloc. In the *Crisis of the Dictatorships* he discussed the decline of 'exceptional' capitalist states in Spain, Portugal and his native Greece, which had been under a military dictatorship. For Poulantzas these countries were dependent on international capitalism especially the United States and the EEC. They were characterised by a dependent form of state, the domination of foreign capital, and the lack of any genuine national independence. In each case there were two important and divided fractions of the ruling class: the 'comprador' bourgeoisie, representing the interests of foreign capital, and a domestic or 'internal' bourgeoisie, based on developing industrialisation (especially light industry), partly representing native capital and partly administering foreign capital. But neither could be considered to represent a genuine 'national' bourgeoisie. The collapse of Mediterranean dictatorships revolved around the level of conflict, and political positions adopted by the 'reactionary' and 'progressive' sectors of the bourgeoisie, one based on foreign capital, the other on indigenous capital. If the 'internal' bourgeoisie formed an alliance with the working class, the dictatorships could be overthrown.

Poulantzas also embarked on a major project to delineate the changes that had occurred in the class structure of advanced capitalist societies in the post-war era. He was concerned about the internationalisation of the capital – mainly American – and its impact on local class structures and alliances. Another of his interests, having both theoretical and strategic implications, was the 'boundary problem' especially in relation to the class position of the petty bourgeoisie. Poulantzas classified professional intellectuals as part of this stratum. But in order to distinguish them from the traditional petty bourgeoisie of artisans and small shopkeepers, he referred to intellectuals as members of a separate new middle class or 'new petty bourgeoisie'. Poulantzas subsequently highlighted the increasing participation of this class in new social movements (housing, transport, environment, etc.). At the same time, this changing pattern of popular rebellion threatened the traditional alliance between the bourgeoisie and petty bourgeoisie.

In the last book before his untimely death, *State, Power, Socialism*, Poulantzas restated his earlier theory of the state and discussed proposals for the transition to socialism in advanced capitalist countries. In developing a political strategy, he was basically sympathetic towards the political changes that had occurred in West European Communist parties during the 1970s. These involved criticism of the Bolshevik model of revolutionary change and a commitment to a democratic, parliamentary road to socialism. But Poulantzas also formulated his own ideas which differed from those of official Eurocommunism. It was not merely a question of socialist parties gaining state power through electoral victories. The crucial problem facing the democratic road to socialism was how to reform the state radically in such a way that 'the extension and deepening of political freedoms and the institutions of representative democracy . . . are combined with the unfurling of forms of direct democracy and the mushrooming of self-management' would prevent the perpetuation of 'authoritarian statism' and enable the working class to move successfully towards socialism.

Poulantzas was a major contributor to Marxist political analysis in the post-war period. But he was not without his critics. In a long-running debate with the British Marxist, Ralph Miliband, his work was criticised for its abstraction, obscure language and paucity of empirical studies of actual capitalist states. Miliband asked the key question which Poulantzas had failed to answer: exactly how relative is relative autonomy? Other critics argued that he only examined the negative workings of capitalist states and ignored their role in welfare provision and crisis management. His theoretical work on fascism was weakened by a careless use of historical evidence. Poulantzas's work on classes in contemporary capitalism was criticised for lacking historical perspective and neglecting social mobility. His preoccupation with class struggle rooted in the relations of production ignored other types of social conflict – gender, ethnic, religious, national and regional – which cut across class divisions.

By the 1980s, the theoretical debate on the nature of the capitalist state was virtually exhausted and had given way to concrete research on national and local power structures. The most balanced assessment of Poulantzas's work and influence was made by the American sociologist E. O. Wright:

> It would be difficult to exaggerate the importance of Nicos Poulantzas's contri-
> bution to the development of the Marxist theory of the state. While there is a
> great deal to criticise in his work, both in terms of the form of the exposition and
> many of his specific formulations, still his ideas have systematically shaped the
> analysis of the state of both his critics and supporters for nearly a decade. (M.
> Maier and D. Gilroy (eds), *Reading Lists in Radical Social Science*, New York:
> Monthly Review Press, 1982)

Main works

Political Power and Social Classes, London: New Left and Sheed and Ward, 1973.

Fascism and Dictatorship, London: New Left, 1974.

Classes in Contemporary Capitalism, London: New Left, 1975.

The Crisis of the Dictatorships: Portugal, Spain, Greece, London: New Left, 1977.

State, Power, Socialism, London: New Left, 1978.

Further reading

Van den Berg, A., *The Immanent Utopia: From Marxism on the state to the state of Marxism*, Princeton, NJ: Princeton University Press, 1988.

Blackburn, R. (ed.), *Ideology in Social Science: Readings in critical social theory*, London: Fontana, 1972.

Clarke, S. (ed.), *The State Debate*, London: Macmillan, 1991.

Hirsh, A., *The French New Left: An intellectual history from Sartre to Gorz*, Boston, MA: South End Press, 1981.

Jessop, B., *Nicos Poulantzas: Marxist theory and political strategy*, New York: St Martin's, 1985.

R

Rawls, John (1921–)

Currently Professor Emeritus of Philosophy at Harvard University, John Rawls is widely regarded, in the English-speaking world at least, as the most influential political theorist of the twentieth century. He has often been credited with a single-handed revival of the tradition of normative political philosophy with the publication, in 1971, of his *A Theory of Justice*. While he has achieved great fame as an academic proponent of liberal justice, Rawls has shied away from any significant public role as an intellectual and has been careful to avoid the cultivation of a celebrity status. After serving in the Second World War, he dedicated his professional life to working out a conception of justice that could regulate social interaction within modern democratic societies. He studied at Princeton University and, after teaching at Cornell University from the early 1950s, became Professor of Philosophy at Harvard in 1976. Though he retired in 1991 he continued to revise and develop his conception of egalitarian liberalism. This culminated in the publication in 1993, of his much discussed second book, *Political Liberalism*.

If we regard citizens of modern pluralist societies as free and equal, then what is the most appropriate conception of justice for specifying fair terms of their co-operation with one another? Rawls's theory offers an answer to this question. He presents, first, a procedure that specifies fair conditions of choice for principles of social justice, and second, an argument for the choice of two substantive principles. He refers to these principles as his conception of justice as fairness and he takes them to represent the most reasonable basis of social unity in a society characterised by the fact of pluralism. In other words, he thinks his principles can be affirmed on moral grounds by all reasonable citizens despite the fact that those citizens actually endorse a variety of incompatible conceptions of a good life.

The procedure of choice that Rawls outlines is an innovative variation on the idea of a social contract as it developed in the tradition from Locke to Rousseau and Kant. Principles of justice that are to regulate the basic structure of society – that is, the political constitution and the most important economic and social arrangements – are ones that would be chosen in an initial act of agreement. We are to imagine ourselves as parties to a hypothetical contract that takes place in an 'original position'. The parties are concerned to further their own interests, but no party is to be advantaged or disadvantaged by the outcome of natural chance or the contingency of social circumstances. So, while the parties know general facts about the political and economic workings of a modern society, they must make their choice behind a 'veil of ignorance' which denies them any particular knowledge of their own actual social position. If the choice is to be made under conditions of fairness, then it must not be infected by the bias that might follow from such particular knowledge. Were the parties to be aware of their own class, sex, race, sexual orientation, of their natural talents, intelligence, strength, of their particular conception of the good, then not only would a moral agreement seem impossible but any agreement that was reached would be the result of a compromise that would favour those social groups who just happen to occupy strong bargaining positions.

Rawls believes that since the original position is designed to represent conditions of fairness that we (real citizens) actually do accept, then the principles chosen by the parties to this hypothetical contract are the ones that should regulate all further agreements regarding the basic structure of society. Since the parties are ignorant of their actual social position, yet concerned to further their own interests, they are motivated to ensure that any inequality should be to the benefit of every social group, most particularly to the group that would be least advantaged by that inequality. Each of the parties is aware that they could be deciding for the worst-off social group. They will, therefore, choose principles that will maximise the life-prospects of that group. This leads Rawls to argue that the parties would choose these two principles, and that they would give priority to the first over the second. *First*: Each person is to have an equal right to the most extensive total system of equal basic liberties compatible with a similar system of liberty for all. *Second*: Social and economic inequalities are to be arranged so that they are both (a) to the greatest benefit of the least advantaged, consistent with the just savings principle, and (b) attached to offices and positions open to all under conditions of fair equality of opportunity. This, so-called 'difference principle' entails that any positions in society which bring advantage may only exist if all are able to pursue them on an equal footing. All of the theory's essentials, including the choice of principles, are laid out in the first part of *A Theory of Justice*. In the second part he draws out some of the implications of the conception of justice as fairness for the political, economic and social institutions of a constitutional democracy. In the third part, he gives an account of how a well-ordered society, regulated by justice as fairness, could generate conditions for its own stability.

Rawls has engaged impressively with critics both of the procedure of choice and of the liberal egalitarian substance of the two principles. His position has been developed most notably however in relation to the account of stability. In a series of essays that were revised and included in *Political Liberalism* he gives an alternative account of stability that takes seriously the plurality of reasonable, yet incompatible, comprehensive religious, moral and philosophical doctrines that are likely to persist over time and to attract a sizeable number of adherents in a just constitutional democratic state. The idea of an overlapping consensus is designed to explain how a political, and not a metaphysical, conception of justice as fairness can be affirmed on moral grounds by all citizens who endorse some such reasonable doctrine.

In the past decades Rawls's work has generated at least three lively series of debates which have been at the heart of recent developments in moral and political philosophy. The initial aim of *A Theory of Justice*, and indeed of the influential essays which preceded it, was to present a theoretically robust conception of social justice as a challenging alternative to the utilitarian moral frameworks that had dominated Anglo-American philosophy for much of the century. Rawls maintained that utilitarianism, by stressing the overriding aim of maximising the general welfare, fails to take sufficiently seriously the inviolability and the distinctness of individual persons. In order to overcome this problem Rawls argues that we must give priority, in our thinking about justice, to ideas of rightness over conceptions of goodness. The right is not determined by the good, or the maximum sum of individual satisfactions; rather the good must be constrained by the right. The basic liberties of each individual must be guaranteed even if this does not maximise the general welfare. While it is arguable that this fundamental shift of emphasis has had a fairly weak impact on political life in the public realm, Rawls has been remarkably successful within academic circles in his efforts to displace utilitarianism from its position of theoretical dominance. In fact, the Rawlsian framework has now become the orthodoxy against which alternative conceptions of justice will have to be judged.

The second series of debates was concerned with the liberal egalitarian substance of justice as fairness. On the one hand, libertarians argued that the second principle is far too egalitarian since it unjustifiably rules out inequalities that are not to the greatest benefit of the worst off social group. This, the libertarian maintains, fails to respect the inviolability of a talented individual by treating natural assets as a common resource. On the other hand, socialists have criticised the priority that Rawls assigns to the first principle, guaranteeing equal basic liberties, over the second, which regulates economic inequalities. While Rawls tries to find a reasonable balance between the values of liberty and equality, there are a number of aspects of his theory which could give it a radically egalitarian critical thrust. For instance, he claims that the political liberties must be guaranteed to be of fair value for each citizen. This could be taken to require a stringently egalitarian distribution of income, wealth and control of material resources.

The third and most recent series of debates has concerned the criticisms of liberalism made by communitarian thinkers. These critics have highlighted a number of possible problems with respect to the philosophical assumptions that underlie Rawls's theory. Most significantly it is claimed, first, that he relies on an untenably individualistic conception of the human self, and, secondly, that he overemphasises the extent to which a liberal state can be neutral between competing conceptions of the good. While the stress, in his recent work, on the political (not metaphysical) nature of his theory may be successful in deflecting the first criticism, it is not yet clear that he can give a convincing answer to the second.

It would be no exaggeration to suggest that much of the work done in normative political theory, at least in the English-speaking world, has, for over twenty-five years, consisted in a series of responses to Rawls's account of justice as fairness. Since the publication of *A Theory of Justice* it has been virtually impossible for normative political theorists to ignore the agenda that Rawls has set. Some have extended and developed his liberal approach to justice, or else produced some variant on it. Others have offered a different perspective on justice, typically presenting it as an alternative to Rawls's liberal framework. Others still, and feminists have been most notable here, have challenged the priority which has been given to theories of justice as a result of the extraordinary impact of Rawls's work.

Main works

A Theory of Justice, Oxford: Oxford University Press, 1971.

'Fairness to goodness', *Philosophical Review*, 84 (1975), pp. 536–54.

'Social unity and primary goods', in Amartya Sen and Bernard Williams (eds), *Utilitarianism and Beyond*, Cambridge: Cambridge University Press, 1982.

'A Kantian conception of equality' in John Rajchman and Cornel West (eds), *Post-Analytic Philosophy*, New York: Columbia University Press, 1985.

'The law of peoples', in Stephen Shute and Susan Hurley (eds), *On Human Rights: The Oxford Amnesty lectures 1993*, New York: Basic Books, 1993.

Political Liberalism, New York: Columbia University Press, 1993.

'Reply to Habermas', *Journal of Philosophy*, 92 (1995), pp. 132–80.

Further reading

Daniels, Norman (ed.), *Reading Rawls: Critical studies on Rawls' 'A Theory of Justice'*, rev. edn with a new preface, Stanford: Stanford University Press, 1989.

Kukathas, Chandran and Philip Pettit, *Rawls: A theory of justice and its critics*, Cambridge: Polity, 1990.

Martin, Rex, *Rawls and Rights*, Lawrence: University of Kansas Press, 1985.

Mulhall, Stephen and Adam Swift, *Liberals and Communitarians*, 2nd edn, Oxford: Basil Blackwell, 1996.

Pogge, Thomas, *Realizing Rawls*, Ithaca, NY: Cornell University Press, 1989.

Sandel, Michael, *Liberalism and the Limits of Justice*, Cambridge: Cambridge University Press, 1982.

Rowbotham, Sheila (1943–)

Sheila Rowbotham was born in Leeds and studied history at St Hilda's, Oxford. She has taught in schools, colleges and for the Workers' Educational Association. She has been Visiting Professor in Women's Studies at the University of Amsterdam and worked for the Popular Planning Unit of the Greater London Council until its abolition in 1986. She now works as Research Adviser in the Women's Programme of the World Institute for Development Economics Research, part of the United Nations University, and as a freelance writer.

Sheila Rowbotham is a socialist-feminist writer and historian best known for her work on, and in, the women's movement. She is the author of a number of highly influential historical studies, a considerable body of theoretical and political articles and essays, published both in academic and popular contexts, and has been involved in many collective and collaborative projects within socialist and feminist movements. Her work is characterised throughout by a refusal to separate analysis of women's oppression and liberation from analysis of class and by an insistence on the interimplication of theory and practical activism. When she writes as a theorist it is emphatically with practical objectives in mind and theory is envisioned not as an absolute truth or blueprint but as a set of maps or an enabling device: 'Making a theory gives you enough bounce to leap up in the air, meet critics head on and land on your feet with an alternative without getting too puffed' (*Beyond the Fragments*, 1979).

As her retrospective accounts of her development as a historian indicate, Rowbotham was influenced both by Marxist theory, which offered a radical alternative to traditional historiography, and by her own involvement in socialist organisations and the women's movement. Much of her work has been explicitly concerned with charting the development of liberation movements, analysing the strengths and weaknesses of radical theoretical and organisational models, and with the development of strategies for meeting the challenges of changing socio-economic contexts.

Rowbotham's first book, *Women, Resistance and Revolution* (1972), outlined a narrative of women's struggles against inequality from the seventeenth century to the late twentieth century and began the exploration of the relationship between women's liberation and the revolutionary left which constitutes one of her recurrent themes. This was followed swiftly by her most influential historical study *Hidden from History: 300 years of women's oppression and the fight against it* (1973), which traces the changing position of women in England within capitalist and male-dominated formations, and the more theoretical *Woman's Consciousness, Man's World* (1973) which presents Rowbotham's analysis of the emergence of feminist consciousness, and her model of socialist feminism as a radical alternative to a male-dominated left which had failed to address the specificity of women's oppression.

These texts had a considerable impact within second-wave feminism, establishing Rowbotham as one of the most powerful voices in the British women's movement but also raising a number of questions about the direction and priorities of that movement. Just as Rowbotham criticised orthodox Marxism's privileging of the economic and social relations of the workplace and neglect of human relations in the family so she took issue with reformist and separatist tendencies within feminism. *Hidden from History*, and numerous articles, in recovering the marginalised history of women's lives and focusing on issues such as birth control and female sexuality as well as work and political activity, fulfilled many of the aims of second-wave feminist scholarship and provided an influential model for feminist history. But Rowbotham's work differed significantly from that of other key feminists of her generation such as Germaine Greer and Kate Millett. Her historical explorations countered the concentration on middle-class, university-educated women's experiences within much second-wave feminism with evidence of the diversity of women's experience. Like bell hooks's later work on African–American women, Rowbotham's histories of working-class women challenged the apparently universal but actually limited model of woman presented in mainstream feminism.

Rowbotham's departure from other feminist models lay not only in the sort of women on whom she focused but in her understanding of the basis of oppression. Her materialist analysis of the impact of social and economic conditions on women's experience resulted in a refusal to endorse the idea that women's oppression could be explained by reference to 'patriarchy' as a universal or fixed structure of male domination. The most critical responses to her critique of patriarchy were not, however, voiced by essentialist feminists but by other socialist–feminist historians, such as Sally Alexander and Barbara Taylor, who, convinced of the inability of Marxist theory to accommodate feminist analysis, had turned to psycho-analytic theory in order to explore sexual difference. More generally Rowbotham has been criticised by some feminists for not attending to the psychic complexity of the personal experience which she foregrounds in her work, but praised by others for avoiding the individualism and ahistoricism sometimes evident in psychoanalytic approaches.

Although it is the feminist strand of Rowbotham's work which has received the most attention, her analysis of Marxist and socialist theory and practice has had considerable impact in debates on the future of radical politics. One of her most influential texts was first published, like much of her work, as a pamphlet. *Beyond the Fragments: Feminism and the making of socialism*, co-written with Lynne Segal and Hilary Wainwright, called for a reappraisal of the forms and priorities of radical politics, criticising the hierarchical and exclusionary structures of traditional Leninist thinking and organising. Presented in the form of three essays based on the authors' different experiences within political organisations and the women's move-ment, the text argued for the development of new forms of organisation based on democratic participation rather than on hierarchical structures of leadership, which would be attentive to material needs rather than abstract principles and able to accommodate people's complex and varied relationships and experiences. Rowbotham's critique of the exclusionary and hierarchical tendencies of Leninism has been retrospectively described as deconstructive in its challenge to Leninism's claims to transcendental truth, through reading it as a historically specific activity, and in its insistence on the multiplicity and contingency of meaning.

Whilst welcoming the articulation of class and gender in the debates initiated by *Beyond the Fragments*, some black feminists criticised the euro-centrism and racism by omission of socialist feminism. In her recent work Rowbotham has broadened the scope of her study to include liberation movements beyond Europe. *Women in Movement: Feminism and social action* (1992) and *Dignity and Daily Bread: New forms of economic organising among poor women in the Third World and the First* (1994), co-edited with Swasti Mitter, both developed from her involvement in the Women's Progamme of the United Nations World Institute for Development Economics Research and can be read as a continuation of Rowbotham's ongoing analysis of the interrelationship of ideas and actions in radical movements.

Rowbotham's prolific output and the diversity of her writings point to her significant contribution to feminist and socialist theory in the past three decades, although she has received less attention in academic surveys of the women's movement than many less widely read feminist thinkers. She has had a profound influence on the development of women's history and feminist historiography and it would be difficult to overestimate the impact of her work, written both individually and in collaboration with others, on the direction of debates within radical political and feminist movements.

Main works

Women, Resistance and Revolution, Harmondsworth: Penguin, 1972.

Hidden from History: 300 years of women's oppression and the fight against it, London: Pluto, 1973.

Woman's Consciousness, Man's World, Harmondsworth: Penguin, 1973.

Dutiful Daughters: Women talk about their lives (ed. with Jean McCrindle), Harmondsworth: Pelican, 1977.

A New World for Women: Stella Browne – socialist feminist, London: Pluto, 1977.

Socialism and the New Life: The personal and sexual politics of Edward Carpenter and Havelock Ellis (with Jeffrey Weekes), London: Pluto, 1977.

Beyond the Fragments: Feminism and the making of socialism (with Lynne Segal and Hilary Wainwright), London: Merlin, 1979.

Dreams and Dilemmas: Collected writings, London: Virago, 1983.

The Past is Before us: Feminism in action since the 1960s, London: Pandora, 1989.

Women in Movement: Feminism and social action, London: Routledge, 1992.

Dignity and Daily Bread: New forms of economic organising among poor women in the Third World and the First, London: Routledge, 1994.

Further reading

Ryan, Michael, *Marxism and Deconstruction: A critical articulation*, Baltimore and London: Johns Hopkins University Press, 1982.

Samuel, Raphael (ed.), *People's History and Socialist Theory*, London: Routledge and Kegan Paul, 1981.

Spender, Dale, *For the Record: The making and meaning of feminist knowledge*, London: Women's Press, 1985.

S

Samuelson, Paul A. (1915–)

Paul Samuelson was born in Gary, Indiana on 15 May. He is perhaps best known for his formidable textbook *Economics: An introductory analysis* (first published in 1948), which in 1992 reached its fourteenth edition. Those not acquainted with the nature of undergraduate economics teaching find it hard to appreciate the absolute centrality of an introductory textbook to the pedagogy of modern economics. Samuelson's version remains the most successful of all the post-war textbooks, forming the basis for the training of five generations of professional economists, and of those taking economics options as part of other degree courses. The front cover of the fourteenth edition is made up of the word *economics* translated into all the languages in which this book has been published (now over forty according to its author). Since most of the other introductory textbooks in economics cover much the same ground as does Samuelson, and were modelled on his own approach, it can safely be said that for all intents and purposes *Economics* establishes the modern canon of what economics is about.

It is extremely difficult neatly to summarise Samuelson's contribution to the substance of economic analysis. Although he singly authored only two books (*Foundations of Economic Analysis* and *Economics*), plus one joint book (*Linear Programming and Economic Analysis*, written with Robert Dorfman and Robert Solow), his reputation amongst professional economists rests more upon the sheer volume and quality of his scientific papers. Economics is an article-driven discipline and Samuelson has played the journal article game assiduously and with effect. There is barely a single field within conventional economics where Samuelson has not made a very significant or central contribution, and most often he has served to define the current contours of that field. This was all recognised in 1970 when he received the Nobel Prize for economics.

Perhaps the best way to begin an appraisal of Samuelsonian economics is with the *Foundations of Economic Analysis* (first published in 1947, though the bulk of it was written as early as 1941). This pre-dates *Economics* and is in many ways more indicative of his overall approach to economics, and thus to the nature of modern economics generally. This is a very 'technical' book. It rather self-consciously parades its mathematical and formalistic credentials, thus prefiguring all current conventional economics. The issue at stake in the book is broadly speaking to define the conditions under which prices formed out of equilibrium can be corrected to correspond to an equilibrium. It is thus concerned with the dynamic properties of the economic mechanism, set in the context of the establishment of an equilibrium for the system as a whole. What this amounts to is a mathematical way of conceiving the nature of the operation of supply and demand schedules in an economic system. Agents are assumed to maximise their objective functions – in Samuelson's particular formulation, making choices that reveal their preferences between possible outcomes – subject to constraints. This established the optimum welfare outcome for the system as a whole. Under these conditions, slight deviations of the variables from their equilibrium values are self-correcting. Different possible static equilibrium situations so constructed can in principle be compared via a Bergsonian social welfare function (a way of combining the welfare of individual economic agents), so that genuine **Pareto** improvements can be discerned (making at least one person better-off without making the others worse-off). To do all of this Samuelson makes liberal use of differential and integral calculus.

This, then, was the first truly mathematical treatment of the properties of a market economy, seemingly building on Adam Smith's discursive treatment, but also quite dramatically changing it. It established a thoroughly neo-classical approach to the market system, with perfect competition taken as the exemplary market form, and it represents much of the rigorous theoretical foundation that still underpins the orthodoxy of modern neo-classical economics.

It is in his *Economics* that Samuelson's other great claim to fame can be found. This book embodies his approach to macro-economics, and particularly his attitude towards the 'Keynesian revolution' with which his formative writing was so closely involved. *Economics* sets out what has come to be known as the 'Neo-classical synthesis' in respect to the Keynesian system. To start with, Samuelson invented a key technique for the representation of a systematised Keynesianism, namely the '45 degree diagram'. One of the features of economics textbooks – a central technique for the way we have all come to 'know' the economy – is the use of diagrammatic representations. Samuelson's, and other textbooks, contain an incredible number of these analytical figures. The 45 degree diagram registers the way shifts in aggregate demand determine output in the context of a multiplier mechanism. This is now a standard technique in introductory economic analysis, though one that is perhaps less popular nowadays as scepticism with the efficacy of 'demand management' has grown in intellectual circles. Nevertheless, it points to the way Samuelson at least was – and probably remains – a Keynesian in his approach to macro-economic matters. But this is a particular version of Keynesianism. The neo-classical synthesis locates its Keynesianism within the intellectual terrain marked out by the *Foundations*. The system is an equilibrating one, where the movement is between one static partial equilibrium position and another. Whether this remains true to the spirit of what Keynes actually meant continues to be heavily disputed in macro-economics, with so-called 'post-Keynesians' challenging the location of any Keynesian system within a Samuelsonian-type equilibrating framework. Those opposed to neo-classical economics in general, and the neo-classical synthesis in particular, reject this outright. For them, the innovative feature of **Keynes**'s own analysis was precisely its rejection of a static equilibrating framework. Uncertainty and risk pervaded the Keynesian economic system, they claim, which undermines confidence in any analysis stressing adjustments towards static equilibrium positions.

So much for the theoretical substance and central tenets of the Samuelsonian system. One thing that should be made clear is the difficulty for the average reader of understanding his books and articles. Even *Economics* is not an easy read; a lot is quite simply beyond an introductory level. It also means that there is no 'Samuelsonian school' of economics. Samuelson has kept himself very much to himself in the grand ideologically driven disputes between schools of economic thought, and he has been modest with his empirical work, his policy advice and economic forecasting. He therefore lacks the 'common touch' so necessary to be in the forefront of economic dispute and policy formation. His intellectual and spiritual home remains very much the universities of Cambridge in Massachusetts, Harvard, where he was a graduate student, and MIT, where he has taught for most of his life. These have provided him with the base to influence the discourse of economics, rather than the direction of economies.

It is interesting, however, to trace the evolution of a textbook like *Economics* through its various editions to gain a little more precise insight into the changing contours of the conventional economics canon. The earliest four editions for instance, provided a more discursive format, explicitly offering the analysis to the 'intelligent citizen interested in a general education' (2nd edn, 1951), and being particularly sensitive to the institutional specificities of the economy (or, rather, the US economy). It was the 1961 fifth edition that signalled a real change in style, however. From then on, the objective was to embrace a thoroughly modern agenda, to establish the book's scientific credentials, the centrality of uncovering the theoretical secrets of the market mechanism, the best of modern thinking, and the like (see the Preface to the 14th edition). Like the trajectory of modern economics it so effectively shadowed, the style lost much of its discursive and institutional feel as it increasingly embraced the tight and formalised structure now followed by every conventional textbook.

But economics are changing and there is a question as to whether *Economics* will be able to adapt to this fast enough to maintain its market lead. A new co-author, William Nordhaus, was recruited for the 14th edition. Although Samuelson was trained as an economist in the era when the American economy was experiencing violent fluctuations, that did not seem to influence much his own understanding of how the actual economic mechanism worked. He was concerned with the new intellectual agenda of 'modernism', understood in terms of the scientificity of physics and the usefulness of mechanical analogies. But we are now entering an era of renewed economic uncertainty and risk, with a potential for violent fluctuations in business activity, where the global market-place is integrating fast as large oligopolistic competitors fight out their strategic battles. Whether an approach to economic analysis that continues to stress the virtue of perfect competition, free trade and partial equilibrium adjustments will remain viable in this new era remains to be seen.

Main works

Foundations of Economic Analysis, Cambridge, MA: Harvard University Press, 1947.

Economics: An introductory analysis, 2nd edn, New York: McGraw Hill, 1951.

Economics (with W. D. Nordhaus), 14th edn, New York: McGraw Hill, 1992.

Further reading

Brown, E. C. and R. M. Solow (eds), *Paul Samuelson and Modern Economic Theory*, New York: McGraw-Hill, 1983.

Feiwel, George R. (ed.), *Samuelson and Neoclassical Economics*, Boston, MA and London: Kluwer, 1982.

Fendry, A., 'Paul Samuelson and the scientific awakening of Economics', in J. R. Shackleton and G. Lockley (eds), *Twelve Contemporary Economists*, London: Macmillan, 1981.

Schumacher, E. F. ('Fritz') (1911–1977)

Fritz Schumacher was born in Bonn. After studying and working in business in Europe and North America during the 1930s he settled in the United Kingdom just prior to the Second World War and eventually became a British citizen. Although he never actually gained a degree he established himself as an economist of high repute, always with vision and often with contrary opinions. During the 1970s he became one of the most widely known 'guru' type figures of the alternative lifestyle movement. This was mainly because of his best-known book *Small is Beautiful*, which advocated an alternative vision for economic society based upon humanistic values, small-scale economic organisation, attention to environmental and eco-logical issues, and perhaps his most important and enduring legacy, the idea of 'intermediate technology'.

Schumacher made many earlier interesting and important contributions in the field of international financial policy, with respect to issues of full employment, with energy policy, and more besides. He was a prodigiously hard worker. When confronted by a new issue he threw himself headlong into its study until he had a detailed knowledge of the field in question. Given his tendency to move rapidly from one area of interest to another, this gave him a breadth of vision, combined with an unquenching thirst to propose 'what should be done', which he used to great effect. He gained a reputation as a deep but free thinker with many ideas about how to reform the economic mechanism and institutions of economic regulation.

It was as a student in England that Schumacher first encountered the serious study of economics. In London in 1929 and at Oxford between 1930 and 1932, he began a project investigating the characteristics of the international banking system, which he carried on as a lecturer at New York's Columbia University. After spells in various business ventures in Germany and the United Kingdom, he was interned early in the Second World War. When released, he eventually found a job at the Oxford Institute of Statistics. It was during this difficult time that Schumacher first developed one of his characteristic 'plans for improving the World': a multilateral clearing office for post-War international payments. This suggestion was published in *Economica* in 1943.

The plan was one of a number of such proposals for international financial co-operation circulating at the time, the most notable being that developed by **Keynes** and proposed by the British delegation to the Bretton Woods conference on post-war international reconstruction in 1944. To some extent Schumacher anticipated Keynes's own proposals, though he never complained about being eclipsed by his more illustrious counterpart. In addition Schumacher worked with Beveridge and other eminent econo-mists (including Michael Kalecki, Nikolaus Kaldor and Joan Robinson) on plans for full employment. His analysis was the basis of the draft for Beveridge's *Full Employment in a Free Society*. All this was part of a then strong 'technicist ideology', which sought to subject all social and economic problems to a technical solution based upon the application of enlightened brain-power. The great strength of Schumacher in this period was that he saw clearly the need to combine technical detail with genuine social and organisational transformation.

After the war Schumacher changed track once again and eventually found a comfortable home at the National Coal Board, where he provided analyses, advice and information on energy matters. It was there that some of his well known critical positions on the nature of conventional economics began to mature. Thinking of energy as primarily a 'capital good' rather than a consumption item, he stressed the conservation of energy sources, particularly coal, since he had calculated a rapid depletion of the then available resources. He was very much against the prevailing trend to substitute nuclear fuel and oil for coal.

After a visit to Burma in 1955 he began to think seriously about the particular problems confronting the developing countries, focusing again on capital goods. The productivity of developing country workers was low because their capital equipment was primitive. But to adopt the most advanced and technologically sophisticated equipment and organisation methods of the advanced countries was expensive, and, although it might increase output and productivity, it would do little for employment. Indeed, it would probably exacerbate already chronic underemployment and unemployment. What was needed instead was a particular form of technology that suited the circumstances of the less developed economies the idea of 'intermediate technology' was born. Although this concept proved difficult to operationalise, it captured the imagination of a generation of radical development economists and Third World politicians alike. So began Schumacher's rise to international fame. He desperately longed for the recognition of his ideas, not perhaps for self-aggrandisement (though he also liked this) but more because he thought of himself as a radical reformer (even revolutionary) with realistic plans that would change the world for the better.

Alongside his economics Schumacher also conducted a wider quest for inner meaning and sense. This spiritual journey again took a number of twists and turns. Schumacher was at one time or another a practising Protestant and a Buddhist, but he died a Roman Catholic. In his early years he could have been described as a capitalist, later he was a Marxist, and then a socialist. Each of these ideological positions provided him with added ethical equipment for his economic analyses. This very important part of Schumacher's life project was brought together in his second significant book *A Guide for the Perplexed*. Issues of morality and ethical judgement were fundamental for economic analysis according to Schumacher. His philosophical position enunciated in that book was a radical (religious) humanism, heavily influenced by St Thomas Aquinas.

Schumacher rather went out of fashion in the late 1970s and during the 1980s, as the world turned against his kind of active interventionary policy-making. Marketisation, liberalisation and deregulation became the renewed currency of economic discussion. But his ideas survive and could be said to be on the verge of a come-back in the mid-1990s. The role of small- and medium-sized business organisation is again at the forefront of economic debate. The large-scale oligopolistic firm is under siege. It is said to be down-sizing, vertically and horizontally disintegrating, and fragmenting into subcontracting chains. Robust industrial districts and regional economies are developing, based upon networks of integrated small firms using appropriately scaled-down, though still 'high-technology' capital equipment – a kind of 'intermediate technology' for advanced industrial countries? 'Mass production' is out, 'flexible specialisation' is in. Increasingly it is being recognised that the relationship between economic analysis and ethical judgement needs to be rethought, but in a newly integrated fashion. And perhaps most importantly of all, the issue of 'sustainable development' – an economic growth path that centrally considers the environmental and ecological impact of economic activity, and which pays close attention to the finite nature of natural and human resources – is surely of central concern once again.

In many ways Schumacher's ideas suffered from his guru-like status. Any guru must provide a populist and simple message that in some way touches the masses with the vision and hope of a better future life. But gurus often become overwhelmed by their popular adulation. Their followers begin to control them, increasingly determining their agendas and activity levels. Such was the case with Schumacher, who only enjoyed this status for a few years before it undoubtedly contributed to his untimely death.

Main works

'Multilateral clearing', *Economica*, 10 (May, 1943), pp. 150–65.

'Public finance, its relation to full employment', in University of Oxford Institute of Economics and Statistics, *The Economics of Full Employment*, Oxford: Blackwell, 1944.

Small is Beautiful: A study of economics as if people mattered, London: Blond and Briggs, 1973.

A Guide for the Perplexed, London: Jonathan Cape, 1977.

Further reading

Wood, Barbara (Schumacher's daughter), *Alias Papa: A life of Fritz Schumacher*, London: Jonathan Cape, 1984.

Schumpeter, Joseph Alois (1883–1950)

Schumpeter was born in Triesch, Austria, the son of a senior army officer, who died when his son was just four; but his mother remarried to a distinguished general seven years later, and this background, plus his exclusive schooling with the sons of aristocrats, moulded Schumpeter's outlook and demeanour in life. Indeed Heilbronner (*The Worldly Philosophers*), whose semi-biographical style benefits from having attended some of Schumpeter's lectures, confides that his mentor is said to have had three wishes in life: to excel as an economist, a horserider and a lover. Intrigued readers must content themselves here with an assessment of his greatness as an economist only.

As a student at the University of Vienna Schumpeter frequently disagreed with his tutor, Bohm-Bawerk, and, on graduating in 1904, was rated a star performer by the then famous economist, Spiethof. From 1909 Schumpeter gained lecturing experience at the universities of Cernovcy in the Ukraine and Graz, Austria. His first work of international renown, *The Theory of Economic Development*, was published in German in 1911. With its incisive approach to the economic nature, status and problems of Third World countries in an era heavily steeped in colonialism, it established his reputation. Full appreciation of his work by English-speaking colleagues, however, had to await the translation of a second edition after Schumpeter took a chair at Harvard, which he occupied from 1932–50. Schumpeter's second internationally acclaimed work, *Business Cycles*, was published in 1939, while *The History of Economic Analysis* (1954) was posthumously edited by his second wife, and fellow economist, Elizabeth Boody Schumpeter.

Although often grouped together with fellow Austrians Menger, Wieser and Bohm-Bawerk, Schumpeter recast their ideas with, amongst others, those of **Marx**, Walras and Weber, to fit his own analysis. Thus in *The Theory of Economic Development* (1911), Schumpeter rejects classical growth theories. For him, there is a difference between growth and development. Growth is the gradual expansion producing more of the same with the same techniques, while economic development happens when new combinations of productive means occur. Innovation is the key, whether it involves production methods, the products themselves, new markets or new sources of supply, or, indeed, the type of industrial organisation within an industry. Essential to this process occurring is not merely the accumulation of new capital and the availability of savings to finance it, but also the presence of an economic entrepreneur/innovator to initiate, undertake and carry through the 'new' method. This entrepreneur is not usually the capitalist, who provides the necessary finance, but, according to Schumpeter, the one who actually engenders the new combinations at the time when the process occurs. After the business has been built up and is functioning in the same way as any other, Schumpeter's innovators lose their status. It is important to note that such innovators are not chosen by social class or background, but by will, talent and leadership. Intellect alone does not define the innovator, because while it may be crucial to the process of invention, it is the innovator/entrepreneur who will deliver economic development.

Schumpeter's work on business cycles sought to explain and analyse the causes of the Great Depression in the wake of the Wall Street crash of 1929. His projected solution to the depression is diametrically opposed to that of his contemporary **Keynes**. Keynes argued that government should give a countercyclical kick-start to the economy, which could otherwise become stuck at an equilibrium level. This was particularly necessary, Keynes felt, when the level fell as dramatically short of full employment as it did in the 1930s. Schumpeter's interpretation of capitalism was that it was intrinsically dynamic and growth-oriented, although he accepted that government expenditure should be used to alleviate social distress. So while they agreed that fiscal policies affect economic behaviour, Schumpeter, in *Business Cycles* argues that taxes beyond a certain percentage, and which vary greatly, will blunt the profit motive. The argument is that, in affecting the individual, micro-economic incentives shape the performance of individuals collectively as an economic society. These ideas reveal Schumpeter to be true to the Austrian paradigm of his tutors. After some reinterpretation, application of this philosophy has spread, to be observed first of all in 'supply side' Reaganomics policy, and then in Thatcherism.

Schumpeter's explanation of the severity of the Great Depression of the 1930s is twofold. First, he argued that the conjunction of the troughs of three different kinds of business cycle had occurred at the same time. Second, he observed another set of contributory factors exogenous to business cycle theory, which he felt reinforced the negative impact on the economic superpowers of that era. He cited the ineptitude of individual governments' economic policies, as well as wider socio-economic and political factors, such as poor harmonisation between governments and developments in Soviet Russia.

Schumpeter argued that apart from a normal business cycle of quite short duration, a 7–11 year Juglar cycle of output and employment occurred, and also a vast Kondratieff cycle over some fifty years. In the last case, the cycle was associated with truly revolutionary inventions such as the commercial exploitation of steam power or the internal combustion engine, or presumably, in today's terms of reference, the harnessing of the information superhighway and its impact on the global economy. The phenomenon of 'swarming' of innovators was the driving force in the upturn of a cycle, and in this Schumpeter relied once again on the innovator for the central role.

The motivation for Schumpeter's visionary innovators, with their new class of products, new markets, new technologies or methods of organisation, is not the welfare of society but their own benefit, and for this, assurance of profit is necessary. Further expectations play a part, in that an innovatory surge will only succeed in a relatively stable or calm period of economic development. The innovator injects a new source of demand for goods of a higher sophistication than hitherto, and one which is required for the new style of production. This process leads to a boom, but as imitators join the trend the profits of the original innovator are dissipated, and the old methods and the need for replacement investment in them become increasingly superfluous. Because this activity has questioned the relevance of previous production methods, products, etc., and also led to marked changes in the pattern of demand for particular types of labour skills and other inputs, old methods and expectations are disrupted. Schumpeter's innovators are a form of elite, and most business people are incapable of following other than existing routines and are thus driven out, or abandon their activities. In this period of uncertainty and change Schumpeter assumes that not even other potential innovators, with their own business plans prepared, can adequately calculate potential profits until the economy stabilises itself. During this process some will succeed, even though new structures both destroy the old and bring uncertainty – which in turn affects the conditions for further innovation. The economy will then gradually move to an even enough keel for the process to begin again.

In *Capitalism, Socialism and Democracy* (1942), Schumpeter rejects Marxian philosophy from a sociological, political and economic perspective, yet paradoxically enough still predicts an almost inevitable rebirth of socialism. Comfortable bourgeois capitalists would betray the necessary virtues of his 'thrusting outsider', the innovative entrepreneur, with the danger that a capitalist economic system would be undermined not by its political opponents, but by a constituent part of its friends.

For his last epic work, *The History of Economic Analysis*, Schumpeter interprets weights and reclassifies economic analysis from the Graeco-Roman period through to the 1940s, and also reveals his choice of Walras as the greatest economist. Historians of economic thought, and Schumpeter scholars in particular, have, in part thanks to the dedication of Schumpeter's second wife, a rare and challenging overview of the entire economic process.

That Schumpeter's work excites interest within a modern theoretical and applied context is evidenced by the study of Malerba and Orsenigo (1995). Despite Heilbronner's claim that Schumpeter achieved greatness in only two of his three areas, and that it was unclear as yet whether he would rank among the greats, Blaug reveals his verdict by including Schumpeter in his book, *Great Economists before Keynes*. Furthermore, nearly a half century after his death, Schumpeter's ideas are still alive and relevant to the age of globalisation (the information technology revolution, and the importance of high value-added production and research and development), and to the developing world still seeking relatively low-cost innovatory methods for the relief of their comparative economic misery.

Main works

The Theory of Economic Development, trans. R. Opie, Cambridge, MA: Harvard University Press, 1934.

Business Cycles, New York: McGraw Hill, 1939.

Capitalism, Socialism and Democracy, London: George Allen and Unwin, 1942.

The History of Economic Analysis, London: George Allen and Unwin, 1954.

Further reading

Blaug, Mark, *Great Economists before Keynes*, Brighton: Harvester Wheatsheaf, 1986.

Eklund, Robert B. and Robert F. Hebert, *A History of Economic Theory and Method*, New York: McGraw Hill, 1990.

Heilbronner, Robert, *The Worldly Philosophers*, London: Penguin, 1991.

Mair, Douglas and Anne G. Miller, *A Modern Guide to Economic Thought*, Aldershot: Edward Elgar, 1991.

Malerba, Franco and Luigi Orsenigo, 'Schumpeterian patterns of innovation', *Cambridge Journal of Economics*, 19 (1995), pp. 47–65.

Simmel, Georg (1858–1918)

Georg Simmel was born in Berlin the youngest of seven children. His parents were of Jewish origin but, before they had met and married, his mother had converted to Protestantism and his father to Catholicism. Simmel was raised a Protestant. His father died when Georg was a boy. Julius Friedländer, a friend of the family and the founder of an international music publishing house, was appointed his guardian. He left Simmel a considerable fortune which enabled him to lead the life of a scholar.

At the University of Berlin he studied history and philosophy. Simmel began to lecture on sociological topics in 1887. His programme for a sociological study of the forms of social interaction was clear in his earliest sociological publications, 'On social differentiation' (1890) and 'The problem of sociology' (1894). Simmel was a prolific essayist and a virtuoso lecturer. He wrote on questions of aesthetics and the philosophy of history and contributed not only to sociological journals but also to literary magazines and newspapers. From 1885 to 1900 he was a *Privatdozent* (a lecturer unpaid except for student fees) in philosophy and for another fourteen years he was an *ausserordentliche Professor* (an honorary, but not remunerated title). Only in 1914 was he finally awarded a full professorship in Strasburg. He died on 26 September 1918.

Simmel was a prolific writer: during his lifetime he published 22 books and over 200 essays and articles. His first works, and his last, were in the field of philosophy. After the publication of his pathbreaking *Philosophy of Money* (1900) he devoted himself for over a decade primarily to the fledgling discipline of sociology. At that point there were still no chair of sociology in Germany. During the last decade of his life Simmel returned to questions of aesthetics and the philosophy of history.

There are many testimonies to Simmel's exceptional brilliance as a lecturer on a very wide range of subjects. But his influence on his contemporaries extended beyond academia. Between 1897 and 1907, Simmel frequently contributed to the Munich *Jugendstil* journal *Jugend*. He wrote not only brief essays but also poems, aphorisms and fables. Aesthetics was for Simmel a lifelong concern and an area from which his thinking drew important resources. Simmel published a short essay on Kant and Goethe in 1906 and Rembrandt in 1916. (Further *Rembrandtstudien* (Rembrandt Studies) were published posthumously in 1953.)

For the Berlin newspapers *Vossische Zeitung* and *Der Tag* Simmel contributed short essays on pregnant themes or emblems of social life. They had titles such as 'The bridge and the door', 'The picture frame', 'The journey in the Alps'. Each attempted to grasp the significance, the general meaning, of particular but common experience. Simmel referred to these as 'Momentbilder *sub specie aeternitatis*' (literally, snapshots viewed from the aspects of eternity). In such writings Simmel anticipates the most vivid passages of the phenomenologists or the most incisive writing of semioticians such as Roland Barthes or Umberto Eco.

As Simmel himself noted in a letter, his specific achievement was inextricably bound up with the Berlin milieu: 'Berlin's development from a city to a metropolis in the years around and after the turn of the century coincides with my own strongest and broadest development.' Simmel is the pre-eminent sociologist of metropolitan social life. Many of his insights are summarised in one of his most famous essays, 'The metropolis and mental life' (1903). One of the most fascinating aspects of his writings is the gallery of social types which he constructed and for which he provided a detailed inventory. Along with 'the stranger' he describes 'the mediator', 'the poor', 'the adventurer', 'the man in the middle' and 'the renegade'. These, together with many essays on the situation of women provide searing portraits of the moral and emotional life of his times.

Simmel's first sociological monograph, *On Social Differentiation* (1890) is an attempt to extend and apply a theory of social differentiation influenced by Herbert Spencer. But Simmel already had more philosophical ambitions. He aimed to provide a foundation for a sociological discipline which would be quite different from the positivist and organicist conception of sociology shared by Spencer and August Comte. Simmel's 'philosophical sociology' would offer general interpretations of history and society which no strictly empirical discipline could provide.

Simmel was writing in the wake of Dilthey's methodological separation of the *Geisteswissenschaften* (human sciences; literally, the sciences of mind or spirit) from the *Naturwissenschaften* (natural and physical sciences). In innumerable essays Simmel developed his own subtle and suggestive views on the role of interpretation in social science and other aspects of the theory of knowledge. Simmel's views on these matters, as on so much else, remained constantly in transition. This characteristic was itself part of his methodological inspiration. In a memorial article published shortly after Simmel's death, Georg **Lukács**, a one-time pupil, developed the view of Simmel as the authentic theoretician of 'impressionism', and compared Simmel's methods and outlook with those of Monet, Rodin, Richard Strauss and Rilke.

Simmel's sociology is always informed by a 'dialectical' approach, by means of which he brings out the dynamic interconnectedness and the conflicts between the social units he analyses. He sees individuals as products of society and as links in the social process. But at the same time there is an equal stress on the connections and the tensions between the individual and society. Simmel saw the atomised conditions of modern life – which he was one of the first to analyse under the heading of 'modernity' – as producing a new freedom for the individual, and a new abstractness in intellectual life. If individuals are produced by society, society is produced only by the interactions of individuals: and the science of society describes the forms of the interactions.

Simmel is often credited with having developed a 'formal' sociology, but his notion of 'forms' is open to misunderstanding. In this area Simmel, like Walter Benjamin, was profoundly influenced by Goethe's writings on natural science. Simmel draws his notion of forms from his study of Kant's categories, but also from his own study of form in art and literature. 'Forms' shape social interaction. Simmel points out that in completely diverse social groups we find the same forms: subordination, competing division of labour, parties, representation, solidarity, together with exclusiveness towards the outside.

In *Philosophy of Money* Simmel explores the way in which money itself shapes, forms and deforms, social interactions. The final essay, 'The style of life', analyses the way in which the ability of money to mediate social interaction, to play its role in relations between people, shapes every aspect of modern life. He shows how it transforms the 'pace of life' and how it breaks down traditional family ties, giving each member of the family a sense of having to act in their own interests. But Simmel also shows how this loosening of traditional, emotional bonds brings a new kind of intellectual life: a new freedom, but also a particular kind of detachment, a blasé attitude which provides a kind of filter against the sensory overload of the modern metropolis. Intrinsic values are replaced by instrumental ones, and the individual person becomes locked into a grid of projects, enterprises and institutions to which is attached no ultimate value or purpose.

Yet Simmel refused to retreat in dismay at the process he analysed. He declared that his intention was to find a more profound and comprehensive basis of dialectical materialism in the very structure of the life-world of human beings. In this way he believed he would rescue the scientific truth hidden in **Marx**'s political eschatology. He shows the myriad ways in which money, the ultimate means, the instrument to any and every purpose itself becomes the ultimate purpose, the value by reference to which the worth of every other product of culture is determined.

Simmel argues that the crisis of modern culture is an inevitable product of cultural development. Culture is tragic: forms, which are necessary products of the process of life itself, inevitably become opposed to the energies and interests of life. The forms of social interaction are antagonistic to the vital energies that created them as the essential condition for the possibility of culture. This pessimism, supported by Simmel's lifelong interest in Schopenhauer, expresses itself in Simmel's view of the 'tragedy of culture', an organising principle of his entire oeuvre. For Simmel, reification is not merely a characteristic of capitalism but was simply part of a perennial 'tragedy of culture'. Nevertheless, such a tragedy took on a specifically modern form in the overrefined, nervous sensibility of modern metropolitan man. Simmel summed up the:

> typically problematical predicament of modern man: the feeling of being oppressed by an infinity of elements of culture because he can neither incorporate them into his own personal culture nor – because they are potential objects of his subjective culture – can he simply ignore or reject them.

A number of Simmel's writings appeared in American periodicals during his life, especially in *The American Journal of Sociology*. He was translated by Albion Small, the founder of that journal and the key figure in the early Chicago School of sociology. G. H. Mead reviewed favourably *Philosophy of Money* and Robert Park actually studied under Simmel in Berlin. Amongst Simmel's students, Georg Lukács was a particular favourite. Simmel's personal influence extended to Ernst Bloch and Siegfried Kracauer, to Karl **Mannheim** and Martin Buber. Finally, in his many writings on postmodernism, the Leeds-based sociologist, Zygmunt Bauman has deliberately revisited many of the sites marked out in Simmel's writings on modernity.

Main works

The Sociology of Georg Simmel, ed. and trans. Kurt H. Wolff, Glencoe: Free Press, 1950. (Includes 'The Metropolis and Mental Life'.)

On Individuality and Social Forms, selected writings, ed. D. N. Levine, Chicago: Chicago University Press, 1971.

The Problems of the Philosophy of History, ed. and trans. G. Oakes, New York: Free Press, 1977.

Philosophy of Money, trans. T. Bottomore and D. Frisby, London: Routledge, 1978; 2nd edn (from amended, 1907 edn of original), ed. D. Frisby, trans. T. Bottomore and D. Frisby, London: Routledge, 1990.

Essays on Interpretation in Social Science, ed. and trans. G. Oakes, Manchester: Manchester University Press, 1980.

Simmel on Culture, ed. David Frisby and Mike Featherstone, London: Sage, 1996.

Simmel on Art and Literature, ed. by David Frisby and Mike Featherstone, London: Sage, 1997.

Further reading

Coser, Lewis, *Masters of Sociological Thought*, New York: Harcourt Brace Jovanovich, 1971.

Frisby, David, *Georg Simmel*, London: Tavistock, 1984.

Frisby, David, *Sociological Impressionism: A reassessment of Georg Simmel's social theory*, London: Heinemann, 1981.

Weingartner, R., *Experience and Culture: The philosophy of Georg Simmel*, Middletown: Wesleyan University Press, 1962.

Singer, Peter (1946–)

Born in Melbourne in 1946, Peter Singer quickly earned himself a certain degree of renown as well as notoriety after the appearance of his book *Animal Liberation* in 1975. A convinced utilitarian, the moral philosophy underlying *Animal Liberation* was later extended to other social issues such as euthanasia and abortion in *Practical Ethics*, a work which also helped augur in the current popularity of applied ethics. He is currently Professor of Philosophy and deputy director of the Centre for Human Bioethics at Monash University, Melbourne, and an editor of the journal, *Bioethics*.

Though he has also published on Hegel and **Marx**, Singer's primary philosophical concern is ethics, to be precise, *applied* ethics. He deplores the turn in twentieth-century moral philosophy towards increasingly improbable and abstract ethical systems. Ethics, in his view, is not an exercise in utopian thought where theory precedes practice: its vocation is to tackle those issues found in the real world.

Alongside this insistence that ethics is an engaged discipline, Singer is also anxious to show that it is neither relative nor subjective. That certain moral principles are relative to time and place does not obviate the fact that they may remain objectively valid for those specific circumstances nor that certain other more general moral principles may be universally applicable. As to the subjectivist's view that ethical positions are expressions of individual taste – personal commendations at best – Singer asserts that no such subjective state is immune from criticism: reason and argument have a role in ethics such that certain ethical perspectives can be shown to be more cogent than others. Having ethical *standards* (as opposed to behaving ethically inadvertently) implies the ability to forward a justification for what one does. Moreover, it must be a justification of a certain type if it is to support an ethical position (the motive of self-interest will not do): the argument must be *universalisable*. Singer's contention is that universalisability, the principle that each individual is deemed *equal* by counting for one and none for more than one, is a feature of all true ethical thinking.

In the modern era, of course, we all adhere to the principle of equality amongst humans (at least in theory). But what does that mean in practice? Not that we are all the same: clearly, there are differences between us in physical and mental endowment (be the latter genetically or culturally determined) that no one deems morally significant. Equality has a different sense here. But what is it? Singer's proposal is that there is no need to establish the principle of equality on the basis of either an *empirical* equality (everyone being a certain colour, gender, or whatever) or an *a priori* equality (being a member of a certain species irrespective of one's individual empirical properties): all that is required to ground a genuine ethic is the notion of *equality of interest*. The chief pre-requisite for any ethical behaviour for Singer is that we treat all sectional interests on a par with our own, no matter whose interests they are: 'Ethics requires us to go beyond "I" and "you" to the universal law, the universalisable judgement, the standpoint of the impartial spectator or ideal observer . . .' (*Practical Ethics*). No empirical fact or *a priori* principle (such as the 'sanctity of human life') can be used to exclude any interest: only those or that without interests at all can justly be excluded.

Giving equal consideration to every interest, however, need not always lead to equal treatment: where there are significantly different interests at hand, commensurably different treatment ought to follow. Conflicting interests will have to be considered impartially, and while attaining such impartiality will never be easy, Singer remains confident that we have the reasoning abilities to transcend our natural parochialism.

That ethics must be universalisable gives us good reason, Singer believes, for favouring a broadly utilitarian position. Singer's reasoning is that, in conflict situations, impartiality demands that one *weigh up* the opposing interests and 'adopt the course of action most likely to maximise the interests of those affected' (*Practical Ethics*). However, Singer substitutes classical utilitarianism's vague and unhelpful criteria of pleasure and pain with the favoured notion of 'interest' or 'preference'. The two elementary preferences for his form of utilitarianism are an individual's continued existence and its avoidance of pain. In place of an ethic that would focus on a person's 'right to life', for instance, Singer's preference utilitarianism states that where an individual is capable of expectations concerning the future, he or she must also have a preference to continue to exist which must not be thwarted. A being that cannot foresee its future (and so have a preference for continued existence), on the other hand, may be sacrificed so long as its death is both *painless* and absolutely necessary to ensure the survival of one that can have such a preference.

The principle of equality leads to some startling implications and Singer is never fearful of pursuing ideas to their logical conclusion. Consistent with his view is the stipulation that no species should receive preferential treatment for its members' interests simply on the basis of their being a member of that species. Notoriously, this leads Singer to compare and often equate the lives of human animals and non-human animals. Significantly, the most important interests possessed by individuals are independent of the categories 'human' and 'non-human': pain, for example, is suffered and avoided by all regardless of colour, gender, or species. If we are ever forced to favour one individual's interests when they are in conflict with those of another, it can only be on the basis of those of their respective properties which *affect the interests either might have*.

Singer puts great emphasis on empirical research over any arm-chair reasoning concerning the abilities and hence preferences of individuals and individual species. Evidence recently confirms that certain species of great ape, for instance, are self-conscious and have language. Such apes are 'persons' in Singer's definition of the term in that, having the capacity for expectations no less than humans, they also have a preference for continued existence that must be respected. Clearly, Singer's definition of 'person' is broader than the orthodox understanding which equates the term with being 'human' alone. But Singer dubs that denotation illegitimate and 'speciesist' as it demonstrates 'a prejudice or attitude of bias in favor of the interests of members of one's own species and against those of members of other species' (*Animal Liberation*). Beyond the great apes, Singer thinks that we can probably extend the category of 'person' to other large-brained mammals like dolphins and whales, as well as to various other mammals such as dogs, cats, pigs and sheep (though with less confidence). If members of these species can indicate a preference for continued existence, then the onus is on us to respect that desire. But while only some animals are persons, almost all animals – certainly all the ones exploited in one way or another by humans – are conscious of pleasure and pain and naturally desire to pursue the one as they avoid the other. Therefore, Singer argues, we are also obliged to ensure that no individual suffers by virtue of our own desire for or use of any particular foodstuff, clothing, cosmetics or even – if we support vivisection – knowledge.

It is not only Singer's approach to the animal question which is informed by the primacy of equality, but also his position on euthanasia and abortion. In the special case of euthanasia, the principle that no species' interests should receive preferential treatment also entitles *humans* to be treated no worse than any other animal, and yet, while we do often terminate non-human lives that have become insufferable, this facility is usually denied to humans. There are many human lives of unremitting physical pain that nobody could seriously think worth living and these are the ones that would benefit from the availability of a properly regulated and informed use of euthanasia.

On the issue of abortion, Singer thinks that a foetus can only be deemed a person and consequently one whose life must be respected if one equates 'person' with 'human being' by definition. In contrast to this view, he contends that if one specifies certain characteristics for being a person as he does, then a human foetus *becomes* a person with a moral claim to continued existence only when it indicates its possession of those characteristics. Before that time, abortion does not frustrate any individual's preference for 'life' and so is not immoral. More controversial, however, is the fact that Singer's thinking here applies as equally to a week-old baby as to a foetus, for no very young infant can have a concept of, and hence a preference for, continued existence.

Singer's *Animal Liberation* is a call for a worldwide movement towards vegetarianism. Political protest can make only slow progress towards such liberation: vegetarianism is a far more successful strategy for it hits the main agents of animal suffering financially. Only when it is unprofitable to exploit animals will it cease: vegetarianism, then, 'is form of boycott' (*Animal Liberation*). In its objective Singer's work has been very effective, converting many to either some version of vegetarianism or at least an awareness of our responsibility for the appalling degree of suffering endured by non-human animals. His approach to abortion and euthanasia has met with even more publicity causing both debate and censure (some of Singer's lectures have been banned in Germany and Austria) worldwide.

Main works

Animal Liberation (1975), 2nd rev. edn, London: Thorsons, 1991.

Practical Ethics (1979), 2nd rev. edn, Cambridge: Cambridge University Press, 1993.

Marx, Oxford: Oxford University Press, 1980.

The Expanding Circle: Ethics and sociobiology, Oxford: Oxford University Press, 1981.

Hegel, Oxford: Oxford University Press, 1983.

Rethinking Life and Death: The collapse of our traditional ethics, Oxford: Oxford University Press, 1995.

Further reading

Frey, R. G., *Rights, Killing, and Suffering*, Oxford: Basil Blackwell, 1983.

Leahy, Michael, *Against Liberation: Putting animals in perspective*, London: Routledge, 1991.

The Monist, 70: 1 (1987).

Philosophy, 53: 4 (1978).

Singer, Peter, (ed.), *In Defence of Animals*, Oxford: Basil Blackwell, 1985.

Skinner, B. F. (1904–1990)

Burrhus Frederic Skinner was born in Susquehanna, Pennsylvania. He gained a first degree in English literature in 1926 and flirted briefly with creative writing before moving, in 1929, to study psychology at Harvard, where he obtained his Ph.D. in 1931. He held positions at the Universities of Minnesota and Indiana before being made a Professor of Psychology at Harvard in 1945, where he continued to work and teach until well into his eighties. Skinner's early work was on rats and pigeons, and he developed several innovative experimental technologies, the best known of which is the so-called 'Skinner's box', in which a rat could be trained to press a lever in certain patterns, or on certain cues, to gain a food reward. Following the Second World War, Skinner increasingly turned his attention to the analysis of human behaviour, leading him into considerable controversy.

Like the great pioneer of behaviourism, J. B. Watson, B. F. Skinner, for all his experiments with rats and pigeons, never doubted that the aim of behavioural science, of psychology, must be the 'control and prediction of *human* behaviour'. He took several assumptions directly from Watson's behaviourism: that human beings can be studied using the same techniques used to study other animals; that introspection can teach us nothing about human behaviour; that mental events or activities, such as having an intention, are 'metaphors or explanatory fictions'; that the very idea of personality is without substance. Behaviourism had turned the attention of professional psychologists away from the inner workings of their minds, in which they had hoped to discover the secrets of consciousness, to the observable behaviour of their fellow creatures. Watson argued that people do what they do not because of some subtle combination of genetic disposition, desire and whim, but because, on receiving a particular stimulus, we do what we did the last time we received that stimulus. Carefully observing behaviour enables the psychologist to predict what a person will do in the future when confronted with that same stimulus. Watson claimed that by controlling the pattern of stimulation (i.e. the environment) he could, given a healthy infant, turn it into a doctor, an artist or an engineer irrespective of any 'natural' abilities it might have.

For Skinner, as for Watson, psychology must confine itself to studying the verifiable facts of behaviour. The attempts of psychologists and philosophers to understand the inner workings of consciousness should be abandoned; indeed they are as quaint and unhelpful as the Aristotelian idea that a falling body accelerates because it feels jubilant as it approaches its natural home. Modern behavioural psychology, like modern physics, knows better. Skinner's 'operant' behaviourism (detailed in *The Behaviour of Organisms* of 1938) was the result of his dissatisfaction with the rather primitive account given by Watson of the relationship between behaviour and the environment, which he felt relied too much on the 'reflex' investigated by Pavlov. Skinner's central insight was that organisms live in dynamic systems and that behaviour has an effect on the environment: actions have consequences. Those consequences then condition future behaviour. A rat in Skinner's box presses a lever, thereby acting on the environment. A peanut appears through a hatch – the behaviour has been rewarded, or 'reinforced' in Skinner's terminology. This reinforcement means that it is much more likely that the rat will press the lever again. If a peanut only appears when the lever is pressed six times, or when the lever is pressed while a red light is on, then the rat will adjust its behaviour accordingly. By these means Skinner managed to elicit amusingly atypical behaviour from his test subjects – he taught his pigeons how to play table tennis.

Skinner identified two types of reinforcement. Positive reinforcement occurs when a behaviour results in the attainment of a pleasant stimulus – food, approval, sex or money, for example. Negative reinforcement occurs where behaviour removes an unpleasant (aversive) stimulus. A man, for example, might buy his wife some flowers. She responds with affection. The behaviour has been *positively* reinforced and the husband is more likely to repeat the action. Another husband finds himself being nagged. He buys his wife flowers and she stops nagging him. The aversive stimulus has been removed and the behaviour *negatively* reinforced. Negative reinforcement should not be confused with punishment, which is what happens when behaviour is followed by an aversive stimulus: the husband comes home with lipstick on his collar and his wife slaps him. For Skinner, reinforcement is much more effective in altering behaviour than punishment, and positive reinforcement better than negative.

In *Verbal Behaviour* (1957) Skinner attempted to explain language acquisition as the product of reinforcement. A baby burbles away to itself until it happens to produce a sound resembling 'mamma'. It is rewarded with cuddles and kisses. Not surprisingly, it 'says' it again. Later, again by chance, it pronounces 'dadda'. Once more this is reinforced. Skinner attributes the whole complex structure of language to this form of operant conditioning. In a devastating review of *Verbal Behaviour*, Noam Chomsky opposed Skinner's view with his own view that the rules of language, or rather of grammar, are innate. Experimental evidence has supported Chomsky rather than Skinner.

Skinner's form of environmental determinism obviously leaves little or no place for the idea of freedom. He boldly confronts the view that freedom is either possible or desirable. Either we take responsibility for planning a society in which 'sociable' behaviour is reinforced or we leave reinforcement to the inefficient, traditional forces of outmoded educational theories, moral discourse and political persuasion. In both cases external forces determine individual behaviour, and the second group has led directly to the problems besetting modern society. Skinner advocated tackling those problems initially in a 'piecemeal' manner, gradually extending the areas in which reinforcement could be applied. He began with education, the treatment of the mentally ill and retarded, and criminal correction. In the America of the 1950s some schools, prisons and mental

institutions implemented his ideas by introducing 'tc
rewarding 'good' behaviour. To a limited degree these
tinue today, with uncertain results.

However, Skinner's ultimate goal was always, as is c
most controversial works, his novel, *Walden Two* (1948) ar
and Dignity (1972), the total transformation of socie
redesigned culture, in which appropriate experts would
reward which would lead inevitably to happiness and harmony. It is a
utopian dream attainable, he claimed, without coercion or oppression. We
will be *rewarded* into sociability. Skinner never tired of claiming that operant
behaviourism provided the technology for controlling behaviour: from
birth we could all be subjected to a regime of reinforcement which made
us behave naturally in socially acceptable ways. Such a regime would make
good behaviour 'natural': it would become impossible for people to conceive of stealing, lying, over-breeding, polluting the environment or
fighting. A system of differential wages and group pressure would
encourage hard work and enterprise.

Skinner's utopia has been attacked remorselessly by both libertarians
and conservatives. Libertarians, such as Chomsky, point out that Skinner's
utopia resembles a well-run concentration camp, or, at best, a mental
institution governed, perhaps, by caring staff; but nevertheless without
the consent or the understanding of the inmates. Skinner gives enormous
power to the technocrats who will plan his society and it would seem that
they are given a freedom of choice and rationality denied to the rest of
humanity. Conservatives bewail the elimination of religion and traditional
morality from Skinner's world. Perhaps the most damaging criticism of
Skinner's work was the attack on the scientific basis of his pronouncements.
For all his claims about his new science of man, Skinner offers us little by
way of experimental proof for his assertions.

Behaviourism has had a lasting impact on the theory and practice of
psychology in the twentieth century, an impact matched only by that of
the contrasting theory of psychoanalysis. Its influence has also been felt
in other disciplines such as the philosophy of mind and anthropology.
No psychologist would now deny that we should study behaviour, or
even that behaviour can, in some circumstances, be controlled by delivering
or withholding rewards. Equally, however, there are not very many
'pure' behaviourists left. It is inappropriate to explain the motion of a
falling body by reference to its intentions, because it does not have any.
Human beings do, and arbitrarily to rule those intentions out of
consideration strikes most researchers as an unwarranted and unscientific
manoeuvre.

...ain works

The Behaviour of Organisms, New York: Appleton-Century-Crofts, 1938.

Walden Two, New York: Macmillan, 1948.

Science and Human Behaviour, New York: Macmillan, 1953.

Verbal Behaviour, New York: Appleton-Century-Crofts, 1957.

The Technology of Teaching, New York: Appleton-Century-Crofts, 1968.

Beyond Freedom and Dignity, New York: Alfred A. Knopf, 1971.

Cumulative Record: A selection of papers, 3rd edn, New York: Appleton-Century-Crofts, 1972.

About Behaviourism, New York: Alfred A. Knopf, 1974.

Particulars of my Life, New York: Alfred A. Knopf, 1976.

The Shaping of a Behaviourist, New York: Alfred A. Knopf, 1979.

Further reading

Block, Ned (ed.), *Readings in the Philosophy of Psychology*, Vol. I, London: Methuen, 1980.

Carpenter, Finley, *The Skinner Primer: Behind freedom and dignity*, New York: Free Press, 1974.

Catania, A. C. and S. Harnad (eds), *The Selection of Behaviour: The operant behaviourism of B. F. Skinner, comments and consequences*, Cambridge: Cambridge University Press, 1988.

Chomsky, Noam, 'Psychology and ideology' (1972), in James Peck (ed.), *The Chomsky Reader*, London: Serpent's Tail, 1988.

T

Tawney, Richard Henry (1880–1962)

During the course of a long and active career, Tawney worked in a number of intellectual areas, as an economic historian, social theorist, moral philosopher and Christian idealist which highlighted his concern at the moral decay and dying social ethic precipitated by modern capitalism. He began his career in working-class education at Toynbee Hall in Stepney, and was, from 1908, a tutor for the Workers' Educational Association in Lancashire and North Staffordshire. Also before the Great War, Tawney worked at both Glasgow and Manchester Universities and he wrote anonymously on education for the *Glasgow Herald* and the *Manchester Guardian*. Throughout his life, Tawney conducted an educational crusade, opposing access on class lines, and his stamp is noticeable on all important educational legislation and policy between the Fisher Act (1918) and the Butler Act (1944). He sat on the Church of England Commission of Enquiry which produced *Christianity and Industrial Problems* (1918). In the same year he was elected fellow of Balliol College, Oxford, and was an unsuccessful Labour parliamentary candidate for Rochdale. Tawney and Sidney Webb represented the union position on the Sankey Commission of enquiry into the coal industry in 1919. Between 1931 and 1949, he was Professor of Economic History at the London School of Economics, and, thereafter, Professor Emeritus. Tawney was prominent in Labour Party circles and was one if its main theorists. Indeed Tawney, Harold **Laski** and G. D. H. Cole were dubbed the 'Red Professors', due to their collective impact on twentieth-century British socialism.

Tawney is correctly placed in a long line of English ethical socialists and his work was underpinned by strongly held moral, Christian and humanist ideals. He was not simply a social democrat, as some have said; and his ethical socialism connected him to Matthew Arnold, John Ruskin and William Morris, each of whom was a savage critic of capitalism and the inequality engendered by industrialism. Tawney's greatest work was completed in the 1920s with the writing of *The Acquisitive Society, Religion and the Rise of Capitalism* and *Equality* which characterise the most important aspects of his moral, philosophical and historical conceptions of the ills of modern society. Tawney was no empiricist, nor was he concerned with the history of individuals. Indeed, Tawney eschewed the classical *modus operandi* of Victorian historians in favour of a theoretical concern with the explanation of social structures.

As a student at Oxford, Tawney fell under the influence of a number of notable figures, not least Sidney Ball, who was the most prominent socialist in Oxford at the time. Tawney's work at Glasgow and Manchester universities brought him into contact with Tom Jones, the economist, and George Unwin, the economic historian, who played an important part in his early development. In more general terms, Tawney was a product of his age, deeply anxious about the problems of the Edwardian world: the crisis of liberalism and capitalism; the spectre of war; agitation for democracy; and the impact of social unrest. At the same time, Tawney's work with the Workers' Education Authority, as well as the time he spent as a soldier on the western front, contributed to sharpen his understanding of the social realities of working-class life. Tawney's social theory was clearly influenced by that of Max Weber.

Although many of Tawney's works were historical, his key interest was in the way modern society had emerged; his writings were invested with contemporary relevance. His first major work, *The Agrarian Problem in the Sixteenth Century* (1912), an economic history examining the impact of enclosures on peasant life, set the historical scene for his emerging critique of contemporary society. *The Acquisitive Society* (1921), outlined his thesis that society was morally 'sick', thus, capturing the pessimistic mood of his age. Here he argued that the emergence of liberalism and secularism had freed capitalism from the shackles of moral obligation. Modernisation, Tawney believed, had seen the demise of social unity and collective purpose and the emergence of acquisitive individualism and the creed of private property. This was, he argued, the basis of a functionless and amoral society. Tawney bewailed the fact that economic life had been removed from its correct place within the moral scheme of social being. Modern societies were governed solely by the desire to acquire wealth and in such societies, Tawney claimed, crucial components of a pre-capitalist social ethic were eroded with acquisition and individual rights replacing giving and mutual obligations. Crucial to this scheme was the fact that human beings, as members of society, became the means to an end, rather than an end in themselves. With this transformation was promoted, in Tawney's view, a society of misery, despair, inequality and moral malaise. In lacking a sustaining social ethic, capitalism had undermined society. Tawney's next and perhaps most famous work, *Religion and the Rise of Capitalism* (1926), was the sum of his attempts to understand the historical context of the sick society of which he was so despairing, and its central theme was not simply the rise of capitalism but, crucially, the withdrawal of past Christian ethics from social and economic life.

Tawney, as well as describing the moral malaise of modern British society, also suggested remedies. It was to this end that he wrote *Equality* (1931). His biographer, Anthony Wright, highlights three central principles of Tawney's social theory: the existence in social and economic life of 'function', 'freedom' and 'equal worth'. Each of these was crucial if society was to be reinvigorated. A functional society, Tawney believed, was anti-thetical to an acquisitive one. His measure of function was neither authoritarian nor pluralistic but was founded on a medieval ideal linking social harmony and moral rectitude. In a correctly functioning and moral society, common purpose and mutual obligation must replace individual rights. The absolute measure of moral decay, for which there must be a practicable solution, was the seemingly unassailable position in society of essentially functionless private property. It was in adopting this position that Tawney most obviously inherited the nineteenth-century tradition of Ruskin and Morris. Tawney viewed political freedom as a fact in British society: what he lamented was the lack of freedom in the economic sphere. He argued that capitalism was irresponsible, arbitrary and tyrannical; in its presence workers were powerless. Unlike some of his socialist peers, Tawney was neither a general critic of the British political system nor a proponent of change by political means alone. His key concern was with obligations and the rejuvenation of society through the creation of participant citizenship. This earned Tawney the label 'guild socialist' and was seen to separate him from Fabianism with its statist and bureacratic emphases. In Tawney's vision, unlike so many critics of left and right, the state was not a living thing, naturally centralising and authoritarian; it was an instrument that could be mobilised for common good. Tawney desired to see capitalism controlled and deployed for social utility; he wished to invest it with function.

R. H. Tawney exercised enormous influence on both individuals and movements during the twentieth century. Dubbed the English **Marx**, Tawney was neither a Marxist nor an anti-Marxist; yet his *Religion and the Rise of Capitalism* is cited as a key influence upon Maurice Dobb, the Marxist economist and economic historian. Tawney's work was not simply about academic production; and his influence reverberated from cloistered halls to the benches of parliament, where he helped to shape the intellectual development of many younger Labour activists, from Hugh Gaitskell to Michael Foot. After his death, however, Tawney's influence waned, mainly because his ethical type of socialism seemed out of tune with the pragmatic, consensual Labour of the 1960s and 1970s. In 1980, Tawney's spirit was resurrected when the 'Gang of Four' left Labour to form the SDP and claimed to take his memory and vision with them. The storm they invoked reminded the left of his fundamental importance within the spectrum of left-wing British politics.

Tawneyism has been criticised on a number of levels. Conservative historians fiercely attacked his conception of capitalism; others accused him of being derivative and lacking originality in either social thought or economic history. Primarily a social theorist, Tawney's aim was to develop 'a general body of ideas' – what Anthony Wright calls a 'consensual social philosophy' – without which durable social reform by democratic means was unachievable. Tawney, then, was a thinker, but not simply an abstract or speculative philosopher. He was also practical, as his contribution to the realities of the modern Labour Party attests. Tawney tried to understand the malaise of modern Britain, on its own terms, and to suggest a new social ethic to encourage the 'respiritualisation' of society.

Main works

The Agrarian Problem in the Sixteenth Century, London: Longman Green, 1912.

The Establishment of Minimum Rates in the Chain-Making Industry under the Trade Boards Act of 1909, London: G. Bell, 1914.

The Establishment of Minimum Rates in the Tailoring Industry under the Trade Boards Act of 1909, London: G. Bell, 1915.

The Acquisitive Society, London: G. Bell, 1921.

The British Labour Movement, New Haven, CT: Yale University Press, 1925.

Land and Labour in China, London: George Allen and Unwin, 1932.

Religion and the Rise of Capitalism (1926), London: Penguin, 1990.

Equality, London: George Allen and Unwin, 1952.

The Attack and Other Papers, London: George Allen and Unwin, 1953.

Business and Politics under James I: Lionel and Cranfield as merchant and minister, Cambridge: Cambridge University Press, 1958.

The Radical Tradition: Twelve essays on politics, education and literature, ed. R. Hinden, London: George Allen and Unwin, 1964.

Commonplace Book, ed. J. M. Winter and D. M. Joslin, Cambridge: Cambridge University Press, 1972.

History and Society: Essays by R. H. Tawney, ed. J. M. Winter, London: Routledge and Kegan Paul, 1978.

The American Labour Movement and Other Essays, ed. J. M. Winter, Brighton: Harvester Wheatsheaf, 1979.

Further reading

Halsey, A. H. and N. Dennis, *English Ethical Socialism*, Oxford: Oxford University Press, 1988.

Ormrod, D. 'R. H. Tawney and the origins of capitalism', *History Workshop Journal*, 18 (Autumn 1984), pp. 138–59.

Reisman, D., *State, Welfare: Tawney, Galbraith and Adam Smith*, London: Macmillan, 1982.

Terrill, R., *R. H. Tawney and His Times: Socialism as fellowship*, London: Andre Deutsch, 1974.

Winter, J. M., 'A bibliography of the published writings of R. H. Tawney', *Economic History Review*, 25 (1972), pp. 137–55.

Wright, Anthony, *R. H. Tawney*, Manchester: Manchester University Press, 1987.

Thom, René (1923–)

René Thom graduated from the Ecole Normale Supérieure in 1946, and five years later completed his doctorate in topology, the study of geometrical properties which are unaffected by changes of shape and size. His main influences at that time were the French geometer Gaston Darboux and the mathematician Henri Poincaré. Thorn's publications in the 1950s were few and far between, but far-reaching in their scope and aspiration. A 1954 paper on transversality was very influential, and in 1958 he was awarded a prestigious international honour, the Fields Medal, for his theory of co-bordism. In 1957 Thom moved from the University of Grenoble to the University of Strasbourg, where he investigated structural stability using topology, and in 1963 he joined the Institut des Hautes Etudes Scientifiques near Paris.

A crucial turning-point in his thinking came when Thom saw affinities between a display of embryological models in a museum and shapes familiar from his mathematical modelling. This sparked an attempt to bridge the disparate disciplines of biology and topology, and led to his investigation of structural archetypes in nature. By 1965 he had concluded that there were only seven ways by which biological processes change from one stable state to another, and all of these can be expressed topographically.

This became the basis of 'catastrophe theory', Thom's most substantial contribution to the history of twentieth-century ideas. Although a draft of his book presenting the theory was completed by 1966, publication was delayed by six years, during which time he refined and developed his thesis. Its eventual appearance in 1972 precipitated much discussion about the social and political implications of his work.

───────────────

When René Thom published *Structural Stability and Morphogenesis* in 1972, several commentators drew parallels with Newton's *Principia*, a book whose principles of motion remained unchallenged for over two centuries. Thom's work was not concerned with motion, but with the nature of change, particularly sudden jumps from one state to another. These are observable in the subatomic world, when electrons leap between energy levels without intermediate stages, and, on a grander scale, when stars go nova. Both cases can be explained by catastrophe theory, Thom's general account of discontinuity.

Catastrophe theory postulates that in a system whose behaviour is governed by no more than four factors, there are only seven different ways in which a catastrophe can take place. This bald assertion caused a considerable stir amongst the scientific community when it was first made public. Hector Sussman and Raphael Zahler launched a damning attack which was summarised in *Science* under the headline 'Catastrophe theory: the emperor has no clothes'. Their main objection was that Thom produced insufficent evidence for his exaggerated claims and was trying to 'deduce the world by thought alone'. Others argued that the emperor's wardrobe was, on the contrary, rather well equipped. Christopher Zeeman extended the model to apply to all manner of catastrophes, including stock market crashes and prison riots. He believed that Thom had evolved not just a mathematical method, but a new language for understanding changes of form and process where they occur. Like all new languages, this one contained many difficult items of vocabulary. Technical jargon such as 'bimodality' and 'hysteresis' were guaranteed to flummox the non-specialist. Small wonder that one non-specialist wrote airily that 'we laymen . . . can happily dismiss catastrophe theory as something else we need not feel guilty about not understanding a single word of'.

Yet the topological pictures of catastrophe theory drawn by Thom were intuitively graspable, and helped popularise its approach. Each of the seven types of catastrophe can be represented by a simple graph (see pp. 344–8). The two-dimensional fold catastrophe graph shows, for example, what happens when a rubber band is stretched until it snaps. The cusp catastrophe graph has a curved surface with a pleat, and can simulate the fitful cycle of waking and sleeping, or the transition of water from liquid to vapour under certain temperature conditions. It is impossible to draw the swallow-tail catastrophe in three dimensions, but a 'freeze frame' of the change shows a folded sheet with an internal curl similar to the bird's tail after which it is named. The surface of the butterfly catastrophe graph is similar to that of the cusp, but with an additional 'pocket' of changing proportions. The other types of catastrophe – hyperbolic, elliptic and parabolic – are much more complex, and can only be accurately displayed on a computer. Nevertheless, they are useful tools for examining transformations in areas such as optics and fluid dynamics. Armed with this sevenfold classification system, catastrophe theory set out to explain the universe. Indeed, Thom self-consciously developed it as a theory of everything, one which focused on things often overlooked by the scientist: 'phenomena of common interest, in themselves trivial . . . the cracks in an old wall, the shape of a cloud, the path of a falling leaf, or the froth on a pint of beer', as Thom put it.

It was inevitable that catastrophe theory should be eagerly applied in physics, chemistry and biology. What surprised many was the swiftness with which it was adopted in the so-called 'soft sciences'. Sociologists used it to look at the erratic actions of crowds. Psychologists referred to it as a means of understanding the violent mood swings of schizophrenics and anorexics. Political scientists enlisted it to study everything from the rise in support for a government policy to the fall of Rome at the hands of the barbarians. Thom's keys, it seemed, unlocked many doors.

Now that the excitement and controversy has abated, many of the rooms remain locked, and the comparisons with Newton seem somewhat premature. Catastrophe theory has scarcely stood the test of two decades, let alone two centuries. It has, we might say, undergone its own catastrophe, and Thom is no longer a fashionable topic for common room discussion.

In his 1959 Cambridge Rede lecture, C. P. Snow referred famously to the divorce between two cultures, the sciences and the humanities. The case of René Thom is a neat illustration of his thesis. Catastrophe theory was Janus-faced, a scientific hypothesis which – although reviled by many scientists – found acceptance with the general public. Why it did so is uncertain. It may have something to do with its combination of mathematical inaccessibility and pictorial simplicity. Or we can perhaps speculate that there was something about its very name which suited the times. The 1960s was a decade of considerable social and cultural upheaval, a period of catastrophic change in many local and global spheres, changes which required explanation. Catastrophe theory provided a sound-byte elucidation.

In this respect we can draw parallels with what has happened more recently with chaos theory. Benoit Mandelbrot is the Thom of the 1990s, a purveyor of abstruse mathematical truths which are nevertheless embraced and misconstrued by laymen who would have difficulty completing a quadratic equation. They differ in one key respect, however. Thom is essentially a structuralist, and his Pythagorean project is to find the topological frames underlying all natural forms. Mandelbrot is a post-structuralist, acknowledging that the world is too chaotic to be deduced by thought alone.

Main works

Structural Stability and Morphogenesis: An outline of a general theory of models, Reading, MA: Benjamin, 1977.

Further reading

Kolata, Gina Bari, 'Catastrophe theory: the emperor has no clothes', *Science*, 15 April 1977, pp. 287, 350–1.

Postle, Denis, *Catastrophe Theory*, London: Fontana, 1980.

Saunders, P. T., *An Introduction to Catastrophe Theory*, Cambridge: Cambridge University Press, 1980.

Woodcock, Alexander and Monte Davis, *Catastrophe Theory*, New York: E. P. Dutton, 1978.

Zahler, Raphael S. and Hector J. Sussmann, 'Claims and accomplishments of applied catastrophe theory', *Nature*, 27 October 1977, pp. 759–63.

Zeeman, E. Christopher, *Catastrophe Theory, Selected Papers 1972–1977*, Reading, MA: Benjamin, 1977.

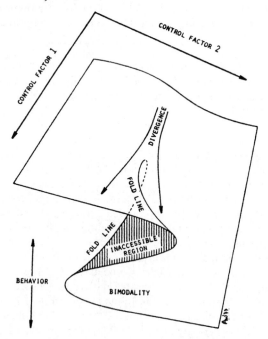

Figure 1 *The Cusp catastrophe graph (Source Woodcock and Davis, 1978)*

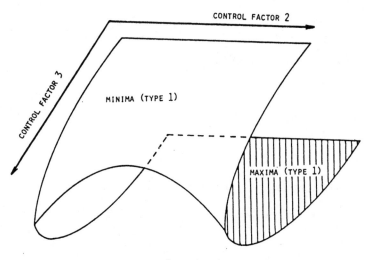

Figure 2 *Two three-dimensional 'slices' of the swallowtail (Source Woodcock and Davis, 1978)*

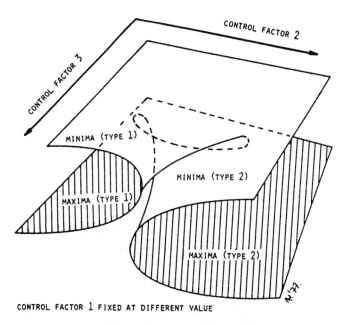

Figure 3 *Catastrophe graph (Source Woodcock and Davis, 1978)*

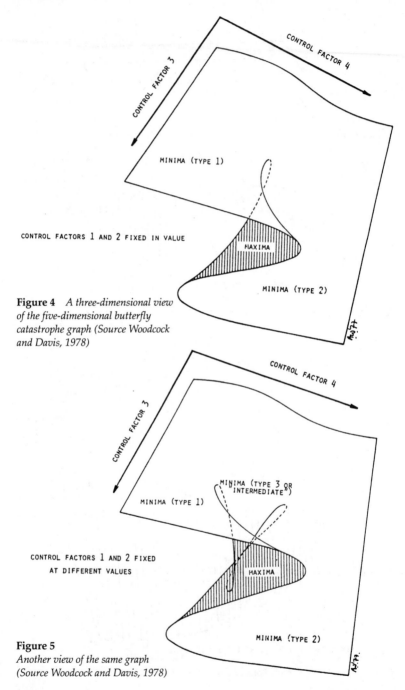

Figure 4   *A three-dimensional view of the five-dimensional butterfly catastrophe graph (Source Woodcock and Davis, 1978)*

Figure 5
Another view of the same graph (Source Woodcock and Davis, 1978)

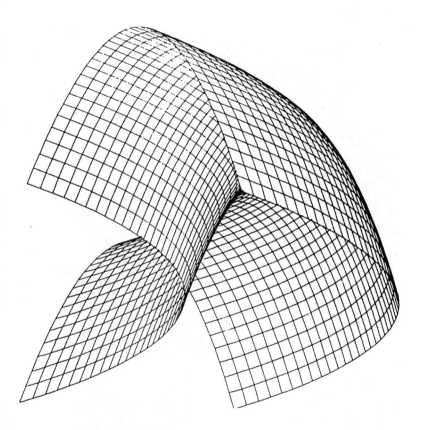

Figure 6 *A computer-drawn projection of the hyperbolic umbilic catastrophe graph (Source Woodcock and Davis, 1978)*

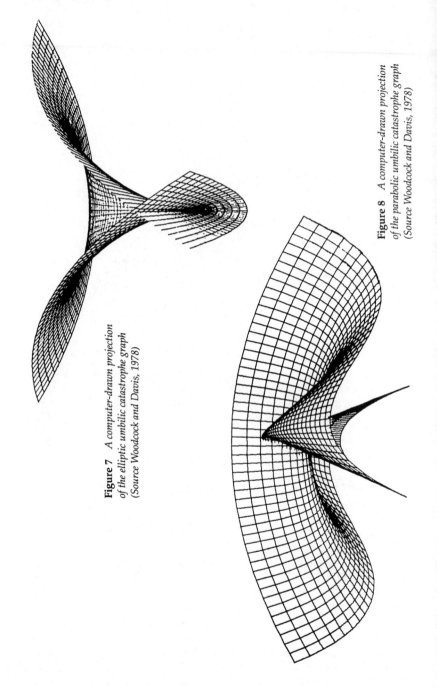

Figure 7 *A computer-drawn projection of the elliptic umbilic catastrophe graph (Source Woodcock and Davis, 1978)*

Figure 8 *A computer-drawn projection of the parabolic umbilic catastrophe graph (Source Woodcock and Davis, 1978)*

Thompson, E. P. (1924–1993)

B. P. Thompson read history at Cambridge during the 1940s; his studies were interrupted by war service (in Italy). Two years after graduating in 1946 he was appointed extra-mural lecturer at Leeds University. During this period, Thompson also emerged as one of the major figures of the British 'old' New Left as a result of his work on the journal *The New Reasoner*, which was formed in response to the Soviet-generated crisis of the European Left in 1956. *The New Reasoner* merged with *The Universities and Left Review* in 1960 to become *The New Left Review*, though by the middle of the 1960s Thompson opposed the 'new' New Left's theoretical critique of English Marxist traditions. The publication of *The Making of the English Working Class* in 1963 made Thompson an authoritative figure in the discipline of social history, and Thompson's academic career moved to the new University of Warwick in the late 1960s. During the 1970s Thompson became a controversial figure as a result of his forceful polemic against **Althusser**'s structuralist Marxism. Although still active as a researcher, Thompson held no academic post during the 1980s, devoting his energies instead to European Nuclear Disarmament (END) and the debates around the nuclear threat and the Cold War which dominated that decade.

Some may place a question mark over Thompson's contribution to social and political theory; in the early 1980s, and as a direct result of his argument with Althusser and his defence of empiricism, Thompson was taken by some to be anti-theoretical. It needs to be recognised, however, that Thompson's socialist humanism was premised on the need for a conceptually and empirically grounded dialogue between the critically interdependent domains of political theory and social history. The argument and significance of *The Making of the English Working Class* exemplifies this aim. In dealing with the formation of a politically radical working-class consciousness during the period 1780–1832, Thompson's primary focus was not on the factory workers who were subjected to the leading and supposedly most alienating edge of industrial modernity, but instead on those whose trades and occupations – stockingers, hand-loom weavers – were destroyed by new forms of production and economic organisation. Thompson's claim for the political value of the consciousness shared by figures at the historical margins, and his consequently famous opposition to 'the enormous condescension of posterity', was an empirically grounded act of revisionism which was conducting a theoretical argument with the functionalist modernisation theory of Talcott **Parsons**'s school, and the latter's assumption of the necessity of economic growth and the regulation of social identity and action to this end. In its account of the relationship between radical democratic traditions within English

Dissent and the emergence of a radical political culture *The Making of the English Working Class* contests a vulgar Marxist view of religion as ideological mystification. Indeed, Thompson's commitment to the moral and affective content of cultural traditions and practices was central to his claim that the English working class was present at its own making. In arguing this, Thompson was advancing a theory of class formation which argued that class was not a thing but a process, that it was produced through experientially grounded social relationships; and that individuals who came to share a class consciousness were moral and intellectual agents who chose forms of belief and action in response to given social circumstances. Thompson was, then, arguing against a powerful determinist strain in Marxism (economism), which held that the economic base determined the superstructure, or the practices and beliefs of people living in a given set of relations of production.

Many of these arguments were to receive more explicit philosophical and theoretical treatment in Thompson's essay 'The poverty of theory' – paradoxically Thompson's great polemic against Althusserian theoreticism. Given the tension between the title of Thompson's essay and its philosophical drive, it is important to specify the kind of theory that Thompson held to be poverty stricken. Althusser's Marxism was, according to Thompson, a variant of those didactic, absolutist and irrational practices which had brought the 'old' New Left into oppositional existence in 1957: in other words, Stalinist ideology reproduced. Indeed, much of Thompson's political and polemical activity as an intellectual was prompted by a resistance to what he saw as irrational absolutisms; from his argument with the editor of the *New Left Review*, Perry Anderson, in 'The peculiarities of the English' (*The Poverty of Theory*, 1965), to his arguments against NATO's domination of North Atlantic and West European politics and the totalitarian implications of its ideology of nuclear deterrance. If Thompson resisted totalitarianism, he promoted the necessity of dialogue – a key term in the multifaceted argument of *The Poverty of Theory*.

At the heart of Thompson's defence of the empirical dimension of knowledge production in *The Poverty of Theory* is the practice of dialogue: knowledge is constructed by means of a dialogue between concepts and empirical evidence, and the product is far richer and more politically enabling than the fruits of empiricism, a positivism with self-denying horizons which refuses to look beyond nominalism and individualism, and which is exemplified by the work of Karl **Popper**. Indeed, it is Thompson's purpose to trace an equivalence between Althusser's anti-empirical theoreticism and Popper's empiricist insistence upon falsifiability – the title of Thompson's essay echoes Popper's *The Poverty of Historicism*, a scientistic argument which argues that history is not real knowledge, but instead mere interpretation. Thompson argues that both Popper and Althusser make historical knowledge impossible and redundant. In so doing, both remove at a stroke the intellectual and interpretive agency, equipped with a sense of 'the logic of process', which engages in a dialogue with the archive of culturally shaped past experience – the empirical raw data of 'historical and cultural materialism.'

Thompson himself engages in this sort of dialogue when re-reading Marx's contribution to intellectual history and social theory in his critique of classical political economy in the *Grundrisse* and *Capital*. Whereas for Althusser these texts constitute Marx's scientific epistemological break from a humanist past, for Thompson these texts reveal Marx reaching the limits of a critique conducted within the terms an internally regulated mechanistic discipline, a discipline shaped precisely by nineteenth-century bourgeois culture (as indeed, Thompson argues in parallel, the mechanistic Althusserian 'Orrery of errors' has been shaped by late twentieth-century university culture). According to Thompson, Marx's critique was unable to show capitalism as capital in the totality of its relations: what was needed for this was the very approach that Althusser was writing out of the Marxist canon – Engels's historically informed cultural anthropology. Thus Thompson affirmed himself as a contributor to a humanist Marxist tradition of active reason, diametrically opposed to Althusser's theological Marxism. By 1978 Thompson had come to see the consequences of 1956 as schismatic in nature; a very different account of the Marxist tradition to the united-but-diverse image offered as late as 1973 in the 'Open letter to Leszek Kolakowski'.

As Kate Soper has observed, *The Poverty of Theory* is an uneven piece of writing: whilst it forcefully restated the case for socialist humanism, it was also both intemperate and unfair to Althusser. Perhaps a more pressing theoretical critique advanced by Perry Anderson centres on Thompson's key defence of human agency: as Anderson points out, there are ambivalences in Thompson's position on structure and agency which make it unclear as to whether we are in fact free agents, or must only think ourselves to be so. This sort of tension has critical repercussions for the inherent moral sense that Thompson claims as the distinctive trait of socialist humanism.

In terms of practical political activity, Thompson will be remembered as a major figure in the British and European peace movements from the 1950s to the 1980s: Thompson was living proof of the fact that English radicalism could be both peculiarly culturally self-centred and outward-looking. Academically, as Harvey Kaye has argued, Thompson's influence needs to be placed in the context of the work of a generation of British Marxist historians such as Christopher Hill and Rodney Hilton. That said, his own research on working-class politics and culture inspired a wealth of new research in social history during the 1970s and 1980s. In addition, Thompson's role in providing an early methodological and political rationale for the emergent discipline of cultural studies should be remembered.

Main works

William Morris: Romantic to revolutionary (1956), 2nd edn, London: Merlin 1977.

Out of Apathy (ed. and contributor), London: New Left and Stevens, 1960.

The Making of the English Working Class, London: Victor Gollancz, 1963.

The Poverty of Theory and Other Essays, London: Pluto, 1978.

Protest and Survive (contributor), Harmondsworth: Penguin, 1980.

Further reading

Anderson, P., *Arguments within English Marxism*, London: New Left, 1980.

Eagleton, T., A. Assiter and G. McLennan, 'E. P. Thompson's *Poverty of Theory*: a symposium', *Literature and History*, 5 (Autumn 1979), pp. 139–64.

Kaye, H. J., *The British Marxist Historians*, Cambridge: Polity, 1986.

McClelland, K. and H. J. Kaye (eds), *E. P. Thompson: Critical debates*, Cambridge: Polity, 1990.

Soper, K., *Troubled Pleasures: Writings on politics, gender and hedonism*, London: Verso, 1990.

Tillich, Paul (1886–1965)

Paul Johannes Tillich was born in Starzeddel, Prussia, in 1886, to a prominent Lutheran pastor. Tillich was himself ordained into the Evangelical Lutheran Church in 1912, and went on to become the foremost Protestant theologian of his generation. He was educated at institutions in Berlin, Tübingen, Halle and Breslau between 1904 and 1912, and taught at universities in Berlin (1919–24), Marburg (1924–5), Dresden (1925–9) and Leipzig (1928–9), before his appointment as Professor of Philosophy at Frankfurt in 1929. He remained there until 1933, when he was forced to flee the country after his criticisms of the Nazis (one of the first non-Jewish intellectuals to leave in such circumstances). Reinhold Niebuhr obtained a post for Tillich at the Union Theological Seminary in New York City, where for over twenty years he taught and wrote prodigiously. The international reputation his work accrued led to a Professorship at Harvard between 1955 and 1962, and a post in the Divinity School of the University of Chicago, where he stayed until his death in 1965.

Tillich wrote in the introduction to *Religious Realization* that the 'boundary is the best place for acquiring knowledge', a phrase he later used to summarise his entire intellectual enterprise. It is indeed an appropriate statement, as his books straddle the boundaries between theology philosophy and psychology.

The boundary between philosophy and theology was one Tillich often traversed. He believed, not unreasonably, that the types of answers we receive from the world are determined by the kinds of questions we ask. Philosophy, on the whole, asks universal questions, and so receives universal answers. 'What is truth?' is a typical philosophical question. The typical philosophical reply is not the resounding silence received by Pilate when he made this enquiry, but an attempt to capture the essence of all true statements, or to outline the truth-conditions in which propositions can be true. So philosophy concerns itself with the things which concern all men. Theological questions, on the other hand, are particularised and spring from a situational concern. The question 'what is suffering?' is not intended to elicit an abstract disquisition on the nature of pain. It can only be satisfactorily answered by some revelation to an individual about the supernal order of things. It would seem, therefore, that we are dealing with two realms of incommensurable discourse. Tillich says, however, that theology is more capacious than philosophy because it can address both the human and the divine, embrace both the finite and the infinite. Tillich's three-volume *Systematic Theology* (1951–63) explores the consequence of this, and many other issues, in considerable depth.

Tillich is most well known for obscuring the boundary between theology and psychology, by importing existentialist ideas into his religious domain. Existentialism was much in vogue after the Second World War as an anti-rationalist, anti-idealist philosophy, and despite offering the self-aware individual the chance for commitment to a cause, it accrued rather negative connotations thanks to the gloomy angst-ridden novels of its literary apologists, such as Jean-Paul Sartre's *Nausea* (1938) and Albert Camus's *The Outsider* (1942). Tillich, however, describes existentialism in a more positive light as 'the most radical form of the courage to be as oneself' in the modern period, and acknowledged that existentialist questions with a small 'the' have been around for some time. Indeed, alienation and meaninglessness are constitutive aspects of man's 'fallen' condition. (The sermons about hell which Stephen Dedalus hears in the third chapter of James Joyce's *A Portrait of the Artist as a Young Man* are, fire and brimstone apart, almost classic statements of Sartrean anguish and despair as most of the punishments involve isolation from oneself and others.) What is important is that the individual finds the courage for self-affirmation in spite of those forces preventing the self from affirming itself.

The chief impetus for this theological leap-in-the-void is the realisation that God is Being Itself, the 'infinite and inexhaustible depth and ground of all being'. This insight is not only available to mystics, as Tillich explains in *The Courage to Be*:

mysticism is more than a special form of the relation to the ground of being. It is an element of every form of this relation. Since everything that is participates in the power of being, the element of identity on which mysticism is based cannot be absent in any religious experience. There is no self-affirmation of a finite being, and there is no courage to be in which the ground of being and its power of conquering non-being is not effective. And the experience of the presence of this power is the mystical element even in the person-to-person encounter with God.

Person-to-person encounters with God are at the heart of Protestantism, and Tillich's work – despite its ecumenical scope and responsiveness – is a substantial continuation of the Protestant tradition. Yet he should not be judged solely in religious terms: he wrote that 'As a theologian I have tried to remain a philosopher, and vice versa', and his union of theology and philosophy is his most distinctive contribution to twentieth-century culture. His early immersion in the German idealists – Fichte, Kant and especially Schelling, whose interest in Christian doctrine counterpointed Hegelian humanism – was shattered by the Great War, a blow for all kinds of utopian thinking. This impelled him, however, to look for something after the catastrophe which could bear witness to the 'experience of the abyss', and he found sufficient gravity in the writings of Nietzsche, Kierkegaard and **Heidegger** to stimulate his own existentialist musings. He thereby found empathy with writers and ideas usually deemed inimical to the Christian faith.

As T. S. Eliot once observed, Tillich's writings offer 'illumination even of subjects apparenfly remote from those with which the author is concerned'. It is this general readability which makes Tillich more influential than his contemporaries Karl Barth, the Swiss theologian, and Rudolf Bultmann, who also brought Christian thinking in line with other forms of twentieth-century thought.

Several of Tillich's works achieved a widespread circulation. The collection of sermons delivered at the Union Theological Seminary during the Second World War, *The Shaking of the Foundations*, contains meditations on 'The Paradox of the Beatitudes', 'The mystery of time', 'The depth of existence' and other matters, in a language which manages to be both orthodox and modern. The work *Courage To Be* is a remarkable synthesis of existentialism and religion. Tillich traces the genealogy of courage from Plato to Nietzsche, and constructs a taxonomy of anxiety (fate and death, emptiness and meaninglessness, guilt and condemnation), providing in the process a religious recuperation of the atheistic despair associated with a Kafka or Camus.

The success of these books, and others, explain the force of Reinhold Niebuhr's eulogy in the *New York Times Book Review* (24 October 1965):

Paul Tillich was a giant among us. His influence extended beyond theological students and circles to include many from other disciplines . . . He combined theological with philosophical and psychological learning, and also, he combined religious insights with an understanding and appreciation of the arts. Thus he displayed to the American communities of learning and culture, the wholeness of religious philosophy and of the political and social dimensions of human existence.

Main works

The Shaking of the Foundations, New York: Simon and Schuster, 1940.

Systematic Theology (1951–63), Chicago: Chicago University Press, 1967.

The Courage To Be, New Haven, CT: Yale University Press, 1959.

On the Boundary, New York: Scribner, 1963.

The Eternal Now, New York: Simon and Schuster, 1963.

Further reading

Ashbrook, James, *Paul Tillich in Conversation: Psychotherapy . . . religion . . . culture . . . history . . . psychology*, Bristol, IN: Wyndham Hall, 1988.

Mahan, Wayne, *Tillich's System*, San Antonio, TX: Trinity University Press, 1974.

Martin, Bernard, *The Existentialist Theology of Paul Tillich*, Albany, NY: NCUP, 1963.

Palmer, Michael, *Paul Tillich's Philosophy of Art*, Hawthorne, NY: Walter de Gruyter, 1983.

Taylor, Mark, *Paul Tillich: Theologian of the Boundaries*, Minneapolis, MN: Augsburg Fortress, 1991.

Tilly, Charles (1929–)

Charles Tilly was born in Lombard, Illinois and studied at Harvard (where he received his Ph.D. in 1958). He researched and taught sociology and history at Harvard, Yale, Ann Arbor and the Massachusetts Institute of Technology, before becoming Director of the Center for Studies of Social Change at New York's New School for Social Research. He recently resigned from there, to become Joseph L. Buttenwieser Professor of Social Science at Columbia University.

Tilly's name will often be found as an editor of research collections. For over two decades, he has been a central figure in collaborative American research in the fields of comparative sociology and history. The interest of his work lies, then, as much in the possibilities opened up by his intellectual strategy, 'at the junction of history, political science, and sociology', as in the substantive results he has achieved. In the late 1980s, Tilly the collaborative researcher added a raft of single-authored books to his output, in which he set out his own comprehensive account of the dynamic development of 'modern' urban life and government, with its political forms and practices in Europe and America.

Tilly once described himself as 'a student of cities, urbanisation, political change, and collective action'. He published, for example, an early study of social groupings in the process of urbanisation: *Race and Residence in Wilmington, Migration to an American City* (1965). Yet his approach has always been deeply rooted in history, and especially the history of social conflict – as was illustrated in *The Vendee* (1964), based on his doctoral thesis, which shows urbanisation as a key to provincial resistance to the French Revolution. By placing the concept of 'contention' (developed, especially, in *From Mobilization to Revolution*) at the centre of his researches into social change in the modern world, Tilly's work has countered the **Durkheim**ian presumption (reflected also in **Parsons**) that disorder and delinquency only express the population's need to receive meaningfulness from above. Rather, Tilly has interpreted the evolution of the modern western world (e.g. in *The Rebellious Century, 1830–1930*) in the dynamic interaction between ordinary people's forms of contention and the growth of the big structures and social interests which form the currency of much social theory.

Contention, the continual claims of subordinate groups against the dominance of others in the social space, brings out the continuity between forms of collective conflict: from routine gestures of complaint, to political contest, to civil war or revolution. It broadens the increasingly shaky Marxist conceptions of 'class conflict' and revolution. Contention is shaped by, and shapes the sociopolitical context in which it occurs. Only at the top end of this continuum, where contention attains a full-scale challenge to sovereign authority, does Tilly refer to a 'revolutionary situation' (or even, à la **Trotksy**, where a significant transfer of power from bloc to bloc ensues, to a 'revolutionary outcome'). Contention stands at the cross-roads, then, between large, given structures, such as state power, and the autonomy of people in history. It is the *channel* by which social groups make claims for their primary, material interests and effect changes in underlying social relations. Yet, passed on in the historical memory and amended by the lessons of present conflicts, the 'repertoires' of contention also belong in the fabric of the social actor's *culture*. Finally, it is *historical* in that the practices of claim-making alter, and themselves adapt to, the context of changing structures and interests.

Tilly's substantive expositions of the development of 'modern' society in Europe and North America concentrate on three focal points: the *activity* of 'state-making'; the evolving *balance* between established power-structures and the resistance of social groups; and social (or revolutionary) pressure for change.

The 1975 symposium on *The Formation of Nation-states in Western Europe* put into practice proposals from Tilly and others (e.g. in his 1971 report *History as Social Science* – edited jointly with David S. Landes) to widen the theoretical diversity and increase the historical sensitivity of American comparative sociology and political science. The collection pursues a more dynamic and historically specific account of the state, which has been the most striking element of modernity. It examines state-*making*: how certain social actors developed power structures which were differentiated from other social forces and networks, and subdued those others. It was this *activity*, and the obstacles it met, that would account for the centralised, sovereign, impersonal, specialised modern state that **Weber** had defined. The state was imposed upon an often resistant environment of decentralised power but homogenous culture. The crucial activities (forming armies, police forces and bureaucracies; tax-collecting; promoting *taxable* economic development; feeding soldiers and towns) all provoked conflict. A combination of force, cajolery and compromise was pursued to overcome the losers: autonomous noble land-holders, free towns, feudal assemblies, rival contenders for statehood and, most of all (echoing Barrington Moore's classic, *The Social Origins of Dictatorship and Democracy*, 1966), peasants. Tilly's own essay, on food supply and public order, demonstrated how, while the state's activities may aim primarily to secure its own power, each produces wider socio-economic repercussions (such as the encouragement of agrarian capitalism), *and* new focuses for contention: the replacement of the localised 'moral economy', with its consensus on the 'just price', by open markets and national-government responsibility for subsistence. The dynamic analysis of sociopolitical development, as the figure below illustrates, stresses systematic relationships between state activities, in a mix of intended and unintended social outcomes.

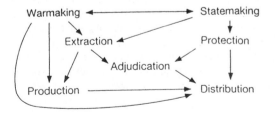

(Tilly, 1992, p. 97)

In *Coercion, Capital and European State, AD 990–1992* Tilly extends earlier findings to an overarching account of the growth of the European state system, and state power in a changing pattern of contention. Capital, Tilly accepts, has been the crucial ascendant social power to which European politics must accommodate. Systematic comparisons bring out how the state and capital have each been reshaped in different ways and time-frames across Europe. Tilly identifies more of a cluster than a simple two-way division, around a strip of early commercial development running from south to north. The most successful state-formation occurred neither *within* nor *too distant* from this strip, but *alongside* it. Where commercial cities achieved much independence (e.g. Holland), state-makers could not extract resources to sustain their power; where commerce was weak or dependent (Hungary, Russia or Spain), state coercion and aristocratic landholders stifled it, obtaining extensive social control of impoverished serf or peasant economies. But where state coercion and the autonomy of capital were in some kind of balance (Britain, France, Germany), an accommodation *had* to be reached between these conflicting powers. This Tilly calls 'capitalised coercion': at the price of ceding some freedom to urban capital, states obtained large financial resources and control over subject populations large enough for the production and manpower needed in their military struggles with their rivals.

The dynamics of modern social and political power have interacted with contention in the wider society. Put schematically, from about the mid-eighteenth century, segmented societies, where contention was communal (e.g. dynastic succession or patron–client relations), were superseded by consolidated, national societies where political power was subject to challenge from countrywide coalitions of classes in *state*-directed forms of contestation (the petition, the mass demonstration, the class-based party, etc.). Tilly's recent works accordingly offer accounts of the evolution of the 'collective-action repertoires' of resistance and their relations with political power. Three concepts embrace the changes: revolution, popular politics and citizenship.

The incidence of revolutionary changes of power (expounded in *European Revolutions*) is related to the path of state-formation and coercion-capital accommodation. 'Capital-intensive' paths (such as Holland's) leave highly decentralised, civic–corporate power, which confines contests to communal forms. 'Coercion-intensive' paths (such as Spain's) leave political contests in the hands of aristocratic or military elites. 'Capitalised coercion' first consolidates the state's centralised order of rule, and then reaches some accommodation with capital and peasant society. Britain's revolution formed a compact, financially effective state, with a coalition of landlords and merchants in control of national affairs. Paradigmatic forms of nation-wide democratic politics superimposed themselves on to this as urbanisation (and continual warfare around the turn of the nineteenth century) took effect (*Popular Contention in Great Britain*). France's early centralisation gave it access to finance which, in pursuit of military survival, the post-revolutionary state enhanced by imposing the mutual obligations of the state and a mass 'citizen' soldiery (*Citizenship, Identity and Social History*).

As regards methodology, Tilly's work has encouraged the best of American comparative sociology to reverse the schematism of post-war functionalist and developmental theories by learning the insights of European conflictual models and historical writing. Even if his larger historical claims are too recent for a judgement of their impact, he stands alongside others (such as Theda Skocpol and Michael Mann) who exemplify current efforts to account for, and identify the limits of 'modern' social and political forms in a genuinely historical fashion.

Main works

The Formation of National States in Western Europe (ed.), Princeton: Princeton University Press, 1975.

The Rebellion Century, 1830–1930, London: Dent, 1975.

From Mobilization to Revolution, Reading, MA: Addison Wesley, 1978.

Where History Meets Sociology, New York and London: Academic Press, 1981.

'War making and state making as organized crime', in Peter Evans, Dietrich Reuschemeyer and Theda Skocpol (eds), *Bringing the State Back In*, New York and Cambridge: Cambridge University Press, 1985.

Coercion, Capital and European State, AD 990–1992. Oxford: Basil Blackwell, 1990.

European Revolutions, 1492–1992, Oxford: Basil Blackwell, 1993.

Popular Contention in Great Britain, 1758–1834, Cambridge, MA: Harvard University Press, 1995.

Citizenship, Identity and Social History (ed.), Cambridge: Cambridge University Press, 1996.

Further reading

Hall, John A. (ed.), *States in History*, Oxford: Basil Blackwell, 1986.

Kimmel, M., *Revolution: A sociological interpretation*, Cambridge: Polity, 1990.

Mann, Michael, *The Sources of Social Power*, Vols I and II, Cambridge: Cambridge University Press, 1986 and 1993.

Skocpol, T., *States and Social Revolutions*, Cambridge: Cambridge University Press, 1979.

Thompson, E. P., *Customs in Common*, London: Merlin, 1994.

Toffler, Alvin (1928–)

Alvin Toffler, the futurist and social critic, graduated in English from New York University in 1949. Inspired by Marxist beliefs, he worked for several years as a welder, a foundry millwright, a punch press operator, a metal finisher and a blacksmith's helper. He wrote for a trade paper and as a journalist for the labour press. After some freelancing, he became a newspaper correspondent in Washington in 1957, and this paved the way for him to become an associate editor of the prestigious business magazine *Fortune* in 1959. Eventually, in 1961, he was able to wed his interests in industry, technology and the future when IBM commissioned him to write a report on the long-term impact of the computer upon patterns of employment. His first book, *The Culture Consumers* (1964), looked at the economy of the arts in the United States. Although reviewed on the front page of the *New York Times Book Review*, it caused little fuss. However, Toffler's next work, *Future Shock* (1969), created immediate tremors of debate. During the five years it took to complete, Toffler ran a course on the sociology of the future at the New School for Social Research and taught on technology and values as a Visiting Professor at Cornell University. He has published several works since *Future Shock*, such as *The Third Wave* in 1980 and *Powershifts* in 1991, which effectively update his earlier groundbreaking study.

Nostradamus, so some claim, could predict the future several centuries ahead. Today's Nostradamuses find difficulties forecasting the next few months, such is the pace of progress. Yet, as we edge nearer the new millennium, the demand for crystal-ball gazing grows. Enter Alvin Toffler. *Future Shock* swiftly became an international best-seller because of its bold and speculative thinking about future trends and the impact of technological developments throughout society.

The shocking thing about the future, of course, is that it is already here. Computers, which not too long ago required entire rooms to house them, can now fit into the breast pocket. The virtual reality explored by science-fiction writers just a decade ago is now with us. Many a soothsayer's prediction has fallen by the wayside, of course, but this short shelf-life of ideas is itself part of the new condition of things. Toffler acknowledges this by commencing *Future Shock* with a chapter called 'The death of permanence', in which he notes the 'fire storm of change' brought about by the rapid advance of information technologies.

This accelerating rate of change triggers a state of shock in the individual and has several immediate consequences for society. First, there is the advent of the throw-away mentality. We may no longer buy paper wedding-gowns and trash them after the nuptials, a fad Toffler observed in the sixties, but we do the same with just about everything else. Second, our sense of identity is much more fragmented, leading to the advent of what Toffler calls 'Modular Man'. All relationships are now brief encounters of one form or other. We change our jobs, our homes and our marriages with frightening speed and unpredictability. Third, our institutions can no longer be relied upon to provide us with continuity. The Orwellian nightmare of a suffocating, self-sustaining bureaucracy never quite materialised. Instead, we live in what Toffler calls an 'ad-hocracy', where organisations are run by temporary 'task-force' management rather than by long-term strategy and design.

Alongside this transience there is a high premium placed upon novelty, and this also induces a societal state of shock. Toffler gives many dozens of examples of the destabilising effects of the new, but two will suffice. There is the unique idea of 'serving wenches in the sky', for instance. This was part of a campaign by TWA in the 1960s to attract more customers to its airline by providing a series of 'theme-flights' in which the stewardesses would dress in period costumes, such as Roman togas or 'Olde English' costumes. This kitsch blurring of boundaries – in this case between travel and entertainment – is observable in many different spheres, and is part of the 'anything goes' aesthetic identified by Jean-François Lyotard as an index of postmodern society. Toffler's forecast about the rise of 'simulated environments' was similarly prescient. In 1970, prior to the advent of the video game and the VCR, the notion that much of the future would be dedicated to the slavish resurrection of the past must have seemed exotic indeed. Yet now most of the major leisure corporations such as Sony and United Artists are geared towards reconstructions of history through the building of theme parks and the provision of ersatz screen adventures. Tourism and heritage is now one of Britain's biggest industries: the 'Oxford Experience' museum in the city of dreaming spires, for example, regularly attracts more visitors than the colleges themselves.

The emphasis placed upon novelty will, according to Toffler, have a deleterious social impact. Diversity is all very well, and the opportunity to design your own Mustang car by permeating a number of stock body parts with a repertoire of custom-built accessory features is certainly welcome to the individual consumer, but what happens when the choices become too great? Overstimulation; information overload; decision stress; also known as future shock. The human body and psyche can only absorb so much change.

Yet Toffler is an optimist, and this optimism is displayed in *The Third Wave* where he re-evaluates his earlier predictions in *Future Shock* and places them in the context of a more global analysis of technological change. According to this revised account, future shock is periodic and occurs whenever societies experience major shifts in their means of production. So the First Wave was agricultural, and established land cultivation as the major source of the economy. This state of affairs was rapidly revised in the eighteenth century by the Second Wave of the Industrial Revolution which shifted the population to the city to work in the new centre of energy, the factory. The Third Wave of change is characterised by its movement away from mass production and consumption and towards diversification.

This sounds like classic Marxism. Toffler is different from Marx, however, in that his work is almost agnostic when it broaches the issue of whether or not society can cope with the technological traumas associated with the Third Wave: 'I don't believe anybody knows the future. . . . What I do is throw out large-scale hypotheses, new ideas, in hopes of stimulating fresh thinking', he confided to a journalist.

In other words, Toffler is a lateral thinker, and it would be a mistake to view his thinking literally. By throwing out provocations, he challenges our preconceived notions of what the future holds (whether it be homosexual parenting, cyborgs or ocean cities). Therefore 'future shock' is not just a transformation of the anthropological concept of 'culture shock'; it is a high-voltage jolt, meant to shake us into an awareness of our present predicament.

It is very difficult to assess Toffler's influence. The massive debate prompted by *Future Shock* immediately propelled Toffler on to the national lecture circuit, where he drew huge crowds from all walks of life to hear his diagnosis of contemporary society and prognostications for its future. He was made into a kind of guru, and during his travels had audiences with heads of states such as Creausescu in Rumania, Trudeau in Canada and Indira Gandhi in India. Prominent organisations, such as the American Telephone and Telegraph Company, rushed to hire him as a consultant. Popularity, though, is not the same as persuasiveness and prestige, as the paucity of critical writings on Toffler testifies. On reflection, though, it is difficult to imagine what form a 'school' of futurists would take, unless it was based solely on statistics or probability. Perhaps there is no future in futurism.

Main works

The Culture Consumers: A study of art and affluence in America, New York: St. Martin's, 1964.

Future Shock, New York: Random House, 1969.

The Futurists (ed.), New York: Random House, 1972.

The Third Wave, New York: Morrow, 1980.

Previews and Premises, New York: Morrow, 1983.

Powershifts: Knowledge, wealth, and violence at the edge of the twenty-first century, New York: Bantam, 1991.

Further reading

Grant, Linda, 'Gurus of the third wave', *Guardian Weekend*, 13 January 1996, pp. 19–21.

Harisalo, Risto, 'Powershift in democracy, public services and local government', *Local Government Studies* (Spring 1993), pp. 16–27.

Lundberg, Louis B., *Future without Shock*, New York: W. W. Norton, 1974.

Naughton, John, 'All change', *Times Literary Supplement*, 31 October 1980, p. 1243.

Stephenson, Hugh, 'Trends and speculations', *Times Literary Supplement*, 8 August 1975, p. 894.

'Of multi-mice and multi-men', *Times Literary Supplement*, 2 April 1971, p. 377.

Trotsky, Leon (1879–1940)

Lev Davidovitch Bronstein was born into a well-off peasant family and became a Marxist activist in his teens. Years of imprisonment, escape and exile followed. He took the name of 'Trotsky' from one of his jailers. At the age of twenty-six his oratory and debating skills brought him the leadership of the Petrograd soviet during the failed revolution of 1905. Joining the Bolsheviks in 1917 after years of criticising **Lenin**'s building of a centralised revolutionary party, he organised the October insurrection and later, against appalling odds, the Red Army's successful defence of the new republic. By 1923, he began to articulate fears about the 'bureaucratisation' of the workers' state first voiced by Lenin in his last years. This brought him into conflict with the increasingly powerful general secretary Stalin, who first expelled him from Russia in 1929 and then, after killing most of his family and close relations, had him murdered in Mexico, where he lived in exile. Variously gifted as a military tactician, historian, dialectician, political journalist and cultural critic, his main legacy as a Marxist theorist is the concept of 'permanent revolution', the possibility of a transition to socialism in a predominantly agrarian country with a small working class, and its economic corollary, 'combined and uneven development'. He produced the first sustained materialist critique of Stalinism and its consequences for revolutionary socialism, and produced both a Marxist analysis of the growth of fascism and the political tactics needed to defeat it, that has yet to be bettered, providing (as Engels suggested theory in general should do) 'a guide to action'.

Although Trotsky's contribution to the success of the revolution was incalculable, his most significant contributions to the theory of socialist revolution are his linked concepts of 'combined and uneven development' and 'permanent revolution', first developed in 1906. The Russian empire was in large part 'pre-capitalist'; a feudal society with the peasantry forming the immense majority of the population. Although there was massive social unrest, the most influential Marxist theorists of the time, such as Plekhanov, believed that this could lead to a bourgeois revolution. It was a commonplace of late nineteenth-century Marxism that no socialist revolution could take place in a country where the means of production had not been sufficiently developed and where a large and organised proletariat did not exist. While Russia lacked the social and political basis for socialism, it was the historic role of the bourgeoisie to destroy feudalism and replace it with capitalist democracy. Only after capitalism had developed to a sufficient level could socialism become a possibility. Political development therefore followed economic development. Large sections of the Russian Social Democratic party, which included both Lenin and Trotsky, Bolsheviks and Mensheviks and representatives of the radical peasants followed the 'stages' theory of revolution. It fell to Trotsky, after only a very few years of political study and activity, to challenge this position through the concept of 'permanent revolution'.

Lenin became one of the first to criticise the 'stages' theory. He pointed out that the Russian bourgeoisie could never fulfil the role assigned to them by Marxists. Numerically weak and wedded to the state, both culturally and politically, they had too much of a stake in the Tsarist state to overthrow it. If there was to be a challenge to the existing order, they would side with the Tsar. Lenin saw an alliance of the peasants and proletariat as one answer to the problem; the peasants had a vested interest in the destruction of an oppressive feudalism if a revolution restored the land to them. Until April of 1917, Lenin himself did not believe that there could be a successful *socialist* revolution in Russia. Trotsky took the argument in an international direction. While he agreed with Lenin that the peasants could never play an independent role, nevertheless, under the leadership of the urban proletariat, a successful socialist revolution was possible. A 'stage' could be skipped. Trotsky argued that Russia, like many other countries in the process of capitalist transformation, was not developing in an 'organic' fashion as the old capitalisms of Britain and Germany had done. The combination of feudalism alongside a rapidly developing capitalism made for a highly volatile social and political mixture. The key point for Trotsky was that this mixture made for a revolutionary situation, but the problems would be insuperable in a national framework. His unique answer was that the revolution would be successful if it could spread to one or more of the developed nations. Here in essence is the answer to why the Russian worker's state could not become a genuine workers' democracy. Although many countries came close to it after the first world war, there were no successful revolutions in Europe and the new state became politically isolated.

After the civil war years saw the decimation of industry and the Russian working class, Trotsky became deeply concerned about the way the party bureaucracy had accrued state power to itself. In exile, Trotsky wrote a vast amount on the growth of Stalinism and its repercussions for international socialism. His last published book was a sustained analysis of Stalinism, *The Revolution Betrayed* (1938). Because of the gains of the October revolution, notably state ownership of the means of production, he called the Soviet Union, a 'degenerated workers' state'. In the international arena, Trotsky felt Stalinism could only play a counter-revolutionary role in the fight for socialism. This was the case in Germany in the inter-war years. Nazism wasn't an expression of a particular national trait or metaphysical 'evil', but had material roots; Trotsky saw fascism as expressing the petty bourgeoisie's despair in a period of capitalist crisis and their fear of organised workers: 'masses of crazed petty bourgeoisie and the bands of the declassed and demoralised lumpenproletariat all of whom finance capital has brought to desperation'. Trotsky saw that fascism needed to smash all working-class organisation, and on that basis argued for a 'united front' of all working-class parties. Revolutionaries should keep their principles and argue their politics, but this did not prevent them from 'marching separately but striking together'. Stalin, on the other hand, initially had the German Communist Party argue that the SDP (the equivalent of the British Labour Party) were 'social fascists' as bad as the Nazis. In order to secure alliances with Britain and France, he then initiated a 'popular front' policy where communists subsumed their politics to the needs of the SDP and similar organisations. Both policies were disastrous. Initially, the SDP and communists far outnumbered the Nazis, but the policy of non-co-operation meant that the Nazis met little real resistance. Trotsky wrote with ever-increasing urgency as the 1930s drew on, but was so vilified and politically marginalised that his warnings went largely unheard. Soon after Hitler came to power, thousands of communists and SDP supporters were sent to concentration camps.

In 1938, Trotsky had predicted that neither Stalinism nor capitalism would survive for long after a major war. In the post-war period the Soviet Union occupied much of Eastern Europe, and the post-war boom enabled the western liberal democracies to deliver major reforms and increasing standards of living. Those Trotskyists who believed that Trotsky could not be wrong were left to explain how a counter-revolutionary force like Stalinism could have successfully overthrown capitalism in a number of countries. Although critical of the regimes in the eastern bloc, 'orthodox' Trotskyists eventually described them as 'deformed workers' states' on the basis of the nationalisation of private property, and saw them as 'transitional to socialism'. Many Marxists (some of whom felt that the proletariat of Western Europe had been 'bought off' by post-war prosperity) looked for inspiration to 'Third World' revolutions in China, Cuba, Africa and Nicaragua. While these revolutions had overthrown imperialism and were examples of combined and uneven development, claiming that they were forms of workers' states (albeit deformed ones), they ran quite contrary to the basic Marxist (and Trotskyist) principle that a socialist revolution would be one led by the self-activity of the working class. In these revolutions, the working class played a negligible role, the key elements being small bands of intellectuals leading large groups of peasants.

A problem of definition arises because Trotsky gave two different descriptions of a workers' state. The first is one in which the relations of production have been changed so that workers have real power through, for example, recallable representatives, workers' councils and militias; whereas the second, seen most clearly in his analysis of the Soviet Union, describes state ownership as the defining characteristic. It is the first that is closest to Marx and Engels. The consequence of following the second definition was that when the states 'transition to socialism' collapsed between 1989 and 1991, many 'orthodox' Trotskyists saw it as a step backwards.

Trotsky's voluminous and diverse writings have inspired some of the most influential theorists in social and political science. His work, despite some of the later mistakes (to some degree the index of his political marginalisation), remains a classic example of 'applied Marxism'; taking Marx's work as a basis and adapting it for the twentieth century. A strong current of present-day Trotskyists follow the consistent principles of the work rather than the letter, producing 'applied Trotskyism' for the post-war period. This leads the best of them to read the collapse of Stalinist-style regimes as the final death of an ideology that stood in the way of the building of a socialist revolutionary alternative to the market.

Main works

Permanent Revolution and Results and Prospects, trans. Brian Pearce, New York: Pathfinder, 1969.

Our Differences, New York: Vintage, 1970.

The Revolution Betrayed, New York: Pathfinder, 1970.

Writings 1934–1940, 6 vols, New York: Pathfinder, 1972–6.

1905, trans. Anya Bostock, Harmondsworth: Penguin, 1973.

In Defence of Marxism, New York: Pathfinder, 1973.

The Challenge of the Left Opposition, New York: Pathfinder, 1975.

History of the Russian Revolution, trans. Max Eastman, London: Pluto, 1977.

The Lessons of October, London: Bookmarks, 1987.

Fascism, Stalinism and the United Front, London: Bookmarks, 1989.

Further reading

Callinicos, Alex, *Trotskyism*, Milton Keynes: Open University Press, 1990.

Cliff, Tony, *Trotsky*, 4 vols, London: Bookmarks, 1989–93.

Deutscher, Isaac, *The Prophet Armed*, Oxford: Oxford University Press, 1954.

Deutscher, Isaac, *The Prophet Unarmed*, Oxford: Oxford University Press, 1959.

Deutscher, Isaac, *The Prophet Outcast*, Oxford: Oxford University Press, 1963.

Hallas, Duncan, *Trotsky's Marxism*, London: Bookmarks, 1984.

Glossary

Permanent revolution This theory argues that in a revolutionary situation, if a newly emerging bourgeoisie in a developing country aligned itself with the old feudal or imperialist order even a small working class would be forced to go beyond the bounds of a bourgeois revolution and create a new socialist society.

V

Veblen, Thorstein (1857–1929)

Thorstein Veblen was born in Wisconsin to Norwegian parents. His family were farmers. He was educated at Carleton College in Minnesota, Johns Hopkins University, Yale University (where he obtained a Ph.D. in philosophy) and Cornell University. Veblen is best known as the author of *The Theory of the Leisure Class*. Although he published other books, it is on this, his first book, that his reputation rests.

The aim of *The Theory of the Leisure Class* is critically to assess 'the place and value of the leisure class as an economic factor in modern life'. Veblen traces the emergence of the institution of the leisure class to the period of the gradual transition from 'primitive savagery to barbarism; or more precisely, during the transition from a peaceable to a consistently warlike habit of life'. The leisure class develops through its predatory acquisition and ownership of private property. Its origins, in other words, are to be found in the predatory activities of warlords, who seized the property of vanquished enemies. The more property they seized, the more power they accrued. Power, as the assertion of superior force, was honorific. To own property, therefore, was a mark of honour. Veblen describes how this developed into a struggle for pecuniary emulation. The more property one had, the more honour one accrued. However, to possess wealth is not in itself a sufficient means to gain and to hold the respect and the esteem of others. To win this, one had to display one's pecuniary strength. 'Conspicuous leisure', according to Veblen, was the principal means openly to display one's wealth and status. Productive work became a mark of weakness. It signified the absence of pecuniary strength. The leisure class's increasing exemption from productive work resulted in exemption itself becoming honorific. To engage in productive work became a sign of inferior status.

Using conspicuous leisure to mark social distinction worked very well in the compact communities of, say, rural Europe. Urbanisation changed this. In the company of urban strangers, conspicuous leisure was no longer a sufficient means to display one's pecuniary strength. The anonymity of urban life demanded a more obvious display of power and status. In the new urban culture, conspicuous leisure was replaced by 'conspicuous consumption', the wasteful use and display of valuable resources.

Veblen argues against the view that conspicuous consumption is little more than harmless and irrelevant display. Such display is the very pageant of power; from its prestige grows authority. He insists that 'the leisure-class scheme of life . . . extends its coercive influence' throughout society as a whole. 'The leisure class stands at the head of the social structure in point of reputability; and its manner of life and its standards of worth therefore afford the norm of reputability for the community'. The example of the leisure class acts to direct social energies away from productive work and into wasteful consumption. Veblen cites the case of those he refers to as 'the scholarly classes'. Although the social equals of the non-scholarly classes, their presumed abilities and attainments, together with their public commitment to leisure class canons of decency, give them a higher status than their pecuniary strength should warrant. As a result, according to Veblen, the scholarly classes

> are unavoidably thrown into contact with classes that are pecuniarily their superiors. The high standard of pecuniary decency in force among these superior classes is transfused among the scholarly classes with but little mitigation of its rigour; and as a consequence there is no class of the community that spends a larger proportion of its substance in conspicuous waste than these.

Veblen also draws our attention to the way in which the canons of conspicuous consumption exercise a distorting influence over the ideal of feminine beauty. The delicate and the diminutive are promoted to display to the world that the women of the leisure class are incapable of productive work. In this way, women are reduced to symbols of 'vicarious consumption'. A woman is little more than a servant, whose task is to put on public display her master's economic power. As Veblen puts it, 'She is useless and expensive, and she is consequently valuable as evidence of pecuniary strength.' Women learn to conform to this standard and men learn to read their conformity as the very epitome of beauty.

Men are not exempt from the dictates of the leisure class canons of good taste. Male apparel must demonstrate the ability to consume without economic restraint. It must also indicate that the wearer is not engaged in productive work.

> Elegant dress serves its purpose of elegance not only in that it is expensive, but also because it is the insignia of leisure. It not only shows that the wearer is able to consume a relatively large value, but it argues at the same time that he consumes without producing.

The very fact that the leisure class denounces useful work as unworthy of human dignity makes them a bulwark against what Veblen regards as the natural evolutionary flow of history. In other words, in an industrial society a leisure class is at best a historical anachronism and at worse a parasitical burden. Such a society depends on productive labour, the very activity the leisure class has learned to despise.

Veblen's analysis is driven by a Darwinian model of cultural evolution. He refers to historical development as

> a process of natural selection of institutions . . . a natural selection of the fittest habits of thought and . . . a process of enforced adaptation of individuals to an environment which has progressively changed with the growth of the community and with the changing institutions under which men [sic] have lived.

The problem with the institution of the leisure class is that it is out of step with the new environment. Its whole lifestyle runs counter to the needs and aspirations of the new industrial culture. As Veblen explains:

> The evolution of society is substantially a process of mental adaptation on the part of individuals under the stress of circumstances which will no longer tolerate habits of thought formed under and conforming to a different set of circumstances in the past.

According to Veblen, the primary circumstances are always economic forces. The privileged position of the leisure class tends to protect it from the full force of economic exigencies. Moreover, given its leading role in terms of taste formation, it is able 'to exert a retarding influence upon social development far in excess of that which the simple numerical strength of the class would assign it'. However, according to Veblen, 'The collective interests of any modern community centre in industrial efficiency. The individual is serviceable for the ends of the community somewhat in proportion to his [sic] efficiency in the productive employments.' Clearly, in such a scheme of things, the leisure class is a burden. 'The leisure class lives by the industrial community rather than in it.' In short, the existence of the leisure class is incompatible with the future development of an industrial community.

———

It is with specific reference to *The Theory of the Leisure Class* that the American sociologist C. **Wright Mills** describes Veblen as 'the best critic of America that America has produced'. Others have been less affirmative in their estimate. Theodor Adorno, for example, is critical of Veblen's dependence on a discredited Darwinian model of human historical development. In the final instance, Veblen's objection to the leisure class is that it is able to escape the economic pressures which force all other classes to accept the constraints of the new industrial conditions. As **Adorno** complains, 'Veblen's outbursts against the "sheltered", whose privileged position allows them to a certain extent to avoid adjusting to a changed situation, amounts to a glorification of the Darwinian struggle for existence.'

Veblen's thesis regarding the role and the significance of conspicuous consumption, the use of goods to mark and maintain difference and distinction, rather than to satisfy 'genuine' human needs, has remained influential in the sociology of culture and in cultural studies. This aspect of this work has been greatly elaborated by the French sociologist Pierre **Bourdieu**.

Main works

The Theory of the Leisure Class (1899), Harmondsworth: Penguin 1994.

The Theory of Business Enterprise, New York: Scribner's, 1904.

The Instinct of Workmanship, New York: Macmillan, 1914.

The Place of Science in Modern Civilisation, New York: Heubsch, 1919.

The Vested Interests and the State of the Industrial Arts, New York: Heubsch, 1919.

Absentee Ownership and Business Enterprise in Recent Times, New York: Viking, 1933.

Further reading

Adorno, Theodor, *Prisms*, London: Neville Spearman, 1967.

Dorfman, Joseph, *Thorstein Veblen and his America*, New York: Viking, 1935.

Dowd, Douglas F. *Thorstein Veblen*, New York: Washington Square Press, 1966.

Dowd, Douglas F. (ed.), *Thorstein Veblen: A critical reappraisal*, Ithaca, NY: Cornell University Press, 1958.

Hobson, J. A., *Veblen*, London: Chapman and Hall, 1936.

Lerner, Max. (ed.), *The Portable Veblen*, New York: Viking, 1948.

Glossary

Leisure class   A term coined by Veblen to denote a dominant class which displays its dominance by 'conspicuous consumption' of goods rather than through ownership of the means of production.

W

Wallerstein, Immanuel (1930–)

Immanuel Wallerstein began his prolific writing career as an Africanist analysing colonial and post-colonial development. His early work was influenced by dependency theory and the historical *Annales* school led by Fernand **Braudel**. His first volume on world-system theory (*The Modern World System*, 1974) was principally written during a year at Princeton's Center for Advanced Study in the Behavioral Sciences. Wallerstein founded the Fernand Braudel Center For the Study of Economics, Historical Systems, and Civilization at Binghamton University of the State University of New York. He was founding editor of the Braudel Center's journal, *Review* which has been the central forum for debate in world-system theory. Wallerstein's intellectual debt to Braudel has been considerable and expressed in Wallerstein's annual period of residence at the Maison des Sciences de l'Homme in Paris. Wallerstein's career project has been a multivolume history of the capitalist world-system.

In collaboration with Terence Hopkins, Wallerstein developed the general approach in sociology which led to the emergence of his world-system theory. Wallerstein's version of world-system theory is directly founded upon dependency theory and its critique of modernisation theory. Like dependency theory, world-system theory is premised on a rejection of country-by-country analysis. Wallerstein restated the structuralist position that the 'world economy' should be analysed as one single system, and not as a mere collection of many national economic systems.

A world economy is defined historically as only one type of social system which, though connected via market exchange, lacks a single overarching political authority. In contrast, there have been 'world-empires' based on a single political structure within a closed economic space, and 'mini-systems' which are small localised cultures and economies.

The current world-system is defined as 'historical capitalism' having its origin in the 'long sixteenth century'. The capitalist world-system expanded from its origin in Europe to encompass the entire world by the end of the nineteenth century. Wallerstein asserts, clearly following **Marx**, that the primary aim of capitalist production is the 'ceaseless accumulation of capital' which is unique to the capitalist mode of production. Capitalism regulates production and economic exchange on a global scale. The 'capitalist world-system' is therefore a 'social entity' with a single international division of labour, whereby world market forces determine the range of possibilities for development for all sectors or areas of the world economy.

Wallerstein's transposition of the analysis of capital from the framework of a national economy to the world market follows work on imperialism by Hilferding, Luxemburg, Kautsky and especially Bukharin's *Imperialism and World Economy*. His formulation of capitalism is situated in neo-Marxism, based upon a reading of Marx emphasising the creation of a world-embracing commerce and market, and production of commodities for sale in this world market.

Nevertheless, Wallerstein regards class relations as the key element to which other social and political divisions, such as racial, ethnic and national, are subordinate. Notwithstanding this, his emphasis on commodity exchange and on the world market led critics such as Robert Brenner to criticise world-system theory as being 'circulationist' and as detracting from the centrality of class analysis. Wallerstein's 'circulationism' has much in common with the position taken by Paul Sweezy and A. G. Frank, while his structuralist perspective on 'center-periphery' relations is similar to that of Paul Baran or Samir Amin. World-systems theory re-states the hypothesis that surplus is transferred between regions of the world-economy, especially from the periphery to the core. This deeply embedded core-periphery structure enabled the 'strong' core states to impose 'unequal exchange' (A. Emmanuel) on the 'weak' periphery.

Wallerstein, however, adds the category of the 'semi-periphery' which stands mid-way in the system hierarchy. This category allows for upward and downward mobility within the world-system, partly depending on the level of autonomy of a state. Unlike dependency theory, world-system theory accepts the possibility of ascent and descent, albeit it regards this as fairly rare and very difficult to achieve. Therefore, the basic three-tier structure of the world-system is quite stable over time.

Within this stability there are periods of rivalry among the powers over the systemic position Wallerstein calls 'hegemony'. A series of powers have held the position of hegemony: the Dutch United Provinces in the seventeenth, the United Kingdom in the eighteenth and nineteenth and the United States in the twentieth century. The hegemonic cycle proceeds through a series of superior economic positions attained sequentially in agriculture and production, trade and commerce, and finally finance. The loss of hegemony proceeds via the same sequence, but in reverse order. This cycle is played out against a background of 'long waves of expansion and contraction in the world economy. Wallerstein adopted Kondratieff's work on price cycles to constitute one of the fundamental aspects of world-system theory.

Wallerstein maintains that modern states are an institutional product of the capitalist mode of production. The capitalist world economy is accompanied by (indeed directly gave birth to) an interstate system composed of theoretically sovereign states, but which in Wallerstein's view are only partially sovereign. The political power structure is hierarchical, based upon unequal amounts of power.

This view of unequal power partly resembles the conventional realist position in international relations theory. However, the difference is that Wallerstein explains this inequality of power strictly on the basis of position in the world market. For instance, 'strong' core states produce 'high-profit' products and exchange them for 'low-profit' products produced by the 'weak' peripheral states. The resulting flow of surplus from periphery to core reinforces the power of the core states in the world-system as a whole.

Wallerstein periodises the history of political and economic development of the capitalist world-system. In its early stage it was 'mercantilist', as European absolutism developed alongside aggressive commercial and industrial policies. Overall, during the first three centuries of the world-system, the basis was laid for what he calls the overarching cultural structure of the system, or its 'geo-culture'. This specific geo-culture came into existence fully only in the wake of the French Revolution.

The main two ideas of this geo-culture are: (1) acceptance of perpetual political change, and; (2) the idea that sovereignty resides in 'the people'. These ideas generated a fundamental contradiction in the world-system, i.e. that between the idea of democracy and the inherent structural inequality of capitalism. Wallerstein contrasts the predominant liberal ideology of the capitalist world-system with the recurrent appearance of 'anti-systemic movements' including revolutionary movements which seek to transform the system.

Wallerstein believes the capitalist world-system is now at a critical historical juncture because the reformist means of containing popular discontent are eroding, along with the legitimacy of separate national states. Beneath this apparent problem, he asserts two fundamental processes: (1) the exhaustion of the cheap labour pool through deruralisation of the world (this idea was prefigured in Luxemburg's work); (2) the reaching of the limits of 'externalization of costs', that is, the practice whereby private capital deflects certain costs of production such as infrastructure, education and environmental costs, onto the state and society at large. This conception of a contradiction between capital accumulation and social welfare and state legitimacy is quite similar to ideas developed by Jürgen Habermas amongst others.

Wallerstein has long maintained the historicity of the capitalist world-system and the inevitability of its demise and replacement by another social system. While he prefers a transition to socialism, he recognises the possibility that the future world-system could be another kind of inegalitarian system, though different from capitalism. The outcome of this transition will be determined in social, cultural and political battles over the next twenty-five to fifty years.

Although Wallerstein's theory has been widely criticised, or even dismissed, by Marxist and non-Marxist social scientists alike, his impact on the fields of development studies, economic history, sociology and international political economy has been substantial. World-system theory is now widely incorporated into teaching as a major theory of world development. Wallerstein's approach gave rise to the formation of the Political Economy of the World-System Section in the American Sociological Association which publishes an annual volume of world-system analysis. The Braudel Center and *Review* have played a key role in developing a distinctive identity for world-system analysis in the social science. In recent years, Wallerstein's work has provoked new debates in the relationship between civilisation and world systems, world economic history, global culture and nationalism.

Main works

The Modern World System: Capitalist agriculture and the origins of the European world-economy in the sixteenth century, New York: Academic Press, 1974.

The Capitalist World Economy, Cambridge: Cambridge University Press, 1979.

The Modern World System II: Mercantilism and the consolidation of the European world-economy, 1600–1750, New York: Academic Press, 1980.

'Crisis as transition', in A. Amin, G. Arrighi, A. G. Frank and I. Wallerstein, *Dynamics of Global Crisis*, New York: Monthly Review Press, 1982.

Historical Capitalism, London: Verso, 1983.

The Politics of the World-Economy: The states, the movements, and the civilizations, Cambridge: Cambridge University Press, 1984.

The Modern World System III: The second era of great expansion of the capitalist world-economy, 1730–1840s, San Diego: Academic Press, 1988.

Geopolitics and Geoculture: Essays on the changing world-system, Cambridge: Cambridge University Press, 1991.

Further reading

Brewer, A., *Marxist Theories of Imperialism: A critical survey*, London: Macmillan, 1990.

Frank, A. G. and B. Gills (eds), *The World System: 500 years or 5000?*, London: Routledge, 1993.

Hout, W., *Capitalism and the Third World: Development, dependence and the world system*, Hants: Edward Elgar, 1993.

Sanderson, S., *Civilizations and World Systems*, London: Sage, 1955.

Shannon, T., *An Introduction to the World-System Perspective*, Oxford: Westview Press, 1989.

Walzer, Michael (1935–)

Michael Walzer is Professor of Social Science at the Institute of Advanced Studies in Princeton, New Jersey. A prominent American Jewish intellectual, he combines in his work, interests in historical and moral theoretical modes of investigation. An undergraduate at Brandeis University, he spent a year as a Fulbright Fellow in Cambridge before undertaking his doctoral studies at Harvard University from 1957–61. He later taught at Princeton University and then, for twelve years, as Professor of Government at Harvard before moving to the Institute of Advanced Studies in 1980. He was politically active in the protest movement against American intervention in the Vietnam War. Due to his involvement, for over thirty years, as a member of the editorial board of the progressive magazine *Dissent*, and, since 1976, as a contributing editor of the *New Republic*, he has been identified with the political left in the United States. While he has written on a wide range of topics (from the relation between religious and revolutionary discourses to the ideas of just war and nationalism), his most influential contributions are to current debates about distributive justice and social criticism.

In *Thick and Thin*, Walzer is explicit in distinguishing between two different kinds of moral argument. Thin arguments invoke a 'minimalist' morality which happens to be shared widely across many, if not all, cultures. This universal moral minimalism amounts to a mutual recognition of similar principles or rules that are reiterated in different ways in a variety of political communities. It is a recognition that the same kind of things are unjust in different contexts; political tyranny, oppression of the poor, the disregard of the basic human rights not to be deprived of life or liberty. Thick arguments, in contrast, appeal to our moral experience in a 'maximalist' sense that depends on the history and culture, the customary practices and the memories of the members of our particular community.

While thin arguments are resonant in creating bonds of moral support for those fighting injustice in other cultures, the more common political practices of social criticism and communal reflection on shared ideals necessarily take place, according to Walzer, in the terms of one specific thick morality. This relation between thin and thick aspects of moral experience has been a constant theme in Walzer's work. He has argued against the view that thin morality is the foundation of a maximalist morality that is thickened up in a particular context. He insists that morality is, on the contrary, thick from the beginning and it is constituted by the shared understandings of the members of a particular community.

Walzer's social and political theory is enriched by the range and variety of historical illustration he uses in weaving arguments for a context-sensitive understanding of moral criticism. This is in no small part due to his training as a historian of ideas. His first book, *The Revolution of the Saints*, was based on his doctoral dissertation. It is an exploration of the political impact of Calvinist ideas in the years prior to the English Revolution. While he continued to work on historical themes in the early years of his career, he also began to write on issues in democratic theory which had been subjects of controversy in the United States during the turbulent years of social protest in the 1 960s. These essays, written over a twenty-year period are available in two collections: *Obligations* and *Radical Principles*.

Walzer's first systematic work of political theory, *Just and Unjust Wars*, appeared originally in 1977. It examined the questions of practical morality that are raised in relation to the realities of war. It is in the moral language we use about war that thin argument takes on a central role. While consideration of thin morality could justify military intervention in certain very specific circumstances, Walzer argues that, in general, states should respect the shared traditions and practices of other historical communities, even if those practices are very different from their own.

Spheres of Justice is Walzer's most important book and it represents the most carefully worked out contextualist theory of distributive justice. It defends an account of justice which is pluralist in two important senses. First, it insists on the cultural particularity, and moral thickness, of criteria of just distribution of social goods. Walzer objects to the philosophical abstraction that is typical of universalist theories of justice, especially the procedural liberalism of theorists such as **Rawls** and Ackerman. Not only are these philosophical approaches insensitive to the cultural creativity of particular historical communities, but they also fail to recognise the fact that their own, supposedly thin, procedures are themselves reflections of some specific thick morality. Substantive principles of justice reflect the shared understandings of the members of particular communities. They differ from one historical context to another and, in this sense, they are always local. We must, Walzer suggests, defend the plurality of cultural creations.

The second sense of pluralism in this account of justice relates more explicitly to substantive principles of distribution. Walzer defends a position of 'complex equality'. This recognises the fact that different social goods have their own distributive logic and this in turn reflects the shared social meanings of the goods themselves. There is, therefore, a plurality of distributive criteria reflecting the fact that each social good occupies its own sphere of justice. The basic principle is that no one should be favoured in the distribution of one social good on account of a dominant distribution of goods in another sphere. In other words, since health care is a recognised social need, it must be distributed only according to the criterion of need. Nobody should receive better health care simply because they have more money, or greater political influence, or a higher education, than another citizen. The approach is politically egalitarian since it draws out social meanings that are genuinely shared. In *Spheres of Justice* Walzer works through a variety of spheres and gives an interpretive account of what justice requires in each of them within his own (American) cultural context. He ends up with the fascinating argument that the shared understandings of his fellow citizens regarding justice are best interpreted as requiring a decentralized democratic socialist society.

In the last decade, Walzer's main concern has been to develop and to defend the interpretive approach to social criticism that is adopted in *Spheres of Justice*. Critics have argued that the defence of complex equality cannot be successful if it is thought of as an interpretation of the shared understandings of American citizens. The democratic socialist account of justice that is presented is simply not compatible, so it is claimed, with the conservatism of an interpretive approach which merely reflects the dominant ideas of a particular culture. Walzer has countered that effective social criticism can only be thought of as an interpretive activity which involves the articulation of some aspects of the thick morality that is constituted by the shared understandings of a particular community. It is not a process of moral discovery or invention but an interpretation of the deepest and most coherent account of the shared ideals that are a necessary constitutive feature of any political community. The true critic invites fellow citizens to think through their ideals and challenges them to aspire to live out of their own deepest moral convictions. Interpretive criticism need not affirm the *status quo* in a conservative manner, nor must it reflect the dominant ideas of a culture. It can, on the contrary, offer a forceful challenge to current practices by revealing the ways in which dominant ideas and social arrangements fail to live up to the moral standards that are deeply embedded in the common life of a people.

Walzer's work, and his fluent style of writing, appeals to students of many disciplines. Not only social and political theorists, but some philosophers, historians of ideas and theologians have been influenced by his ideas. The value of his reflections on citizenship and democracy, on nationalism, pluralism and ethnicity, on the relation between political revolution and religious thought, have long been recognised. *Just and Unjust Wars* remains one of the standard works in the ethics of war, and the defence of complex equality in *Spheres of Justice* has received much attention as one of the most brilliant accounts of the theory of distributive justice. Since the publication of the latter, Walzer has emerged as one of the most important of the so-called communitarian critics of contemporary liberal theory. His political egalitarianism allied to his interpretive approach to criticism have made for an original and thought-provoking combination. The emphasis he places on the shared moral ideals that are constitutive of communities has given him an authoritative voice in contemporary debates between universalists and contextualists.

Main works

The Revolution of the Saints: A study in the origins of radical politics, Cambridge, MA: Harvard University Press, 1965.

Obligations: Essays on obedience, war and citizenship, Cambridge, MA: Harvard University Press, 1970.

Regicide and Revolution (ed.), Cambridge: Cambridge University Press, 1974.

Radical Principles: Reflections of an unreconstructed democrat, New York: Basic Books, 1980.

'Philosophy and democracy', *Political Theory*, 9 (1981), pp. 379–99.

'Pluralism in Political Perspective', in Michael Walzer *et al.*, *The Politics of Ethnicity*, Cambridge, MA: Belknap, 1982.

Spheres of Justice: A defence of pluralism and equality, Oxford: Basil Blackwell, 1983.

'Liberalism and the art of separation', *Political Theory*, 12 (1984), pp. 315–30.

Exodus and Revolution, New York: Basic Books, 1985.

Interpretation and Social Criticism, Cambridge, MA: Harvard University Press, 1987.

The Company of Critics: Social criticism and political criticism in the twentieth century, London: Peter Halban, 1989.

'The communitarian critique of liberalism', *Political Theory*, 18 (1990), pp. 6–23.

'Nation and universe', in Grethe B. Peterson (ed.), *The Tanner Lectures on Human Values, XI*, Salt Lake City: University of Utah Press, 1990.

Just and Unjust Wars: A moral argument with historical illustrations, rev. edn, New York: Basic Books, 1992.

What it Means to Be an American, New York: Marsilio, 1992.

Thick and Thin: Moral argument at home and abroad, Notre Dame and London: University of Notre Dame Press, 1994.

Further reading

Bader, Viet, 'Citizenship and exclusion: radical democracy, community and justice. Or, what is wrong with communitarianism', *Political Theory,* 23 (1995), pp. 211–46.

Dworkin, Ronald, *A Matter of Principle,* Cambridge, MA: Harvard University Press, 1985.

Galston, William, 'Community, democracy, philosophy: the political thought of Michael Walzer', *Political Theory,* 17 (1989), pp. 119–30.

Miller, David and Michael Walzer (eds), *Pluralism, Justice and Equality,* Oxford: Oxford University Press, 1995.

Thigpen, Robert B. and Lyle Downing, 'Beyond shared understandings', *Political Theory,* 14 (1986), pp. 451–72.

Warnke, Georgia, 'Social interpretation and political theory', in Michael Kelly (ed.), *Hermeneutics and Critical Theory in Ethics and Politics,* Cambridge, MA: MIT Press, 1990.

Weber, Max (1864–1920)

Max Weber, a German academic, is regarded, along with **Marx** and **Durkheim**, as one of the three great classical writers who laid the foundations of sociology. Though his first lectureship was in law he combined outstanding scholarship in history, economics, jurisprudence, sociology and philosophy to develop his theories of the nature of capitalism and economic change. His main intellectual influences were German, and, as such, his writing was informed by the work of Karl Marx, though always developed along independent lines of enquiry. It is often believed that he wrote in opposition to Marxist thought, but he was sympathetic to many of its propositions and diverged mainly in his rejection of pure economic determinism. Weber can be best described as a bourgeois liberal. He was a fervent supporter of the nation-state and believed that, rather than revolution, political power invested in government was the best way of advancing the economic position of the working class.

Weber made four major contributions to sociological knowledge, his analysis of power, his theory of the origins of capitalism, his treatise on class and status and his advice on methodological development in the social sciences. However, the important, underlying theme in the first three of these areas is the forces that mould society and bring about social change. He believed that the predominant force since the late Middle Ages in Europe was rationalisation: the replacement of sacred, magical explanation by secular, logical explanation and the shift from traditional, patriarchal structure to legal-rational organisation. Rationalism is the philosophy that assumes all action has a knowable and understandable cause; that there is a logical reason for everything. Weber believed that modernity – the era that began in the late eighteenth century – was essentially characterised and determined by rationalisation. He saw rationalisation as an irreversible process, that gradually replaced the superstitious practices of traditional society with the rational structure and utilitarian principles of modern society.

The importance of rationalisation in Weber's analysis of society can be made clearer by studying his analysis of power. In *The Theory of Social and Economic Organization*, Weber argued that power exists in three forms: power, authority and legitimacy. Power is the capacity of the actor to achieve his or her will in the face of resistance from others. It assumes the existence of conflict. Authority and legitimacy are forms of social control that go a long way to prevent conflict from arising. Power is probably only exercised on a temporary basis until the actor's will is imposed. Authority can be far longer lasting. It may be maintained by coercion, but this is a weak form of authority because sanctions breed resistance. A key factor in the success of authority is legitimacy. People may come to accept authority without question if they believe it is legitimate. Legitimacy removes the need for surveillance and leads to a more stable social order than authority based on sanctions.

Weber described three forms of legitimate power: traditional, charismatic and legal–rational. The first is based on habit and the assumption that authority has always existed in that form and cannot exist in any other form. It is typical of primitive societies and medieval Europe, and still exists in many ways in a smaller form. For instance, women still perform the bulk of household chores despite emancipation in other areas of work.

Charismatic power rests on the extraordinary character of the leader. It contains elements of the sacred or supernatural – Christ and the growth of Christianity are perhaps the most obvious examples of charismatic power.

Although Weber construed charisma as an individual possession, it can extend beyond the person to the symbols and myths of the faith. Thus, Christ's disciples and the symbol of the cross became invested with charismatic power. It is a revolutionary power and an important concept, because Weber saw it as the driving force for change. Charisma withers when it becomes convention. Once established, it gives way to either traditional or legal–rational authority.

Legal–rational authority is based on the application of reason. There is an explicit, logical reason for each and every action, which most people accept as fair and necessary. Weber believed that the apotheosis of legal–rational authority in society could be found in bureaucracy, the dominant mode of organisation in modern capitalism. A bureaucracy is a formal, hierarchical organisation, dedicated to particular goals. Each member of staff has a fixed and limited area of authority and is accountable to his or her manager. Communications are usually recorded and filed. Access to jobs and advancement is by expertise and qualifications, and all actions are based on objective assessment – there is no room for emotion or sentiment in decisions.

Weber felt rationalisation brought mixed benefits. He noted in his early research how bonded labourers in nineteenth-century Germany sought to become wage labourers for the independence it offered, despite a net loss in terms of material comforts and security. Traditional society was oppressive, but it offered the comforts of communal life and spiritual solace, whereas modern society was increasingly materialistic, overorganised and alienating. Weber felt that where rational authority was used to oppose traditional authority, progress was possible and positive, but if rational authority *replaced* traditional authority it would eventually stifle freedom and further change. Bureaucracy was the most efficient means of co-ordinating the complexity of action under capitalism, but it controlled and alienated people. Employees were at risk of becoming cogs in a machine more important than they themselves. As rationalisation achieved greater and greater control over social and economic life, reason would become redundant and with it the debate necessary for democracy.

The second of Weber's main contributions to sociology was his analysis of the ideological factors that encouraged modern, rational capitalism. In *The Protestant Ethic and the Spirit of Capitalism*, he argued that Protestant religions inculcated the values and beliefs that nurtured the development of capitalism. This is not a claim for ideological determinism; Weber recognised that capitalism also required money, technology and political centralisation. *The Protestant Ethic* is a comparative study of capitalism in countries with different religious influences. Countries where Calvinism was strongest appeared to be those where capitalism thrived in its most rationalist form. Weber believed this was because Calvinism encouraged hard work and discipline and frowned upon the pursuit of personal enjoyment. The Calvinist notion that they were among the 'elect', the small number of people chosen to receive eternal grace, meant that they based their lives on ascetic religious principles. To do otherwise would be to show doubt and loss of faith and, therefore, no evidence of salvation. In addition the Lutheran notion that vocation could apply not just to religious calling but to secular pursuits meant that worldly success could be another sign of salvation. To make money was to serve one's Christian vocation, but to spend money was to be guilty of self-indulgence. Consequently entrepreneurs saved money and accumulated capital.

The distinction between ideological determinism and Weber's view of the influence of religious ideology on economic change is an important one. Weber argued for 'elective affinity' between ideas and socio-economic groups. That is that ideological beliefs and group interests meet and embrace one another. Group aims may be furthered by being imbued with a moral purpose, and ideological doctrine may be developed by the ideas and interests of converts. Weber suggested, for instance, that Calvinism might be more prominent amongst entrepreneurs, and Pietism, which praised frugality and humility, more prominent amongst lower paid workers. In this way Weber opposed the economic determinism of the Marxists. For him ideological power was as important as economic power and not a reflection of it.

In *Economy and Society*, Weber extended his interest in power and economic change to a study of social class. Marx attributed a fundamental role to class and class consciousness in economic change. Weber was critical of the notion that members of a class would share common aims and sensibilities and unite as a political group. He felt class boundaries were hard to define because there were three dimensions of stratification – class, status and power – which created groupings rather than clear strata. Class, the most important of the dimensions, is based on ownership of property and opportunities for income. It is an economic form of stratification that groups people according to their position in the labour market. Status refers to 'estate' or the social group into which one is born. It confers social esteem. Power refers to the likelihood that some groups have more political power than others. The three forms of stratification all contribute to the life chances of individuals.

In contrast to Marx, who thought a person's social class was determined by his or her relationship to the means of production, Weber thought a person's relationship to the means of distribution of wealth was more important. Consequently members of a given class might share life chances, but not the joint action in production which might encourage class consciousness and political action.

Methodology was Weber's fourth main area of contribution to social science. He argued that since the social sciences were concerned with 'spiritual' or ideological phenomena, it was necessary to try to understand why individuals chose particular courses of action. This attempt to 'get inside the heads' of individuals past and present should not rest entirely on empathy – in fact Weber was very critical of the use of intuition – but should enable researchers to construct hypotheses which they could then test using empirical observations and logical analysis. In this sense Weber was both an idealist and a positivist. His comparative analysis in *The*

Protestant Ethic was a good example of how a hypothesis about the relationship between ideology and social action could be tested by contrasting the consequences of the presence and absence of Protestantism.

Despite Weber's faith in empirical research he did not think it was possible to get a completely accurate picture of social reality. He thought observations and the choice of subject to observe were always coloured by the researcher's point of view and cultural values. It was a problem that Weber grappled with unsuccessfully. He argued for 'value-free' social science, but his only practical advice was that researchers should make a firm separation between their academic work and their political activity. Objectivity is not much increased by the absence of factional interests if unconscious biases remain.

Weber's contribution was fundamental to the development of social and political theory. His typologies of class and power formed the conceptual building blocks of sociology and his theories of economic change, most notably of the role of ideology in driving change, are still important. The contemporary debate on the nature of society – whether we are in the era of modernity or post-modernity – has led to Weber being widely acknowledged as the greatest writer on modernity. Legal–rational authority and bureaucratic organisation are the hallmarks of modernity. In many ways, Weber's fears about the growth of rationalisation appear to have been justified. Bureaucracy within organisations may be decreasing, but industrial corporations have grown in size and power and exert a more global dominance over human behaviour. The extent to which rationalisation has stifled freedom of thought and cultural innovation is debatable. Some contemporary writers have argued that western society has entered a post-modern era which is critical of reason and characterised by a growing diversity in culture and the nature of capitalism. This would not surprise Weber. Throughout his work he championed the power of human values and beliefs to influence economic change.

Main works

Gerth, H. H. and C. Wright Mills, *From Max Weber: Essays in sociology*, London: Routledge and Kegan Paul, 1948.

The Methodology of the Social Sciences, New York: Free Press, 1949.

General Economic History, New York: Collier, 1961.

Economy and Society, Berkeley: University of California Press. 1978.

The Protestant Ethic and the Spirit of Capitalism, London: Allen and Unwin, 1978.

The Theory of Social and Economic Organization, New York: Oxford University Press, 1947.

Further reading

Giddens, A., *Capitalism and Modern Social Theory,* Cambridge: Cambridge University Press, 1971.

Lash, S. and S. Whimster (eds), *Max Weber, Rationality and Modernity,* London: Allen and Unwin, 1987.

Parkin, F., *Max Weber,* Chichester: Ellis Horwood, 1982.

Schroeder, R., *Max Weber and the Sociology of Culture,* London: Sage, 1992.

Winch, Peter (1926–)

Peter Winch taught at University College, Swansea, and Birkbeck College, London, before becoming Professor of Philosophy at King's College London; latterly at the University of Illinois, Urbana–Champaign. As interpreter of **Wittgenstein** for a wider audience of social theorists and philosophers, he has been active in moral as well as purely epistemological matters.

Winch's *The Idea of a Social Science* (1958) was among the earliest statements of interpretative social theory in post-war Britain, and formed one of the key critiques which led to the demise of Durkheimian or American functionalism. Winch introduced into social theory the fundamentals of the philosophy of Wittgenstein through attacking a number of perspectives claiming to establish a social science. The book is perhaps now difficult to read in the light of later more detailed elaborations on this theme. Over-simplistic conceptions of personal motivation, such as those of Mill and **Pareto**, are strictly castigated as reductionist attempts to produce laws of the human mind. By contrast, Winch attempts to provide an alternative perspective deriving from a radically different epistemology defining action as both conscious in character and governed by socially available rules for creating intelligible meanings for others. This is the central paradox of Wittgensteinian social theory – that people know what they are doing, and yet depend on choices from a recipe of rules available in, and specific to, their culture. Any version of motivation which assumes simple mental dispositions consequently misses the complexity of the meaningful rules on offer to actors. Action always involves choices which could have been different. Conscious rule-following necessarily involves people's ability to correct themselves when they do things wrongly, and therefore implies the corollary that they might make a deliberate mistake. Social 'scientific' models that assume a set of determining structural 'facts' which unconsciously determine people's actions are therefore misconceived and inappropriate as a sociological perspective, for they replace conscious decisions with causes defined in terms that people themselves would not recognise.

Winch is not trying to define 'society' purely in terms of individual action, and explicitly rejects Karl **Popper**'s notion that everything is the outcome of individuals' decisions (social structures being merely the sociologist's model of the statistical consequences). There are social relations which appear as social institutions, but they consist of rule-bound modes of thinking which provide society's members with forms of action. Social relations are thus defined as radically different from the relations between natural objects familiar to laboratory scientists, for they are dependent on people choosing to follow the rules involved and putting into practice the ideas they contain. Our social relations, he says in a famous formula, are permeated with ideas about reality: 'indeed, "permeated" is hardly a strong enough word: social relations are expressions of ideas about reality'. War is an institution whose character stems from accepting rules (and breaking them): but the same could be said of the social identity of a monk or a police officer. Failure to understand social action therefore derives from conceptual difficulties about rules and ideas: 'sociologists who misinterpret an alien culture are like philosophers getting into difficulties over the use of their own concepts' (*The Idea of a Social Science*).

In a famous paper 'Understanding a primitive society' (1964/1977) Winch pursued the implications of this approach for the understanding of other cultures. He chose as the key case study the central African people, the Azande, and their witchcraft, based on the superb fieldwork of Sir Edward Evans-Pritchard in the 1920s. He criticised those who wish to discount or explain away apparently irrational cultures. Following Wittgenstein, he rejected the argument that beliefs, such as the Azande's explanation of unexpected (and undeserved) misfortunes as the product of witchcraft, are irrational in denying some external objective reality. Nor are they guilty of logical contradictions, for example in holding that witchcraft is hereditary, even though they confine their accusations to one person rather than whole families or clans sharing common descent. This criticism misses *the point* of the belief and its associated actions. The Azande have perfectly intelligible and, by western standards, acceptably practical explanations for many events, including accidents and natural disasters. It is when these everyday forms of reasoning can provide no explanation that they turn to ideas of human but mystical malice in the form of witchcraft, a force to be investigated by divination and defeated by magic. Winch points out that these forms of detection (divination using poisons on chickens and other methods) are not meant to be refuted. As

Wittgenstein had said, we cannot talk of error or stupidity as long as magic is not presented as a form of proto-science, that is, an opinion open to challenge and disproof. Winch agrees: such beliefs are not scientific hypotheses, and the rituals associated with them are not practised because of some sort of intellectual inadequacy. The demand for logical coherence in belief or consistency in action stems from a mistaken notion that the Azande are following scientific procedures in their accusations of witchcraft and use of countermagic. The crucial notion in Winch's work is that all cultures, ours as well as the Azande's, contain many different world-sustaining language games, and to subject them all to the uniform criticism of a single, scientific world-view is to miss their diverse purposes and methods. Winch is not an irrationalist or idealist, denying that there is an external world against which we can test ideas, but he is simply pointing out that such tests are not part of many important areas of belief and action. Moreover, the idea of such an external reality is not exclusive to science (religion, for example, contains the idea of an independent and higher reality). But we have been misled or dazzled by the dominance of science in our culture: to judge one set of beliefs by the standards of another is to commit a category mistake (1964/1977). In order to find out why we do not share the definitions of reality in other cultures, we must first understand the point of those beliefs and the actions which they involve for members of that society. If we are taking our own concept of thinking, with its rules and conventions, as a paradigm of what it is to have a point, then we shall misunderstand.

Much of the subsequent, rather unsatisfactory discussion of Winch involved considerable misreadings of his work. The association of his position with complete relativism, for example, ignored his 1960 paper against ethical relativism and the concluding sections of the Azande paper which deliberately set out a kind of universal human experience that underlies all cultures and provides the basis for mutual understanding. He clearly decries those who believe in the total relativism of complete cultural determinism without such cross-cultural elements, or universal 'limiting concepts': rather predictably these turn out to be life, death and sex.

Peter Winch has had a considerable impact on subsequent developments in sociology and anthropology, for many rejecting both functionalism and the rigidities of structuralist theories welcomed the more flexible concepts of meaning in the interpretative or hermeneutic tradition of Wittgensteinian perspectives. Others, exploring the possibilities of relativism or non-judgemental approaches to non-western cultures, were also heartened by Winch's ideas. He was fiercely attacked by Jarvie and **Gellner**, partly on the grounds that relativist tolerance of opinions which seek to destroy ours is unwise, and partly because cognitive relativism is self-contradictory in supposing a level of rational knowledge of other cultures sufficient to assert their uniqueness and interpretative opacity. To understand so much and not compare or contrast cultures is seen as wilful. Nevertheless, the result of Winch's intervention has been to make it harder for social theory to avoid the necessity of understanding before judgement.

Main works

The Idea of a Social Science and its Relation to Philosophy, London: Routledge and Kegan Paul, 1958.

'Nature and convention', *Proceedings of the Aristotelian Society*, 20 (1960), pp. 231–52.

'Understanding a primitive society', *American Philosophical Quarterly*, 1 (1964), pp. 307–24, repr. in B. R. Wilson (ed.), *Rationality*, Oxford: Basil Blackwell, 1977.

Studies in the Philosophy of Wittgenstein (ed.), London: Routledge and Kegan Paul, 1969.

Ethics and Action, London: Routledge and Kegan Paul, 1972.

Trying to Make Sense, Oxford: Basil Blackwell, 1986.

Simone Weil, 'The Just Balance', Cambridge: Cambridge University Press, 1987.

The Political Philosophy of Intellectuals (eds), New York: Cambridge University Press, 1990.

'Certainty and authority', *Philosophy*, Supplement 28, ed. A. Phillips Griffith (1991), pp. 223–37.

Wittgenstein: A religious point of view?, ed. Norman Malcolm, Ithaca, NY: Cornell University Press, 1994.

Further reading

Gellner, E., 'Winch's idea of a social science', in I. C. Jarvie and J. Agassi (eds), *Cause and Meaning in the Social Sciences*, London: Routledge and Kegan Paul, 1973.

Hollis, Martin, 'Witchcraft and winchcraft', *Philosophy of the Social Sciences*, 2 (1972), pp. 89–193.

Hollis, M. and S. Lukes (eds), *Rationality and Relativism*, Oxford: Basil Blackwell, 1982.

Horton, Robin, 'Professor Winch on safari', *European Journal of Sociology*, 17 (1976), repr. in his *Patterns of Thought in Africa and the West. Essays on Magic, Religion and Science*, Cambridge: Cambridge University Press, 1993.

Wittgenstein, Ludwig (1889–1951)

Wittgenstein was an extraordinary character, and at least part of his fame as a philosopher stems from his charismatic and compelling personality. Born into a wealthy, talented, but troubled family (three of Wittgenstein's four brothers committed suicide) Wittgenstein studied engineering in Berlin and then Manchester. Engineering led him to an interest in the foundations of logic and mathematics and on the advice of the philosopher and mathematician, Gottlob Frege, he became a student of Bertrand Russell in Cambridge (1912–13). In the First World War he served with the Austrian artillery on the Russian and Italian fronts. The notebooks he kept during this period became the source for his first published work. the *Tractatus Logico-Philosophicus* (1921, with an English translation following in 1922), the only one of his books to appear during his lifetime. The *Tractatus* was meant to be the final word in philosophy and so, logically, Wittgenstein abandoned the subject. From 1920–6 he taught in village schools in Austria and after a period as a gardener in a monastery he spent two years designing and supervising the construction of a house for his sister. In the late 1920s he became dissatisfied with the conclusions of the *Tractatus* and returned to philosophy. He was a fellow of Trinity College Cambridge from 1930 to 1936, and professor from 1939–40. During the Second World War he worked as a hospital porter in London and as a laboratory assistant in Newcastle. The major statement of Wittgenstein's later philosophy appeared after his death in *The Philosophical Investigations* (1953). Much of his work from the 1930s and 1940s, contained in his copious notebooks or in the form of lecture notes taken down by his students, has appeared since his death, a process which continues. Wittgenstein's unique lecturing style and many behavioural quirks are well caught by Norman Malcolm's *Ludwig Wittgenstein: A memoir* (1966). In his *Autobiography*, Russell wrote of Wittgenstein, 'he was perhaps the most perfect example I have ever known of genius as traditionally conceived, passionate, profound, intense, and dominating'.

Although the early and late philosophy of Wittgenstein differ in many ways, they are united by a concern with language, and particularly with the problem of what can be said meaningfully. According to the *Tractatus*, the world is made up of independent, simple 'atomic' facts and the job of language is to 'picture' these facts. By this Wittgenstein means that there will be some logical or structural similarity between language and what it depicts, as there is a relationship between a map and the land it represents. A statement is true or false to the extent that it corresponds to a 'state of affairs' – an arrangement of atomic facts. Although this structure is obscured by the conventions and muddle of ordinary language, it is possible to imagine a perfect language, in which the structure would be laid bare.

Wittgenstein, in the *Tractatus*, draws a boundary around what can be said without straying into nonsense. Outside that boundary we find ethics, religion and metaphysics – indeed everything other than the statement of simple facts (and the 'tautologies' of mathematics and logic). Although without sense, these are not unimportant, indeed Wittgenstein states that when we have answered all scientific questions, the 'problems of life remain completely untouched'. But these are things which cannot be talked about, which, in the famous closing words of the *Tractatus*, 'we must pass over in silence'.

In the later philosophy the attempt to identify a logically perfect language is abandoned in favour of a painstaking description of the different ways in which language is used in a variety of 'language games'. Giving orders, describing an object, play acting, cursing, greeting and playing are all given as examples of language games. In playing a language game we employ tools – words and sentences that are as different in design and purpose as the tools used by a workman. The point of Wittgenstein's descriptions is not to give some overarching account of language, but rather to lay language open to us, to bring home to us the truth that language is a *social* phenomenon, only understandable, therefore, in its *social* context.

Language games do not have a set of features in common which we could extract and present (as the *Tractatus* had done) as the definitive constituents of *all* language. Rather they are linked by what Wittgenstein calls a 'family resemblance'. Game A might have some properties in common with B, and B with C, without A and C having any thing in common. Understanding a language game involves not grasping an abstract principle, but entering into a 'form of life', the whole network of social relations in which an activity is embedded. We learn to play language games not by being taught an abstract rule, but through practice, through *living*.

The very possibility of language itself is posited on social interaction. Wittgenstein's 'private language argument' denies that we could learn language by associating sounds with impressions or feeling experienced 'internally'. Meaning comes rather through the ways in which words are used; we agree about the meaning of a word when we find that we 'apply' it in the same way. In this Wittgenstein comes close to the behaviourism of J. B. Watson and B. F. **Skinner**.

Truth, in the later Wittgenstein, comes not from a correlation between a statement and 'the facts', but is the function of a language game and embedded in a form of life. Philosophical error comes from trying to apply the type of discourse appropriate to one language game to another. This clearly suggests a form of relativism, and Wittgenstein's influence on social theory has reflected, above all else, this aspect of his thought.

Wittgenstein has been perhaps the most influential philosopher of the twentieth century, an influence not confined to the analytic tradition of Anglo-American philosophy to which he belongs. The strict distinction between sense and nonsense, and the general scientism of the *Tractatus* was important in the early development of the logical positivism of the Vienna Circle, which in turn, through A. J. Ayer's *Language, Truth, and Logic,* helped to shape Anglo-American philosophy. (Wittgenstein's affinity with logical positivism is most in evidence in the *Philosophical Remarks,* written in 1929–30, where he closely follows their line that the meaning of a statement is related to its method of verification.) However, it is probably the case that Wittgenstein's reputation among *philosophers* now stands at its lowest point since the 1950s.

Wittgenstein's work has exerted a far greater influence outside the narrow boundaries of 'pure' philosophy, particularly in the field of social theory. Perhaps the main conduit for that influence has been the work of Peter Winch. **Winch**'s *The Idea of a Social Science* (1958) applied the explicitly Wittgensteinian concepts of 'form of life' and 'rule following' to attack the prevailing positivist view of sociology. In place of the 'scientific' approach to social relations, which attempted to locate causal connections at the heart of social interaction, Winch, argued that we must endeavour to reach a 'meaningful understanding', based on the *meanings* given by individuals for their actions.

Wittgenstein has also been given a prominent position in the development of sociological theories of science, particularly those of Thomas Kuhn and Paul Feyerabend, which account for science as a 'form of life', understandable as a series of social practices within a tradition, or 'paradigm'. Wittgenstein's influence has been criticised by Ernest **Gellner** (*Words and Things,* 1959), who has defended rationalism in sociology against what he takes to be the relativism and idealism inherent in the later philosophy. Finally, Wittgenstein's philosophy, both early and late, has been appropriated by religious thinkers, drawn by the overt mysticism of the *Tractatus,* or by the insulation from rationalist criticism offered by locating religion within a specifically religious language game.

Main works

Remarks on the Foundations of Mathematics, ed. G. H. von Wright, Rush Rhees and G. M. Anscombe, Oxford: Basil Blackwell, 1956.

The Blue and Brown Books, ed. Rush Rhees, Oxford: Basil Blackwell, 1958.

Philosophical Investigations, ed. Rush Rhees and G. E. M. Anscombe, Oxford: Basil Blackwell, 1958.

Tractatus Logico-Philosophicus, trans. D. F. Pears and B. F. McGuinness, London: Routledge and Kegan Paul, 1961.

Lectures and Conversations on Aesthetics, Psychology and Religious Belief, ed. Cyril Barrett, Oxford: Basil Blackwell, 1966.

Zettel, ed. G. E. M. Anscombe and G. H. von Wright, Oxford: Basil Blackwell, 1967.

On Certainty, ed. G. E. M. Anscombe and G. H. von Wright, Oxford: Basil Blackwell, 1969.

Philosophical Grammar, ed. Rush Rhees, Oxford: Basil Blackwell, 1974.

Philosophical Remarks, ed. Rush Rhees, Oxford: Basil Blackwell, 1975.

Remarks on Colour, ed. G. E. M. Anscombe, Oxford: Basil Blackwell, 1977.

Remarks on the Philosophy of Psychology, 2 vols, ed. G. E. M. Anscombe, G. H. von Wright and Heikki Nyman, Oxford: Basil Blackwell, 1980.

Culture and Value, ed. G. H. von Wright, Oxford: Basil Blackwell, 1980.

Last Writings on the Philosophy of Psychology, ed. G. H. von Wright and Heikki Nyman, Oxford: Basil Blackwell, 1982.

Further reading

Grayling, A. C., *Wittgenstein*, Oxford: Oxford University Press, 1988.

Kenny, Anthony, *Wittgenstein*, London: Allen Lane, 1973.

Kerr, Fergus, *Theology after Wittgenstein*, Oxford: Basil Blackwell, 1986.

Pears, David, *Wittgenstein*, London: Fontana, 1971.

Phillips, Derek L., *Wittgenstein and Scientific Knowledge: A sociological perspective*, London: Macmillan, 1977.

Winch, Peter, *The Idea of a Social Science and its Relation to Philosophy*, London: Routledge and Kegan Paul, 1958.

Glossary

Language game A group of related linguistic usages and social practices sharing some common function. Religion, science, telling jokes and giving orders are all examples of 'rule governed' language games.

Wright Mills, Charles (1916–1962)

Wright Mills's academic career, although confined to the United States, nevertheless allowed him access to wider political debates. After graduating from the University of Texas, where his early influence was Jamesian pragmatism, Wright Mills studied at the University of Wisconsin, where he met and was greatly influenced by Hans Gerth, a Frankfurt School emigré who provided a pathway into European political thought and the theories of, amongst others, Karl **Marx**, Karl **Mannheim**, Thorstein **Veblen** and Max Weber. Wright Mills went on to teach at the University of Maryland for a short period, but it was at Columbia University that he was to consolidate his political thought via his work with other Frankfurt School emigrés, including Theodor **Adorno**, Max Horkheimer and, perhaps most significantly, Herbert **Marcuse**, whose populist tone and immediacy Wright Mills's work seems to echo. Other influences were no less important; his work with Robert Merton, for example, confirmed Wright Mills's theoretical convictions that individuals were not simply manipulated unquestioningly by their political masters, nor were they actively and democratically involved as is characteristic of a just society. Wright Mills was Professor of Sociology at Columbia when he died at the age of forty-five.

In his short life and career, C. Wright Mills made a significant mark on twentieth-century American political and sociological thought. Perhaps more than any other American commentator, he connected academic debate with everyday sociopolitical problems. This ability to make connections meant that Wright Mills was always fiercely critical of abstracted academicism, which he saw as pervasive in much western university life, whilst being equally suspicious of political projects and dogma. His theoretical world-view was informed by the failures of Stalinism, but equally by a 'small town' romanticism of pre-industrial, pre-bureaucratic middle class America.

The refusal to adopt extreme micro- or macro-analyses was a leitmotif of Wright Mills's major works, which he captured in his critical formulations of 'grand theory' and 'abstracted empiricism'. Grand theory is taken to be theoretical ideas and projects which bear no obvious link to the 'real' world. Here Marxist economism and functionalist conservatism are both key targets, Wright Mills being deeply suspicious of all-embracing theories of social and political life. Abstracted empiricism was for Wright Mills the use of social research, but without any clear theoretical underpinnings. For Wright Mills most survey research was constructed and administered in abstract from wider political debate, and the result was a body of research without analytical value or social application. Here Wright Mills was applying sentiments similar to the American field theorist Kurt Lewin, whose formulation, 'there is nothing more practical than a theory', reflects the interdependence of theory and research technique.

Wright Mills's main contributions to twentieth-century critical thought rely on his identification of known social and political problems, and the need to reframe the discourse that surrounds them. An example of this is his classic reframing of unemployment as a 'public issue' and not a 'personal trouble' (failure). Underlying the impetus to reframe analysis in this way was Wright Mills's conviction that modern mass society had stripped individuals of a critical faculty, the ability to think reflexively. This connects with Veblen's earlier discussion of 'drift' in his *Theory of the Leisure Class*, where drift represents the insidious loss of engagement in decision-making and critical thought with the bureaucratisation of *fin-de-siècle* Europe and America. Wright Mills's focus extended to the linguistic obfuscation that characterised American policy and society. The influence of Marcuse and his notion of one-dimensional thought and language is noticeable here. Wright Mills isolated the nature of science and laboratory work as the new language of understanding, the dominant and only 'legitimate' mode of thought, with the result being that 'other (non-scientific) terms and other styles of reflection, seem mere vehicles of escape and obscurity'. As science becomes the common denominator for our understanding of the world, social and political issues will increasingly be viewed as susceptible only to these techniques; this itself, according to Wright Mills, being an ideological reframing of social and political questions.

Alongside Wright Mills's seminal work in *The Sociological Imagination*, where he discusses the need to nurture a sociological world-view which connects the everyday with structural phenomena, his more substantive works include *White Collar*, where an image of a dispossessed American middle class is portrayed. Shorn of meaning in both work and leisure, the growing middle mass of white-collar America, although salaried, is politically emasculated and culturally stultified. Wright Mills compares the 'new' credentialled middle classes with the 'old' autonomous middle classes of pre- and early-industrial society. Nineteenth-century farmers are adopted as the archetype of the 'old' middle class: fiercely independent, entrepreneurial and politically engaged, if not informed. The decline into what William Foote Whyte later dubbed 'Organisation Man', is lamented by Wright Mills, who is concerned primarily with the changing relationship between the middle classes and an increasingly strong social elite, the growing gap between major entrepreneurs, a shrinking 'lumpen bourgeoisie' and bureaucratised white-collar workers. It is notable that no companion volume charting the fate of blue-collar workers was ever attempted, which reflects Wright Mills's affinity with the work of the early Marx, which emphasised the impact of capitalist industrialisation on the labour process, more specifically the image of alienated humanity. This is at the expense of Marx's later emphasis on economic exploitation, an examination of which would have called into the frame the fate of blue-collar workers.

In *The Power Elite*, Wright Mills portrays the American military–industrial–political complex as the main beneficiary of the drift of power from the American middle and working classes. For Wright Mills, a non-economistic theory of power is posited, suggesting that a small elite network connects the prevailing triangle of forces in US society. The role of this elite is to sustain an anti-democratic polity via a hermetic controlling of countervailing powers, entailing a permanent war economy to fund the political process, which in turn evens out the peaks and troughs of American capitalism. The analysis in *The Power Elite* carefully avoids suggesting neo-Marxist causal connections between economic imperatives and state personnel; the power elite is seen ultimately to represent its own interests, and by implication can find fertile ground in socialist as well as capitalist states. Wright Mills's work directly counters pluralist and elite pluralist theories of political decision-making (for example, J. K. Galbraith's *American Capitalism*), and sees part of the activities of the power elite as the obscuring of a manipulative social and political order through the mass media. Fiercely critical of Charles Cooley's prediction that more technology and communicative mechanisms would lead to more open and contested discussion (a view later embraced by Daniel **Bell**), Wright Mills summed up the influence of the mass media as, 'the violent banalisation and stereotyping of our sense organs'.

The overall impact of Wright Mills can be seen in the critical studies of elites that he spawned in the United States and Britain; his wider legacy lies in his blueprint for theorising the hidden forces that shape broad social and political changes, to illustrate the political causes of apparently personal problems. There has been criticism of his writing, however, as being populist and lacking in empirical support, and at times polemical. Paradoxically, he is also criticised for avoiding any political project, and his refusal to make explicit his humanist Marxism has led to complaints that his work is itself a form of abstracted theorising – a charge he laid against other academics. Despite the criticisms, Wright Mills's work remains an influence in sociological analysis as it represents a watershed in political and social theory, especially in the context of 1950s America. Wright Mills was one of the first writers to provide a deeply critical image of the American state, working practices, bureaucratisation and the mass media. His profile has perhaps suffered because of his refusal to align himself with a theoretical tradition; neither the western Marxist *Kulturkritik* of his emigré colleagues at Columbia, the influence of Mertonian sociology, nor the early attachment to pragmatism seemed to have had a dominant place in his later work, which to some extent defies categorisation, save for a close link with Veblen's equally populist brand of social observation and a belief in the need to link what look like isolated phenomena with broader social and political processes. Wright Mills is likely to continue to influence the development of a sociological world view. The substantive relevance of his work on American elite society and the changing middle classes seems less likely to survive, as the Western middle classes become increasingly diverse and social elites internally fragmented.

Main works

From Max Weber (ed. with Hans Gerth), London: Routledge and Kegan Paul, 1948.

White Collar: The American middle classes, New York: Oxford University Press, 1951.

Character and Social Structure (with Hans Gerth), New York: Harcourt Brace, 1953.

The Power Elite, New York: Oxford University Press, 1956.

The Sociological Imagination, New York: Oxford University Press, 1959.

'A Letter to the New Left', *New Left Review*, 5 (1960), pp. 18–23.

Further reading

Bottomore, T., *Elites and Society*, Harmondsworth: Penguin, 1964.

Bottomore, T. and R. Bryn, R. (eds), *The Capitalist Class: An international study*, Hemel Hempstead: Harvester Wheatsheaf, 1989.

Domhoff, G., *Who Rules America?*, Hemel Hempstead: Prentice Hall, 1967.

Eldridge, J., *C. Wright Mills*, London: Tavistock, 1983.

Horowitz, I. L. (ed.), *The New Sociology: Essays in social science and social theory in honor of C. Wright Mills*, New York: Oxford University Press, 1964.

Scott, J., *Who Rules Britain?*, London: Polity, 1991.

Young, Iris Marion (1949–)

Iris Marion Young is an untiring political activist, a contemporary philosopher, feminist academic and Associate Professor of Public and International Affairs at the University of Pittsburgh. Young has written on democratic theory, theories of justice, feminist social theory, female bodily experience and the politics of difference. In addition to her political activism and academic writings, Young has edited significant collections of essays by feminist philosophers linking ethics and social policies.

Much can be gleamed about Young from the evolving content of her publications. The essays by Young, collected and published in *Throwing like a Girl and Other Essays in Social and Political Theory* (1990), are representative of both her intellectual development and the evolution of feminist theory from the 1970s to 1990. In one of her early essays, 'Throwing like a girl', Young brings together Simone **de Beauvoir**'s feminist account of the Other and Maurice Merleau-Ponty's phenomenological account of the lived body. In applying Merleau-Ponty's phenomenology of the body to women's particular situation in western societies, Young demonstrates that women live their bodies as both subject and object. But in the slightly later essay, 'Pregnant Embodiments', Young pushes beyond the subject/object distinction and, in so doing, begins to transform the existential methods of phenomenology. She resists the transcendence and immanence distinction of existential phenomenology, seeing it as a form of the subject/object split which inhibits active awareness of one's own body. The decisive case here is the pregnant woman who can both passively watch the changes in her body and actively experience them for herself; this pregnant experience does not involve estrangement as existential phenomenology had asserted.

In a third essay Young moves beyond traditional phenomenology to a highly significant account of women's 'breasted experience'. She argues for the ethical and political importance of the sexed mother, building upon the psycholinguistic account of mother–child *jouissance*. This account of the sexed mother means that the mother and child can experience sexual pleasure; mother and child together have the ability to feel fulfilment in a joyful continuity. In contrast the non-sexed mother of the traditional heterosexual economy of pleasure has ensured that women's sexuality remains the sole property of men; women have no pleasure without men. Western political theory has maintained a crippling separation between motherhood and sexuality, supporting the conception of a unified subject against the polymorphous flesh; the unerotic love of the mother means that the child must sublimate its erotic relation to the mother and that the mother must give without taking. Against this essentially patriarchal account Young's breasted experience suggests that motherhood and sexuality flow together; the mother gives pleasure at the same time as she takes pleasure. The ethical implication is that the conception of woman as the self-sacrificing nurturer disappears. The political implication is that Young offers a model for a more human justice than patriarchal theories of justice which force self-sacrificing on to women and men. Instead she imagines a new social ethic of care in which all persons can take pleasure in caring for others.

As evident in the larger course of her writings Young has moved on to postmodern concerns. While building upon her earlier studies of embodiment she has developed an alternative theory of justice to the liberal theory of distributive justice with its ideals of abstract freedom and formal equality. In *Justice and the Politics of Difference* Young focuses upon issues revealing the substantive content of justice. She challenges the presumption that justice is a question of distribution rather than of oppression and domination. With this distinctive challenge Young's political philosophy differs from not only the liberal tradition of Rousseau, Mill and **Rawls** but from the post-Enlightenment tradition of much critical theory, notably of Jürgen **Habermas**. Although similar to Habermas in deriving her method from the social and political concepts of critical theory Young resists what she sees as Habermas's modern commitment to a homogeneous public. Young contends that democratic theorists generally assume a homogeneous public and so fail to consider institutional arrangements for including people not culturally identified with white European male norms of reason and respectability. Hence political theories of liberal democracy have not adequately addressed the problem of an inclusive participatory framework.

Young argues that, in contrast with the political theory of modern liberals, normative theory and public policy should undermine group-based oppression by affirming rather than suppressing social group difference. Her vision of the good society is the differentiated, culturally plural network of contemporary urban life. Her goal is a principle of group representation in democratic publics, along with group differentiated policies. Hence Young resists those feminist theories of embodiment which retain an ideal of a shared subjectivity and unified desires over the basic opaqueness and assymmetry of subjects and their desires. She fears the suppression of difference and of concrete otherness.

With her distinctive passion for the postmodern Young argues that the desire for community among the members of radical organisations, especially of anti-urban groups, is dangerous. Desire for community produces homogeneity; it directs energy away from political goals, creating a clique atmosphere which excludes difference. Instead Young proposes an ideal of urban life, nurturing diversity and co-operation in providing services conceived, distributed and administered justly. Some critics claim that Young is against community and friendship, but arguably she has realistic doubts concerning the transparency and affection of face-to-face relationships.

The critical problem attributed to Young's political and social theory ironically constitutes the distinctiveness of her position: her rejection of identity and community for difference and diversity is criticised as often as it is celebrated. Seyla Benhabib confronts Young. Having her foot in the modernist camp of Habermasian critical theory yet her heart in feminism, Benhabib is sympathetic with but ultimately critical of Young's post-modernist account of difference over identity, multiplicity over unity, heterogeneity over homogeneity. She argues that Young overstates her case in objecting that the self, as a unified centre of desire, is a mere fiction. Is it necessary or wise to undermine the coherent core of individual self-identity? Benhabib's counterassertions to Young appear sound: 'not all difference is empowering; not all heterogeneity can be celebrated; not all opacity leads to sense of self-flourishing'. These may be grounds for caution, for a weaker version of the postmodern story. Reason, identity and unity need not be thrown out completely, while accepting the urgency in criticising exclusionary politics and social policy which ignore concrete needs. After all, in Young's own account of Kristevan *jouissance*, she recognises that the child must separate from its joyful continuity with the maternal in order to enter language and become a self. The consequence of this separation, of the primal repression of *jouissance*, is both the identity and the difference of individual persons. Thus Young's proposals for a social ethic of care and a politics of difference – both continuity and discontinuity – are not so easily realised.

Young's influence on social and political theory is evident in her recent edited volumes of essays by various other feminist philosophers, in which she has selected and brought together writings on current feminist ethics and social policies. What Young demonstrates, with this collection of feminist voices, is the inadequacy of both contemporary ethical theory and current social practices. She reveals the indelibly liberal colours of feminist ethics and the failure of social policy, especially in the United States, to address the specific and distinctive needs of women, of groups differentiated by race, gender, ethnicity. Young's most salient influence lies in suggesting the inadequacy of the liberal notions of individuality, freedom and equality which emerge in feminist confrontations with theory and practice. Justice to be just in substantive ways needs a politics of difference. Yet this politics is tough to think of and even tougher to implement.

Main works

'Throwing like a girl: a phenomenology of feminine body comportment, motility, and spatiality', *Human Studies*, 3 (1980), pp. 137–56; repr. in Jeffner Allen and Iris Marion Young (eds), *The Thinking Muse: Feminism and modern French philosophy*, Bloomington, IN: Indiana University Press, 1989, pp. 51–70.

'Humanism, gynocentrism and feminist politics', *Women's Studies International*, 8 (1985), pp. 173–83; repr. in Azizah Y. al-Hibri and Margaret A. Simons (eds), *Hypatia: Reborn*, Bloomington, IN: Indiana University Press, 1990.

Throwing like a Girl and Other Essays, Bloomington, IN: Indiana University Press, 1990.

Justice and the Politics of Difference, Princeton, NJ: Princeton University Press, 1990.

DiQuinzio, Patrice and Iris Marion Young (eds), *Hypatia*, special issue on 'Feminist ethics and social policy', Part I (Winter 1995); Part II (Spring 1995).

Further reading

Benhabib, Seyla, 'Women and moral theory revisited', in *Situating the Self: Gender, community and postmodernism in contemporary ethics*, Cambridge: Polity, 1992.

Kristeva, Julia, *The Powers of Horror: An essay on abjection*, trans. Leon S. Roudiez, New York: Columbia University Press, 1982.

Weir, Alison, 'Toward a model of self-identity: Habermas and Kristeva', in Johanna Meehan (ed.), *Feminists Read Habermas*, London: Routledge, 1995.

Glossary

Politics of difference Instead of difference being a description of the attributes of a group, it is a function of the relations between groups which intends emancipation not exclusion. Moreover, difference is not a category which separates groups; the group 'women', for example, has overlapping experiences with such group differences as race and class. A politics of difference assumes that every social group has differences cutting across it.

Index

Abraham, Karl, 162
Achebe, Chinua, 77
Ackerman, R.J., 377
Adorno, T.W., 1–5, 10, 75, 88, 130, 132, 143, 200, 228, 370, 393
Alexander, Sally, 312
Althusser, Louis, 5–9, 39, 63, 128, 173, 242, 302, 349, 350–1
Amin, Samir, 373
Anderson, Perry, 350–1
Anglicanism, 182, 266, 269
Annales School, 41–3, 372
anti-foundationalism, 60
anti-psychiatry, 178, 180
anti-semitism, 10, 79, 182
Aquinas, St. Thomas, 210, 212, 214, 319
Arendt, Hannah, 9–13
Aristotle, 142, 210, 214, 333
Arnold, Matthew, 337
Aron, Raymond, 13–16
Arrow, Kenneth, J., 16–21
Austin, J.L., 30
Ayer, A.J., 30, 211, 391

Bachelard, Gaston, 5
Bacon, Francis, 297
Ball, Sidney, 338
Balzac, Honore de, 199
Baran, Paul, 373
Barker, Ernest, 182
Barth, Karl, 33, 35, 354
Barthes, Roland, 39, 325
Baudrillard, Jean, 175, 217
Bauer, Bruno, 242
Bauman, Zygmunt, 328

Beatles, 156
Beauvoir, Simone de, 22–5, 397
Beckett, Samuel, 3
behaviourism, 333, 335, 390
Bell, Daniel, 25–9, 395
Benhabib, Seyla, 132, 399
Benjamin, Walter, 75, 200, 326
Bentham, Jeremy, 71, 135–6, 264
Bergson, Henri, 315
Berlin, Isaiah, 12, 29–33
Bernstein, Edouard, 202
Bernstein, J.M., 132
Beveridge, William, 318
Bhabha, Homi K., 113
Blache, Vidal de la, 41
Blaug, Mark, 323
Bloch, Ernst, 197, 200, 328
Bloch, Marc, 40–1
Boas, Franz, 246
Bohm-Bawerk, Eugen von, 321
Bolshevism, 191, 203, 253, 276, 304, 363–4
Bonhoeffer, Dietrich, 33–6
Bourdieu, Pierre, 36–40, 371
Bowles, S., 150
Bradley, F.H., 266
Braudel, Fernand, 40–4, 372
Brecht, Bertolt, 199–200
Brenner, Robert, 373
Bretton Woods Conference, 318
Bruner, Jerome, 296
Bryant, P., 295
Bryce, James, 184
Buber, Martin, 328
Bukharin, Nikolai, 373
Bultmann, Rudolf, 35, 354